Ernst von Bunsen

**The Keys of Saint Peter**

The House of Rechab

Ernst von Bunsen

**The Keys of Saint Peter**
*The House of Rechab*

ISBN/EAN: 9783337336400

Printed in Europe, USA, Canada, Australia, Japan

Cover: Foto ©Thomas Meinert / pixelio.de

More available books at **www.hansebooks.com**

# THE KEYS OF SAINT PETER

OR

## THE HOUSE OF RECHAB

CONNECTED WITH THE HISTORY OF

## SYMBOLISM AND IDOLATRY.

BY

ERNEST DE BUNSEN.

LONDON:
LONGMANS, GREEN, AND CO.
1867.

*The right of translation is reserved.*

# PREFACE.

A MYSTERIOUS SILENCE rules over the period of nearly five hundred years, which separates the events chronicled in the Old Testament from those that are recorded in the New Testament. Yet the New and the Old hang together. There are Scriptures, which refer to these times, and they form part of the Greek version of the Hebrew Canon, of the Septuagint, which was published during the three last centuries of the pre-Christian era.

That Alexandrian collection of holy writ was pre-eminently, if not exclusively, the Canon of the Apostles, and of their Divine Master. Those Scriptures which were excluded from the Hebrew Canon, for reasons hitherto not generally known, form not a supplement, but the very centre of the Greek Canon, and they explain, why the Septuagint is a freely handled version, and not a literal translation of the Hebrew Canon.

These Scriptures were called Apocrypha, because they referred to what had, in earlier times, been hidden. Can it be proved, that some of these Scriptures were composed, essentially in the form we now possess them, before the captivity, during the same, and during that eventful period, which commenced with the return to the holy land, and which culminated in the commencement of the Christian era? If so, in what connection do these records of things hidden stand with 'the preaching of Jesus Christ,' that is, with 'the revelation of the mystery, which was kept in silence since the world began,' although, from the beginning, God had spoken 'through the mouth of his holy prophets?'

These are problems, the importance of which is obvious, and which ought to be generally acknowledged. We try to prove, that the Apocrypha, or hidden wisdom, was gradually recorded, in spite of a party in the Jewish Church, which was always opposed to the promulgation of tradition, and thus to the principle of universality. These and other principles were always supported by the Rechabites, or Kenites, who, although from the beginning separated from the Hebrews, formed with the latter the people of Israel. These two parties merged into the Christian Church. Although their hostility never entirely ceased, concord by compromise was rendered possible through symbols, which suggested more than they defined the right interpretation of Divine mysteries, the keys of which were confided to St. Peter.

The author wishes gratefully to acknowledge his deep obligation to many of the writers in Smith's 'Dictionary of the Bible.' Although it was not possible, often to quote passages from that valuable work, the information therein contained has been freely used, and has often suggested new combinations, or assisted the author of the present Volume in framing them.

Abbey Lodge, Regent's Park:
*February* 1867.

# ANALYTICAL TABLE

OF

# CONTENTS.

### PREFACE.

Five hundred years between Old and New Testament.—Apocrypha then published in Babylon and Alexandria.—Connection with the preaching of Jesus.                                                                      PAGE V

### INTRODUCTION.

Origin of fire.—The cloud a centre of superhuman intelligence.—Submission to the same led to symbols, ignorance of their meaning led to idols.

xiii

### CHAPTER I.

#### THE HOUSE OF RECHAB.

Kenites, descendants from Cain, called Rechabites, sons of Jonadab, and descendants from Hemath.—Jonadab, David's nephew.—The Rechab or chariot of Israel, refers to tradition, of which Elijah the Tishbite, that is, the stranger, or Rechabite, and also Elisha, were fathers.—Rechabite families of Scribes.—Jabesh-Gilead inhabited by Rechabites.—Hamath the Great, a rival to Zion and Gerizim, and inhabited by Rechabites.—Jethro, Caleb, Joshua.—Rechabite, or Kenite origin of the house of David.—The house of Rechab, or house of tradition, traced back to Moses and to Abraham, because to Jethro and to Melchizedec, who represents pre-Abramitic Monotheism, of Eastern origin.—Kenite and Hebrew tradition contrasted.—Both separately represented by the double Aaronic lines of Eleazar and of Ithamar, that is, by the Sadducean and Pharisean sacerdotal lines.—Jabez 'more honourable than his brethren.'—Gerizim and Zion.       .       .       .       .       1

### CHAPTER II.

#### MIGRATIONS AFTER THE FLOOD.

Twofold record of post-diluvian genealogies in Genesis.—Land of Canaan or Kenaan, called after the lowland of the Indus, or Nod.—Eastern origin of the Kenites.—Shemitism originated in the subjugation of dark coloured Africans by white coloured Asiatics.—Grammar and Dictionary of Shemitic languages thus explained.—Hieratic and demotic languages the necessary consequence.—Shemites represented post-diluvian humanity, and Israel the catholicity of mankind . . . . . . PAGES 13–21

## CHAPTER III.

### HIGH CASTE AND LOW CASTE.

Patriarchal history marks a twofold stream, originating in diversity of colour and of caste.—Sarah and Hagar represent freedom and serfdom.—Sign of Hagar and sign of Cain.—Ishmael.—Mission of Abraham.—Eliezer of Damascus, that is, dwelling of Mesech.—Eliezer and Hadadezer.—Melchizedec the Kenite priest.—Table of high castes and low castes in the patriarchal family.—Both castes among Kenites and Hebrews.—Egyptians and Shepherd rulers —Zoan and Hebron.—Philistines and Phœnicians.—The 'I Am.'—Seth-Baal . . . . . 22–45

## CHAPTER IV.

### SONS OF GOD AND SONS OF MEN.

Kenites and Hebrews were Aryan or Asiatic leaders of non-Aryan or African tribes.—History of Israel a continued fight for supremacy between cognate races.—Kenites and Hebrews contrasted in the book of Job.—Job and his three friends were Kenites.—Elihu the Hebrew.—Chaldeans and Sabeans.—Chedorlaomer.—The adversary, or the Satan, and the sons of the Gods minister before Jehovah.—Union of Kenite and Hebrew priesthood.—Job and Melchizedec . . . . . . 46–57

## CHAPTER V.

### KENITE AND HEBREW RECORDS IN GENESIS.

The Elohist is the Hebrew, and the Jehovist the Kenite chronicler.—Origin of Jehovah-worship.—The 'generations' in the fourth and in the fifth chapter of Genesis compared . . . . . 58–66

## CHAPTER VI.

### THE AARONITES.

Thamar, descendant from the Anakim of Hebron.—Eleazar and Ithamar.—The priestly courses in the time of David.—The possessions of the Aaronites, in the time of Joshua, lay exclusively in Judah, Simeon and Benjamin.—Household priesthood and hereditary priesthood.—Battle of Gibeah, the cause of the substitution of the younger for the older line of Aaronites.—The massacre at Nob.—Two high priests.—Royalty introduced as a guarantee against hierarchical feuds and oppressions.—Abiathar's rebellion leads to the re-establishment of the senior line.—Hebrew and Kenite tradition represented by Aaronites . . . . . 67–74

## CHAPTER VII.

### SYMBOLISM AND IDOLATRY IN ISRAEL.

Different symbols admitted in the same sanctuary.—Gradual interpretation of symbols necessary.—Spirit of caste.—Secrecy led to tyranny, and tyranny to ignorance.—Thus symbols became idols.—The first symbols were not made with hands.—The works of nature witnessed and revealed God's glory.—Ideas gave birth to symbols.—The ark a symbol of the universe.—Star-symbolism of the East, introduced into Egypt before Abraham.—Ashtaroth-Karnaim.—Images of Terah and Laban, Aaron and Micah.—Beginning of idolatry, that is, misunderstood imagery, preceded by the transition from recognised to unrecognised symbols.—Moses forbade all imagery.—Balaam, the Kenite, distinguishes Jacob, or the Kenites, from Israel, or the Hebrews. —Moses is recorded to have pointed out the Babylonian captivity, as the close of Israel's idolatry.—Jeremiah declares that God has said 'nothing' to the fathers concerning sacrifices.—Ezekiel, and the statutes that were 'not good.'—Human sacrifice commanded in the Pentateuch.—All prophets protest against sacrifices.

The presence of God symbolised in the ark.—The cloud and the incense. —Urim and Thummim.—The Shechina symbolised the dwelling of the Spirit of God in man.—Solomon's catholicity based on the recognition of all existing symbols.—Unrestricted symbolism became the source of idolatry, because the interpretation of the symbolised mysteries was not generally taught.—Zadok the enemy of tradition and catholicity.—The matrimonial metaphor applied to the record about Solomon's strange women. —Toleration, liberty of conscience, unity without uniformity, the key-note of Solomon's policy.—The brazen and fiery serpent.—Its history and interpretation.—The symbol of fire.—Fire of Jehovah.—Nadab and Abihu.— Eldad and Medad.—Korah.—The everburning altar.—Non-Mosaic origin of sacrifice.—Moloch and other fire gods.—Red-heifer and scapegoat.—Egyptian imagery introduced by Jeroboam.—Priests and Levites follow Rehoboam.—Jezebel and Elijah.—Cause of Israel's captivity.—African imagery vitiated Asiatic symbolism.—African origin of sacrifices.—Babylon the link between East and West . . . . PAGES 75–126

## CHAPTER VIII.

### JOSHUA THE KENITE HIGH PRIEST.

'Sons of Belial,' a term marking the hostility between Kenites and Hebrews.—The Levite at Gibeah.—The sons of Eli.—Hannah's song of praise.—'Saints.'—'An adversary.'—Origin of Psalm cix.—Satan, the adversary, provokes David to number the people.—Joshua's Kenite descent. Zechariah's vision about Joshua and the Satan . . 127–146

## CHAPTER IX.

### KENITES AND PSALMS.

History of Israel is the history of Kenites and Hebrews.—Psalms show traces of a double stream.—Rules for testing the Kenite or the Hebrew authorship of Psalms.—David turns the house of oracles into the house of prayer.—Prayer enjoined and taught by precept and example.—Relations between Hiram and David and Solomon.—Council of priests and Levites.—David's sons were priests.—Asaph.—Doctrines in the Psalms which are not contained, or not so fully developed in the Pentateuch     PAGES 147-161

## CHAPTER X.

### KENITES AND PROPHETS.

Kenite origin of prophetic institution in Israel.—Prophets the representatives of the people.—Their office was, to interpret sealed visions, and sealed books, by the Apocalypse of the Apocrypha.—Prophetic colleges, or national seminaries of theology.—The key of knowledge given to the people.—Council of the Seventy.—Nathan and Zadok.—Prophets rose when Sadducees fell.—David, Hezekiah, and Josiah.—Eliakim the Kenite high priest.—Jeremiah and the crystallisation of tradition.—Prophets were reformers.—Promise of the Kenite Branch, the God-with-us.—Bethlehem     162-179

## CHAPTER XI.

### PARTIES IN THE JEWISH CHURCH.

Tribal and family distinction during the captivity.—Party spirit, and party organisations at their height in the time of Ezra.—Principles and organisations of the Sadducees, the Pharisees and the Essenes and Therapeuts       .        .        .        .        .        .     180-202

## CHAPTER XII.

### SECRET TRADITION.

Moses and the Seventy.—Dark sayings of old.—Proverbs.—Scribal organisation.—Organs of tradition.—Genealogies.—Stewards of Divine mysteries.—Scribal pairs, the heads of Kenite and Hebrew Scribes.—Shemaia, Abtalion, Hillel, Gamaliel.—Cabbala.—Revisions of holy writ.—Synagogues.—The Great Synagogue.—Hidden Wisdom.—Genûsim, or Apocrypha.     203-220

## CHAPTER XIII.

### THE APOCRYPHA.

Book of Job.—Song of Songs.—Ecclesiastes.—Wisdom of Solomon.—Apocrypha of Moses.—Wisdom of Sirach or Seraiah.—Book of Daniel.—Identity of Daniel the priest and Daniel the prophet.—Titles of Persian kings.—Book of Ezra, Esther, and Nehemiah.—Vistâspa.—Purim massacre in 516-515 B.C.—Book of Tobit.—Nineveh still the capital after 516.—Book of Judith.—Principal events from 536 to 490 B.C.—Maccabees.—Sibylline oracles.—Book of Enoch.—Psalm-book of Solomon.—Hebrew Canon without the Apocrypha is a sealed book      .        .        .     221-233

## CHAPTER XIV.

### TARGUMS OR PARAPHRASES.

Onkelos is Aquila.—Mishna and Talmud.—Oral law and written law.—Concord and compromise.—Oracles of the Fathers.—Targumists and Prophets.—The Targum of Moses . . PAGES 234–247

## CHAPTER XV.

### THE SEPTUAGINT.

The Seventy.—The law full of hidden wisdom.—Targumistic convocation at Alexandria.—Systematic re-formation of holy writ.—The Zohar.—Philo. 248–260

## CHAPTER XVI.

### MESSIANIC EXPECTATIONS.

Eden.—Rebekah's twins.—Jacob's blessing.—Balaam.—The keys of David.—The servant of God.—Kenite and Hebrew expectations contrasted.—Divine incarnation.—The world and the Son of God . 261–271

## CHAPTER XVII.

### THE SON OF DAVID.

The Branch.—Catholicity of the Gospel.—Herod and the Pharisees.—Herod and the Kenites.—The leaven of the Pharisees.—The baptism in Jordan.—Conveyance of the Holy Ghost.—The incarnation.—Judas.—The Sun of righteousness . . . . . 272–292

## CHAPTER XVIII.

### THE CONVERSION OF ST. PETER.

Simon Jonas.—Fishers of men.—'Our fish Jesus Christ.'—Symbol of the Holy Presence.—Christ walking on the sea.—St. Peter and the sons of Zebedee.—Parable of the talents.—The wicked and slothful servant.—The unprofitable servant.—The good servant.—The ensample of the flock. 293–313

## CHAPTER XIX.

### THE CONVERSION OF ST. PAUL.

Saul's education.—Visions, trances, and ecstacies.—Ananias.—The gulf between Saul and St. Paul . . . . 314–321

## CHAPTER XX.

### THE CONVERSION OF ST. JAMES.

Situation after the crucifixion.—Date of the crucifixion.—Rise of the Samaritans under Simon Magus.—Jesus about fifty years old.—Agrippa the Sadducee.—Martyrdom of St. Stephen and St. James in 41 A.C.—Eusebius and the Acts.—St. Peter's first journey to Rome in 41 A.C.—St. Peter and Philo and Aquila in Rome.—St. James the brother of the Lord.—St. James the Nazarite.—St. James and St. Paul.—St. James and the Sadducees.—Martyrdom of St. James.—'James and the brethren.'—St. James the secret friend of St. Peter . . . . . PAGES 322–352

## CHAPTER XXI.

### THE APOCALYPSE OF THE APOCRYPHA.

Manifold measures and manifold fashions.—The faith of Roman Christians.—The first Christians at Rome.—Epistle to the Romans.—St. Paul in the Roman prison.—Epistle of Jude.—Early Apocrypha.—A Jewish writer in the reign of Claudius.—The Assumption of Moses a retrospect of Jewish history.—The body of Moses.—Conclusions.—The book of Jubilees.—The Apocalypse of Ezra.—Vision of the Roman eagle.—The Church as a woman.—The woman and the city.—The Messiah.—The new heaven and the new earth.—Apocalypse of Ezra compared with Book of Daniel and Apocalypse of St. John . . . . . . 353–396

## CHAPTER XXII.

### SYMBOLS, MIRACLES, AND CREEDS.

Concealment of the truth in Scripture.—Key to the symbol of Holy Writ.—Historical and ideal element.—No sudden abolition of symbols, or cessation of miracles.—From the outward to the inward.—The visible and the invisible Church.—The tree of life.—The tree of knowledge.—The Serpent in Eden.—The Mystery of Babylon.—'Through knowledge cometh life.'—Jonah and the kikayon.—The tree of life and of knowledge on Egyptian Monuments.—Dogmas are symbols.—Primacy of the Pope.—Parties of progress and of stagnation in the Church.—The keys of St. Peter, and the mission of the Popes.—The 'holy Catholic Church' . 397–422

## APPENDIX.

New Dates in New Testament Chronology.

# INTRODUCTION.

FROM THE BEGINNING man was, and felt himself to be, a free agent. Conscious of his liberty and of his powers, man gradually became the ruler 'over the fish of the sea, and over the fowl of the air, and over the cattle, and over every creeping thing that creepeth upon the earth.' But by contemplation and experience he perceived also, that there were powers in nature, over which he had no command. The earth, with its supposed motionless stability, would not present itself as a problem, even to the wisest of men. But whence the motion of air and water, and, above all, whence the origin of fire? This was not altogether a mystery to him. By an act of his own, he could originate the most powerful of nature's elements. Yet fire was observed, as suddenly issuing forth from a dark cloud, and as penetrating into the earth. This fire from heaven was a mystery, and man considered the cloud as the dwelling-place of a non-human intelligence, higher than his own.

Experiencing how this submission to superior powers harmonised with his innermost feelings, an undefined but irresistible longing led man to mark by outward deeds his dependence upon the mysterious and the invisible. He worshipped in different forms the unknown. All meteoric phenomena, which we know to be caused by temporary changes in the atmosphere, from the clouds to the rainbow, were regarded as mysterious manifestations of superior powers. But, as they suddenly appeared, so they disappeared. And though snow and hailstones seemed, at first sight, to be inhabitants of other regions, yet both melted into water, and ceased to be mysteries. It was not so with meteoric stones. As they fell to the ground, light accompanied their path, and if they were dug out of the ground, they had in most cases lost their heat, but they had not lost their value as visitors from another world. Meteoric stones were the first idols, because symbols of incomprehensible powers.

As man acknowledged the superiority of incomprehensible agents, as he became more conscious of their reality, he was led to picture to himself the forms of such primary causes. He fashioned images, to represent the ideas he had conceived. In the beginning, images were symbols. Man did not regard them as original realities, but as emblems. The visible was but the garment of the invisible. Thus, light and warmth had been discerned as necessary conditions to life. Yet neither the fire, which man could produce, nor the light of the sun, moon, and stars, was by thinking man regarded as a cause, but as an effect. Images were the creations of his own self, and yet they represented, what his mind had conceived of the most sublime, of the ineffable. They formed a visible centre of attraction, well qualified to draw forth, to develope and to fix his purest thoughts and emotions.

There was danger in worshipping the invisible and the unknown, through the medium of works made with hands. Superiorly gifted, and more perfectly instructed men, would teach their fellow creatures to regard images in their true character. And as these images became household gods, the father of the family would instruct the son in the mysteries which they represented. Yet, in course of time, when tribes migrated to distant lands, and intermixed with other races of mankind, the original tradition would be altered, for better, or for worse. Symbols would be differently interpreted, the love for the visible would wrongly direct, or chase away, the awe of the invisible; the outward symbol would lead to a merely outward religion. Profiting by the ignorance of the people, the few who were initiated in the mysteries of symbolic worship, would create a caste privilege, of that which ought to belong to all. The priest would usurp the duties which originally devolved on the father of the family, and the chiefs of the tribes. Moreover the knowledge of One God was neither aboriginal nor universal. The migrations of mankind would, therefore, lead, if not to an interchange of images, at least to a mixture of the different conceptions, of which they were originally the representatives. Thus the symbols of the One God might even become the symbols of many gods. Symbols would become idols.

But in the beginning it was not so. The recorded early history of the Israelites would be inexplicable, if, in the time of the Patriarchs, idols had been anything else than symbols. The idea which symbols embodied, and which originally they conveyed, thus became engrafted on mankind, and was transmitted from generation to generation. So long as symbols were rightly understood, as visible manifestations, or rather, as suggestive representations of the invisible, so long were all crystallisations of ideas beneficial and necessary. They were the revered heirlooms of the human family, the uniting links between tribes and nations. But, in course of time, the traditional interpretation was either entirely lost, or it was concealed by a few, as the pearl of great price. In the earliest ages to which history refers, long before the art of writing was known, verbal tradition was the only conveyancer of knowledge. Signs were gradually invented, to assist memory. These signs were only understood by the few who had received the education of the most privileged members of their community. They were inherited by the son from the father, by the family from the tribe. Hence symbols became mysteries. They required to be interpreted by those who possessed the key of knowledge, they were the memorials of a hidden wisdom. Thus emblems became hieroglyphics, history took the form of allegory, and symbols were degraded into idols.

To restore symbolism, by the removal of idolatry, this was the mission of prophets. Their office was that of reformers. It was not so much their duty to announce and establish what was new, as to proclaim the old in a new form, to harmonise the just appreciation of the past with the exigencies of the present.

In order to consider the origin and development of the prophetic office, the connection between prophets and scribes, and of the latter with ancestorial tradition, we must trace the origin and development of the mysterious union between the Rechabites, or Kenites, and the Hebrews.

From this new point of view it may be possible to explain the relations between the Hebrew and the Greek Canon. The exclusion of the Apocrypha from the Hebrew Canon has not been sanctioned by the Catholic Church. The Hebrew or Protestant Canon of Holy Writ, without the Apocrypha of the Greek Canon, is a sealed book. Scripture requires to be interpreted. The word of Scripture is a symbol of the truth, not the truth itself. Canons of interpretation, which are to commend themselves to the conscience of every man, can only be framed in conjunction with the unwritten tradition of the Church. Christianity is the Apocalypse of the Apocrypha.

# THE
# KEYS OF ST. PETER.

## CHAPTER I.

### THE HOUSE OF RECHAB.

*Errata.*

Page 3, lines 3 and 6 from foot, *for* Judea, *read* India.
Page 119, line 2 from foot, *read* ' to Isaac's sacrifice.'

and of (by) the first of the captives. The Rechabites, or Kenites, descendants from Cain, went, therefore, into captivity with the Hebrews.

Jonadab, whom the Rechabites in the time of Jeremiah called their 'father,'[4] is stated to have been 'the son of Rechab,'[5] from which it does not follow that Rechab was Jonadab's progenitor. Since among the Kenites the Shimeahites are mentioned, it is probable that Shimeah, the brother of David, was also connected with the Rechab-

---

Gen. v.    [2] Num. xxiv. 22; Judg. iv. 11 (Hebrew text).
[3] 1 Chr. ii. 55.    [4] Jer. xxv. 6, 10.    [5] 2 Kings x. 15.

few who had received the education of the most privileged members of their community. They were inherited by the son from the father, by the family from the tribe. Hence symbols became mysteries. They required to be interpreted by those who possessed the key of knowledge, they were the memorials of a hidden wisdom. Thus emblems became hieroglyphics, history took the form of allegory, and symbols were degraded into idols.

To restore symbolism, by the removal of idolatry, this was the mission of prophets. Their office was that of reformers. It was not so much their duty to announce and establish what was new, as to proclaim the old in a new form, to harmonise the just appreciation of the past with the exigencies of the present.

In order to consider the origin and development of the prophetic office, the connection between prophets and scribes, and of the latter with ancestorial tradition, we must trace the origin and development of the mysterious union between the Rechabites, or Kenites, and the Hebrews.

From this new point of view it may be possible to explain the relations between the Hebrew and the Greek Canon. The exclusion of the Apocrypha from the Hebrew Canon has not been sanctioned by the Catholic Church. The Hebrew or Protestant Canon of Holy Writ, without the Apocrypha of the Greek Canon, is a sealed book. Scripture requires to be interpreted. The word of Scripture is a symbol of the truth, not the truth itself. Canons of interpretation, which are to commend themselves to the conscience of every man, can only be framed in conjunction with the unwritten tradition of the Church. Christianity is the Apocalypse of the Apocrypha.

*Errata.*

Page 3, lines 3 and 6 from foot, *for* Judea, *read* India.
Page 119, line 2 from foot, *read* ' to Isaac's sacrifice.'


Bunsen's Keys.

THE

# KEYS OF ST. PETER.

## CHAPTER I.

#### THE HOUSE OF RECHAB.

In one of the most ancient records of Genesis, Cain is called Kenan.[1] The connection between Kenan and the Kenites is proved by two passages in holy writ, where 'Cain' stands for 'Kenite.'[2] Again, the Kenites are identified with the Rechabites. We are told in Chronicles, that 'the house of Rechab' contained 'families of the scribes which dwelt in Jabez,' and they are called the 'Kenites that came from Hemath,' or Hamath, 'the father of the house of Rechab.'[3] According to the Septuagint, which is confirmed by the targum of Jonathan, the 71st Psalm was dedicated to 'David, of (by) the sons of Jonadab, and of (by) the first of the captives.' The Rechabites, or Kenites, descendants from Cain, went, therefore, into captivity with the Hebrews.

Jonadab, whom the Rechabites in the time of Jeremiah called their 'father,'[4] is stated to have been 'the son of Rechab,'[5] from which it does not follow that Rechab was Jonadab's progenitor. Since among the Kenites the Shimeahites are mentioned, it is probable that Shimeah, the brother of David, was also connected with the Rechab-

---

[1] Gen. v.    [2] Num. xxiv. 22; Judg. iv. 11 (Hebrew text).
[3] 1 Chr. ii. 55.    [4] Jer. xxv. 6, 10.    [5] 2 Kings x. 15.

ites. Shimeah had a son Jonadab, who is described as 'very subtil,' or very wise,[1] that is, as we may interpret, as initiated in the wisdom in which Solomon excelled 'the children of the East,' and the wisdom of Egypt. This Jonadab, the son of Shimeah, was therefore probably the father to whom the Rechabites referred.

Another Jonadab was the contemporary of Elijah and Elishah.[2] It is not improbable, that he also was a Rechabite. Josephus states, that Jehonadab had been Jehu's 'friend of old,' and that he was 'a good and a righteous man.'[3] Jehu cannot have doubted his 'zeal for the Lord,' of which the king boasted, for Jonadab accompanied the latter on his mission of destruction against the priests of Baal. Yet Jehu is not quite sure of Jonadab's fidelity to him, for he asks: 'is thy heart sincere, as my heart is towards thy heart?' Jonadab having affirmed this, Jehu said: 'And is it so, then give me thine hand,' whereupon the king shook hands with him, and made him sit in his chariot. Jonadab can hardly have entirely agreed with Jehu, whom Josephus reports to have said on this occasion: 'that it was a most excellent and a most pleasing sight to a good and righteous man, to see the wicked punished.' But, as Josephus adds, Jonadab was persuaded by Jehu's arguments to go with him to Samaria. It was not an enterprise against Judah, with which country the Rechabites, or Kenites, as we shall see, were closely connected, but against the Royal family of Israel, because of its connection with Ahab's Canaanitish, or Hamitic, queen Jezebel, through whose influence new symbols of worship had been introduced in Judah as well as Israel. The Shemites, perhaps the Hebrews as well as the Kenites, considered the spread of Hamitic or Egyptian mode of worship to be subversive of the religion of Jehovah. It was essential, in their opinion, to eradicate by fire and sword the notion, that the sun not only symbolises,

---

[1] 2 Sam. xiii. 2.   [2] 2 Kings x. 15, 16.   [3] Ant. ix. 6, 6.

but is, the one God, whom the Hamitic nations worshipped under the name of Baal. Jehu, whom Elijah was ordered, in the vision at Horeb, to anoint as king over Israel, was to be, together with Elisha, the destroyer of those who bowed unto Baal. These facts tend to confirm the Jewish tradition, that Jonadab, probably a Kenite, like his namesake, David's nephew, was the disciple of Elijah and Elisha.

Both of these prophets are in the Bible referred to as the 'father,' as 'the horseman,' or leader, of 'the chariot,' or Rechab, of Israel.[1] We shall now try to prove, that by this appellation Elijah and Elisha are designated as fathers of tradition. The mystic tradition of the Jews, the Mosaic, and pre-Mosaic, origin of which has hitherto been regarded, at most, as a non-proven probability, was, according to the Talmud, divided into two parts, the one theoretical, the other practical. The former was called 'the history of creation,' and probably began with the mystic interpretation of Genesis; for one of the earliest works on secret tradition, referred to by Jewish authors, bore the title: 'Midrash, let there be light.'[2] The second part was called 'the history of the Chariot' or of 'the Rechab,' and it is often referred to as 'the holy Merkabah.' The first part could not be communicated to any of the uninitiated, whilst the Rechab was the canon of tradition applied. This interpretation of the Rechab or 'Chariot' of Israel receives a remarkable confirmation by the fact, that the same symbol, possibly derived originally from the sun, as the conveyancer or chariot of light, was used in Judea. The Buddhistic essays on theology, called Sutras, were, from the commencement, divided into sutras of great vehicle, and sutras of small vehicle. Also in Judea the records of tradition were the chariots of the law. Fathers of the house of Rechab were, therefore, fathers of tradition. This conclusion will be con-

---

[1] Comp. 2 Kings ii. 12; xiii. 14; and Boulduc, 'De Eccles. ante Leg.' iii. 10.
[2] Appendix to Gelinek's translation of Frank's Cabbala, p. 229.

firmed, if we succeed in proving, that 'the house of Rechab' is another name for the house which, according to Proverbs, Divine wisdom has built and supported by 'seven pillars,' or organs of tradition. The tradition, or Rechab, was transmitted by the fathers to the sons, by the teachers to their pupils, and it formed the mystery of Scribes, or the learned in Scripture, who, as such, were called 'Sons of Rechab.' For this reason the Kenites or Rechabites had ' families of Scribes.'

Such fathers of Scribal tradition were Elijah and Elisha, as well as Jonadab. Thus, through the Rechabites a connection can be traced between the tradition in the time of David, and that of which Elijah was a father. What we know of Elijah confirms his assumed connection with the Rechabites. Without laying too much stress on the nomadic habits, the fiery zeal, and the austerity of the great prophet, his Rechabite descent is convincingly proved by the signification of the word tishbite. For the tishbite means, undoubtedly, 'the stranger,' and the Rechabites were always to live as 'strangers' in the land.[1] The Hebrew word tôshâb is used, in several of the most ancient parts of the Bible, as stranger, foreigner, or sojourner.[2] Elijah was 'of the inhabitants of Gilead,' and it is not improbable, that Jabesh or Jabez in Gilead was his native place. For, as the Rechabites had a dwelling in Jabez of Judah, another in the south of Arad, in the wilderness of Judah, so their settlements in the north, beside Zaanim, near Kadesh, may have included Jabesh in Gilead, the native country of Elijah 'the stranger.'[3] This probability is heightened by the history of that town.

After the destruction of the tribe of Benjamin, at the battle of Gibeah, the men of Jabesh-Gilead not having gone up to fight the rebel tribe, all the inhabitants of that town were slain, and the virgins given in marriage to

[1] Jer. xxxv. 7   [2] Lev. xxv. 6; Ex. xii. 45; Ps. xxxix. 12.
[3] 1 Kings xvii. 1.

the 600 Benjamites that escaped. Saul defended the city against the Ammonites, and its inhabitants afterwards showed their gratitude to the Benjamite ruler, by taking down the bodies of Saul and of his sons from the walls at Bethshan, by burning them, burying the bones under a tree, and observing a seven days' fast. From this we gather, that the men of Jabesh, who did this, could not have been Hebrews, that is, descendants from Eber and other trans-euphratian tribes. As the Hebrews never burnt their dead, this only recorded instance of the bodies of Israelites being burnt, is a conclusive proof of our assertion, that the inhabitants of Jabesh in Gilead belonged to some of the Kenite families that came from Hamath. This is confirmed by Balaam's saying of 'the Kenites,' that 'Cain' will have 'to be burnt,' that is, partly destroyed and partly led captive. The prophet would not have referred to the burning of the Kenite bodies, unless this was the Kenite rite of burial.

The book of Amos furnishes us with a striking confirmation of the above interpretation.[1] The prophet refers to 'Hamath the Great' as a rival city of Zion and Gerizim. 'Woe to them that are careless on the Zion, and to them that are secure on the mountain of Samaria, to the first named of the first among the nations,[2] to them that come from the house of Israel. Pass ye unto Calneh, and see, and from thence go ye to Hamath the Great, and go down to Gath of the Philistines; are they better than these kingdoms, or is their border greater than your border? Ye who consider yourselves far removed from the day of trouble, whilst he have brought near the dominion of violence.' At that time, 'Joseph,' that is, Ephraim and Manasseh, the tribe which had shared with Judah the privilege of first taking their inheritance,[3] Ephraim 'the first-born' of the Lord, was in affliction. But the careless and the secure on Zion and

---

[1] Amos vi. 1-14.  [2] Comp. Ex. iv. 22; Jer. xxxi. 9, &c.
[3] Josh. xv.-xviii.

on Gerizim, whilst 'they chant to the sound of the harp,' whilst they compare their 'music on stringed instruments' with 'that of David,' whilst they 'drink wine in bowls, and anoint themselves with the best oil,' they are 'not grieved for the wound (breach) of Joseph. Therefore now shall they be led away captive at the head of the captives.'

Amos declares, that God despises 'the pride of Jacob,' and that he will 'deliver up the city (Jerusalem), with all that is therein.' 'If there remain ten men in one house, they shall die. And if one be carried away (by) his cousin, and (by) him that burneth him, to bring the bones out of the house, and shall say unto him (that is) within the house: Is (there) yet (any) with thee, and he shall say: Not one, then shall he (the former) say: Silence, for the name of the Lord may not come over my lips.' Finally the prophet announces, that the God of hosts will cause a nation to rise against 'the house of Israel,' oppressing, or driving away the same, from 'the district (or entrance) of Hamath, unto the brook of the wilderness.' Thus Amos foretells, that, by a relative of the Hebrews, by a race akin to the inhabitants of Jabez in the time of Saul, and to the inhabitants of Hamath, whom we shall prove to have been originally cousins to the Hebrews, the rite of burial was to be performed on the slain Israelites according to a non-Israelitic custom.

In the days of Amos, Hamath was still the principal city of Upper Syria, as it had been in the time of the Exodus. The Hamathites are designated as those who enter into Israel's possessions. The Samaritans or Cuthcans can be shown to have been, at least, a race cognate to the Hamathites, or Rechabites, if not identical with them. We may therefore assume, that the affliction, the wound, or breach, of 'Joseph,' that is, of one of the tribes representing the Kenite branch among the Israelites, was somewhat connected with the exclusive and domineering principles of the Hebrew branch, ruling on Zion as well as on Gerizim, before the Assyrian invasion. If Kenites formed a component part of Israel, the Kenite conquerors would naturally perform the funeral rites on those of the fallen, who, like them, were descendants from Cain.

The kingdom of Hamath, during its independence, extended from 'the entrance of Hamath,'[1] near the sources of the Orontes, to the defile of Daphne below Antioch. Toi, king of Hamath, made formal submission to David, after his victory over Hadadezer, king of Zobah,[2] and the country of Hamath formed part of Solomon's kingdom, inasmuch as Solomon built store-cities in Hamath.[3] The Hamathites were a Hamitic race, mentioned in Genesis among the descendants from Canaan,[4] and generally allied with the Hittites. The Hittites, or descendants from Heth, in the genealogies of the sons of Noah, are recorded as descendants from Canaan, and they are enumerated, with the Kenites, among the non-Hebrew tribes who inhabited the land of promise before Isaac was born. Thus the non-Hebrew origin of the 'Kenites that came from Hamath,' that is, of 'the house of Rechab,' is confirmed.

Although the Kenites, and others, were established in the promised land before the immigration of the Hebrews, yet some of these non-Hebrew tribes became early associated with the trans-euphratian highlanders, the descendants from Abraham, and formed an integral and important part of their community. The marriage of Moses, the Hebrew, with Zipporah, the Kenite, daughter of a Midianite priest, is the first recorded proof of this communion in the post-patriarchal time. The fact, that Zipporah was a descendant of Keturah, the concubine of Abraham, shows, in the outset, that the two streams had met before. Again, Caleb, 'the son of Zephunneh the Kenezite,' was of non-Hebrew origin. Kenaz the Edomite was a descendant from Esau, who received the name

---

[1] Num. xxxiv. 8; Josh. xiii. 5, &c.  [2] 2 Sam. viii. 18.
[3] 2 Chr. viii. 4; comp. 1 Kings iv. 21.  [4] Gen. x. 18.

Edom, and became, according to the genealogy, the grandfather of Amalek. Caleb the Kenezite, together with Joshua or Jehoshuah the son of Nun, probably a descendant from Shuah, son of Keturah, and therefore a Kenite,—these two Israelites, whose ancestors were of non-Hebrew descent, among all the men that came out of Egypt, from twenty years old and upward, were alone to see the promised land, because they had been perfectly obedient to Jehovah. Of Caleb it is written: 'My servant Caleb will I bring into the land, into which he has come, and his seed shall possess it, because that another spirit did lead him, and that he was perfectly obedient unto me.'[1] Because of this Divine command, the city of Hebron and its neighbourhood became the inheritance of Caleb,[2] forty-five years after he had advised the Israelites to enter the promised land. Thus a descendant from an Edomite, whose ancestors may, like Joshua, long before the conquest, have formed part of Israel's community, received 'a part among the children of Judah'[3] in the holy land.

It was a descendant from Moses the Hebrew, and Zipporah the Kenite, who symbolised the union of the Hebrew and the non-Hebrew race, which, combined, formed the people of Israel, in all parts of its history. As if to refer to the connection between the Hebrews and the Kenites, the eldest surviving son of Moses and Zipporah was called Eliezer, which name, in the time of Moses, as in the time of Abraham, can be shown to have referred to the union of Hebrews and non-Hebrews. Eliezer's son was called Rechabiah, literally, 'the chariot,' that is, the tradition of Jehovah. According to the Targum, Rechabiah, or Rechab, was the father of the sons of Jonadab, that is, of the Kenites from Hamath. 'Eliezer had none other sons, but the sons of Rechabiah were very many.'[4] As Aaron

---

[1] Num. xiv. 24; xxxii. 11, 12.   [2] Josh. xiv. 6, 14.
[3] Josh. xv. 13.   [4] 1 Chron. xxiii. 17.

was brother to Moses, the Mosaic descendants from Rechabiah were cousins to the Aaronic descendants from Eleazar and Thamar, the first Hebrew high priest's only surviving sons. Thus it is confirmed, that the prophet Amos refers to the people of Hamath, to the Rechabites of Mount Gerizim, as the 'cousins' of the Israelites, whose bodies were by them to be burnt in the same strange manner in which the inhabitants of Jabesh Gilead had burnt the bodies of Saul and of his sons. At that time Jabesh Gilead was a city of the Israelites, and it is highly probable, that, after the massacre of its male inhabitants, the Rechabites pitched their tents in or near that place. For in the time of Saul it was a Rechabite city.

Kenites cannot be shown ever to have become Hebrews, with whom they lived in union. They were originally, and they continued to live as 'strangers' within the gates of the Hebrews. Thus Caleb's descendents are enumerated in the list of the families of 'the Kenites, that came from Hamath, the father of the house of Rechab.'[1] Among these is Salma, or Salman, the father of Boaz, and founder of the house of David, who married Rahab or Rachab of Jericho. Josephus merely calls her an 'innkeeper,' and states nothing against her character, from which circumstance it may be assumed, that the matrimonial metaphor has been used by the Hebrew chronicler, in this as in other instances, in order to mark the spreading of influences which he supposed to be idolatrous.[2] We shall show, that, probably in all, certainly in the principal instances, the charge of immorality is raised by Hebrews against Kenites, who, like their kindred, the Hittites, readily received strangers among them. In the time of Ezra, and already in the time of Josiah, when the hidden book of the law was incorporated in the Mosaic writings, the admission of strangers was either restricted or absolutely prohibited. In Deuteronomy the Ammonite and the Moabite were alone excluded from the congregation;

---

[1] 1 Chron. ii. 50-55.   [2] Judg. ii. 17; viii. 33; comp. 1 Sam. ii. 22.

and the history of Ruth shows, that this injunction was not, at that time, inserted in the written law. But in the time of Ezra a party spirit can be shown to have prevailed, which was far more narrow and uncompromising, than the spirit of party still traceable in the records which refer to earlier times. Soon after the return from the captivity, immediately after the Purim massacre, every marriage with a stranger was regarded as an abomination. It can be fully established, that the final revision of the canon took place under circumstances which were adverse to a just appreciation of the house of David, that is, of the Kenite line, always opposed by the Hebrew or Sadducean line, to which Ezra belonged. It is probably owing to these hostile influences, that Rahab has received an epithet which prophets invariably used as the symbol of idolatry.

The Kenites had not separated from the Hebrews, ever since the time of Moses. The great lawgiver, who had implicitly followed Jethro's advice, urged the Kenites, not to separate themselves from the Hebrews, but to share, on equal terms, the benefits of the Lord, and to be 'the eye' of Israel. Addressing Hobab, his brother-in-law, from whom Heber the Kenite descended,[1] Moses said: 'Leave us not, I pray thee. Since thou knowest, where we are to encamp in the wilderness, therefore thou shalt be to us instead of eyes.'[2] It is not stated, how this knowledge of Israel's future wanderings to the promised land had been conveyed to the Kenites. Had they seers among them, like Balaam, and had the Lord, through such Kenite seers, 'spoken good concerning Israel'? This conjecture will become highly probable, when we shall have pointed out, that the first seer of Israel's future, of whom we have any knowledge, was a Kenite, a contemporary of Moses; that the prophetic institutions were introduced in the time of Eli and Samuel, the Kenites; that David, foremost among the first Hebrew prophets, was a Kenite; that in his time the oracles began to be

---

[1] Judg. iv. 11.  [2] Num. x. 31.

given through prophets, instead of through the medium of the Urim and Thummim; that the Kenites introduced Jehovah worship into Israel; that the leading prophets of Israel were Kenites; and that, already in the patriarchal time, Job, the Kenite, referred to his eye being enlightened by the lamp of God, to his walking through the darkness by the Divine light, to 'the secret of God' as being in his tabernacle. Job was 'eyes to the blind, and feet to the lame, father to the poor, and searcher of the unknown.'[1] Was 'the secret of God' in the tent of the Kenites, during the forty years that Moses dwelt among them? Did Moses receive his first revelations concerning his future mission, through Kenite 'searchers of the unknown?' We have, perhaps, sufficient reason to think so. The connection between the Kenites and the tribe of Judah, which formed the vanguard of Israel during its wanderings, rather confirms this view.

The house of Rechab is the house of tradition. Through the Rechabites, or conveyancers of tradition, through the Scribes, among whom prophets took the lead, tradition can be traced back to Jethro and Melchizedec, and thus to Moses and to Abraham, the inhabitant of Ur of the Chaldees. Although the tradition of Melchizedec, and that of Abraham, must have been essentially the same, yet the greater of the two, the Kenite Melchizedec, represents pre-Abramitic Monotheism. Kenite priestly succession has transmitted Kenite pre-Abramitic tradition; whilst Hebrew tradition, since the time of Moses and Jethro, has transmitted a mixed tradition, the non-Kenite elements of which may be, in a general sense, designated as Egyptian. Hebrew tradition is Eastern tradition mixed up with Western tradition. The non-Kenite element of Mosaic tradition must therefore be more clearly defined as of Western or African origin. The black-skinned ravager of the West, Chedorlaomer, was the common enemy of Melchizedec and of Abraham, and also of the Eastern

---

[1] Job xxix. 15, 16.

Shepherd-rulers in Egypt. The black man was the adversary of the white man, in the land between the Nile and the Euphrates. Pure Eastern and pre-Abramitic tradition was mixed up with, and opposed by, impure Eastern tradition in the West. Yet the latter, or Western element was necessarily predominant in the time of Moses and Jethro. The elder son of Aaron represented the least pure tradition. Because the tradition of Melchizedec, of Abraham, of Jethro, and of Moses was of one and the same Eastern origin, therefore the successors of Jethro and of his contemporaries, the Rechabites, or Kenites, represent the Abramitic covenant, as well as that made 430 years later on Sinai.

The double Aaronic line represents the more restrictive principles of the Mosaic, and the Catholicism of the Abramitic covenant. To the line of Eleazar the Sadducees, and to the line of Ithamar the Pharisees and Essenes can be shown to have always belonged. The Kenite high priestly line was so much more venerable than the Hebrew line, as Abraham was greater than Moses, and as Melchizedec was greater than Abraham. It is for this reason, that Jabez, that is, the Kenite, in holy writ, is recorded to have been more 'honourable than his brethren.'[1] 'Honourable men' were men of wisdom.[2] Hence it follows, that Kenites and Hebrews, the descendants from Melchizedec and from Abraham, originally were the conveyancers of one and the same wisdom.

The house of Wisdom, built on seven pillars, that is, as we shall prove, on the unbroken chain of tradition, represented by the names of Adam, Methuselah, Shem, Isaac, Levi, Amram and Moses, the house of tradition, 'the house of Rechab,' was confided to the care of two cousins, whose ancestors came from the East, to Kenites and Hebrews, to the guardians of Mount Gerizim and of Mount Zion, both living more or less peacefully together, till the fight for supremacy dissolved the bonds of common origin, and ancestorial tradition.

[1] 1 Chron. iv. 9.     [2] Josh. vi. 13.

## CHAPTER II.

### MIGRATIONS AFTER THE FLOOD.

THE double stream of Hebrew and of Kenite tradition, dating from the Abramitic period, is marked by a twofold record of post-diluvian genealogies. The book of Genesis furnishes us, in the form of genealogies, with the names of the different settlements of the Shemites after the Flood. In the tenth and in the eleventh chapter we find a Jehovistic and an Elohistic version of the post-diluvian genealogies.[1] We shall later prove, and now assume, the identity of the Jehovistic and the Kenite, as of the Elohistic and the Hebrew version. The Kenite account contains some additional names. Elam and Assur are mentioned as first sons, or earlier settlements of the Shemites, and Lud and Aram, and his sons, are given as following between Arpachshad and Shelach. But the two latter names, as well as the two following, Heber and Peleg, are identical, and follow in the same order in both lists. The lists of Shemitic genealogies, or settlements, start from the highland of the Caucasus. At the foot of this mountainous district, were the kingdoms of Chaldea, Assyria, and Persia. To these countries the names of the genealogies, four of which are only recorded by the Kenite, evidently refer.[2] For Elam, which word has been etymologically identified

---

[1] The word Jehovah is in the English authorised version translated by 'the Lord,' and Elohim, by 'God.'
[2] After Bunsen's 'Bibelwerk,' and Pleyte's 'Religion pré-Israelite.'

with Iran, is the Elymais of Ptolemy, which he describes as situated on the Eastern shore of the Tigris, in Eastern Babylonia. Assur was a tribe inhabiting the sources of the Tigris, and belonged to the kingdom of Ninus. Arpachshad or Arapachitis, extended to the foot of the Armenian mountain. Lydia was a land in Asia Minor, and Aram was, at first, the name of the Armenian highland, before it was applied to Syria.

The first name which both lists have in common, is Arpachshad, Arapachitis, bordered in the East by Elymais, in the South by Assyria, in the West by Lydia, and in the North by Armenia. The next name is Shelach, which means 'emigration.' The tribes followed the Eastern bank of the Tigris, and crossed that river, as the name Eber, son of Shelah, implies. The tribes then divided, and to this 'division' refers the name Peleg. Part of the Shemite immigrants started for the Yemen, that is, for the Arabian shores on the Indian Ocean and the entrance of the Persian Gulf, and the other branch returned to the Caucasus, following the right bank of the Tigris, and traversing Mesopotamia. To these fertile plains refers the name Réhu, given as the 'son' of Peleg in the genealogy. These tribes spread to Osroëne, or Serug, as the Syrians called it, and of this settlement the name Serug, father of Nahor, is the traditional memorial.

No doubt exists as to the situation of Osroëne, or Serug, and the present Seruj, in the plain between the upper Euphrates and the Belik. A little to the East lies, between the Khabour and the Euphrates, the present town of Harran, which has been identified with Haran 'the city of Nahor.' To the north of Harran, forming a triangle with it and with Seruj, lies Urfah, and, though the identification of it with Ur is disputed on high authority, yet, according to the geographical interpretation of the names in the genealogies, for which geographical interpretation there seems to be sufficient reason, we should expect 'Ur of the Chaldees' to have been situated, as all other names of the lists are, near to the names which precede and follow it.

As it is impossible to assert, that the genealogies of the tenth and other chapters in Genesis contain nothing more than the lists of human descendants, and as in various instances the names of tribes and nations, of their habitations, and not of individuals, have undoubtedly been recorded, the above-traced connection of genealogical names with known geographical districts, allows us to regard the genealogies as records of settlements, as landmarks of tribal migrations. We can thus follow the Shemites from the mountain range spreading between the Caspian and the Black Sea, to the Western bank of the Tigris, where a separation of tribes took place towards the south-eastern part of Arabia, and towards Northern Mesopotamia, the ancient Padan Aram, that is, to 'the cultivated district at the foot of the hills,' where 'Ur of the Chaldees' was situated, from whence Terah and Abram started, 'to go into the land of Canaan.'

'The land of Canaan' was in later times, and perhaps from the earliest times, used in a narrower and in a wider sense. It changed its limits at different times, and included, at one time, the maritime plains of Philistia, in the South of Canaan proper, and of Phœnicia to the north of it, thus extending to the entire sea-coast from Zidon to Gaza. Canaan, or the 'low land,' denotes in the Bible the country West of Jordan and the Dead Sea, and between those waters and the Mediterranean. In comparison with the land East of Jordan, 'the land of Gilead,' Canaan might be called a lowland; but the high level of many parts of it seems to point to another origin of this name. If we succeed in proving the descent of the Kenites from Cain, and their migration from Nod, that is, the lowland of the Indus, to the land between the Euphrates and the Nile, the importation of the name Canaan by the Eastern lowlanders will be a sufficiently established hypothesis. Not only does the name Kenites or Kenaanites mean lowlanders, but the name Samaritan means the same thing. Like the Lithuanian Zemaitis, and the Greek chamaítios, Samaritan means lowlander. The importance of this identity is evident, as the Samaritans were of the stock of the Perizzites,[1] and thus, like the Kenites, descended from the pre-Abramitic inhabitants of Canaan.

Canaan seems to have been an ever-varying local definition of countries occupied by Canaanites, or Kenaanites, the descendants from Kenan, or Cain. Thus C'na, the Greek name for Canaan, was by the Greeks used for Phœnicia, and, by the later Phœnicians, not only for Phœnicia proper, but for the Punic colonies in Africa. In the Septuagint, a similar extension is given to the name.[2] We regard, therefore, the land Canaan, in its wider sense, as the country 'between the river of Egypt unto the great river, the river Euphrates.' When that country was promised to Abram's seed, before even Isaac had been born, it was inhabited by 'the Kenites, and the Kennizites, and the Kadmonites, and the Hittites, and the Perizzites, and the Rephaims, and the Amorites, and the Canaanites, and the Girgashites, and the Jebusites.'[3] The Hittite and the Jebusite and the Amorite dwelt 'in the mountain' (of Judah and Ephraim), and the Canaanite 'by the sea and by the *side* of Jordan,' when the spies of every tribe of Israel entered Canaan. At that time the Amalekites dwelt in the southern part of the land, that is, between the southern hill ranges of Palestine and the border of Egypt. But we know, that already before Isaac was born, Chedorlaomer smote the Amalekites in these regions; we cannot, therefore, account for the omission of the Amalekites in the above list. Balaam is recorded to have stated, that 'Amalek was the firstborn of the nations,' whilst in the tenth chapter of Genesis Zidon is called 'the firstborn of Canaan.' That this cannot be

---

[1] Epiph. Haer. i.    [2] Ex. xvi. 35; Josh. v. 12; comp. v. 1.
[3] Gen. xv. 18-21.

understood in the genealogical sense is probable, inasmuch as the name Sidonians is, in the books of Joshua and of the Judges, used as the generic or collective name of the Phœnicians or Canaanites.

Among the pre-Abramitic inhabitants of the southern maritime plains of the Mediterrranean were the Philistines, or 'emigrants,' who are mentioned in Genesis as a pastoral tribe in the neighbourhood of Gerar.[1] They are stated to have come from Caphtor,[2] and may be identified with the 'Caphtorims which came out of Caphtor' (Kebt-Hor, Coptos), and who expelled the nomadic Avims from their territory, and occupied it in their place,[3] being descendants from Mizraim. Of Mizraim, as of 'Cush, it is now generally admitted, that they are not personal but geographical names. From being a nomadic race cognate to the Egyptians, the Philistines, that is, the Tok-Karu (Carians), and the Shayratana (Cherethim and Cretans) of Egyptian monuments, had become a seafaring nation by a long separation, during which they probably occupied the sea-coast between the mouths of the Indus and of the Euphrates, as also the southern and western coasts of Arabia. From these latter coasts, according to earliest tradition,[4] came the Phœnicians, who are proved to have been of the same stock as the Kenaanites, and whose language was essentially the same. The Phœnicians, the Philistines, and the Kenites, were cognate races.

This is confirmed by the fact, that Canaan was the native name of Phœnicia. Among the pre-Abramitic inhabitants of Canaan were the Kadmonites, whose name is a synonym of the 'Bene Kedem,' or 'sons of the East,' often mentioned in holy writ. That they came from the East, is confirmed by the name of Cadmus, or 'man of the East,' the leader of the Phœnicians, who taught the

---

[1] Gen. xxi. 32-34; xxii. 1, 8.   [2] Amos ix. 7; Jer. xlvii. 4.
[3] Deut. ii. 23.   [4] Herod. vii. 89.

letters of the alphabet to the Greeks. It is possible that the Kenaan of the West was already called 'holy land' before the time of Abram. The name of Cain is connected with the 'paradise,' that is, with the highland, where God's presence was manifested. That presence had followed Cain on his wanderings. He had received a sign, a symbol or an earnest, that he should never die. The holy presence followed the highlander to the lowland of Nod, and to the holy land of the West, where the Kenites called one of their cities, probably their capital, Cain, which is enumerated among the possessions of Judah, in the time of Joshua.[1] Ages before Moses, the Egyptians called Palestine *Ta-Neter*, that is, the holy land. At that time the Cheta, that is, the Hittites, were among its inhabitants. We know that they inhabited the land before Abraham.

The Eastern origin of the pre-Abramitic inhabitants of Canaan or Kenaan, including the Kenites, or Kenaanites, which name we propose as a substitute for Canaanites, can be proved from Genesis, and confirmed by those Aryan migrations which are recorded in the Vedas, and in the Avesta, compendiums of the most ancient Eastern tradition.

These Aryan records refer to a common Bactrian home, and to an aboriginal Aryan home. The latter was probably situated on the highland of Pamer, between the sources of the Amu-Daria (Oxus), the Sir Daria (Jaxarthes), and the Kashgar-Daria or Tarim. This table-land forms the centre, from which the Thian Shan radiates to the North-East, the Himalaya to the South-East, and the Hindoo Koosh to the South-West. It is supposed by some,[2] that the ancestors of the Chinese inhabited this Airyana or Aryan home, from whence, wherever it lay, the Bactrian Aryans certainly came. From the Bactrian home which is called Heden, from Bakhdi, with the capital of

[1] Josh. xv. 57.  [2] Knobel especially.

Bactra, two great emigrations are recorded to have taken place. The tribes of Cain, or Kenan, went to the East, towards the upper Indus, where, according to the epic poems of the Vedas, after long conquests, the Eastern Aryans subjugated the non-Aryan inhabitants of these lowlands, who have been called Turanians or Cushites, belonging to the so-called Hamitic stock. From the Indus they later spread to the Sutlej and the Ganges, where, at a still later period, the Brahminic system was founded. The descendants from Seth, after the separation of the Kenites, migrated to the South-West of Eden, and we will call them the Western Aryans. Their wanderings are marked by successive settlements, all traceable in the direction from East to West, a list of which has been preserved in one of the most ancient traditions recorded in the Vendidad, which forms part of the Avesta. The western frontier of the Western Aryans was marked by Ragha 'with three castles,' which commanded the Caspian passes. Like the Eastern Aryans, the Western Aryans subjugated non-Aryan tribes. The Aryans in the East and in the West formed naturally the higher castes of a mixed race, to which, after the Flood the name of Shem refers. Whilst the Shemitic race united Aryan tribes and non-Aryan tribes, it kept up, by its castes, the distinction between the Aryan home and the non-Aryan home, between Asia and Africa.

The races which inhabited, in prehistoric times, among others, the important region from the Indian Ocean to the Mediterranean, were dark-coloured Africans, till they were subjugated by the white-coloured Asiatics, when they became a mixed white and black race. Two facts support this theory at the outset. As the Aryans advanced towards the South-East and the South-West, in Iran as well as in India, the language of the people gradually became the language of the wise, that is, of the higher castes. This is perhaps best explained by assuming, that the lower, or African castes increased in number, whilst the Aryan castes decreased. The dictionary became more African, and the grammar remained Asiatic. The formation of the Egyptian language may, perhaps, be explained by an early Asiatic transformation of the African stock, at a time when the formation of the mixed Asiatic and African the so-called Semitic languages, was in a state of transition. The difference between the Egyptian language, on the one side, and the Semitic languages, that is, the Arabic, the Aramean and the Hebrew on the other, may be sufficiently accounted for, by longer continued African influences in the former, and longer continued Asiatic influences in the latter case. Yet the Egyptian grammar is essentially Asiatic or Aryan, and when a popular or demotic African language was formed in Egypt, the ancient hieroglyphic language was distinguished as the sacred language, as the priestly or hieratic idiom, the language of the initiated. In like manner, the African or Cushite dialect became the language of the 'Wise' in Assyria and in later Babylonia, when the, essentially Aryan, Semitic language had become the language of the people. For this reason Daniel had to be taught the 'tongue' and 'learning of the Chaldeans.'

Because the Asiatics, or Aryans, after the Flood called Japhetides, constituted the ruling castes of subjugated non-Aryan or African races, they did not, for some time, form independent empires. Strengthened by the non-Aryan element, the white race could venture on that colossal combat with the black race, which made the mixed or Semitic race alternately dependant, from the North and from the South. Japhet, the Asiatic highlander, dwelt and ruled in 'the tents' of Shem, the half Asiatic and half African, and Canaan, the African lowlander in Asia, was his servant. The Japhetides were the rulers, or Aryas, in the mixed Semitic and nomadic community, whilst the Hamiks were the servants of the former. Thus Israel consisted of representatives of Japhet, of Shem, and of Ham. Because Shemites represented the entire postdiluvian humanity, Israel was always a mixed community, and symbolised the catholicity of mankind.

## CHAPTER III.

### HIGH CASTE AND LOW CASTE.

IF the origin of the Shemite race can be traced to a combination of Asiatic and African tribes, and if the Aryans, or Japhetides, formed the high castes, and the non-Aryans, or Hamites, the low castes of the mixed Asiatic and African race, then two independent streams must be traceable in Hebrew history.

That history begins with Abram's migration from Ur of the Chaldees, which seems to have been caused by the hostile advance of Hamite races. For the name of Chedorlaomer, or Kedar-el-Ahmar, that is, Kedar the Red, points to a Hamitic origin. As he was king of Elam, this Shemite tribe must have been subjugated at an early period. It is highly probable that Abram's name marks a general migration from regions which had become untenable. The name of his father, his wife, and his nephew, who all went to Haran, represent various tribes, at least of later times. Sarah's name, which probably signifies 'the contentious,' supports the assumption, that a larger number of emigrants left the highlands. A small family party would hardly have ventured to settle in the rich plain of Moreh, or in the mountain-fastness of Ai, seeing that the Kenaanite was already in the land. A famine caused the emigrants to go to Egypt, where, in all probability, the rule of the Hyksos, or Shepherds, had been established long before. It is certain that these shepherds were Aryans, who, like the Shemites, had subjugated non-Aryan tribes on the Indus, or in some districts to the west of that river. As such, they would naturally welcome the Aryan immigrants from the north, whose ancestors had once lived together in Central Asia. The episode about Sarah, when divested of the conventional form of a mere family record, may point to the desire of the Egyptian and of the Philistine kings to rule over the contentious tribe. A fusion of the cognate Hebrews, Egyptians, and Philistines, was with difficulty prevented, in a country where the low caste, or African element predominated, and might soon have overpowered the ruling Asiatic element. Abraham, the leader of the conquering race, must have increased the number of his African dependents. He went out of Egypt richer than he had entered it, as the separation of Lot implies.

Whether we regard the name of Abram, 'father of the mountain,' and the name of Abraham, 'father of many nations,' as exclusively referring to an individual, or whether, as in the case of the sons of Adam, of Noah, and of Jacob, we recognise in it also the collective name of a plurality of persons, the records of Abraham's history enable us to distinguish two separate streams, originating, we suggest, in a diversity of colour and of caste. Sarah was 'free,' but Hagar, the Egyptian, was a 'bondwoman,' a slave. Sarah, or Saraï, belonged to Abram's family before he left Ur of the Chaldees; but Hagar was made over, as a slave, by Sarah to Abram. Hagar was not a concubine, as Keturah is represented to have been; for the concubine was free before her marriage. The rivalry between Sarah and Hagar, and between their offsprings, seems to denote, that Abraham vainly tried to unite discordant elements. Many of the traits transmitted to us, gain in lucidity and in force, if we assume, that, between Sarah and Hagar, there was a difference of caste, that is, of colour. We may here suggest, that the names of Abraham, of Sarah and of Hagar possibly represent the same threefold division to which the postdiluvian names of Japhet, of Shem, and of Ham refer. At least, we regard Abraham as a representative name of the high caste, Sarah of the mixed caste, and Hagar of the low caste. The Aryan mountain chief a descendant from the Aryans in Bactria, from the ancestors of all Indo-European nations, was a ruler of mixed tribes, belonging partly to the Northern or Aryan, and partly to the non-Aryan, Cushite, or Turanian race, of Southern origin. It is immaterial, whether we regard Sarah as representing, like Abraham, the pure white, that is, the high caste, or the half caste, which can hardly have existed in those early times. The fact remains, that freedom and serfdom are symbolised by Sarah and by Hagar. The ancestors of Abraham, of Sarah, and of Hagar, had lived together on the Aramean highlands, in the time of the Flood, and, before that event, in the present Bukhara. There was a time, when no human link existed between the North-Eastern and the South-Western cradle of mankind, between Central Asia and Africa.[1] It is this early separation, which best explains the fact, that no tradition of the great northern Flood can be traced among the Egyptians. The traditions of the latter confirm the distinction of an Asiatic and of an African centre of mankind. The black race and the white race were, by the Egyptians, both subdivided in two classes—the dark one, in the red and the black; the white one, in the yellow and the white. We now proceed to trace the high-caste descent, and the low-caste descent, in the descendants from Hagar and from Sarah.

The first addition to the family of 'Abram, the Hebrew,' was the fruit of his union with Hagar. Ishmael was the firstborn son of Abraham in Canaan. The prospect thus opened to Hagar, 'the Egyptian,' to become the ruling element among the Abramites, to exchange freedom for serfdom, is described as the maid's despising her barren mistress. The jealousy between the rivals necessitated the flight of Hagar from the plains of Mamre towards Egypt, her home. The importance of this event is perhaps

---

[1] Comp. Job xv. 18–20, 28.

underestimated, so long as the figurative or representative form of the family record is altogether denied. To Cain 'a sign' had been given, which preserved him and his descendants, after the separation. So likewise Hagar received 'a sign' of God's presence, on the road to Egypt, which crossed the desert of Shur. The angel of Jehovah commanded her to return, and promised, that her son Ishmael, though a man of the wilderness, and in spite of the opposition of his enemies, should 'dwell in the East of all his brethren.'[1] After the birth of Isaac this promise was confirmed. God promised, that he would 'make him fruitful, and multiply him exceedingly,' so as to become 'a great nation,' and the progenitor of twelve princes.[2] Thus, the first of those many nations was born, of which Abraham was to be the father, according to a promise made after the birth of Ishmael.

Ishmael settled in Egypt and married a daughter of the land. As the Egyptians were Kenites, that is, descendants from Cain, from the Eastern Aryans, and as his name must be connected with tribes, it is immaterial whether Ishmael's Egyptian wife, or another, became the mother of his twelve sons, and of his daughter Mahalath. Ishmael's 'firstborn' was Nebaioth, or Nebajoth, after whose name, according to Jerome, the land between the Euphrates and the Red Sea, which, according to Josephus, the twelve sons of Ishmael inhabited, was called Nabatea. These Nabaioth, if Jerome's assertion is correct, must be identified with the Nebathæans of Arabia Petræa, and with the Nabat of Chaldea, who originally seem to have inhabited the regions about the Euphrates and Tigris, and who were, according to Arabian tradition, the founders of Babylon and of Nineveh. In the sixtieth chapter of the book of Isaiah, 'the rams of Nebaioth' are mentioned together with 'the flocks of Kedar,' and with the men from Sheba or Saba, the Sabeans, with whom the Neba-

---

[1] Gen. xvi. 12.     [2] Ibid. xvii. 20.

thæans must be identified. Now, Kedar, or 'black-skinned man,' was the second son of Ishmael, and the name of a tribe inhabiting the North-West of the peninsula and the confines of Palestine. The kingdom of Sheba, in Southern Arabia, was so called after a son of Joktan, the son of Eber. 'The companies of Sheba' are, in the book of Job, connected with 'the troops of Tema,' a tribe called after a son of Ishmael; and Jeremiah connects Tema with Dedan and Buz. But the Sabeans are mentioned as among the enemies or adversaries of Job; and we shall see that the cause of this hostility lay in their being Hebrews, that is, Aramæans, and as such opposed to the 'men of the East,' to the Bene Kedem, the Kadmonites, and other Kenaanite tribes, who inhabited the land Canaan, or Kenaan, before the time of Abram's immigration. We shall try to prove that, in the Patriarchal period, to which the book of Job refers, Kenites and Hebrews, Eastern and Western Aryans, among whom were men of low degree and men of high degree, lived together, and fought for the possession of the land between the Nile and the Euphrates.

The heart's desire of Abraham, the Aryan chief, must have been, to see the Aryan element spreading in those favoured regions. The northern immigration was checked by an adverse race from the South, and the mixed race inhabiting the central districts, became alternately dependant on its northern or southern neighbours. Between the time of the Flood, and the Abramitic descent of highlanders upon the so-called lowlands of the Euphrates and Tigris, these central regions had been the battle-fields between contending parties. Elam, once a Semitic settlement, between the Mesopotamian plain and the high table-land of Iran, had become the seat of a powerful government under Chedorlaomer, perhaps the Babylonian monarch, who is called 'the Ravager of the West.' He was probably 'the leader of certain immigrant Chaldean Elamites, who founded the great Chaldean empire of

Berosus, in the early part of the 20th century B.C.[1] Allied with three other kings, or local governors, the 'King of Elam,' at a distance of two thousand miles from his own country, subjugated the kings of Sodom, Gomorrah, Admah, Zeboim, and Zoar, and annihilated, thirteen years later, after their rebellion, these five princes of the lowland. Lot was taken, and though Abram rescued him and his possessions with 318 men, and with the assistance of the Amorites, his allies, yet the circumstances under which the tribes of Abram were placed, after the return from Egypt, seemed adverse to the fulfilment of the Divine promise. Nevertheless Abram believed in that promise, and he regarded it as his mission, to spread the knowledge of his God.

In Ur, the 'fire,' or the 'light' of the Chaldees, the seat of Chaldean learning, Abram had been taught, as we may assume, the mysteries of antediluvian tradition. Josephus states, that Abram 'was a person of great sagacity, both for understanding all things, and persuading his hearers, and not mistaken in his opinions. For which reasons he began to have higher notions of virtue than others had, and he determined to renew and to change the opinion all men happened then to have, concerning God. For he was the first to publish this notion,—that there was but one God, the Creator of the universe; and that, as to other (gods), if they contributed anything to the happiness of men, that each of them afforded it only according to his appointment, and not by their own power.'[2] According to the Jewish historian, the proclamation of Monotheism was an innovation. But the distinction which he makes between Abram's renewing and changing the religious belief of mankind, corroborates our view, that these districts were inhabited by men of high degree, and by men of low degree, by Aryans and non-Aryans, by white and by black populations; and that to the higher

[1] Rawlinson's Herod. i. 436 f.     [2] Ant. i. 7, 1.

castes, at least to the initiated, the doctrine of one God was known, whilst it was unknown to the lower castes. A religious revival among the Aryans, and a conversion among the Hamitic or Turanian descendants, this was the mission of Abram. The traditions which Abraham, the Hebrew, and Melchizedec, the Kenite, represented, reached far beyond Ur, like those of which Moses, and Jethro, Shammai and Hillel, St. James and St. Paul were the organs. These traditions reached beyond Egypt, beyond Palestine, and beyond Cilicia; they came from the East. In the conviction of Abram, the promise about his seed possessing the land, could only be fulfilled by Aryan blood. Although Ishmael had been 'brought up, in order to succeed in the government,' yet Abram's stay in Egypt had confirmed him in his ancestorial belief, as Josephus informs us, that the wisdom of the Egyptians could not be compared with that of the Aryans, notwithstanding the Aryan influence which the Hyksos exercised in the land of the Nile. The tradition of the Egyptian priests had been vitiated by non-Aryan influences, and required a renewing from Eastern sources. It was only the Aryan stock, in Canaan, which could realise the promised moral and material conquest. Everything pointed to such a consummation, and a Divine communication confirmed Abram in his conviction. 'The word of the Lord came unto Abram in a vision,' and announced that he who was born in his 'house,' should not be the heir, but one who should come out of his own 'body,' and thus be of his own blood and colour.

The mysterious and isolated introduction of 'Eliezer of Damascus' compels us to assume, that the servant born in the 'house' of Abram, who was not of his own 'body,' and who yet was considered by Abram, before the birth of Ishmael and Isaac, as the 'son of possession,' that is, as the heir, was of non-Aryan descent. Yet the origin of the name Damascus apparently contradicts this view. It has been shown, that Damascus, in Hebrew Dammasec, originally meant Dormesec, that is, the dwelling of Mesech, the son of Japhet.[1] By this interpretation of the name Damascus, the statement of the Damascene historian Nicolaus, which is recorded by Josephus, becomes important, that 'Abram reigned at Damascus, being a foreigner, who came with an army out of the land above Babylon, called the land of the Chaldeans. But, after a long time he arose, and removed from that country, also with his people, and went into the land then called the land of Canaan.'[2] From this it follows, that Damascus was no longer, in the time of Abram, inhabited by descendants from Mesech, or that these had degenerated into a non-Aryan nation. Either the people of Damascus were then Egyptians, or a race cognate to them, over which Abram, the Eastern chief, ruled in the same manner, as the Eastern shepherds ruled in Egypt. For Abram is stated to have been 'a foreigner' at Damascus. Therefore the 'house' of Abram, and those over whom he ruled, were men of low degree, and the Patriarch could say: 'I go childless, and the son of Mesech is my house, Damascus—Eliezer.' The two latter names were probably a marginal reference, later taken into the text, when the original meaning, of what was so long transmitted by verbal tradition, had been forgotten. The name Eliezer is identical with Hadadezer, which appears to have been an official title, like Pharaoh, and means 'assisted by God.' For Hadad originally was the indigenous appellation of the Sun among the Syrians.[3] The Hebrew writer substituted the name El for Hadad. In the Septuagint Eliezer is called 'the son of Mesek.' The original tradition and interpretation of the text was probably: 'the son of Mesech is my house.'

Not the non-Aryan tribes, over which Abram had ruled at Damascus, not 'his people' that he 'removed' from Damascus to Canaan, were to be heirs of Abram, but

[1] Bunsen's Egypt; comp. 'Bibelwerk.'  [2] Ant. i. 7, 2.
[3] Macrob. Saturnal. i. 23; Plin. xxxvii. 11.

one that should come out of his own 'body.' Ethnologically interpreted, this means, that Abram should become the ruler and father of tribes of the same descent as his own. The promise about Sarai, henceforth to be called Sarah, no longer 'the contentious,' but the 'princess,' does not exclude this interpretation. 'I will bless her, and give thee a son also of her, and will bless her, that she become nations; kings over nations shall come from her.' Thus two distinct covenants were made with Abraham. Before we try to prove that the one referred to the black, the other to the white race, we must consider the mysterious connection between Abraham and Melchizedec.

Abram having, with his allies, beaten Chedorlaomer and his tributary kings, and pursued them unto Hobah, which is on the left hand of Damascus, he was met on his way from Hobah to the plain of Mamre, by the King of Salem, who was 'a priest of the Most High God,' and who with these words hailed the Eastern conqueror: 'Blessed be Abram of the Most High God, creator of heaven and earth, and blessed be the Most High God, who hath delivered thine adversaries into thy hand.' Melchizedec 'brought forth bread and wine,' probably as an offering to God, and Abram gave to Melchizedec a tithe of all. Jewish tradition has seen in Melchizedec, that is, in the Melech-Zadok, in 'the king of righteousness,' its own ancestor Shem, thereby recognising the King of Salem as the organ of antediluvian tradition. But the comments on Melchizedec made by the writer of the Epistle to the Hebrews, absolutely exclude the identity of the priest and king with any son of Noah. Whatever meaning be given to the declaration, that Melchizedec had neither father nor mother, reminding us of what was said of Levi, who yet was 'an instrument of wrong,'[1] it certainly excludes, as his angelic descent, so his descent from any one of

---

[1] Deut. xxxiii. 8-11; comp. Gen. xlix. 5-7.

the fathers of tradition, which are enumerated in the Hebrew genealogies. Like Jethro and Balaam, Melchizedec was unconnected with the Hebrew stream of tradition.

If we succeed in proving the existence of a Hebrew and a non-Hebrew sacerdotal order, and if the latter order was represented by Jethro, the Midianite priest, and descendant from an Abramitic tribe, our supposition, that Melchizedec represents the Kenite descent, will gain a footing at the outset. To establish the identity of Melchizedec's and of Jethro's order of priesthood, we have first to point out the connection in which Melchizedec is placed with the Kenaanites, whose discomfiture by Chedorlaomer had been avenged by Abram. For 'the king of Sodom went out to meet him after his return from the slaughter of Chedorlaomer, and of the kings that were with him, at the valley of Shaveh, which is the king's dale.' It is probable, that Melchizedec and the king of Sodom formed one party, at any rate, they were jointly interested in the victory. The five kings of Southern Canaan, whose possessions had been saved by Abram, belonged to the Kenaanites, whose settlements, after the Flood, extended from Zidon in the North, to Gaza in the West, and to Lasha in the East, near the North-Eastern shore of the Dead Sea.[1] These Kenaanites, or Kenites, we have identified with descendants from Kenan or Cain, with the Bene Kedem or 'sons of the East,' the original Aryan dwellers in the lowland of the Indus, where they subjugated non-Aryan tribes, which they led, at different times, to the Western regions between the Nile and the Euphrates, among which were the Kenaanitish settlements between the Mediterranean and the Dead Sea, to which the kingdom of Sodom belonged, in the time of Melchizedec. Moreover, we have traced the Kenites, through the Midianites, to Keturah, and to

[1] Gen. x. 19.

Abraham. Thus we are in a position to assume, that the Kenite order of priesthood, which Jethro represented, is identical with the sacerdotal order of Melchizedec.

The Kenite order was unconnected with the Levitical order, whose beginning was in the time of Aaron, whilst the beginning of the former was unknown, reaching to pre-historical times. Again, to the Kenites, or Rechabites, the promise was given by Jeremiah, that 'Jonadab, the son of Rechab, shall not want a man to stand' before the Lord 'for ever.' Like the sons of Levi, they were chosen to 'stand before' God in the sanctuary; but at the time when Abram 'stood before the Lord,'[1] their ancestor Melchizedec was already a priest of the Most High God, to whom Abram gave tithes, and who blessed Abram. The priesthood which Melchizedec represented, had no historical beginning, no beginning of days, and as it was an everlasting priesthood, Melchizedec could be said to have 'no end of life,' and to 'abide a priest continually.' As Balaam identified Cain with the Kenite, and as the Korahites were identified with Korah, so the writer of the Epistle to the Hebrews identifies Melchizedec with his successors in the eternal priesthood. He 'that had the promises,' was blessed by One 'whose descent or pedigree is not counted' from the Hebrews. 'And without all contradiction the less is blessed of the better;' and 'Levi, also, who receiveth tithes, hath payed tithes through Abraham.' In the collective, or representative sense, it could be said, about the time of the destruction of Jerusalem, and the practical ending of the Levitical priesthood, that 'here,' that is, among the Hebrews, to whom the Epistle is written, 'men that die receive tithes; but there, One receiveth them, of whom it is witnessed that he liveth.' This had been witnessed by the Kenite king, David, who recognised 'a priest for ever, after the order of Melchizedec,' and who may well have regarded

---

[1] Gen. xviii. 2.

Abiathar as the living representative of the everlasting priesthood. For Abiathar was, like David, of Kenite descent, and as, after the discomfiture of David's and of Abiathar's adversaries, David had made him high priest at Jerusalem, the Royal Psalmist could sing, 'The Lord stretcheth forth the staff of thy power from Zion; rule thou in the midst of thine enemies.' It is to a high priest of the same Kenite line, as we shall see, that the promise of the servant of God, 'the branch,' the Messiah was made.

It is because of his spiritual birth, analogous to that of Isaac, that Melchizedec is said to have been 'like unto the Son of God,' and consequently to abide 'a priest continually.' He is declared to be among 'the living,' like Abraham, Isaac, and Jacob. Though dead, yet even now he speaketh. This honour of an everlasting priesthood, is not a privilege of carnal descent, for 'no man taketh this honour unto himself, but he that is called of God, as was Aaron.'

The two covenants, made with Abraham, referred to the different nations, of which he was to be the Father. Of these, Ishmael and Isaac are, by the genealogist, stated to have been the respective progenitors. The following table points out, which were, or were supposed to be, the low-caste descendants and the high-caste descendants from Abraham.

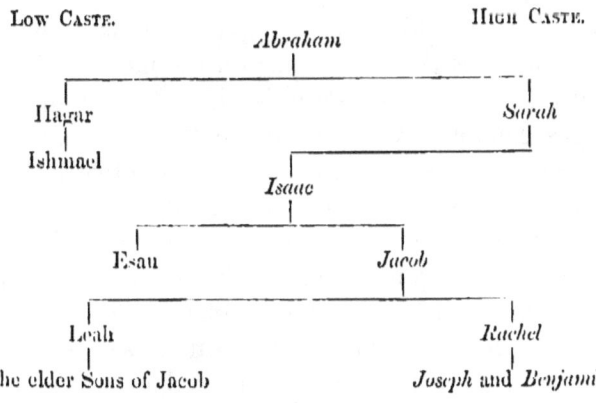

Hagar, Ishmael, Esau, Leah, and the ten elder sons of Jacob, were by race, and therefore by caste, separated from Sarah, Isaac, Jacob, Rachel, Joseph and Benjamin. Of Hagar we know, that she was an Egyptian, and that she was a bondwoman, as compared with Sarah, the free woman. Ishmael married an Egyptian, but Isaac did not take a wife 'of the daughters of the Kenaanites' among whom Abraham dwelt, but of his father's country and kindred. Esau, born 'reddish,' as if of Egyptian blood, 'and all hairy like skins,' was 'a man of the field, skilled in the chase,' and had married Hittites of low degree, and the daughter of Ishmael, who was also of low caste. Jacob the 'plain' and 'upright' man, 'dwelt in tents,' like his father and his grandfather Abraham, and was sent to Padan Aram, in order, we may assume, to make a high-caste marriage. His smooth hands had to be covered with skins, in order to pass for his brother; though younger, Jacob ruled over Esau. Again, Leah was plain, and Rachel was fair. The jealousy between the ten elder sons of Jacob by Leah, and the children of Rachel, is best explained by difference of caste. It is thus, that we can account for Reuben's taking Joseph's part; for he married Bilha, Rachel's maid, who, we may assume, belonged to the white race. And Judah was best qualified to act the part of a mediator, by his connection with his non-Hebrew wives. Again, Levi, the signification of whose name, as a 'link' between his parents, well symbolises a mixed origin, represents the white race on his father's side, and the dark race on his mother's side. Although mixed marriages cannot have been uncommon, the annihilation of the Shechemites proves how a fusion between the high caste and the low caste tribes was abhorred.

The low caste, formed by the non-Aryan, or Ethiopian races, which were conquered by the white race, at different times and places. formed an element of the Kenite and of the Hebrew community. But it seems, that the Kenites were more especially connected, if not identified

with men of low degree, for reasons which we shall later
more minutely consider. It is probable, that the pure
high caste element had nearly, or entirely, dwindled away,
under Ethiopian or low caste predominance. We shall
point out, that the accession of the Kenite branch of the
Aaronites, in the person of Eli, led to the participation of
the men of low-degree in the honours which the men of
high degree had regarded as their exclusive privilege.

This Kenite revolution, which, as we shall see, had been
prepared by the rebellion of the Korahites in the time of
Moses, must be connected with the reign of the Shepherd
Kings in Egypt. Like the Bene Kedem, the Kadmonites,
and other pre-Abrahamitic tribes, which we comprise
under the collective name of Kenites, the Shepherds, or
Hyksos, who ruled in Egypt, were a nomadic race, that
came from the East. The Kenites lived as strangers
among the Israelites, and so the Shepherds lived as strangers among the Egyptians. Yet the Egyptians,[1] whose
kings lived at Memphis and had built the most famous
pyramids before the Shepherd invasion, had likewise come
from the East in pre-historical times. They were a cognate race to the Shepherds, as the Kenites were a cognate
race to the Hebrews. Like the Kenites and the Hebrews,
the old inhabitants of Egypt can be proved to have been
a mixed race of Aryans and non-Aryans, of white and
black. Their hatred of the yellow and the white race
strangely contrasts with their own pride of race. This
apparent incongruity can, however, be explained. The
Eyptians hated the Nigritians, the black-skinned men, as
infinitely below them, and they hated the higher caste
races, because of their superiority. The mixed Asiatic
and African tribes or nations, with whom they came in
contact, were Eastern Nomads, whilst the Egyptians had
become exclusively tillers of the soil, during their long
residence in the land fructified by the Nile. The shepherd

[1] See Mr. Poole's articles on Egypt, &c., in Smith's Dictionary.

occupation was by them treated with contempt, as one befitting only men of low degree. And yet they suffered the Israelites to settle as shepherds in Goshen. It was an exceptional act of toleration, which permitted the Israelites to live unmolested in a non-Egyptian frontier district, near the mouth of the Nile, in spite of the fact, that 'every shepherd' was 'an abomination unto the Egyptians.' Like Abraham and Isaac, Jacob and his family tribes lived as strangers in every part of the land which had been promised to Abraham's seed. Goshen seems to have been inhabited by other strangers, and also by Egyptians. It formed the Western border of Kenaan.

We have seen, that already in the time of Abraham, Chedorlaomer, whose African descent cannot be doubted, had to be pursued to Damascus. At that time, it is well nigh certain, that the Shepherd Kings ruled in Egypt, residing at Memphis and at the stronghold of Avaris or Zoan, on the Eastern bank of the Nile. For Zoan had been built by the Shepherds, but 'seven years' after Hebron, or Kirjath-Arba, from the inhabitants of which, the Anakims, Abraham purchased the cave of Machpelah. This burial-place of the Patriarchs became the possession of Kenites, in the time of Caleb, and was the residence of the Kenite king David. The connection between Zoan and Hebron strongly confirms the connection between the Kenites and the Shepherds of Egypt. Other Shepherd tribes had entered and had left Egypt before Abraham entered Kenaan. Such were the Philistines or 'emigrants' from Capthor, descendants from Mizraim, who settled near Gazar. We have seen, that they were a cognate race with the Phœnicians and the Kenites, with the former of which the Shepherds of Egypt are generally identified. 'It is probable, that the immigration into Egypt, and thence, at last, into Palestine, was part of the great movement, to which the coming of the Phœnicians from the Erythræan Sea, and the Philistines from Capthor belong.'

Long before the Shepherds of Egypt, the Philistines,

the Phœnicians, and the Kenites, in the wider sense of the word, had left the East, Cushites had settled on the shores of the Indian Ocean, and had been subjugated by the Aryans. It was this first meeting of the black and of the white race, which caused the formation of those mixed races of high caste whites and low caste blacks, which were destined to play so important a part in history by their alternate settlements in the West. To the same mixed high caste and low caste race, the Hebrews and the Kenites belonged. No wonder that the Shepherds befriended the Israelites. Joseph probably represented the pure high caste, and served as minister under a high caste Shepherd—Pharaoh. He received an Egyptian name, and married the daughter of a priest whose name, Potiphera, implies that he worshipped the sun at On, where the Shepherd king Apepi had built a temple. The name of Joseph's wife, Asenath, is of doubtful etymology, but there is good authority for connecting it with Neith, the mystic goddess of the Egyptians, on whose temple the famous inscription stood: 'I am all that was, is, and is to come; no mortal removed my veil; the sun was my child.'

The Pharaoh of Israel's oppression must have been of a native, or Theban, dynasty. This is confirmed by the change of policy towards the Israelites, and by the remarkable fact that, according to Manetho as transcribed by Africanus, the 17th dynasty, the one which preceded the rule of Aahmes—who overthrew, and probably expelled the Shepherds—consisted of Shepherds and of Thebans. Thebes, probably founded by a colony of priests, the principal town of Egypt before the incursion of the Eastern Shepherds, set up the Pharaoh, who, fearing a war with a foreign foe, and that the Israelites would join the enemies, oppressed them by forced labour, and afterwards killed their male children. But Moses received the Divine call, and led the children of Israel out of Egypt, probably about the time when the Shepherds were expelled. The Israelites followed the cognate race, which had permitted them to live as strangers in the land of the Nile.

We have pointed out the Eastern origin of the Shepherds in Egypt, and of the Kenites; the connection between the two, of which the record about Zoan and Hebron is the culminating proof; the relations between Jethro the Kenite, and Moses the Hebrew, who was brought up in all the wisdom of the Egyptians, and whom the daughters of Jethro supposed to be an Egyptian.[1] At a time when the Hebrews had entirely lost the tradition of Abraham, Isaac, and Jacob, Moses was summoned, whilst living among the Kenites in Midian, to go to the oppressor of the Hebrews, and to lead them out of the land of bondage into the land of promise. He was to tell them that he was sent by ' I am,' that is, by Jahveh, which name has been incorrectly turned into Jehovah. ' I am ' was a Divine name, understood by all the initiated among the Egyptians. It was the god of light or fire, which was symbolised by his child, the solar lamp. The worship of the Sun by the Egyptians, in the time of the Shepherds, and by the Phœnicians and Philistines, was the worship of One invisible God, symbolised by the visible source of created light and life. It is, therefore, quite immaterial, whether the identity of the Hebrew Jahveh, or 'He is,' and the Phœnician Yakveh, or 'He gives life,' be admitted or not.

The 'I am' of the Egyptians, the 'I am' of the Hebrews, and the 'I am,' or Jao, of the Greeks, that is, ' He who is and who shall be,' are all identical.[2] Again, it can be proved that the name of the Deity during the rule of the Eastern Shepherds, and which was almost certainly introduced by them into Egypt, was Seth, or Sutech. Shepherd kings added this name to their own, as the earlier Pharaohs had added the name of Ra, the Sun. And on numberless monuments, bas-reliefs, and scarabæi, the name

---

[1] Ex. ii. 19.  [2] Colenso's Pentateuch, v., App. iii.

of Seth has been preserved to this day, though it was generally mutilated after the expulsion of the detested Eastern rulers. We shall see, that the name of Seth, as an appellative of the Deity, is of Eastern origin. According to Hebrew tradition, the Divine soul (spirit) of Seth had tabernacled in Moses. And Balaam, the Kenite seer, can be shown to have connected the rising of Israel with the rising of Jacob, that is, of the Kenites, and with the rule, not with the destruction, of 'all the sons of Seth.' According to the reading of the Septuagint, as interpreted by the Targum called after Onkelos, Seth was in Egypt identified with Baal, the Sun God, the two names appearing combined on Egyptian monuments.[1] The Sun was regarded as the child of the uncreated light 'I am,' in the time of Joseph, by the initiated. But the people, in Egypt as in Palestine, worshipped Baal or Seth as God. Thus symbols became idols. In the time of Moses the name of Jahveh had been forgotten by the Hebrews, though it was known to the Kenites in Midian. Men of high caste, among whom the priests probably stood foremost at all times, understood that the Sun was but the symbol of uncreated light, and they knew, that the different names given by Eastern nations to the Sun God, referred to visible signs or symbols of the invisible and ineffable Being, whom the Phœnicians called 'Intelligent Light,' and who was first proclaimed among the Aryans in Central Asia, as 'the living Creator of all,' and 'the Father of all truth.'

It is impossible to assert, either that the genealogy of the patriarchs is not a family record, or that the ethnological element must be altogether excluded from the same. We have seen, that Esau cannot have been the grandfather of Amalek, since Amalek existed as a tribe in the time of Chedorlaomer, and is called 'the first of the nations,' by Balaam. Again, if the above-traced distinction of race is admitted, it would be difficult to

---

[1] 'Religion des pré-Israélites,' 127.

explain, in the literal sense, the birth of the twin sons of Rebekah. Accepting the three patriarchs, and their wives, as individuals, we may assume, that the names of the latter, like those of the twelve sons of Jacob, represent also the names of different tribes, of which Isaac and Jacob were chiefs. The uniform custom among the Israelites, of representing a people by the symbol of a woman, confirms this hypothesis. It must have been for some such reason, that Paul speaks of the record about the two sons of Abraham as ' an allegory,' that is, as a document not to be taken in its literal sense. He has not merely compared, but identified Hagar with Arabia, whilst he only compares Arabia with Jerusalem, ' which now is and is in bondage with her children.' On the other hand, he insists on the personality of Isaac, and by saying, that Isaac was born after the spirit, he implies that he regarded the spiritual birth as a complement of the birth ' after the flesh.' The argument that pervades this passage is, that freedom and not serfdom was promised, and that, historically, Isaac represents liberty, and Ishmael bondage. In how far superiority of race was the cause of this distinction, history clearly shows, and thus marvellously confirms the patriarchal genealogy of the Hebrews.

It cannot be asserted, that the elevation of the sons of Kohath, above the sons of Gershom, the eldest son of Levi, had anything to do with difference of caste connection. Moses, the Kohathite, having become the leader of the Hebrews, it was natural that he raised the second line above the first. Yet other reasons may be assigned for this preference. Gershon was born unto Levi before Jacob's descent into Egypt. The name Gershonites may be interpreted so as to point to their having, like the Kenites, lived as ' strangers.' Even if we prefer the other signification of Gershon, as the ' expelled,' the name would naturally refer, either to the Aaronic line of Ithamar, which, as we shall see, was separated from the high priestly office, up to the time of Eli, or to the expulsion of the Kenites from Eden in the time of Cain. The connection between the Gershonites and the Kenites, thus rendered probable, can be proved beyond the possibility of a doubt, and by this fact can be explained the peculiar nature of the sin with which the sons of Eli have been charged.

Whether we regard the narratives transmitted to us about the patriarchs, exclusively as family records, or also in the light of tribal development, and of caste distinction, the fact remains, that Jacob was separated from Esau, as Isaac had been separated from Ishmael, and as Joseph and Benjamin were separated from the other sons of Jacob. Again, as, by unjust means, the blessing of Isaac had been diverted from its proper channel, so Jacob was by deceit misled into his union with Leah. The same injustice led to the separation of Joseph, and then of Benjamin, from their father, and from their elder brethren by Leah. It was injustice, which caused Jacob to flee from Padan Aram, where he had served Laban for fourteen and for six years, and from whence, according to ancient tradition, he was summoned by Deborah, the nurse of his mother Rebekah. It was not till after Jacob's union with the fair Rachel, that the servant felt himself strong enough to fight for his liberty and independence. If Rachel be regarded as the representative of the white race, or high caste, it will follow, that the infusion of this element into Jacob's family led to his freedom and subsequent dominion. But we do not here found any argument on this more or less probable hypothesis. We have to deal with the fact, that among the possessions which Jacob had acquired in Padan Aram, were two wives, two concubines, eleven sons and a daughter. With these, excepting Rachel, who, as also Deborah, had died on the way, Jacob settled at Hebron, the burial-place of his ancestors. A few years after Jacob and Esau had buried their father, in the cave of Machpelah, Jacob went into Egypt, where his son Joseph was the Prime-minister of the Shepherd Pharaohs, to whose connection with the Kenites we have referred. Before Jacob left Hebron, formerly Kirjath-Arba, and which had been built seven years 'before Zoan in Egypt,' the stronghold of the Aryan Shepherd Kings, his grandson Gershom, or Gershon, eldest son of Levi, was born.

As in the case of Ishmael, and of Esau, and of Leah and her descendants, the elder branch of the descendants from Levi, for a reason not stated, was deprived of its birthright. The younger was preferred to the elder. Hebrew history is the record of the triumphs of secundogeniture, and Kenite history the documentary proof, that 'Jabez was more honourable than his brethren,' that even Abraham acknowledged the superiority and primogeniture of Melchizedec. Kohath, the second son of Levi, like Isaac and Jacob and Rachel, became the progenitor of a privileged class. The Kohathites enjoyed an official superiority over the Gershonites. The sons of Gershon are recorded to have been Libni and Shimi or Shimei. But in Chronicles Shimei is declared to have been, not the brother, but the son of Libni, and the latter is asserted to have been the son of Merari, Levi's third son.[1] In the same book it is recorded, that David recognised the seniority of the Gershonites over the Kohathites.[2] Not only are the former shown to have enjoyed an official superiority over the Kohathites, but Asaph the Gershonite[3] was by David acknowledged as a seer. He received an hereditary office,[4] and his words were put on a par with those of David.[5] That the Kenite king should thus honour the elder branch of Levites, favours the view, that the Gershonites or 'strangers' were connected, if not identical with, the Kenites, who, although they formed tribes before Isaac was born, lived as 'strangers' among the Hebrews.

---

[1] 1 Chr. vi. 21.   [2] Ibid. xxiii. 7.   [3] Ibid. vi. 39.
[4] 2 Chr. xx. 14; Ezra ii. 47.   [5] 2 Chr. xxix. 30.

It was upon a 'stranger,' a Gershonite, upon 'one of the sons of Asaph,' that, 'the spirit of the Lord came in the midst of the congregation,' and enabled Jehaziel to prophesy to Jehoshaphat, to 'all Judah,' and to the 'inhabitants of Jerusalem,' that they would see the presence of the Lord in their camp, who would cause the Moabites to destroy the enemies of Judah. On this occasion 'the Levites of the children of the Kohathites, and of the children of the Korhites stood up to praise the Lord God.' The Korahites of those days were by descent connected with Caleb the Kenezite,[1] that is, with a cognate tribe of the Kenites and other pre-Abrahamitic inhabitants of Kenaan, who, as non-Hebrews, lived as 'strangers' with the descendants from Abraham. These strangers or Kenites, we have identified with the Korahites. At the time when a prophet arose from among the Gershonites, or strangers, in Israel, a Korahite, or Kenite Levitical line was acknowledged, by the side of the Hebrew or Kohathite line of Levi. This is in accordance with the statement, that Korah, like Cain, never died, and with the established fact, that the Kenites or Korahites never wanted a man to stand, or minister before the Lord, and that they were represented by the junior Aaronic line of Ithamar. As the Gershonites were placed under the superintendence of this Kenite sacerdotal line, to which Eli belonged, we can now assert, that the Gershonites were connected with the Kenites, and must be identified with them, as regards their non-Hebrew descent. The question, in what sense Gershon was the first-born son of Levi, will be answered differently by those who insist on the literal sense of the genealogies, and by those who regard these lists equally as family and as tribal records. In either case, we may assume that Levi's eldest son represented the tradition of his mother Leah, whom we have connected with Esau and Ishmael, with the ancestors of the Edomites, that is, of the Kenites.

[1] 1 Chron. ii. 43.

God works by means, and this according to selection. Science, and history, and its interpretation by such a man as the Apostle Paul, alike prove, that the white race, as being the most highly gifted, has been, and is, a chosen instrument in the hand of God. Whatever be its primary cause, the difference of blood is a fact. Convinced of his calling, the white man spread over the world, conquering and to conquer.

According to the allegory about the sons of Adam, as contained in Genesis, the Western Aryans, who did not follow the Kenites to the land of Nod, were the first believers in One God. This is confirmed by the Avesta, the holy tradition of the Western Aryans, the ancestors of the Hebrews, as the Vedas are the holy tradition of the Eastern Aryans, the ancestors of the Kenites in Kenaan. But also to the Eastern Aryans, to the tribe which at the time of the great Aryan separation, is recorded to have rejected Monotheism, even to Cain 'a sign' was given. Whether or not it was a visible symbol or mark, it was a sign, a promise, a pledge unto life. Cain was never to die. The Kenites, as the Ishmaelites in the time of Abraham, and as the Korahites in the time of Moses, were to be represented in all ages by their successors, the guardians of their traditions, whether or not they referred, already in the earliest historical times, to immortality. Melchizedec, the Kenite, or Eastern Aryan, was a contemporary of Abraham, the Western Aryan, and can hardly have been the first proclaimer of the One God, in the land between the Nile and the Euphrates, in which different tribes of Asiatics, mixed with subjugated Africans, had settled before Abraham entered it. The ancestor of the Hebrews understood the language of the Kenaanites, and lived on good terms with them, whilst converting those who were serving other Gods, to the worship of Jehovah. The ancestor of the Kenites, Melchizedec, though he represents the Eastern and Kenite sacerdotal tradition, undoubtedly represents the Monotheism of the Western Aryans, from whom Abraham descended. The descendants from Cain had become believers in the most high God, the Creator of heaven and earth, before Abraham's time. Both Kenites and Hebrews believed in One God, when the brother tribes of the Aryans, after long separation, met again in the regions between the Nile and the Euphrates. The Kenites and the Hebrews met as cognate races, keeping up their distinctions, without forgetting their common origin. We shall see, that the tradition of Melchizedec and of Abraham, about Jehovah, was preserved by Kenites, and that these disciples and descendants of Melchizedec, through the Kenite priesthood, revealed to Moses that knowledge, which prepared him to see in the burning bush, the manifestation of the God of Abraham, of Isaac, and of Jacob.

## CHAPTER IV.

### SONS OF GOD AND SONS OF MEN.

BEFORE the Abramitic immigration into Kenaan, mixed tribes of Asiatics and of Africans had settled in the land. The dominion of the white Kenite and of the white Hebrews over the black Ethiopian, continued undisturbed for many centuries. The book of Job refers to the remote time, when the ancestors of the Kenites lived in Eden, unmolested by the presence of strangers. For thus said Eliphaz to Job: When the earth was alone given to the 'fathers' of 'wise men,' who have not hidden but transmitted the tradition, then 'no stranger passed among them,' they were yet unopposed by 'the wicked man,' by the adversary, who 'dwelleth in desolate cities and in dwellings which no man inhabits,'[1] that is, in desert places and caves. We shall prove, that these fathers of antediluvian tradition were Kenites, or sons of the East; that the adversary who opposed them, in the time of Job, opposed also the Hebrews, and that this adversary of the white race was Ham, the representative of the black race.

Kenites and Hebrews are contrasted with each other in the book of Job. This will become evident, if it can be shown, that not only Job, but also his three friends, were Kenites and not Hebrews. For it is absolutely certain, that Elihu was a Hebrew. Like Job, who was 'the greatest of the sons of the East.' Bildad 'the Shuhite,' or properly, the Shuchahite, as a descendant from Keturah, is an ancestor of Jethro the Kenite, and therefore one of the Bene Kedem or 'sons of the East,' who inhabited the

[1] Job xv. 18-20, 28.

land between the Nile and the Euphrates, the land of
Kenaan in its widest sense, before the Abramitic immigration. Eliphaz 'the Temanite' was a descendant of
Teman, the son of Esau and Adah, and probably also of
Tema, son of Ishmael, after whom an Arabian tribe was
called, which already existed in the time of Job,[1] and
which Jeremiah connects with Dedan and Buz.[2] Now
Esau, as we have seen, is in the genealogies erroneously
stated to have been the grandfather of Amalek, the
Amalekites being mentioned as a tribe before Esau was
born. But the genealogy is right, if ethnologically interpreted, in so far as it connects Esau and the Edomites with
Amalek 'the first of the nations.' In the book of Judges
the sons of the East are invariably connected with the
Amalekites and the Midianites.[3] From this it follows,
that they belonged, in all probability, to the Bene Kedem,
a supposition which is confirmed by the fact, that they
inhabited part of that land in which the Nabathæans
dwelt, whom we must, on various grounds, connect, if not
identify, with the Kenites. For of the Nabathæans it is
recorded by Diodorus Siculus, the Silician historian in
the time of Julius Cæsar, that the Nabathæans neither
sowed seed nor planted fruit tree, nor used or built
houses, and that they enforced these transmitted customs,
under pain of death.[4] This description corresponds not
only with what Jeremiah has transmitted, about the
anti-agricultural habits of the Rechabites, or Kenites, but
it is in literal harmony with the hostile acts of the sons
of the East, and of the Amalekites and the Midianites,
which are recorded in the book of Judges. 'When
Israel had sown, the Midianites and the Amalekites and
the Sons of the East came up against them, and they
encamped against them, and destroyed the increase of the
earth all the way towards Gaza, and left no sustenance
in Israel, neither sheep, nor ox, nor ass. For they came

---

[1] Job vi. 19.     [2] Jer. xxv. 23; comp. Is. xxi. 13, 14.
[3] Judg. vi. 3, 33; vii. 12.     [4] Diod. Sic. xix. 94.

up with their cattle and their tents, and came in multitudes like grasshoppers, that neither they nor their camels could be counted, and they came into the land to destroy it.¹ We may, therefore, assert, that Eliphaz was also a Kenite.

Zophar is called 'the Naamathite,' and may, therefore, safely be connected with Naam, or Naham, one of the sons of Cain, the ancestor of the Kenites. A striking confirmation of Zophar's descent from Cain is contained in the genealogical record in Genesis, according to which the same name of Naam, with the Jehovistic ending, that is, Naamah, was borne by the daughter of Lamech and Zillah, by the sister of Tubal-Cain.² The Naamathites were, therefore, descendants from Cain, and also from Tubal, if Tubal was originally the name of a person, or tribe. It is probable that Tubal is derived from the Persian *tûpal*, which means iron, and that Cainites or Kenites were, in the period to which the name of Lamech refers, workers in iron, as the men of Tubal were coppersmiths in the time of Ezekiel.³ According to Josephus, the men of Tubal were called Iberians, that is, inhabitants of a tract of country between the Caspian and the Black Sea. They are the *Tuplai* of Assyrian inscriptions,⁴ and as *Tibareni* are connected with the Moschi. Both were later called Scythians, that is, Turanians, who inhabited in early times the land between the Indus, the Persian Gulf, the Mediterranean, and the Caucasus, that is, generally speaking, the land inhabited by the Kenites, or sons of the East.

Having proved, that Job and his three friends were all Kenites, that is, descendants from Cain, it is evident, from the independent position which is assigned in the book of Job to Elihu, 'son of Barachel, the Buzite,' and thus to a nephew of Abraham,⁵ that as a Hebrew, Elihu is con-

---

¹ Judg. vi. 3–5.   ² Gen. iv. 22.   ³ Ezek. xxvii. 13.
⁴ Rawlinson's Herod. i. 535.   ⁵ Gen. xxii. 21.

trasted with the Kenites, or sons of the East, among whom Job was the greatest. Job lived in the land of Uz, or Huz, that is, in the land between the Dead Sea and the Aleanitic Gulf, which the Edomites inhabited in the time of Moses,[1] and of which 'not a footbreadth' ever belonged to Hebrews. This remarkable fact leaves no doubt on the connection between Job and the Kenites, and the identity of these with the sons of the East. We have now to prove our assertion, that the adversary of the Kenites and the adversary of the Hebrews is Ham.

Kenites and Hebrews, both Aryans by descent, had become, through conquest, a mixed race, not of half-castes, but of Asiatics and Africans. The Kenites as well as the Hebrews represented the pure Aryan element in their higher castes, and the Hamitic element in their lower castes. Not only Job, but his three friends, and also Elihu, the Hebrew, were men of wisdom, and, as such, representatives of the higher or Aryan castes. Among Job's enemies the Sabeans and Chaldeans are mentioned by name, whilst the description of the customs of his adversaries shows them to have been of a nomadic race, very much akin to the Kenites. The Sabeans, whatever be their origin, were comprised under the collective name of Joktanites, and as such, were connected with the Hebrews. So were also the Chaldeans, notwithstanding their non-Hebrew origin, inasmuch as Chesed and Buz are mentioned as brothers.[2] But in like manner Job, the Kenite, and Elihu, the Hebrew, were descendants from two brothers, from Cain and from Abel and Seth. Representing the white race, both Job and Elihu had to rule over Hamite tribes, in regions which were contiguous to purely Hamitic settlements. The Kenites, at the time to which the book of Job refers, seem to have lived exclusively in tents, for in every instance in which the name 'house' occurs, it ought to be translated 'dwelling.' Again, it is only in

---

[1] Deut. ii. 5; comp. Lament. iv. 21.  [2] Gen. xxii. 21, 22.

the first chapter, the later composition of which is highly probable,[1] that the children of Job are described as drinking wine, and his oxen as ploughing the fields. These are anti-Kenite habits and occupations, of which there is not the least trace in any other part of the book.

But although nomads, Job and his friends were exposed, as much as the Hebrews inhabiting Arabia, to the depredations of other nomadic tribes, who may, or may not have been of Eastern origin, but who certainly were mixed up with Hamites. It is certain, that the Chaldeans, who attacked Job, were Cushites, and therefore, non-Kenites. The same may be said of the Sabeans, or dwellers in Southern Arabia. Of some of his adversaries Job said, that their fathers he would have 'disdained to have set with the dogs' of his flock. They were thin (not dark) from 'want and hunger;' they 'gnawed the wilderness, the old desert and desolation;' they 'cut up mallows' by the bushes, and juniper roots for their meat; they were driven forth from among men, they cried after them as after a thief; in deserted valleys they must dwell, in holes of the earth and in rocks; among the bushes they roar; under the nettles they were gathered together, children of godless, yea of base men, expelled from the earth.'[2]

These godless men, of low degree, we have sufficient reason to identify with Hamites. For in the passage already quoted,[3] 'the stranger,' who, in earliest times had not lived among the Asiatics, 'the wicked man,' the adversary, is likewise described as living in desert places and caves. That the adversary of Job was of African descent, is confirmed by the Hamite origin of the name Chedorlaomer, Kudur-el-Ahmar, or 'Kedar the red,' who is probably identical with the 'Kudur mapula,' whose name is found on Chaldean bricks, and who, as 'mapula' implies, was 'the ravager of the West.' If we assume,

---

[1] Comp. Ezek. xiv. 14, where Job is mentioned after Daniel.
[2] Job xxx. 1-8; comp. xxiv.   [3] Ibid. xv. 18-20, 28.

that 'the red' was later substituted for the original title, the name Kedar may be connected with the Hebrew word Kedar, which means 'the black-skinned man.' In the time of Job, as in the time of Abraham, the adversary was Ham. The Hamites, the godless men, not only interfered with their property, but also with their faith. For, in the days of Job, 'the sons of God came to stand before the Lord, and the adversary (the Satan) came also to stand before the Lord. And the Lord said unto the adversary: From whence comest thou? And the adversary answered the Lord and said: From going to and fro on the earth, and from walking up and down on the same.' This is what the Hamites had done, who were gradually conquered on the Indus, and returned to the West under Aryan rule. They had gone to and fro, from West to East, and from East to West. 'And the Lord said unto the adversary: Hast thou noticed my servant Job? For there is not on the earth a man, like him, pious and upright, fearing God, and eschewing evil. And he does still hold fast his piety, and thou movedst me in vain against him, to destroy him. And the adversary answered the Lord, and said: Skin for skin, yea, all that a man hath, will he give for his life. But put forth thine hand, and touch his bone and his flesh, whether he will not curse thee to thy face? And the Lord said unto the adversary: Behold, be he in thine hand, only his life preserve. And so the adversary went away from the presence of the Lord.'[1]

'The sons of God,' or more literally, the sons, servants or worshippers 'of Elohim,' that is, of the gods, together with their 'adversary,' presented themselves before 'the presence of Jehovah,' to stand or minister before him. This is perhaps what Abraham desired, when he said unto God: 'Oh that Ishmael might live before thee.'[2] A similar union is described in the book of Genesis, as having

---

[1] Job ii. 1–7.    [2] Gen. xvii. 18.

taken place before the Flood. Then 'the sons (or servants) of Elohim saw the daughters of men that were fair (or 'the fair daughters of men'), and they took any to wives, according to their pleasure.'[1]

Whilst the men of Japhet, the Aryans, were exclusively of 'high degree,' and the men of Ham, the non-Aryans, exclusively of low degree, the upper castes of the men of Shem were, as we tried to explain, of white descent, and the lower castes of dark descent. We suggest, that for this reason we can trace in the Bible the mysterious distinction between 'sons of Adam,' the *ammîm*, and 'sons of man,' the *îsh*, of the 'rich' and the 'poor.'[2] Before the Flood, the sons, or servants of the gods, of Elohim, that is, the descendants from Cain, migrated from the plains of the Indus, the country of Nod, to the Aramean highland. To this immigration the notice seems to refer, that the Nephilim, giants, or powerful men, were then on the earth, that is, in the land of Kenaan. It was because of their descent from Cain, who had fallen away from God, that the Kenites were called Nephilim, which word literally means 'apostates.' They had gone away, or departed 'from the face of Jehovah.'

Like the passage in Genesis, that in the book of Job, may be interpreted as referring to the union of Hebrews and Kenites. The high-caste Hebrews, sons, or servants of God, married daughters of men, that is, of men of low degree (sons of Belial), as all the Kenites were called by the Hebrews, although the Kenites had, like the Hebrews, high castes, and consequently 'daughters that were fair.' As the priests of the Kenites and of the Hebrews always belonged to the high caste, the passage in Job refers to the joint appearing of the Hebrews and of the Kenites before 'the presence of Jehovah.' They both wished 'to worship the same God, in the same sanctuary, 'to stand

---

[1] Gen. vi. 2.
[2] Ps. xlix. 1, 2; Luke i. 52, 53, &c. This distinction has been first pointed out in the Genesis of the Earth and Man, p. 88 f.

before Jehovah,' before his 'face.' Already in the time of Abraham, to 'stand before' the Lord was understood to refer to sacerdotal ministration in the sanctuary.[1] The Hebrew Targum called after Jonathan, interprets this phrase as 'to minister' before the Lord. We are, therefore, entitled to apply this interpretation to the passage in the book of Job, and venture to hope, that every doubt about this interpretation will disappear, by our later consideration of the vision of Zechariah, where Joshua and the 'adversary' are described, as 'standing before' the angel of the Lord's presence.

In the early Patriarchal time, to which the book of Job refers, the Kenites and the Hebrews in the land of Kenaan, had a common adversary in the Hamites. Ham in Canaan, or, in the language of genealogy, Canaan the fourth son of Ham, was ever since the Flood, in these regions, and before that event, in Eastern countries, 'one of the least servants of his brethren,' that is, of Japhet and Shem. These Lords, or Aryas, of Ham, are represented by Job, the Kenite, and by Elihu, the Hebrew. Both were descendants of the white Aryan race, their ancestors having lived together in Central Asia. What had been accomplished on the Indus, and in other Eastern districts, that is, the subjugation of non-Aryan, black, or Hamitic races, was to be done between the Nile and the Euphrates. Aryan Shepherd Kings had established their rule in Egypt, but 'the black-skinned man,' the Kedur, or Kedar, later called 'Mapula,' or 'the ravager of the West,' was the great 'adversary' of the Aryans in the land of Kenaan. He and his black host were 'base' men, 'men of low degree,' and 'godless men,' who opposed 'the sons of God,' and claimed the privilege of ministering unto the same God in the same sanctuary.

By their contact with the Aryans, with the servants

---

[1] Gen. xviii. 22.

of Jehovah, non-Aryan, Hamitic, that is, African races had been brought to the knowledge of the One God. Already before the Flood a fusion of the two races had been effected, probably, as we shall see, at the time to which the name of Jared in the antediluvian genealogies refers. Thus, Aryan Monotheistic tradition was transmitted through two distinct channels, through one white, and through one dark race. In the time of Job these two organs of tradition claimed recognition of their respective priesthoods, on equal terms. Those Adamites of high degree, who regarded themselves as the 'rich,' and called themselves sons, or servants, of God; and those whom they distinguished by the name 'sons of men,' that is, as the *ish*, as 'men of low degree,' as the 'poor,' both the Aryan and his non-Aryan adversary, or Satan, strove, in the time of Job, as in the time of Abraham, for supremacy in these favoured lands.

The two hereditary sacerdotal lines of Aaronic descendants, can be shown to have been respectively the organs of a two-fold tradition. The union of the Kenite and the Hebrew, which was symbolised by the marriage of Moses and Zipporah, recognised Kenite tradition as of the same origin as Hebrew tradition. The tradition of Melchizedec and that of Abraham was the same. During a long separation the Kenite branch, ever since the departure of Cain from Eden, had carefully and reverently preserved, through its hereditary organs for the transmission of ancestorial tradition, the 'sign' or symbol which God had given to that branch of the Aryan family, which migrated to the lowlands of the Indus, to the Eastern Kenaan, from whence different tribes migrated, at different periods, in the Western Kenaan. However much the tradition of the Kenites had been leavened by the tradition of the fathers from whom it separated in Central Asia, that Eastern race, whose fidelity to commands received and transmitted by their forefathers, stands without parallel in history, continued everywhere, and at all times, to venerate the outward sign or symbol of Cain, interpreted as the same had been by Melchizedec. Before the time of Abraham, when the Hebrew and the Kenite stream first met, to conquer their common adversaries, the Kenites had become believers in 'the Most High God.' The Kenite 'king of righteousness,' Melchizedec, 'a priest of the Most High God,' brought out 'bread and wine' as a sign or symbol of worship. This interpretation is clearly implied by the narrative. After so signal a Divine intervention, for the purpose of delivering into the hands of Abraham the adversary, Chedorlaomer and his host, the Kenite priest brought out bread and wine, as the mystic elements of Divine presence. If it could be said of Levi, that he paid tithes in, or through, Abraham to Melchizedec, so can it be said, and in a more literally true and still higher sense, that all who stood before the great priest paid their dues through Melchizedec unto the Most High God. In the visible symbol of bread and wine they worshipped the invisible presence of 'the Creator of heaven and earth.' This was the tradition of the Kenite priesthood, to which Jethro belonged, with whom Aaron and all the elders of Israel ate bread 'before God.'[1] We may assume, if we cannot assert, that the sign of Melchizedec was the sign which God gave unto Cain, and which was connected with the promise, that he who hid himself from the presence of God, might move about on God's earth, ever changing his abode, with the restlessness of fugitives and strangers, as the Kenites ever did, and yet, that he would be preserved from the attacks of the adversary, because of his faith in that presence of God which he dared not to behold, and which he worshipped through a sign. Whether or not the sign of Melchizedec was the sign of Cain, it certainly was connected with the worship of Jehovah, even the name of whom had been forgotten by the Hebrews in Egypt. It was during the long stay of

---

[1] Ex. xviii. 12; comp. Ps. lxxv. 8.

Moses, the Hebrew, with Jethro, the Kenite, that the deliverer of the Israelites was called.

The Kenites and the Hebrews may have had different symbols for the representation of the same ideas; but, in the eyes of Moses, such and similar differences did not stand in the way of union. The Kenites and the Hebrews agreed where they could do it, and disagreed where they could not. Nevertheless, and although they never abandoned their distinctive customs, they offered to the world the sublime spectacle of brethren zealous for the preservation of their peculiar traditions. They fought for supremacy, even with unhallowed zeal, and yet believed in the precept of the Kenite king, David, that it is good and pleasant 'for brethren to dwell together in unity.' We shall show, that the Kenite and Hebrew tradition, whose essential identity was manifested by the union of Melchizedec with Abraham, and of Jethro with Moses, was represented respectively by the line of Ithamar and by that of Eleazar.

We have pointed out, that both Job and Abraham were men of the North-East, and that their common adversary was the black-skinned tyrant of the South-West, represented by Chedorlaomer. Again, we have seen, that Melchizedec was the title of a man of the East, a contemporary of Abraham. If, then, it could be asserted, that Job, who cannot have lived after Moses, was likewise a contemporary of Abraham, it would become probable, that the greatest man of the East, and the righteous King, were the same person. The value of this identity would be, that we should know, which were the doctrines of Melchizedec. But as both Job and Melchizedec were Kenites, we may assume, that their doctrines were essentially the same. Though we cannot assert the identity of both persons, the fact remains, that the most pious, upright and God-fearing man on the earth, the King of Salem, or Shaveh, most probably of Mount Gerizim, blessed Abraham, and received tithes from him. Although unconnected with any genealogical descent, Melchizedec represents a priesthood, which reaches back to pre-historical times. To this priesthood of the descendants of Cain, an unrecorded early promise had been made, of everlastingly standing as ministers before the Lord.[1] Thus interpreted, the book of Job contrasts Kenites and Hebrews with their common adversary of the black-skinned race, men of high degree with men of low degree, rich with poor, pious or godly men with base and godless men, Sons of God with sons of men.

[1] Comp. Ps. cx. with Jer. xxv. 19.

## CHAPTER V.

### KENITE AND HEBREW RECORDS IN GENESIS.

The Kenite and the Hebrew traditions, the two streams of common origin, early divided, reunited in the time of Moses, and yet never losing their distinct features, are marked by the Jehovistic and by the Elohistic records in the Pentateuch, and especially in Genesis. We shall here assume, what we have tried to prove in another work, that the Avesta and the Vedas refer, like the book of Genesis, to the first preaching of Monotheism, and of Divine sonship, among mankind; not to the creation, but to the renewing, bârâ, of heaven and earth, and to the renewing of man to the image of God. About the time of the separation of Cain from Eden, in the time of Seth and Enos, the name of Jehovah commenced to be called upon, or to be proclaimed. It has been pointed out, that the 4th and 5th chapters of Genesis contain a double list of the genealogies of Cain, only the former of which contains the name of Jehovah in the superscription. The name Jabal, in the Jehovistic list, might be a compound of Jah or Jehovah. Jabal is stated to have been 'the father of such as dwell in tents, and of such as have cattle.'[1] Could the name Jabal be connected with Jehovah, it would prove, that the Kenites, that is, the men of Jabesh, and their tribes, were called after Jehovah. They were nomads, even at the time when this account was written, and possibly Jehovists.

According to the tradition of the Septuagint and of the Vulgate, Jochebed, the mother of Moses, was not the aunt, but the cousin of Amram. This leads us to suggest, that

---

[1] Gen. iv. 20.

the mother of Moses was of Kenite descent. As such, Jochebed would be called a cousin of Amram, the Hebrew, in the same ethnological sense, in which the Kenite children of Hamath are by Amos called the cousins of the Hebrews. As the name of Jochebed is an acknowledged compound of Jehovah, which name we only find in the list we try to identify with the Kenites, the Kenite connection of Jochebed becomes probable. It is admitted, that no argument can be exclusively based on the two isolated passages in the Pentateuch, where the name of Jochebed occurs. The name of Jehovah in the pre-Mosaic times was only used in the family of the ancestors of Moses on the mother's side. Assuming the Kenite descent or connection of Jochebed, we can understand, how the Hebrew, or Elohistic, writer in Genesis could assert, that the name of Jehovah was 'not known' to Abraham, Isaac, or Jacob.[1] It was, therefore, evidently his intention, to teach the people, that God was only known to the patriarchs, as 'El Shaddai,' or God Almighty, and not as Jehovah. In the book of Job, the latter name is never connected with the former, which there so frequently occurs. It is explained by these facts and conclusions, that, according to the Elohist, God revealed himself to the patriarchs as El Shaddai, whereas the Jehovist records the revelation of God to Abraham through a vision, by the mediation of the Divine Word, as 'Jehovah, who had brought him out of Ur of the Chaldees.'[2] Again, Jacob is recorded to have declared, that if he returned to his father's house in peace, 'Jehovah shall be his God.'[3] It is needless to add, that the name of Jacob, like that of Judah and others, may be taken to be a compound of the name Jehovah. Although the organs of the Elohistic or Hebrew tradition did not reveal God to the people as Jehovah, the organs of the Jehovistic or Kenite tradition did so, as their compound names, and the histories of Moses, of the patriarchs, and of Jethro imply.

---

[1] Ex. vi 2.   [2] Gen. xv. 7.   [3] Ibid. xxviii. 21.

The name Jehovah was transmitted, and gradually made known, for a long time exclusively, by Kenite tradition, in the pre-Mosaic, if not pre-Abramitic times. It was in the time of Samuel, when the Kenite line of Eli occupied the sacerdotal see, that the name of Jehovah first began to be made the name of the national God of Israel, whilst the more prominent place assigned to prophetic schools, if not their introduction, marks the growing influence of prophets, the leading guardians and promulgators of tradition. Thus the way was prepared for the ascendancy of the Kenite house of David. It is the king after Jehovah's own heart, who forms the link between what Moses really taught, and the teaching of the prophets. Elijah and Jeremiah, the Kenite fathers of tradition, protested against the idolatries, especially of sacrifices, which Jehovah had 'not commanded,' and which were introduced by the spiritual leaders of a nation, which had gone 'backwards and not forwards,' since the days of Moses. Great progress was made in the establishment of Jehovistic principles, during the captivity, when a descendant of the Royal house of David, and therefore a Kenite, the prophet Daniel, still farther developed and applied the principles of Kenite tradition, of which the fullest record is to be found in the prophecies of the unknown prophet of the captivity, which form the latter part of the book of Isaiah.

We have pointed out, that the 'seven pillars' which Divine Wisdom has built, refer to the transmission of tradition, through the unbroken chain, formed by the seven organs of tradition, from Adam to Moses. The latter received the tradition of the former, directly through Amram, who received it from Levi, and thus from Isaac, Shem, Methuselah, and Adam, according to the age assigned to these individuals in holy writ. History shows, that from time to time prophets arose, to proclaim God's revelations to mankind. What prophets announced, recognised organs of tradition transmitted from one generation to another. Those who were fully initiated in the mysteries of tradition, those who had been, in every generation, the most revered conveyancers of the mysteries proclaimed by prophets, were considered as landmarks of the past, as epochs of tradition, as renewers of the same. By applying and developing the treasure committed to their keeping, the appointed organs of tradition became creators of new or mystic signs, for the visible transmission of the invisible.

In order to mark the unbroken chain of tradition, it was considered of the highest importance among the Israelites, as among Eastern nations generally, to preserve exact lists of generations, in the form of genealogies. These are not lists of lineal individual descendants from Adam and from Noah, but they mark the principal migrations of tribes. Thus the names of the children of Shem mark the gradual conquest of Shemitic tribes from the Persian gulf to the Mediterranean. It is important to observe, that the chiefs of tribes must have been regarded as chiefs of tradition, at a time, when each father of a family was a priest. The tribal chiefs occupied the place, which was assigned to the 'chiefs of the fathers,' in the time of Ezra. This tribal organisation led to a Scribal organisation, consisting of scholars, teachers, and chiefs, or fathers of tradition. Such an organisation is implied by the distinction of the 'rabs,' the 'rabbis,' and the 'rabbonis,' a classification offering an exact parallel to that of the Magi, who were originally not priests, but belonged to the prophetical order, and were divided, according to unanimous tradition, ever since the undefined time to which the name of Zoroaster refers,[1] into disciples, 'harbeds,' teachers, 'mobeds,' and the more perfect teachers of a higher wisdom, the 'destur mobeds.' This scribal organisation, which can be proved to have existed among the Jews after the captivity, and which

---

[1] See Rapp's 'Religion und Sitte der Perser,' p. 21, in *Zeitschr. der deutsch. Morg. Ges.*

was probably in force much earlier,[1] must have been headed by the high priestly lines of the Aaronites. As these represented a twofold stream of tradition, that of the Hebrews and of the Kenites, the scribal tradition would naturally be represented by two names, or by 'pairs,' the existence of which can be proved only in the last centuries of the pre-Christian era.

But although the traditional chain was in later times marked by the names of individuals, it was evidently, at first, connected with collective, or with representative titles. The twofold stream of Kenite and Hebrew tradition enables us to account for the similarity, and possibly also for the divergence in the genealogical lists contained in the fourth and in the fifth chapters of Genesis. These are two versions of the same antediluvian tradition.[2]

| Jahveh | God created | Seth |
|---|---|---|
| Adam | Man | Enos |
| 'Son of the earth.' | | 'Man.' |
| (generic name for mankind.) | | (generic name for mankind.) |

*Genealogies before the Flood.*

| GENESIS IV. | GENESIS V. |
|---|---|
| *Jehovist narrative (Kenite).* | *Elohist narrative (Hebrew).* |
| 1. Kajin, Abel, Enos, or 'the usurper.' | 1. Kènan. |
| 2. Chanokh, or 'the initiated.' | 2. Mahalalêl. |
| 3. Irad, or 'the founder of cities.' | 3. Jéred. |
| 4. M'echújaêl, or 'struck by El.' | 4. Chanokh. |
| 5. Metúshaêl, or 'the man of El.' | 5. Metushelach. |
| 6. Lémech, or 'the adolescent.' | 6. Lamech. |
| Dispersion of mankind. | 7. Noah, 'rest,' or 'water.' |
| | Dispersion of mankind. |

[1] Is. xxix. 10.  [2] Bunsen's 'Bibelwerk,' v. pp. 47, 305 f.

We have first to consider the different names given to the Deity. The historical tradition commences with Cain, that is, with the great separation in Eden. The name Enos corresponds with the name Adam, and so does Seth with Jehovah. We have pointed out, that Seth was the name for the Deity, which was introduced into Egypt, long before the time of Moses, and most probably by the Eastern Shepherd rulers. A third name for the Deity is introduced in these genealogies, the name of Elohim; it occurs but once in the fourth chapter,[1] where the Jehovistic writer introduces it, for the purpose of showing, when men began to call upon the name of Jehovah. From this it has been conjectured, that the name Elohim preceded the name Jehovah. Indeed the Elohistic writer of the fifth chapter of Genesis, declares in Exodus,[2] that God was not known to the patriarchs as Jehovah, but as El-Shaddai. El-Shaddai has the double meaning of 'the God of the pastures' and 'the God Almighty.' As the avocation of shepherds preceded that of tillers of the ground, the name El or El-Shaddai is probably more ancient than the two names of Jehovah and Elohim recorded in the pre-Noachian genealogies. But was El a more ancient appellation of the Deity than Seth? This question cannot perhaps be decided. They both refer to primitive times. Whilst El originally referred to the pastures, Seth referred to the shepherds. El and Seth may therefore, perhaps, be regarded as essentially identical. But though El had preceded Elohim, though the worship of many Gods had been a retrograde development, according to the Elohist's own showing, yet, when the records of Genesis were finally fixed, at the time of Jeremiah and of Ezra, it was in the interest of the Elohist party, which we hope to identify with the non-Kenite or Hebrew party, to declare in the Elohistic, or Hebrew, record that the Gods,

[1] Gen. iv. 25.    [2] Ex. vi. 3.

the Elohim, had created the heavens and the earth; and that, when man was to be created, the Gods said: 'let us now make man in our own image.' For these reasons, it would seem, the name of El or 'the God' was excluded in the Elohistic genealogy, and the name Seth, from the name of the Creator was lowered to the name of a creature, of a son of Adam, begotten by him 'in his own likeness, after his image.'

This Elohistic view about the human origin of Seth, is confirmed by the two verses which close the fourth chapter, that is, the Jehovistic genealogy. Seth and Enos follow after Cain, according to the Jehovist, and they precede Cain, according to the Elohist. As the names from Cain to Lamech are identical in the two lists, we may assert, that the names of Seth and Enos were, by the Elohist, placed between Adam and Cain, either from ignorance, or because the writer's object was, to show, that Seth had never been a name for the Deity. The final revisers of the Jehovistic genealogy in the fourth chapter, seeing, that the Elohistic genealogy commenced the list of the descendants from Adam with Seth and Enos, added these two names, for the purpose of harmonising the two accounts, and also, in order to prove, that, before the separation in Eden, before Cain, that is, in the time of Enos, according to the Elohist's genealogy, men began to call upon the name of Jehovah. Wishing, the more prominently to point out the transition from Polytheism to Monotheism, and the revelation of Monotheism in Eden, the Jehovistic writer, in these verses only, introduces the name Elohim or gods, in order to contrast it with the name Jehovah, the God above all Gods.

Thus we may distinguish, even now, three distinct traditions about the creation of man.

| Seth | Elohim | Jehovah |
|------|--------|---------|
| Enos | Adam | Adam |
| Kénan | Kénan | Kajin |

The different names of Kênan and Kajin for Cain, lead us to the suggestion, that the Jehovistic or Kenite tradition is more ancient than that of the Elohist. For whilst Cain is by the former called Kajin, the son of Adam is by the latter called Kênan, which name points to the later, the Abramitic time, when the Aramean highlanders met with the Kenaanites in the land of Kenaan. The three names following after that of Cain, are the same in both lists, but the Elohist, or the Hebrew, enumerates them in an inverted order. In the absence of any explanation, we suggest the following. Chanokh is a representative name, signifying 'the initiated.' We assume, that there was, among the Kenites on the Indus, an organisation of men of wisdom, of conveyancers of secret tradition, of initiated, and that such an organisation, though it probably existed among the Hebrews, was a distinct one, till a reunion of the Eastern tribes had been effected, in the time to which the name of Jared refers. We are expressly told, that, at some indefinite period before the Flood, 'the sons (or 'servants') of Elohim, saw the daughters of men that were fair, and they took any to wives, according to their pleasure.'[1] According to Arabian tradition, the intermarriage between the descendants of Seth and of Cain took place in the time of Jared. As this name signifies 'the founder of cities,' it well accords with the time 'when men began to multiply on the face of the earth.' We have, therefore, some ground for our suggestion, that the organisation of the initiated, to which the name of Chanokh in the genealogies may refer, was the fruit of the reunion of Eastern tribes which had separated in the time of Cain. This explanation seems to be confirmed by the name Mahalalêl, which, in the form of M'echújaêl, follows upon Irad (Jered) in the Kenite list. From this we infer, that the above name, which means 'struck (or 'marked?') by God,' and

[1] Gen. vi. 2.

which was given to the descendants of Cain, was introduced in the Kenite genealogy, in order to mark the re-union of the once united tribes. The next two genealogies of Metúshaél (Metushelach) and Lémech (Lamech) present no difficulty, as they form parallels in both lists. But according to Jehovistic tradition, the dispersion of mankind took place in the time of Lamech, whilst the Elohistic chronicler introduces the name of Noah, which refers, by its etymology, to the Flood, whether his name signifies 'rest' or 'water.'

The comparison of the antediluvian genealogies has confirmed our assertion, that the Jehovistic writers in Genesis represent the Kenite tradition. It is to the latter that we owe the ethnological and geographical information, contained in the tenth chapter of Genesis, whilst it is proved by the Jehovistic, as well as by the Elohistic narrative about the announcement of the Flood, and the prevalence of the same, that the tradition about this event was preserved by Kenites as well as by Hebrews. Kenite tradition, as we have shown, was preserved among Israel by the descendants from Melchizedec, from Jethro, and from David.

## CHAPTER VI.

### THE AARONITES.

ELEAZAR and Ithamar, after the death of Nadab and Abihu, the only surviving sons of Aaron, and of Elisheba, daughter of Amminadab, prince of the tribe of Judah, are in the genealogies shown to have been grandsons of Pharez, 'one of the twin sons whom Tamar bare unto Judah.' Tamar, after whom the youngest son was probably called Ithamar, by compounding the mother's name with the initial of Jah, was a descendant from the Anakim, or sons of Anak, who ruled in Kirjath-Arba, later called Hebron. They were a race of 'giants,' so called, either from their stature, or, more likely, from their strength, and were among the original inhabitants of the land between the Nile and the Euphrates, though, unless identified with the Rephaim, they are not mentioned by name in the passage in Genesis, where the promise of the land to Abram is recorded. A branch of the Anakim were the Talmai, descendants of the third 'Son' of Anak, who were slain or expelled from Kirjath-Arba, by the men of Judah, under Caleb's command. The same name Talmai, or Tholmai, was given to the son of Ammihud, king of Geshur,[1] whose daughter was married to David, and was the mother of the fair Absalom, and of the beautiful Thamar. The identity of the names Thalma and Thamar, points to a common origin, and thus it becomes probable, that Thamar the wife of Judah, and great grandmother of the Aaronites, was a descendant of

---

[1] 2 Sam. iii. 3, &c.

the Anakim. This probability is strengthened by the fact, that the Anakims of Geshur in Bashan, were allowed to live in the territory allotted to Manasseh.[1]

Moses appointed Eleazar as 'prince over the priests of the Levites,' and 'overseer of them that keep the charge over the sanctuary.'[2] Both 'Eleazar and Ithamar executed the priest's office,' or rather, 'became priests.'[3] They were assistants of the high priest, as Nadab and Abihu had been, till they were killed by the fire. Lots were drawn, one by one, in the time of David, between their respective descendants, for these and similar offices. David divided, or separated, Zadok of the sons of Eleazar, and Abimelech (Abiathar) of the sons of Ithamar, 'according to the appointment in their service.' Sixteen 'chief men' of the sons of Eleazar, and eight of the sons of Ithamar, were appointed as 'chiefs' of the sanctuary, and 'chiefs of God.' As the lots were drawn alternately for the two Aaronic lines, we may assert, that the eight priestly courses of the junior line were the following: Jedaiah, Seorim, Mijamin, Abijah, Shecamiah, Jakim (Eliakim), Jeshebeab, and Immer.

After the settlement at Shiloh, all 'the cities of Judah,' and many cities 'of the tribe of Benjamin,' were given to 'the sons of Aaron.'[4] In the book of Joshua the names of the Aaronic cities are given, and it appears, that nine were in Judah and Simeon, and thirteen in Benjamin. Although Ephraim, the tribe of Joshua, was the leading tribe at the time of the territorial division, yet the Aaronites had no possessions in that tribe. The only recorded exception is, that Phinehas received an allotment of his own, a hill on Mount Ephraim.[5] This exclusion of the Aaronites from Ephraim is difficult to explain. For to this tribe belonged Shiloh, and also Shechem, with Ebal and Gerizim. We may, therefore, assume at the

---

[1] Josh. xii. 13; 1 Chr. ii. 23.   [2] Num. iii. 32.   [3] 1 Chr. xxiv. 2.
[4] 1 Chron. xvi. 57–60; comp. Josh. xxi. 9, 13–19.
[5] Josh. xxiv. 33.

outset, that the Aaronites were, by family ties, exclusively
connected with Benjamin, Judah and Simeon. Had any
of the high priestly families settled in Ephraim, the
history of this tribe would probably have been very
different, and Hosea would not have lamented, that the
Epraimites 'refused to return' from the captivity.[1] To
the downward course of Ephraim, the upward course of
Judah and of Benjamin forms a surprising contrast.

Household priesthood was succeeded by hereditary
priesthood, among the Israelites, as among the Egyptians.
In both nations there was but one high priest, and the
law of succession was hereditary. At a time when the
existence of Levites as a consecrated tribe is more than
doubtful, since no trace of such special calling can be
found in Genesis, Moses established an hereditary priesthood in the family of Aaron. The tribal organisation must
have led to the settling of all sacerdotal descendants in
one or more tribes. We know, that their possessions lay
exclusively in Benjamin and Judah and Simeon. At the
census on Sinai, the tribe of Simeon was exceeded in
numerical force only by Judah and Dan, but in the time
of Joshua it had fallen to be the weakest of all tribes, and
it never rose to any political importance. It shared the
fate of Judah, and followed its leadership. Of the two
rival tribes, Judah and Benjamin, soon after the conquest
of Canaan, Benjamin rose to power, became the leading
tribe, defied all others, and was annihilated in the battle
of Gibeah, under the high priesthood of Phinehas, a son
or grandson of Eleazar. During the time that Phinehas
'stood before,' or ministered before the house of God,
probably the sanctuary at Shiloh, the men of Gibeah in
Benjamin, sons of Belial, worthless men, or men of low
descent, committed an unpardonable offence against a
Levite, sojourning on the side of Mount Ephraim, and
against his concubine out of Bethlehem Judah. This

---

[1] Hos. xi. 1-8.

'folly,' which the tribe of Benjamin had 'wrought in Israel,' caused all other tribes to demand the extradition of the offenders, in order that, by putting them to death, they might 'put away evil from Israel.' The demand having been refused, the children of Benjamin gathered themselves out of the cities unto Gibeah, to go out to battle against the children of Israel.' Among the 400,000 men of Israel, that went out to fight against the 26,700 men of Benjamin, Judah was ordered, by a Divine oracle, to go up first of all. After a three days' battle, the Benjamites and their cities were all but utterly destroyed. Hereupon the Israelites swore in Mizpeh, that none of them should 'give his daughter unto Benjamin to wife.' Nevertheless, seeing that God 'had made a breach in the tribes of Israel,' and agreeing, that 'there must be an inheritance for them that be escaped out of Benjamin,' the tribes of Israel, beside Benjamin, advised the remnant to take wives from among 'the daughters of Shiloh,' and to 'go to the land of Benjamin.' Following this advice, the Benjamites kidnapped some daughters of Shiloh, at an annual festival, which was held at a place in the north of Bethel, and went with them to the cities of Benjamin, which they repaired, and re-inhabited.[1]

The tribe of Benjamin, in the time of Saul, supported the senior Aaronic line of Eleazar. Thus it becomes probable, that this line was already connected with that tribe at the time of the battle of Gibeah. If so, the house of Eleazar, that is, the family of Phinehas and Abishua, must have shared in the degradation of Benjamin. That this was the case, is asserted by Josephus. He writes, that Abishua, the son of Phinehas, followed his father in the sacerdotal office; but that Abishua's descendants, from Bukki to Ahitub, the father of Zadok, lived according to the rank of private persons, 'during the time that the high priesthood was transferred to the house of Ithamar.'[2] Hence-

---

[1] Judg. xix.–xxi.     [2] Ant. viii. 1, 3.

forth the line of Ithamar, whose lot was cast, as we shall see, with the tribe of Judah, shared with the line of Eleazar, and thus with the tribe of Benjamin, the honours of the Aaronic inheritance. Thus the prophecy about Benjamin, which is recorded in Genesis,[1] may be said to have received its historical fulfilment by the tribe of Benjamin. Like a 'wolf,' this tribe had in the morning, in the early part of its history, 'devoured the prey,' and in the evening 'divided the spoil,' that is, the Aaronic inheritance.

The connection which the remnant of the Benjamites had formed with Ephraim, became a cause of this tribe's strength. Under the leadership of Ehud, the Benjamite, it had been foremost in Israel's fight for independence. The last judge, or liberator, in Israel was Samuel, son of Elkanah, of Ramthaim-Zophim in Mount Ephraim. Seeing how the representatives of the senior Aaronic line, since the battle of Gibeah, had been degraded, Samuel raised Saul, a layman belonging to the least of all the families of Benjamin, to the Royal dignity. Thus commenced the restoration of the tribe of Benjamin to power. The Benjamite king was supported by Zadok, the priest at Gibeon in Benjamin, and the representative of the senior Aaronic line of Eleazar. This is implied by the Biblical narrative. For Zadok and twenty-two captains of his father's house, together with many priests, joined David at Hebron, after the discomfiture of Saul and of his allies. As Zadok supported Saul, and as the tribe of Benjamin supported the elder line, so it can be shown, that Abiathar was the ally of David, and that his tribe Judah supported the junior line of Ithamar.

At Saul's command, which Zadok did not resist, and which he may have called forth, a bloody deed of shame was wrought in Israel. At Nob, 'the city of priests,' close upon the border of Judah, and within sight of Jeru-

---

[1] Gen. xlix. 27.

salem, all the priests of the house of Ahimelech, who was 'of the sons of Ithamar,'[1] that is, eighty-five priests of Zadok's rival line, were slain. Abiathar alone escaped, and fled to the forest of Hareth, in Judah, where David had gone to dwell, on the advice of the prophet Gad. David invited Abiathar to abide with him, as Saul sought the life of both of them. For Doeg, the Edomite, had accused Ahimelech, the father of Abiathar, of having conspired against Saul, by enquiring of the Lord for David, also by giving him victuals, together with the sword of Goliath, and by not informing Saul of his whereabouts. The successful flight of Abiathar, the preservation of the line of Ithamar by David, led to the translation of the ark from Kirjath-Jearim 'the city of the woods,' in Benjamin, to Jebus, the former city of the Jebusites, in Judah, which was probably not called Jerusalem before the time of Solomon. The future of this, then obscure, city of Judah, 'the holy city,' depended on the rescue of Abiathar by David. Had the line of Ithamar been utterly destroyed, as Saul intended, the line of Eleazar, although its succession had been interrupted, would have claimed, through Zadok, its representative, 'a young man mighty in valour,' not only the exclusive succession in the high priesthood, but the selection of Gibeon, or some other city in Benjamin, as the seat of the national sanctuary.

The plot at the sanctuary of Nob having failed, a compromise between the two rival lines, and between the two rival tribes, seems to have been effected by David, who did not underrate the political power of Zadok, and of the tribe of Benjamin. The king anointed 'over the house of Judah,' divided the sacerdotal honours between Abiathar, to whom he gave the ark and the ephod, and Zadok, who received the tabernacle, both being high priests, respectively at Jerusalem and at Gibeon. But the compromise thus made, between the Aaronic line of

[1] 1 Chron. xxiv. 3; comp. 2 Sam. viii. 17.

Benjamin and that of Judah, was merely a truce. Samuel had foreseen, that although his revered spiritual father Eli had, by force of circumstances, succeeded in raising the line of Ithamar to a participation in the Aaronic office, yet, that lasting peace could not be established between the rival Aaronites, except by the elevation of a layman to the Royal office. Thus royalty was introduced as a guarantee against hierarchical feuds and oppressions.

Instead of extinguishing the fire, this new institution poured oil into the flame. Abiathar joined Adonijah, David's eldest surviving son, who had set himself up as his father's successor. But a junior son of David, Solomon, Nathan's pupil, was joined by Abiathar's great rival Zadok, by whom, with the recorded consent of the dying David, the third king was anointed. The success of this plot re-established the line of Eleazar, as exclusive holders of the high priestly office, whilst Abiathar was 'thrust out from the priesthood,'[1] and exiled to his 'own fields' at Anathoth in Benjamin. The degradation of Abiathar was regarded as the fulfilment of the recorded prophecy, according to which the rule of the house of Eli was to be cut off, when 'an adversary,' or 'a rival,' that is, a representative of the senior line of Eleazar, would be set up in the habitation of God. In those days there was not even to be 'an old man,' that is, an elder, of the house of Ithamar. God would raise himself up 'a faithful priest,' who shall do according to what is in God's heart and soul, and build him a lasting house, and walk for ever before God's anointed. The remnants of the house of Ithamar will 'crouch to him for a piece of silver, and a morsel of bread, and shall say: Put me, I pray thee, into one of the priest's offices, that I may eat a piece of bread.'[2] At that time Benjamin would again 'devour the prey' without 'dividing the spoil.' This prophecy about the uninterrupted possession of the high

---

[1] 1 Kings ii. 27.  [2] 1 Sam. ii. 31-36.

priesthood in the line of Eleazar, stands in direct connection with the earlier prophecy to that effect, which had received an unexpected interpretation by the accession of Eli and of his successors. But, during the captivity, the prophet Ezekiel turned that promise into a command, ordering, that only the men of the house of Zadok, that is, of Eleazar, should enter into the most holy place.[1] This connection would not be overlooked by the final reviser of the Hebrew canon, by Ezra, the scribe and priest of the line of Eleazar.

From the above investigation it follows, that, probably ever since the time of Joshua, certainly during the reigns of Saul and of David, the line of Eleazar was mainly supported by the tribe of Benjamin, and the line of Ithamar by the tribe of Judah. The leading families were followed by the leading tribes, and the transfer of the national sanctuary from Shiloh to Gibeon, and from Gibeon to Jerusalem, marks the struggles for leadership, between the tribes of Ephraim, of Benjamin, and of Judah. If Judah and Benjamin were the tribes to which the descendants of the two sons of Aaron belonged, we shall be able to illustrate from this point of view the mysterious fact, that these two tribes separated from the ten tribes under Jeroboam, and to explain why only men of Judah and Benjamin returned from Babylon, and formed that hierarchy, which is not correctly called a theocracy. The light which may thus be thrown on these important events of Jewish history, confirms the view above expounded, about the peculiar mission assigned to Judah and Benjamin, as the cradles of that sacerdotal aristocracy which has been so instrumental in moulding the character of mankind.

---

[1] Ezek. xl. 46; xliii. 19; xliv. 15; xlviii. 2.

## CHAPTER VII.

### SYMBOLISM AND IDOLATRY IN ISRAEL.

We have pointed out, that in the earliest ages, to which history refers, symbols, signs, or images, were regarded as imperfect, but as revered representations of ideals. Rightly interpreted, they were well qualified to assist the mind, in the effort of realising, what superiorly endowed men had conceived. Tradition and Scripture prove, that man was led, through the symbol, to the reality, through the visible to the invisible. By the mixture of different races, the necessity arose, to harmonise dissimilar, and even adverse customs. The symbol facilitated, for a time, this work of compromise. It was found, that different symbols represented the same, or nearly the same ideas. They all pointed to the fact, that man is dependent on higher powers. Thus union in essentials was regarded as more important than union in non-essentials; unity and not uniformity was aimed at, universality was founded on liberty of conscience.

Not the spirit of charity, but physical force, at first gained for different symbols admittance into the same sanctuary. Different races ministered before the Lord, the unknown God, through a household priesthood, and later through a hereditary priesthood. Public worship, first domestic, then tribal, and later national, as it assumed larger proportions, so it became regulated by wider views. Stewards of Divine mysteries discovered, that, what was absolutely incomprehensible to the multitude, in times of old, by gradual preparation and interpretation, could be rendered comprehensible and useful to the unlearned

by the learned. However much they might have been
desirous, not to hide what they had heard from their
fathers, the wise men of every generation knew well, that
a premature revelation of religious mysteries, whilst it
must necessarily do harm to unprepared and unworthy
recipients, could not fail to jeopardise the safe transmission
of that tradition, of which they were the chief recognised
organs. Whilst this fact must be borne in mind, we must
not lose sight of the other, that the necessary institutions
of hereditary priesthoods, and corporations of the learned,
engendered a spirit of caste, which deprived the people
of their birthright. Secrecy led to tyranny, and tyranny
to that ignorance, which during long ages prevented the
revelation of things kept secret. Thus symbols were
gradually degraded to idols.

Jewish history confirms this view. The ancestor of
the Hebrews, accompanied by members of his family,
and probably also by a larger community, was a descendant from those who 'dwelt on the other side of the
flood in old time,' that is, on the Eastern side of the
Tigris. Of his father, Terah, it is recorded, that he and
his family 'served other gods.'[1] The Hebrew chronicler,
to whom it was forbidden to make any graven image,
meant by these words, to convey the tradition, which
has been preserved through independent Arabian channels, that Terah was a maker of images. For the
Hebrew word âbad signifies 'to make,' and also 'to
serve,' or to worship. It is the interpretation of Scripture, it is tradition, that can alone decide, which sense of
the word is the right one. Scripture without interpreting tradition, is a sealed book. Thus, again, the word
Asherah has the double meaning of image and of grove,
so that we cannot be certain, whether Abraham planted
a grove or erected an image at Beer-sheba.

The erection of a sanctuary, among the Hebrews, was

---

[1] Josh. xxiv. 2.

in the time of Abraham, and thus originally, connected
with the setting up of an image, that is, of a symbol.
Much light is thrown on the nature of symbolism in the
time of Abraham, by the interpretations of Mār Jacob,
bishop of Edessa in the seventh century.[1] He asserts, that
there was a mystery about the exodus of Terah and his
sons from the land of the Chaldees. One of the reasons
why Scripture records that Haran died ' whilst Terah his
father was living in the land of his nativity, in Ur of the
Chaldees,' is stated to have been, ' that when Abraham
burned the celebrated temple of Kenan, the God of the
Chaldees, Haran ran to extinguish the flames, and he fell
down and died there. When, not long after, it became
known to the Chaldees, what had happened, they pressed
Terah to deliver up Abraham, his son, to be slain, or
they threatened him, that they would destroy all his
family, if he did not obey. Since, therefore, Terah was
pressed by them, he took flight from the land of the
Chaldees with all his house.' Ephraem, called ' the
prophet of the Syrians,' in the fourth century refers
already to the tradition of the church about the temple
of Kenan. ' And when they were in the land of the
Chaldees, the Chaldees had a celebrated and magnificent
temple, in which was placed Kenan, a graven God, which
they worshipped; but the true God, they knew not. . . .
And when Abraham saw, that, for a moment, Terah
turned away from this, in his zeal he took fire, and
burned the celebrated temple of Kenan, the graven image
of the Chaldees. But Haran, the brother of Abraham,
entered to extinguish the flames, and deliver the graven
image from the burning, and he fell there and died.'[2]

From this we may conclude that, pressed by the
African element represented by the Chaldees, and led
by the Divine Spirit, the Asiatic leader left Ur of the
Chaldees. How long before the time of the Hebrew

---

[1] See Phillips on Mār Jacob, 1864.   [2] Eph. Syr. i. 156.

Patriarch, worship through symbols was practised, cannot be determined. But there is evidence to show, that the first symbols were not made with hands, and that heavenly bodies, or nature's elements, were the earliest symbols of the Deity, as well as of the Deities. It is an acknowledged fact, that all the most ancient religious systems were founded on symbolism, that is, that they expressed even the most ineffable conceptions, through the medium of beggary elements. The works of nature were regarded, not only as the witnesses, but as the revealers of God's glory. Thus Asaph the Kenite Psalmist exclaims: 'that thy name (or spirit) is near, thy wondrous works declare.'[1] Nature was studied, with a view to discovering, which of the elements might be regarded as the fittest symbols of supernatural agency, as effects of superhuman intelligence. Ideas gave birth to symbols, and these transmitted fixed and gradually crystallised religious conceptions, as the good deposit, the heirloom of mankind. If the object of all pre-Israelitic religions had been nothing beyond nature-worship, it would be quite incomprehensible, how Philo, Josephus, Clement of Alexandria, Origen, and the Rabbis, could have looked upon the ark as nothing more than a symbol of the universe. Thus they all regard the seven candlesticks as symbols of the seven planets. Again, unless the ark was a collection of symbols, pointing to the universe and its mysteries, the Latin word for the latter, arcanum, would not be connected with the Latin word for the ark. After its destruction by Nebuchadnezzar,[2] another ark would have taken its place in the temple of Jerubbabel and Joshua, unless the symbol was supposed to be no longer requisite.

Fire was regarded as the sublimest symbol of uncreated light, before a deeper knowledge about the heavenly bodies led men to worship the Deity through the symbols of the sun, of the moon and the stars. The star

---

[1] Ps. lxxv. 1.      [2] 2 Esdr. x. 22.

symbolism, and astronomical science generally, including the signs of the zodiac, were certainly imported into Egypt from the East.[1] This was done long before Abraham, as is proved by the name of Ashtaroth-Karnaim, the city where the Rephaim were slain by Chedorlaomer. An image, or asherah, was made to represent a heavenly body, an ashteroth, which had been regarded as a symbol of uncreated light, suggested to man by the terrestrial fire, which he had the power to originate. Thus in Egypt, and also in the land between the Nile and the Euphrates, the ashteroth, that is, either the moon, or Venus or Sirius, was represented by a cow. 'The throne of the cow,' or ashtaroth, referred to 'the queen of heaven,' to Baal-ti, the wife of Baal, the Sun-God. Among the Egyptians the cow was the symbol of Sirius, the brightest of all fixed stars. Therefore the hieroglyphics represent a star between the horns of a cow.[2] To this comparatively late combination of Eastern and Western symbolism, the name Ashtaroth-Karnaim refers; for it means: 'the throne of the cow with two horns.' The images which Terah is said to have made, or rather to have served and worshipped, may, therefore, be connected with Eastern symbolism. The 'other gods' which Abraham's father served, were different symbols, images or asherahs of the One God.

Similar images, or teraphim, were in the possession of Laban. Unless they had been regarded as symbols of Jehovah, Isaac would not have sanctioned Jacob's marriage with a daughter of Rebekah's brother. Of such value were these household gods held to be, that Rachel did not venture to leave her father's home without them, on her flight with Jacob. The teraphim represented the Divine Presence in a figure, that presence which, in later times, the Israelites believed to be manifested by the

---

[1] Bunsen's Egypt, Germ. ed. i. 40; v. 4, p. 8 f.
[2] Brugsh in D. Morgenl. Ges. ix. 3, &c.

cloud, and by angels. Jacob remembered, that on his lonely journey from Beer-sheba to Haran, a stone of the country, possibly a meteoric stone held in general reverence, had by him been used as a pillow, during the night of his vision, had been set up as a pillar, and consecrated with oil. So far from taking offence at the household images of Rachel, Jacob ordered his household, on the journey from Shechem to Bethel, only to put away 'the gods of the foreigner,'[1] that were among them. And lest they should be tempted to use their precious metal for the moulding of other images, all the followers of Jacob gave up their earrings, and their master buried them under the oak, probably a sanctuary at Shechem.

The practice of moulding silver and gold into images, and of engraving mystic signs thereon, is several times referred to in the Pentateuch, and in the book of Judges. Aaron moulded the calf from the gold which the Israelites had stolen from the Egyptians; and Micah the Ephraimite, a devout believer in Jehovah, stole his mother's silver, who, when it had been returned by her son, gave the precious metal, which she had 'wholly dedicated unto Jehovah,' into the hands of a founder, 'who made thereof a graven image, and a molten image, and they were in the house of Micah.' Here they were kept, together with the ephod, till the Danites stole them, who must have believed, that in securing them, they secured the presence of God. And yet Micah, who had been instrumental in the making, that is, the engraving of these symbols, and had consecrated one of his sons as a priest, to minister in the 'house of gods,' was more sure, that the Lord would do him good, when he had 'a Levite' to his priest. This Levite was of Bethlehem-Judah, and went to sojourn, where he might find a place. He consented to be unto Micah 'a father and a priest,' and the young man, who had stood before the Lord in the domestic sanctuary,

---

[1] Gen. xxxv. 2-4; comp. Josh. xxiv. 14.

'was unto him as one of his sons.' This priest was Jonathan the son (descendant) of Gershom, the firstborn son of Moses (not Manasseh) and Zipporah, the Kenite. Danites, that is, descendants from Bilhah, Rachel's maid, having by force taken Micah's images, Jonathan, whose voice the Danites knew, consented to follow them, and, under his auspices, Micah's graven image was set up in 'the house of God' at Shiloh, 'until the day of the captivity of the land.'[1]

All the names mentioned in this narrative, Micah the Ephraimite, Jonathan the descendant from Gershom, that is, of the 'stranger,' and the Danites, descendants from Bilhah, point to the high-caste descendants from the Patriarchs. Ephraim is the representative of Joseph, whose mother was the fair Rachel; Gershom was a direct descendant from Moses and Zipporah, and Bilhah, from whom the Danites descended, was probably of the same race as Rachel. As Joseph was minister to a Pharaoh of the Shepherds, whom we have pointed out as a cognate if not identical race with the Kenites, and as the Kenites were the first possessors of Bethlehem-Judah, to which city the priest Jonathan belonged, it may be asserted, that the above names refer to Kenites. And this becomes important, by the reference of Jeremiah to the sanctuary at Shiloh, where God caused his name to 'throne' in times of old, although, because of the wickedness of the people he had 'cast away' from his presence all the seed of Ephraim. Jeremiah was a descendant from the priests that were at Anathoth, and as the fields of Abiathar were there, it is certain, that Jeremiah, like the latter, was connected with the Kenite line of Ithamar. To have gone after other gods, to their own hurt,[2] was one of the sins which the Israelites had committed, and because of which the prophet threatened them with the punishment the Ephraimites had received.

---

[1] Judg. xvii. and xviii.    [2] Jer. vii. 6, 12–14.

The engraven symbol which Jonathan, the priest, had set up in Shiloh, had not been displeasing to God; for Jeremiah declares, that God's name throned in that place. But during the nearly thousand years, which elapsed between the time of Jonathan and that of Jeremiah, symbols had become idols, that is, they were worshipped as realities, and no longer as symbols.

How soon this degradation of symbols took place, cannot be determined. We have no sufficient reason to doubt the identity of El and the Elohim of the Israelites, and the Baal and the Baalim of some of the earliest settlers in the land. And we shall see, that there are some reasons for assuming, that the name Jehovah was transmitted to Moses through the instrumentality of the Kenite organs of tradition. As the whole of the Pentateuch, in the form in which we possess it, was certainly not written before the time of Josiah; and as Ezra finally revised or recomposed the Scriptures, which had perished, or from which the truth had perished,[1] doing this under circumstances unfavourable to the Kenites, the record in the book of Numbers, about the Baal-worship among the Moabites and the Midianites, both descendants from Terah, who himself 'served other gods,' must be read with caution. The forty years' residence of Moses with Jethro, his marrying Zipporah, and the solemn uniting of Aaron, and of all the elders, with Jethro, in eating bread before the Lord, —these facts are difficult to explain, if during the time of Moses the people of Israel bowed to the gods of the Moabites and Midianites, and consequently, either 'all the chiefs of the people,' or 'all the men that followed Baal Peor,' were hanged up before the Lord against the sun. Accepting the fact, it seems reasonable to assume, that the prohibition, not to make any graven image, was vigorously enforced among the Israelites, whilst their co-

---

[1] Jer. vii. 28.

descendants from Terah continued to worship the Lord through symbols. Aaron had re-introduced a symbol of the Deity, but he did not share the fate of those who had worshipped before that symbol. He was consecrated as high priest, though afterwards deprived of his high priestly robes, which Eli-Sheba gave to Eleazar. The stern upholding of unsymbolised Monotheism, had become a necessity among the Hebrews, after their long residence in Egypt, where symbolism prevailed to a perilous extent. But it does not follow from this, that the symbolical worship of the Moabites and the Midianites was an idolatrous worship. We must not, therefore, literally interpret the record, according to which, that worship led to the most outrageous profligacy. For we have already pointed out, that the matrimonial metaphor is in such cases invariably resorted to, by the Hebrew Chronicler. No offence is taken at Terah's having served other gods, but Israel's doing so is defined as going 'a whoring after other gods.' The change from legal to illegal symbols, is described as a falling away, as adultery. Unless we thus figuratively interpret the narrative about Baal-Peor, it will remain inconceivable how Moses could have viewed the promised land from a Moabite sanctuary, and how he could have been buried in Moab, at a place facing Beth-Peor, that is, the abode of Baal-Peor.

It is a strong confirmation of the view, that the Midianites cannot have been idolaters in the time of Moses, if it has been proved, that the entire house of David is, like the Midianites, of Kenite descent. The wars between Midian and Moab, on the one side, and Israel on the other, were caused by their not separating peaceably, as their ancestors Lot and Abraham had done. Both branches of the Abrahamitic family wished to possess the same land. Before commencing this war of annihilation, the contending parties consulted the same prophet, Balaam, who came from Aram, from Mesopotamia, 'out of the mountains of the East.' His recorded visions and interpretations declare that Jehovah, who alone knows and predicts the future, has decided in favour of Israel. The non-Hebrew prophet was probably one of the Chaldean Magi, that is, one of the wise men from the East, of the Bene Kedem, or sons of the East, whose ancestors had settled in the West. Balaam's knowledge about Jehovah is thus accounted for. The Amorites, and the Moabites, and the Midianites, were sore afraid of the Israelites, of the nomadic tribes that threatened to eat down all in the land of the Kenites, 'as the ox eateth down the grass of the field.' They wished to drive these intruders away from the land, and the seer was asked to 'curse Jacob' and to 'rebuke Israel.'

But Balaam cannot curse whom God has not cursed, nor rebuke whom God does not rebuke. From the top of the rocks, and from the hills, the seer saw 'a people that dwells separated, and does not let itself be reckoned among the (other) nations.' This people is called Jacob and Israel. 'The man with the closed eye,' the 'hearer of Divine speech,' who 'beholds the visions of the Almighty,' and 'whose eyes are opened when he falls to the ground,' never mentions Jacob without Israel, although he regards them as a united people. Jacob has 'tents,' and Israel has 'dwellings,' but both will be ruled by one king, and from one kingdom. This king, who will be greater than Agag, that is, than the Pharaoh, or king, of Israel's enemies, will ascend as a star out of Jacob, and his sceptre shall arise out of Israel, and shall smite the foreheads of Moab, and destroy, that is, according to the Targum of Onkelos, 'rule over' all the sons of Sheth or Seth. We shall see, that, 'the sons of Seth,' and 'the sons of God' are identical expressions, and that Jacob is, by Balaam, identified with the Kenites. The promised ruler is to be a Kenite, as David was. Those of Edom and of Seir, the descendants from Esau, who had kings before the children of Israel had any,[1] and the aboriginal inhabitants of Edom, the Horites, descendants from Seir, whose name refers to their having dwelt in caves, like the Kenites,[2] are to become the possession of the future Kenite king in Israel. History fulfilled this prophecy of Balaam, when David, the first Kenite king, conquered Edom, ' putting garrisons throughout all Edom,' and when 'all they of Edom became David's servants,'[3] having been, as Balaam describes them, 'his enemies,' because his rivals. Although David conquered Edom, and Solomon equipped his merchant fleet at Elath and Eziongeber, the seaports of Edom, yet Edom did not continue to be Israel's possession,[4] and even Hebron, the ancestorial place of the Hebrews and Kenites, was taken by the Edomites, during the Babylonian captivity.[5] 'Not so much as a footbreadth' of the land belonging to the Edomites, the 'brethren,' of Israel, was lastingly to belong, with God's sanction, to Israel.[6]

Thus clearly does the Kenite prophet refer to the temporary possession of Edom and Seir by David, who ruled over all the sons of Seth, that is, over the Kenites. Through the Kenite King, the star arising out of Jacob, Israel did rise to power, as Balaam had foretold. 'And he that comes out of Jacob shall rule, and he shall destroy those that flee from the cities.'[7] He who rules over those that dwell in 'tents,' over the nomadic Kenites, makes war against the inhabitants of cities, against the Hebrews. This prophecy was fulfilled when David fought against Saul, Judah against Benjamin. We are now no longer surprised to find, that the seer has distinguished in the united people, that came out of Egypt, the non-Hebrew stream of the Kenites, as Jacob, dwelling in tents, and the Hebrew stream as Israel.

[1] Gen. xxxvi. 31.  [2] Num. xxiv. 21.  [3] 2 Sam. viii. 14.
[4] 2 Kings xvi. 6.  [5] Ant. xii. 8, 6, &c.  [6] Deut. ii. 5.
[7] Num. xxiv. 17-19.

Speaking in the language of genealogy we should say, that 'Jacob' refers to the descendants from Rachel, and 'Israel' to the descendants from Leah. Jacob and Israel whom God brought out of Egypt, are by Balaam compared to a unicorn, or rather, a buffalo. Thus the same figure is taken, which Moses is recorded to have used in blessing Ephraim, whose 'horns' were to push down the people, both the ends of the earth.'[1] Unless we have failed in tracing these two streams in Hebrew history, the separate mention of Jacob and of Israel must be thus interpreted.

It is a confirmation of this view, that the prophecy, whose furthest horizon is the Babylonian captivity,[2] points to the great king as coming out of Jacob, the originally non-Hebrew part of Israel, as a star arising from among the Kenites. But from the Kenites, who had been incorporated with the Hebrews, without giving up their peculiar customs and traditions, Balaam distinguishes not only the Kenites of Edom, but other Kenites, or descendants from 'Cain,' that dwelt in other parts of the land, and who were to be led away into captivity by Asshur. We shall see, that the men who returned from Babylon to the holy land, were men of Judah, accompanied by some of Benjamin. The former were Kenites, so was the high priest Joshua, their spiritual leader. These all believed in the approaching fulfilment of Kenite prophecies about the return after the scattering. With the Kenite Psalmist they believed, that the 'heritage' of Israel was 'the worship of Jacob,' whom God loves.[3] That Kenite worship of Jacob was introduced into Jerusalem by Joshua the Kenite high priest, when the Lord had 'turned away the captivity of Jacob.'[4] It was then, if not already in the time of the Kenite king David, that the Kenite Psalmist, the Son of Korah,

---

[1] Deut. xxxiii. 17; comp. Job xxxix. 9.
[2] Num. xxiv. 22, 23.   [3] Ps. xlvii. 4.   [4] Ibid. lxxxv. 1.

exclaimed about the Kenites' stronghold and sanctuary: 'Her foundations are upon the holy hills; the Lord loveth the gates of Zion more than (or, first among) the dwellings of Jacob. Very excellent things are spoken of thee, thou city of God. I will think upon (or, I will call by name, or, I will claim) Rahab and Babylon with them that know me (or rather, as my fellow-worshippers); behold, the Philistines also, and they of Tyre with the Morians (Ethiopians, or rather, those of Moriah, the Samaritans) they are born there. And of Zion it shall be reported, that he was (or, that they all were) born there, and the Most High shall stablish her.'[1] The same preference before Israel is ascribed to Jacob by David, when he said, that 'all the seed of Jacob' were to 'magnify,' and 'all the seed of Israel' to 'fear' the Lord.[2] Again, the Psalmist declares, that God 'showeth his Word unto Jacob, his statutes and ordinances unto Israel.'[3] Asaph states, that whilst fire was kindled in Jacob, which may possibly mean, whilst Jacob abstained from image worship, God's heavy displeasure came against Israel.[4] Jeremiah denounces commandments which God had not commanded, and which still were promulgated in his name. Again, Ezekiel speaks of 'statutes that are not good.' The distinction between Jacob and Israel is similar to the distinction between Moses and the children of Israel. God made known his 'ways' unto Moses, and only his 'acts' unto the children of Israel.[5]

The Babylonian captivity is indirectly, but clearly, referred to in the book of Deuteronomy, as the close of Israel's idolatry. Here we are told, that Moses looked forward to a time, when Israel would have worshipped idols, would have 'suddenly perished' as a nation, and have been scattered among the other nations of the earth. At that time, that is, after the Babylonian captivity, if the Israelites would, with all their hearts,

---

[1] Ps. lxxxvii.     [2] Ibid. xxii. 23.     [3] Ibid. cxlvii. 19.
[4] Ibid. xxviii. 22.     [5] Ibid. ciii. 7.

and with all their souls, truly seek the Lord their God, they would find him.[1] It is in this book, which contains the hidden law of Moses, as revealed in the time of Josiah, that the seeking and finding of God is made dependant on man's loving his Maker with all his heart, and with all his soul, and with all his might.[2] This injunction was to be taught diligently to the people; they were to be bound for a sign upon the hand, to be as frontlets between the eyes, and to be written upon the posts of the houses, and on the gates. So little was this mode of seeking the Lord known to the people, that the first four books of Moses contain only one passage, on this all-important subject. In referring to the first, the provisional tabernacle, erected by Moses outside the camp, the narrator has recorded, that every one who 'sought the Lord' went out unto the same.[3] Here only the idea and the phrase occurs, whilst in all the five books of Moses nothing is said about prayer. The priests performed certain acts before the people, and this was called worship. No wonder, that the symbols of worship, the ark, the brazen serpent, and others, were more and more misunderstood, and idolised, instead of being revered as the figurative interpreters of Divine mysteries.

To this idolatry Jeremiah refers, when he declares, that, ever since the days of the exodus, the people had been, and were, stealing, murdering, committing adultery, swearing falsely, burning incense unto Baal, and walking after other gods, whom they knew not. Yet they came and stood before God, in the house which was called after God's name, and said: 'deliver us,' that they might do all these abominations. 'Is this house, which is called after my name, become a den of robbers in your eyes?' 'Seest thou not what they do in the cities of Judah, and in the streets of Jerusalem? The children gather wood, and the fathers kindle the fire, and the women knead

---

[1] Deut. iv. 26–29.   [2] Ibid. vi. 5.   [3] Ex. xxxi. 7.

dough, to make cakes to the queen of heaven, and to pour out drink offerings unto other gods, that they may afflict me.' 'Thus saith the Lord of hosts, the God of Israel: Put your burnt offerings unto your sacrifices, and eat the flesh thereof. For, nothing have I spoken with your fathers, and nothing have I commanded them respecting burnt offerings and sacrifices, in the day that I brought them out of the land of Egypt. But this is the word, which I commanded them: Obey my voice and I will be your God, and ye shall be my people, and walk entirely in the way that I command you, that it may be well unto you. But they hearkened not, nor inclined their ear, but walked in the councils, in the stubbornness of their evil heart, and went backward and not forward; . . . truth is perished, and cut off from their mouth.'[1]

Thus the prophecy of Moses, about the idolatry of Israel, up to the time of the captivity, is spoken of in the light of its fulfilment, by the great prophet of the captivity, by the contemporary of those, who found and proclaimed the hidden book of the law of Moses, by Jeremiah, a prophet like Moses, and who has most probably written that part of the second law, of Deuteronomy, which contains what had been unknown to the high priest and to the king of his time. Already, two centuries earlier, Amos had spoken, in the name of God, about the abomination of Israel's sacrifices. 'I hate, I despise your feast days, and do not like to smell your festive assemblies. Though ye offer me burnt offerings and your meat offerings, I do not accept it graciously, and I do not regard the peace offering of your fatted calves.' 'Have ye offered unto me sacrifices and offerings in the wilderness forty years, ye of the house of Israel? And now ye bear the tabernacle of Moloch, and your images Chiun and Remphan,[2] the star of your gods, which ye made for

---

[1] Jer. vii.

[2] Acts vii. 43. Chiun and Remphan were foreign divinities worshipped in Egypt, possibly introduced by the Shepherds.

yourselves. Therefore will I cause you to go into captivity beyond Damascus, saith the Lord, whose name is the God of hosts.'[1]

The language of Ezekiel confirms the charge of Jeremiah, and the prophecy of Moses, recorded in Deuteronomy, that the period between the exodus and the captivity, was one of idolatry. As if referring to the words of Moses, Ezekiel said, in the name of the Lord: 'I lifted up mine hand unto them in the wilderness, that I would scatter them among the people, and disperse them in the countries. Because they had not executed my judgments, but had despised my statutes, and had polluted my sabbaths, and their eyes were after their fathers' idols, I gave them also statutes that were not good, and judgments whereby they should not live, and I polluted them by their own gifts (of sacrifice), in that they caused to pass through the fire all that opened the womb.'[2] It is impossible not to connect, in some way or another, this passage with some that are recorded in the books of Moses. 'And the Lord spake unto Moses, saying: Sanctify unto me all the firstborn, whatever openeth the womb among the children of Israel, both of man and of beast: it is mine.'[3] 'Moreover every devoted thing (kherem) that a man shall devote unto the Lord, out of all which he hath, out of man and out of beast, and out of the field of his possession, shall not be sold, and shall not be redeemed; every devoted thing is holy of holies to the Lord. Every devoted thing which shall be devoted out of man, shall not be redeemed, it shall surely be put to death.'[4] Thus an exception was made to the general command not to kill, not even a slave, as a punishment.[5] It was to be regarded as an honour, that the firstborn was devoted, that is, killed unto the Lord. The act of devotion was the act of killing the object to be sacrificed.

---

[1] Amos v. 25–27.  [2] Ezek. xx. 25, 26.  [3] Ex. xiii. 2.
[4] Lev. xxvii. 28, 29.  [5] Ex. xxi. 20.

Whether or not we regard this commandment as one of the statutes that 'are not good,' thus much is certain, that the Israelites were led by these injunctions, whether orally transmitted, or in writing, to commit the abomination of human sacrifices, even in Jerusalem.

For thus spoke Jeremiah, in the name of Jehovah: 'The children of Judah have done evil in my sight, saith the Lord, they have set their abominations in the house which is called by my name, to pollute it. And they have built the high places of Tophet, which is in the valley of the son of Hinnom, to burn their sons and their daughters in fire, which I commanded them not, neither came it into my heart.'[1] 'They have forsaken me, and have estranged this place, and have burned incense in it unto other gods, whom neither they nor their fathers have known, nor the kings of Judah, and have filled this place with the blood of innocents. They have built also the high places of Baal, to burn their sons with fire for burnt offerings unto Baal, which I commanded not, nor spoke it, neither came it into my mind.'[2] As in the time of Abraham,[3] children were first slain, and then burnt. It is remarkable, that in the book of Deuteronomy alone, the above practices, which in Leviticus were only forbidden with reference to Baal,[4] are prohibited as not pleasing to Jehovah. 'Thou shalt not do so unto the Lord thy God, for every abomination to the Lord, which he hateth, have they done unto their gods; for even their sons and their daughters they have burnt in the fire to their gods.'[5] This injunction may, therefore, be classed among those, which were first made known in the time of Josiah, the contemporary of Jeremiah, the probable writer of those parts of Deuteronomy, in which the newly proclaimed book of the law of Moses was inserted.[6]

---

[1] Jer. vii. 30, 31.
[2] Ibid. xix. 4, 5; comp. Ps. cvi. 37, 38; 2 Chr. xxviii. 3.
[3] Gen. xii. 10.  [4] Lev. xviii. 21; xx. 2.
[5] Deut. xii. 31.  [6] Comp. Colenso's Pentateuch, v. 285 f.

Such were the idolatries and abominations which according to Deuteronomy, Moses foretold, that Israel would commit during the time between his death and the Babylonian captivity. Immediately before this event, Jeremiah declared, that God had commanded 'nothing' respecting any sacrifices. He could not have made so sweeping an assertion, if he had believed, that any of the sacrifices enjoined in the books attributed to Moses, were ever sanctioned by God. If there were exceptions, and if he did not regard the entire sacrificial ritual as composed of statutes which were 'not good,' though given in the name of Jehovah, he must have qualified this and other remarks against every kind of sacrifice. A similar unqualified censure of every kind of sacrifice, of every attempt to atone for iniquity in any other way than by forsaking it, is contained in the book of Isaiah. 'To what purpose is the multitude of your sacrifices unto me? saith the Lord: I am full of the burnt offerings of rams, and the fat of fed beasts, and I delight not in the blood of bullocks or of lambs, or of he goats. When ye enter and appear before my face, who requires of you to tread my courts? Henceforth bring no more vain meat-offerings; incense is an abomination unto me; new moon and Sabbath, feast-congregation, iniquity and feast assembly, I will not. My soul hateth your new moons and feasts, they are a burden unto me, I am weary of bearing them. And though ye spread out your hands, I yet hide mine eyes from you; though ye make much prayer, yet I hear you not; your hands are full of blood, wash, purge yourselves, remove from mine eyes your evil doings, cease to do evil, learn to do good, strive after right.'[1]

'Pollute ye no more my name with your gifts and with your idols,' said Ezekiel to the Israelites who served 'wood and stone,'[2] instead of offering 'sacrifices of righteousness.'[3] That 'righteousness of the Lord' consists,

---

[1] Is. i. 11–17.  [2] Ezek. xx. 31, 39.  [3] Deut. xxxiii. 19.

according to the definition of Balaam, in a life of obedience to the voice of God, of charity and humility, and not in sacrifices of any kind. The Kenite seer was the first who enjoined the presentation of the human body as a living sacrifice.'[1]

Sacrifices are first ordered, and then counterordered and condemned by Balaam. Balak, the king of Moab, together with his allies, having consulted the seer Balaam, the latter ordered him to build seven altars, and to sacrifice seven bullocks and seven rams. Whilst Moab sacrificed, the prophet saw Israel 'encamped according to its tribes,' that is, he saw, by lifting up his eyes, what was being done in Israel. No sacrifices are mentioned as being offered to God; we may therefore assume, that in his prophecy about Israel, he contrasts, for this reason, the lovely tabernacles of Israel, with the altars and burnt offerings of Moab. More fully instructed by the 'divine speech,' which he had heard and proclaimed, Balaam had soon an opportunity of giving better advice to Balak, with reference to sacrifices. The same king, whom Baalam is recorded to have assisted in offering burnt-sacrifices of rams and bullocks, seeing in the war hereupon ensuing, that he was hardly pressed, and regarding his want of success as a proof, that what he had offered was not sufficient to procure him the favour of God, he once more consulted the seer, and said: 'Wherewith shall I come before the Lord, bow myself before the God in the height? Shall I come before him with burnt offerings, with calves of a year old? Will the Lord be pleased with thousands of rams, with ten thousands of rivers of oil? Shall I give my firstborn for my transgression, the fruit of my body for the sin of my soul?' Balaam answered: 'It has been shown to thee, O man, what is good, and what the Lord requireth of thee. Nothing else than to do what is right, and to practise charity, and to walk humbly

---

[1] Rom. xii. 1.

with thy God.' The knowledge of how to do right, of 'the righteousness of the Lord,' was imparted, by the Midianite or Kenite seer, to the king of Moab.¹ It consists in no outward dedication. As Jeremiah declared, that God had commanded 'nothing' about sacrifices, so Balaam declared that God requires 'nothing else' than the offering of man's heart; yet the same man had first advised the king of Moab to sacrifice. This must have been a Moabitish custom at that time. The conjecture is not unwarrantable, that, during the last stage of the journey of the Israelites to Canaan, that is, 'from Shittim unto Gilgal,' when, as Micah states, this scene between Balak and Balaam occurred, the Israelites had not received any commandments about sacrifice, and that the commandments, later introduced in the books attributed to Moses, were by prophets not regarded as having received the Divine sanction.

We shall see, that the earliest protest against sacrifices in Israel, was made by David, the first of the three kings of whom it is said, in the wisdom of Sirach, that they alone were 'not faulty,' or 'failed not.' Before we do so, we must more minutely consider the symbolism connected with the ark. We have already observed, that, according to universal and uncontradicted tradition, recorded by Philo, Josephus, and the Fathers, the ark symbolised the universe, different parts and elements of which were symbolised within the sanctuary, by the candlesticks, the coverings and other things belonging to the same. As God is present in the universe, so was his presence symbolised in the ark. But as he thrones invisibly and unapproachably in heaven, so the holy of holies was separated from the other part of the sanctuary, the inner veil performing the office of the barriers around the holy mountain, upon which the Lord descended in fire, when he communicated the law, 'through the me-

¹ Micah vi. 5–8.

diation of angels.' The cherubims who, with the flaming sword, guarded the way to the tree of life, in the garden of Eden, towards the East, and which Moses saw on the Mount, were represented in gold on the mercy seat, where God met with Aaron. Between the cherubims shone the glory, so that these symbolised the Lord's descent in fire. Ezekiel describes having seen them in a vision, 'like burning coals of fire,' from which 'lightning' issued forth.[1] Next to the mercy seat with the cherubim, there were only the stone tables of the covenant in the ark. Thus the cherubims and the stone tables pointed to the manifestation of God in the bush, through fire, and through the word. Darkness enshrouded these symbols of God's presence, and pointed to 'the thick darkness' in which God was, when he spoke to Moses, that is, to the cloud.

The presence of God in the dark place, in the veil of the cloud, which hid the brilliancy of Divine light, was symbolised by the cloud of incense within the sanctuary, with which the cloud above the sanctuary may, perhaps, be connected. That cloud was the only generally visible sign of God's presence. In the Mosaic records it is directly connected with the wanderings of Israel. When the cloud appeared, the Israelites were to rest. Thus the invisible rest, or indwelling of God's glory, the Shechina, was symbolised by its temporary outward sign, the Kabôd. The latter was the forerunner of the former. Israel was led from that which was visible and without, to that which invisibly abides within the holy of holies. And yet the cloud was but a symbol, and not the real conveyancer of God's presence. As Israel came to its rest, in Shiloh, the invisible Divine rest came unto Israel. Only once is it recorded in Deuteronomy, that the cloud was seen over the door of the tabernacle.[2] And in the books of Joshua, Judges, and Samuel, no cloud is stated to have appeared, although its reappearance in Solomon's temple is described.[3]

[1] Ezek. i. 13, 14.   [2] Deut. xxxi. 15.   [3] 1 Kings viii. 10, 11.

According to the book of Exodus, Moses received the Divine command, to offer incense, through Aaron, on the altar of shittim wood, covered with gold, which stood before the inner veil, covering the ark of the testimony, before the mercy seat.[1] The cloud of incense was a symbol of God's presence. If incense had been originally, among the Hebrews, intended as the symbol of prayer, some injunction to pray would have necessarily been recorded in the books of Moses. The golden altar and the fiery coals, which were placed on the same, were symbols of that Divine presence, which had been manifested to Moses, as to Abraham, through the medium of fire. To enter into the cloud, in which 'the glory of the Lord appeared,'[2] that is, to come before God's presence, was, in the times of Moses, the privilege of Moses and Aaron only, whilst neither the priests nor the people were permitted an approach, which would have been destruction to them.[3] In order to seek the Lord, the people had, at first, to go without the camp. They went to the sanctuary, as they later went to a seer, for the purpose of asking God questions, through the priests. The Divine oracles were proclaimed through the mysterious instrumentality of the Urim, that is, a symbol of light, possibly connected with Ur, the fire or light of the Chaldees, probably typified by the Scarabees, and through the medium of the Thummim, or golden image of truth.[4] But already about two years later, Moses set up the tabernacle in the very centre of Israel's camp. The time came, when the Lord promised, through the mouth of his holy prophets, that he would 'create upon every dwelling place of Mount Zion, and upon her assemblies, a cloud and smoke by day, and the shining of a flaming fire by night,' and when 'upon all, the glory shall be a defence.'[5] At first, men tried to hide themselves from the presence of the Lord, or fled from it like

---

[1] Ex. xxx. 1-7.   [2] Ibid. xvi. 10.   [3] Ibid. xix. 18-24.
[4] But see Mr. Plumptre in Smith's Dictionary.   [5] Is. iv. 5.

Cain and Jonah. Even Job was troubled, or 'trembled' before it; but David could proclaim the secret of the Lord, that if the Divine Spirit abides in man, he is not cast away from God's presence, which, though it cannot be seen, may be felt by man. The Shechina symbolised God's dwelling in man.

It cannot be ascertained how soon it was known to the Israelites, at least to the men of wisdom among them, that God 'dwelleth not in a temple made with hands.' David must have known this. For Stephen said of him, that the king after God's own heart 'prayed, that he might find a dwelling for the God of Jacob.' Stephen, the martyr, would not have given so exceptional a character to David, nor would the martyr of Riblah, the high priest Seraiah, whom we suppose to have been the writer of the original Wisdom of Sirach, have connected with David the names of only Hezekiah and of Josiah, as the kings that were 'not faulty,' and forsook not 'the law of the Most High,'[1] unless they had been foremost among those who tried to stem the tide of idolatry, by restoring symbolism to its pristine purity. In the tabernacle which David erected at Jerusalem, there was no symbol but one, and that was invisible. David must have regarded the ark as the symbol of the heart of man, in the darkness of which God's glory, that is, God's spirit, dwells, through which God meets with man, and communes with him. He sought for a suitable dwelling for the God of his forefathers, and his Shepherd led him to regard his heart as the temple not made with hands, wherein the Lord does dwell, as the place of his rest. But Solomon built a house to the God whose throne is heaven, and whose footstool the earth. He did so with diffidence, well knowing, that the house which he had builded was not suitable for Him, whom the heavens cannot contain. If God indeed is to dwell on the earth,

---

[1] Ecclus. xlix. 4.

it can only be in answer to the prayer, that he would remember the promise made to Moses, about causing the Divine name, or spirit, to dwell in a chosen place of the chosen land.[1] Again, Solomon knew, that 'prayer and supplication' in the sanctuary, by whomsoever offered, cannot avail, unless he who prays knows individually 'the plague of his own heart.' The temple which Solomon built, was to be 'a house of prayer unto all nations,' for 'all the people of the earth,' that they might know and fear the name, that is, the spirit, of the Lord, turn unto him 'with all their heart, and with all their soul,' and know that 'the Lord is God, and none else.'[2]

The king who thus prayed, the pupil of Nathan the prophet,[3] who may have composed this prayer, laid the foundation for a universal Church. He whose wisdom excelled that of all the men of the East, did not allow any difference of symbol, or of its interpretation, to stand in the way of unity, between all parties in Israel, nor between Israel and all other nations. Not the form of symbols, but the high conceptions which were embodied by them, Solomon regarded as essentials. Thus he paved the way to a dangerous ritualism. The temples which he erected to Moloch, to Chemosh, and to Ashtaroth—that is, to the Sun- or fire-gods of the Ammonites, and of the Moabites, and to the Assyrian Astarte, to the moon, were, in themselves, not objectionable symbols of the One God, the uncreated light, reflected by the sun, the moon, and the stars, and symbolised by fire. Nor can we assert, that the later practised abominations of human sacrifices were connected with the worship of Moloch, when the same was tolerated, if not sanctioned, by Solomon. Indeed, such acts cannot be attributed to so wise and so piously-minded a man. But the unrestricted symbolism which David's son permitted and encouraged, whilst it

---

[1] Deut. xii. 11.   [2] 1 Kings viii. 22 f.; comp. Is. lvi. 7.
[3] 1 Kings iv. 5 in Heb.; comp. Ewald, iii. 116.

would not be misunderstood or misapplied by the learned, became a stumblingblock to the unlearned. The symbolical meaning of images was either not generally known, or it was confounded and forgotten, and thus symbols became idols. Whether this was already the case during Solomon's reign, is uncertain. His own wisdom, and that of Nathan, may have preserved Israel and its king from such a degradation of the emblems of worship. But a new influence had sprung up, from the day when Zadok, the high priest, anointed him.

The man from whom the Sadducees derived their name must, like these, have been an enemy of tradition and of catholicity. In his eyes, what Solomon did, was not better than what was later described as going ' a whoring after other gods.' If there are reasons for assuming that the use of the above matrimonial metaphor led to the description transmitted to us about the abominations at Baal-Peor, the conjecture is allowed, that what is said about Solomon's intercourse with ' strange women,' must be figuratively interpreted, with reference to his admitting and acknowledging other symbols of worship than those which had been previously sanctioned. As the influence of the line of Eleazar continued long after the death of Zadok, the records of Solomon's reign, finally revised by Ezra the Sadducee, must be read with caution; and all the more so, since important works of that time have been lost, though they are referred to in Scripture. Such are: 'The book of the acts of Solomon;' 'the book of Nathan the prophet, the book of Ahijah the Shilonite, the visions of Iddo the seer.'[1] Toleration, the key-note of Solomon's reign, was intolerable to Zadok and his followers. And as the sacrificial ritualism expanded, notwithstanding the rebuke of prophets, who condemned them altogether, care would be taken to exaggerate the importance which Solomon had attributed to burnt-

---

[1] 1 Kings xi. 41; 2 Chr. ix. 29.

offerings and sacrifices. It is, perhaps, to be attributed to similar influences, that the vision is recorded to have appeared unto Solomon, after he had sacrificed at Gibeon, the former sanctuary of Zadok.

Before Abiathar's banishment, Zadok was high priest at Gibeon, where the tabernacle of the wilderness was set up without the ark. It is not unimportant to enquire, whether at Gibeon some other symbol may not have represented the Divine presence, which had been symbolised ever since the time of Moses. There was but one symbol, that could have taken the place of the ark and of the cloud. It was the brazen and fiery serpent. A grander symbol had never been set up, had never helped to work such miracles. It was the one type, which was destined to receive, by its historical fulfilment, a significance so sublime, that no other symbol can be compared to it. The fiery serpent made of brass, was put before the eyes of the children of Israel, as a symbol, after that the image of the golden calf had been condemned and destroyed. Its primary object was, to heal the Israelites that were bitten by fiery, or 'burning' serpents, as the Hebrew term is literally translated in the Vulgate, and by Onkelos. The explanation, that they were so called, because their sting was burning, is excluded by the text. These burning serpents, or fiery serpents, have been compared with the 'fiery flying serpents' or dragons, which are mentioned in the book of Isaiah,[1] among the animals of Egypt. This interpretation is not excluded by the Wisdom of Sirach or Seraiah, the martyr of Riblah. According to the tradition which he possibly has sanctioned,[2] the Israelites were bitten by 'venomous dragons,' by 'grasshoppers and flies,' as well as by 'crooked serpents' and 'wild beasts.' The existence of flying serpents, whose wings may have shone like fire in the sun, is confirmed by the representation, on Egyptian monuments, of winged serpents en-

---

[1] Is. xxx. 6; xiv. 29.
[2] Wisdom xvi. 5-13. We shall substantiate this conjecture about the author.

compassing the globe. It is under the symbol of a winged serpent, that the Egyptians represented Kneph, the Spirit of all good, who by the Greeks was called the Agathodaemon. If there were, in early times, flying serpents, whose wings looked fiery, they would particularly recommend themselves as symbols of the Spirit, of which fire was regarded as the purest and most perfect symbol, because of the mystery of its origin, and of its propagating power, for good or for evil. We suggest, that for this reason, because of the connection of serpents with what either was or appeared like fire, the serpent was, among the Egyptians, not only the symbol of the good spirit, but also of the evil spirit, at once the emblem of wisdom, and of subtlety. The same two-fold symbolism of the serpent is to be found in Greek mythology. As the symbol of good the serpent represented the Divine attributes of Ceres, the goddess of agriculture, of Mercury, or Hermes, and therefore most probably of the Indian God Sâramêya, son of dawn,[1] and of Aesculapius or Asclepios, the God of healing. As the symbol of evil the serpent represented, in the East, the winter, caused by the cloud, which by harbouring the rays of the sun, for a time prevents the action of the rays, till they reappear, driving away the clouds, and causing the rains to fall. Light and darkness, life and death, were represented by the same symbol of the serpent. The same symbolical conceptions are embodied in the Biblical account about the fiery serpents of death, and the fiery and brazen serpent of life.

Fire was known to the early Israelites as the symbol of the Deity. The Lord descended in fire, spoke through the medium, or in the presence of fire, and the fiery cloud symbolised the presence of Jehovah. Ever since the time of Noah, offerings were made through fire, and the fire on the altar, in the first instance, lighted by fire which 'came out from before the Lord,' was ordered never to go out.[2]

[1] Max Müller on Science of Language, ii. 462 f.
[2] Lev. ix. 24; vi. 9, 13.

In the temple of Solomon it was, at the dedication, also kindled by 'fire from heaven,' which the children of Israel worshipped, praising the Lord.[1] Only fire from the perpetually burning fire on the altar, was to be used in the Hebrew ritual. For that fire had been miraculously kindled by the uncreated light. No burning of incense, no kind of sacrifice, was declared by the Mosaic ritual, to be efficacious, that is, well-pleasing to God, unless the fire had been taken from the ever present symbol of perpetual adoration, from the burning altar. To impress this doctrine on the minds of the Israelites, and to ensure their obedience to this decree, it was deemed necessary to prove, that disobedience is death. The consuming quality of fire, as well as its preserving quality, had to be demonstrated by a miracle. Nadab and Abihu, the eldest sons of Aaron, made use of 'strange fire,' for burning incense, that is, they did not take the fire from the altar, as God had commanded, and the consequence of this act of disobedience was, that 'fire (lightning) went out from the Lord and devoured them.'[2] On other occasions the lightning, issuing forth from the clouds, where God was, the fiery messengers that do his pleasure, were known to act as instruments of destruction. But in this case, fire from heaven, which had kindled, once and for ever, the fire on the altar, destroyed those, who stood before the Lord, offering incense through fire of their own creation. In the time of Abraham this was not considered culpable. Abraham took the fire, for Isaac's sacrifice, not from any altar where it was continually burning. Yet, in the covenant which was made 430 years later, such a transgression was declared to be as unpardonable, as, in the later covenant, the sin against the Holy Ghost was pronounced to be, the one which could never be forgiven.

Even in the time of Moses, different views were held on the communication of God's Spirit, which the fire

---

[1] 2 Chr. vii. 1, 3.    [2] Lev. x. 1 f.

symbolised. It is recorded in the book of Numbers: 'And it came to pass, that the people raised wicked complaints before the ears of the Lord, and when the Lord heard it, his anger was kindled, and the fire of the Lord (the lightning) struck among them, and consumed the uttermost parts of the camp. Then the people cried unto Moses, and when Moses prayed unto the Lord, the fire sunk' (into the ground).[1] Moses and Aaron had alone been initiated in the mystery of the fire, which attested the Lord's descent on Sinai. The people believed, that it was owing to the exceptional approach of Moses to the cloud, in which the fire was, that the Lord's spirit had rested on the Shepherd of Israel.[2] To approach the cloud, was by them supposed to be a necessary condition of the Spirit's communication. The barriers erected round the mount, were to prevent the people's breaking through, and thus approaching the cloud, which would have been to them instant death. So the people were told in the name of the Lord. These views were, however, not held by all, as the story of Eldad and Medad, of Nadab and Abihu and of the tribe of Korah prove. Although the two eldest sons of Aaron were supposed to have been struck by lightning, in consequence of the 'strange fire' which they used, yet Eldad and Medad, two of the seventy elders chosen by Moses, did not consider it necessary to follow the command of Moses, recorded to have been made in the name of God, to assemble at the tabernacle, and to stand with Moses before the cloud, in which Jehovah would descend, for the purpose of communicating to them the spirit which was upon Moses, and which had made him the shepherd of the flock. Eldad and Medad opposed this decree, maintaining, as their conduct implies, that it was not necessary to approach the cloud, in order to receive the Spirit of God, the possessors of which could alone prophesy. They were not punished for their dis-

---

[1] Num. xi. 1-3.     [2] Comp. Num. xi. 25; Is. lxiii. 11.

obedience, and the result showed that they were right. Whether or not, the institution of the seventy elders, as a corporation of initiated, owed its origin to the 'wicked complaints' which the people made, the successful opposition of two of Israel's elders proves, that the people clamoured for a participation in the knowledge and the government of the initiated. Far from being opposed to this, Moses encouraged it. He admitted, by his words and deeds, that the possession of spiritual gifts did alone qualify for the offices of rulers and overseers; he declared it to be God's will, that he should not alone 'bear the burden of the people,' but that these should share in this responsibility, which he felt himself to be 'too heavy' for him. Moses did not insist upon the necessity of standing before the sanctuary, in order to receive the Divine Spirit; and when 'one of his young men,' or rather, with the Septuagint and the Fathers, 'one of his chosen ones,' one of the seventy elders, when Joshua asked Moses, to forbid the prophesying of Eldad and Medad, he replied: 'Art thou jealous for my sake? What would I, that the whole people of the Lord prophesied, and that the Lord would give his Spirit over them.'[1] That was the fire which the 'prophet like Moses' came to kindle.

Not many years later, it became evident, from the rebellion of Korah, Dathan and Abiram, and the 250 men who followed them, that the spirit of opposition, shown by Eldad and Medad, had spread in the camp, and had rendered impossible the maintenance of the established government. These 250 men are stated to have been 'princes of the assembly, councilmen, and respected persons.' Addressing themselves to Moses and Aaron, they charged them with taking too much upon themselves, or rather, with going 'too far.' They asserted, that 'the entire congregation is holy altogether,' and that the Lord 'is in the midst of them.' They asked: 'wherefore, then, lift ye up yourselves above the congregation of the Lord?'[2]

[1] Num. xi. 16–29.     [2] Ibid. xvi. 3.

In reply, Moses argues, that they, being all members of the privileged class of Levites, separated by the Lord from the congregation, to 'stand before and to serve the same,' ought not to consider that 'too little,' nor to demand 'even the priesthood.' He sent for the chief conspirators, Dathan and Abiram, but, like Eldad and Medad, they would not obey him. The time had come, to put an end to this spreading spirit of disobedience, or to give up the government to men in whom the people confided. 'Fire from heaven,' that is lightning, again destroyed the children of disobedience. The censers of all these men, who, for their sins, had 'paid' or 'done penance,' with their lives, were to be 'a memorial unto the children of Israel, that no stranger, who is not of the seed of Aaron, come near to offer incense before the Lord, that it may not be done to him as to Korah and his company.'

From this it follows that Korah and his company, though officiating as Levites, were not of the seed of 'Aaron the Levite,' and that the burning of incense was a privilege of the priests, the Cŏhanim, that is, of those who were permitted to 'draw near' to the Divine presence. This privilege had been extended to the seventy, who were chosen among the elders, overseers, princes of the assembly, councilmen and respected persons.[1] To the larger council of delegates, the 250 men who followed Korah belonged, and Moses admitted, that they had the right to 'stand before' the congregation, and to serve the same. But Moses refused to enlarge the smaller council of the seventy initiated elders. He knew, that the people could not apprehend the mysteries which he entrusted to the safe keeping, and the secret transmission of those, whom he had chosen among the delegates of the people. In order to be kept secret, tradition could only be communicated to a limited number. So convinced were the later Rabbis of this, that when they ingrafted the interpretation on the letter, and by vowel

[1] Comp. Num. xvi. 2, 16; Deut. xvi. 18.

points, they transmitted the tradition through the Scripture, and recorded, that the Spirit of the Lord having rested on the seventy, 'they prophesied and afterwards no more.'[1] The question now arises, why these followers of Korah are called 'strangers, who are not of the seed of Aaron?' We know, that the Kenites, or Rechabites, were strangers, and yet members of Israel's congregation. 'As ye (are). so shall the stranger be before the Lord.[2] Although descended from a non-Hebrew race, they were scribes, and some of them priests.

It is now easy to prove, that the 'princes of the assembly, councilmen and respected persons,' who followed Korah, were Kenites, and that, in consequence of their rebellion, the command was given, and probably enforced for a time, that no strangers, though sharing the privileges of the Levites, were to be priests. Korah, the son of Izhar, the son of Kohath, the son of Levi, in the genealogies, which are more than lists of family descent, is shown to have been a cousin to Moses and Aaron. We have seen, that the inhabitants of Hamath, and of Jabesh Gilead, were Rechabites, and are called 'cousins' of Israel by the prophet Amos. Again, the name of Korah is connected with Hebron, the Kenite city,[3] with Edom, that is Edom proper, of which not a footbreadth ever belonged to Israel, and with Esau, whose non-Hebrew connection we have pointed out. The Kenite descent of the Korahites is confirmed by the New Testament. For by Jude, the brother of James, one of those cousins of Jesus who were late believers in the Son of David, Korah is coupled with Cain and Balaam, the Kenite seer.[4] Like Cain, Korah never died.[5] The descendants from both, the Kenites and the Korahites, continued to live as strangers in Israel, and they were held up as patterns to idolatrous Israel, by Jeremiah, who promised, that 'Jonadab the son of Rechab shall not want a man to stand before

---

[1] Num. xi. 25.   [2] Exod. xii. 19; Num. ix. 14; xv. 15.
[3] 1 Chr. ii. 43.   [4] Jude 11.   [5] Num. xxvi. 11.

me for ever.' Thus Jeremiah abrogated the command, recorded in the book of Numbers, that no 'stranger who is not of the seed of Aaron' shall come near before the Lord. Although in the days of Elkanah the grandson of Korah, an eternal high priesthood was foretold to Phinehas, yet the son of Elkanah, the Levite of the Korahites, or Kenites, the judge and prophet Samuel, ministered unto the Lord before Eli, the priest of the Kenite line of Ithamar, whilst the grandson of Phinehas was separated from the priesthood. Joshua, the Kenite, was among the seventy elders, whom Moses chose for the transmission of secret tradition. But 250 other elders among the Kenites demanded, that the Kenites should also be represented in the priesthood. They perished, yet 'the children of Korah died not,' and we have seen, that the junior Aaronic sacerdotal line of Ithamar was the Kenite line.

Another act of disobedience in Israel, similar to that of Nadab and Abihu, and of the followers of Korah, was punished in a like manner. In deciding which way to go, through the wilderness, Moses followed the Divine commands, as revealed through the instrumentality of the cloud, in which God's glory was enshrined. So implicitly did the Israelites believe in this symbol of Divine presence, of that presence which was promised to go with the Israelites, that to be 'discouraged,' on the way which the cloud pointed out, to speak against Moses, who followed that cloud, was understood by the people, after that they had been bitten by fiery serpents, to be the same thing as to speak and to sin against God. In their affliction, whilst many Israelites were dying, they discovered 'the plague of their hearts,' and asked Moses that he would pray for them. Then God heard from heaven his dwelling-place, and forgave, but not unconditionally. Even those, who had been bitten by fiery serpents, might be healed, if they but looked upon the fiery serpent which God commanded Moses to make of brass, and to put it upon a pole. As we are expressly told, that this symbol should be a 'fiery' serpent, we must assume, that Moses made it of brass, for the purpose of lighting a fire within the same. If so, it follows, as a matter of course, that he took the fire from the altar.

The ever-burning altar, symbolising the perpetual presence of the Lord, was now set up, in the midst of a dying multitude, as the source of life to the obedient, and as the source of death to the disobedient. To look up, was to live; to refuse to obey this command, was to die. Obedience was the condition of God's pardon. God gave 'to every man according to his ways,' for he knew their hearts.[1] Did they regard the fire as the symbol of the Divine Spirit? Did they remember, that even among the Egyptians the serpent was the symbol of the good Spirit, and also of the evil Spirit? Now that they had been bitten by fiery serpents, did they regard these as the symbols of the evil Spirit? Then let them turn their eyes from the symbol of evil to the symbol of good; let them direct their hearts to the visible sign of the invisible Spirit, or Word, of God, 'unto the name of the Word of the Lord,' of that Word or Spirit of God, which the revered traditional interpretation, recorded more than a thousand years after this event, proclaimed to be 'the Saviour of all.' The Israelites were 'restored to health' by 'the Word of the Lord, which healeth all things. For thou hast power of life and death, thou leadest to the gates of the lower world, and leadest upwards.' Of this Word of the Lord, the 'fiery' or 'burning serpent' which Moses made of brass, was the symbol, inasmuch as it pointed to a Divine agency then actually at work. 'For he that turned himself towards it, was not saved by the thing that he saw,' by the lifeless object, 'but by thee (the Divine Word), that art the Saviour of all.'[2] The fiery serpent was the symbol of the eternal Word or

---

[1] Num. xxi. 4-9; comp. 1 Kings viii. 38, 39.
[2] Wisd. xvi. 7; comp. Targum of Jonathan.

Spirit of God, and it was the type of the future living manifester of that Spirit, of the incarnate Word; of him that should baptize 'with the Holy Ghost and with fire; of him that should manifest by his life and death, the perpetual presence of God in man; of the Son of Man who was to be lifted up, 'as Moses lifted up the serpent in the wilderness.'

This sublime symbol of Divine presence had become an idol, in the time of Hezekiah. Instead of an aid to faith and worship, it had become an object of faith and worship. For some indefinite time before the reign of the son of Ahaz, the children of Israel 'had been in the habit of burning incense to it;' thus worshipping the serpent, as the Phœnicians are known to have done, and as the Chinese still do, whose kings are by them conceived to receive bodies of serpents when they enter heaven. So subversive of true religion did Hezekiah consider the brazen serpent, which 'he called,' or, rather, whose 'name was called,' Nehushtan, that is, 'a brazen thing,' that he caused to be destroyed, what had been preserved, with reverend awe, for nearly a thousand years. The people knew not, what was well known to its spiritual leaders, that their fathers in the wilderness were not saved by the lifeless symbol, but by the living Divine agency which it represented. According to a late tradition, the brazen serpent had been set up in the temple. This becomes highly probable, when we consider that Zadok, before he was Solomon's high priest in Jerusalem, had been high priest at the sanctuary of Gibeon, whilst the tabernacle at Jerusalem, in which Abithar officiated, contained the ark. If Zadok introduced the brazen serpent into the sanctuary at Gibeon, and he must have done so, as the Divine presence had so long been symbolised, he would set it up in the temple of Jerusalem, on his removal to the same. By assuming that the brazen fiery serpent was introduced in the temple at Jerusalem during, or after, the high priesthood of Zadok, we can best explain, why the ark was, at some time before the reign of Josiah, removed from the temple.[1] Hezekiah having destroyed the brazen serpent, Josiah re-introduced the ark. The brazen and fiery serpent had never been hidden from the people, like the ark, but it was the visible symbol of the invisible presence, as the ark which David and Solomon triumphantly introduced, was the symbol of that presence which only the high priest could see. God was known to be present by his Spirit, and this Divine Spirit was symbolised by fire. In looking up to the fire of the mystical serpent, the Israelites looked up to 'the Saviour of all.' Thus, one of the sacerdotal mysteries had been popularised.

The fiery serpent's symbolical meaning was easily understood in the time of Moses, since fire was then generally, if not universally, acknowledged as the sublimest symbol of the Creator. Like the fire-god of the Phœnicians, of the Sepharvaim, the Moabites, the Edomites, and other Eastern tribes and nations, as also like the Greek fire-god Dionysus, Moloch was worshipped under the symbol of a rising flame of fire. This flame was imitated in the stone pillars, erected in honour of these supposed incorporations of the fire.[2] The face of Moloch, the fire-idol, was that of a calf or a cow, according to tradition. As the cow, with a star between its horns, is represented on Egyptian hieroglyphics, it is probable that the images of Moloch and of the star, which the Israelites made and worshipped, were a twofold representation of heavenly bodies, the symbols of uncreated light. Perhaps the star was the interpretation of the cow; for, in Egypt, the latter represented Sirius. But as, in other countries, the cow represented Venus, or the moon, it is not improbable that the Septuagint translators substituted Remphan, or Renpu, for Chiun, know-

---

[1] 2 Chr. xxxv. 3.   [2] Mover's Phön. i. 9.

ing that both had been worshipped in Egypt, and with a view to render the passage more intelligible to the Hebrews in Egypt. Aaron's golden calf, which, in the book of Tobit, is called 'the heifer Baal,' whether it was an image of Apis at Memphis, or of Memphis, or of Monevis, On, or of Heliopolis, must have been connected with celestial symbolism, or with fire. In course of time, and possibly already in the time of Moses, the Eastern fire-symbolism was still more degraded. Not enough, to have represented heavenly bodies, the symbols of uncreated light, by images of animals, living animals were offered as sacrifice, being slain and burnt. Plutarch informs us,[1] that the Egyptians offered a red heifer to Typhon, instead of a human victim. They took care that the animal selected had neither a black nor a white spot. And yet they chose those animals which were supposed to contain the souls of the wicked. For this reason, the head of the victim was charged with malediction, and cast into the river. Through this sacrifice Typhon, the representative of evil, was to be appeased, and evil prevented. A similar rite is recorded to have been instituted by Moses, as 'a statute for ever,' for the Hebrews as well as for the strangers, or Kenites, sojourning among them.[2] The Egyptian origin of all bloody sacrifices among the Hebrews, against which the Kenites protested, is confirmed by the above traced similarity, and by that between the scapegoat for Azazel, and the red heifer of the Egyptians, who took away the sins of the land. Plutarch writes, that, at the time when 'the great offering of purification' was celebrated, that is, during the dog-days, droughts, or other national calamities, a red heifer, on whom the sins of the people had been laid, was driven into the wilderness, the supposed abode of Typhon, the evil Spirit. If the impending disaster was not soon removed, the animal was slain. On this, or on similar rites among the Egyptians,

[1] De Isid. et Osir. 31.  [2] Num. xix.

Herodotus writes: 'When the animal has received the seal (or mark), it is led to the altar where it is to be sacrificed; they light a fire, then they pour wine on the altar, over the victim, and slay it, whilst they call upon the Deity. They then cut off its head, and pull down the skin from the body of the animal. They pronounce a long curse on its head, and carry it away. In such places where there is a market, and where Greeks come to trade, they take it to the market, and sell it at once; but where there are no Greeks, it is thrown into the river. The curse which they pronounce is as follows: May all the evil which hovers above the sacrificers, or which menaces Egypt, pass into this head.'[1]

The red heifer, which, according to the book of Numbers, Moses commanded to be offered, without the camp, as a 'propitiatory sacrifice,' was not deemed sufficient to make an atonement for sin, perhaps because not every Israelite made use of the 'water of purification.' Therefore, one goat was, by lot, to be separated for the Lord, and the other for Azazel, which name is usually translated as the scapegoat. The goat allotted to the Lord was to be offered for a sin offering, but the scapegoat was to be 'presented alive before the Lord, to make an atonement with him.' He was to be sent to the wilderness for Azazel, which name, in the book of Enoch, is given to an evil spirit. But the blood of the other goat of the sin offering for the people, was to be sprinkled within the veil, upon the mercy seat, and before the mercy seat, where the Lord appeared in the cloud.[2] We now continue to point out, what reasons we have for asserting the non-Mosaic but Egyptian origin of sacrifices.

If Joshua did forbid, in the name of God, all sacrifices on any other than one altar,[3] then even such men as

---

[1] Herod. ii. 39; comp. Pleyte, 154.
[2] Levit. xvi.
[3] Josh. xxii. 29.

Samuel and Elijah acted contrary to God's declared will. As it is impossible to assume this, we are bound, either to regard the above, and similar passages,[1] as later interpolations, or to assert, that Samuel and Elijah did not sacrifice, as they are recorded to have done. The latter course seems to be the more warrantable one. For, not only is Joshua reported to have forbidden sacrifices on any other than one altar; but this altar was 'not' to be 'for burnt offering nor for sacrifice;' the 'pattern of the altar of the Lord' which their fathers made, was to be 'a witness.'[2] This was the tradition of Joshua, a Kenite by descent. We have seen, that Balaam, the Kenite seer, proclaimed that 'the righteousness of the Lord' consists not in, nor is aided by sacrifices; that God requires of man 'nothing else' than, by obeying God's voice, to do what is right, to practise charity, and to walk humbly with his God. As Samuel and Elijah were Kenites, we cannot believe them to have sacrificed animals. Moreover, the assumption, that Samuel and Elijah did not sacrifice, is confirmed by the remarkable fact that in all the passages where 'the book of the law' is mentioned, which was known to Joshua, no reference whatever is made to any kind of sacrifice having received the sanction of the lawgiver. Again, leading prophets condemn them in the strongest terms. But the culminating proof of the non-Mosaic origin of sacrifices, and of the Kenite opposition to the same, lies in the fact, that the Psalms which, in the name of God, protest against all sacrifices, were written by David, the Kenite king, and by Asaph, the Kenite seer. So entirely was Asaph put on a par with David, that the reforming king, Hezekiah, commanded the Levites 'to sing praise unto the Lord with the words of David, and of Asaph the seer.'[3]

Joshua had erected but one altar, and this was not to be for burnt offerings and sacrifices, but for a witness and

---

[1] Josh. ix. 30, 31; xiii. 14.   [2] Ibid. xxii. 26.
[3] 2 Chr. xxix. 30; comp. Neh. xii. 46.

a testimony. The fire on the altar was to symbolise the Spirit of the Lord, his witness to and in man. This Kenite tradition was faithfully transmitted by the Kenite pupil of a Kenite high priest, by Samuel, the spiritual son of Eli. Saul having been anointed as king, feared the people, and obeying their voice, did not prevent the Israelites from sacrificing. 'And Samuel said: Hath the Lord delight in burnt offerings and sacrifices, as in obeying the voice of the Lord? Behold, to obey is better than sacrifice, and to hearken (to the voice of the Lord), than the fat of rams; for disobedience is a sin of (against) divination, and stubbornness is iniquity and idolatry.'[1] The prophet was the organ of the Divine voice; to disobey a prophet was, therefore, the same as to disobey the voice of the Lord, and by stubbornness to be led into iniquity and idolatry. The Divine presence was, in the days of Samuel, believed to be not only symbolised, as by the fire on the altar, by the fiery serpent of brass, and by the ark, but to be manifested by a human being, by a prophet like Moses. Obedience was the saving test, both in the time of Moses and in the time of Samuel.

Obedience is opposed to sacrifice by David. 'Sacrifice and offering thou didst not desire; burnt offering and sin offering hast thou not required, mine ears hast thou opened.' David's ears had been opened to hearken unto the voice of the Lord. What had been denied to Israel, during the forty years in the wilderness, had been granted to David. The Lord gave him 'an heart to understand, and eyes to see, and ears to hear.'[2] To the opened ears of David, God's will was revealed, almost in the same words which were uttered by Balaam. God requires not sacrifice of any kind. 'Then said I: Lo, I come; . . . I delight to do thy will, O my God, yea, thy law is within my heart.'[3] It is in the sanctuary which contains the fleshy tables of the heart; in this holy place that God

---

[1] 1 Sam. xv. 22.  [2] Deut. xxix. 4.  [3] Ps. xl. 6–8.

will meet with man, and that he will deposit the statutes which are good. Sacrifice is not even a symbol, unless it is understood as an outward sign of inward dedication. Sacrifice has been superseded by obedience. Through the mouth of David, as through his holy prophets of all ages, God reproves not man because he does not sacrifice at all, or not enough, but because he does sacrifice. 'Not for thy sacrifices do I reprove thee, for, behold, thy burnt offerings are continually before me . . . Will I eat the flesh of bulls, or drink the blood of goats? Offer unto God thanksgiving, and pay thy vows unto the Most High, and call upon me in time of trouble.'[1] 'Thou delightest not in sacrifice, else would I give it; thou delightest not in burnt offering. Sacrifices well pleasing to God, are a broken spirit; a broken and a contrite heart, O God, thou wilt not despise.'[2]

The deep import of these words is unmistakable. The principle is laid down which was proclaimed by the prophet Hosea, and which was to receive the highest sanction, that God will have mercy, or, as the Septuagint has rendered it, that God 'is well pleased' with mercy, and that he is not well pleased with sacrifice; that 'the knowledge of God is more than burnt offering.'[3] It is the will of man that must be broken, the spirit of man must be brought into subjection to the spirit of God, so that the Divine Spirit may testify to the spirit of man. Obedience, such as God delights in and requires, cannot be enforced; it is a free-will offering of man, whom God has created a free and self-responsible creature. It lies with man to will and to do, or not to will and not to do of God's good pleasure. 'Truth in the inward parts,' the honest desire to hear and to obey the voice of God, who said 'nothing concerning sacrifices' to the fathers of Israel,—this is what God requires man to offer as a well-pleasing sacrifice. Through this faith Abel's sacrifice was greater, or more

[1] Ps. l. 8–15. [2] Ibid. li. 15–17. [3] Hos. vi. 6, 7; comp. Matt. ix. 13.

pleasing to God, than that of Cain. It was by faith, not by any outward act, that Abel 'obtained witness, that he was righteous, God testifying of his gifts.'[1]

This Divine testimony, concerning the different gifts offered by the two brothers, declared it to be immaterial, whether 'pleasing gifts' or 'not pleasing gifts' were brought as a sacrifice to God. Because God 'looked graciously' on Abel and not on Cain, he also looked graciously on the sacrifice of the one, and not on that of the other. The nature of the outward symbol of dedication was declared to be a matter of indifference. For thus 'said the Lord unto Cain, Why art thou wroth? And why is thy countenance fallen? Is it not this wise? Though thou bring pleasing or unpleasing gifts, sin is lurking at the door, and after thee is her desire, but thou shalt become ruler over her.' The fruit of the ground was, in itself, no more worthy of God's gracious look, than the firstling of the flock and the fat thereof. Both Cain and Abel offered the best of what they possessed. But the heart of the one was proof against sin, and that of the other was not yet. Still Cain was promised that victory over sin, by forsaking it, which is the only sacrifice required by God.[2] Although Cain went away from God's presence, the fugitive and vagabond, going to and fro in the earth, and exposed to the hostility of strangers, received a life-preserving sign from the Lord, a gift, which caused the lost son to return to his father's presence. The righteousness which avails has been proclaimed ever since the days of Cain, and of Balaam, the Kenite. It is not connected with sacrifice, but with that mercy of God, which calls sinners to repentance.

Balaam, Samuel, Asaph and David are the first who

---

[1] Gen. iv. 4-7; Heb. xi. 4.

[2] 'Behold, if thou doest well, thou art accepted. But if thou doest not well, sin lieth at the door. Thou turnest to it, and it hath dominion over thee.' Thus the text is quoted by Mär Jacob, bishop of Edessa in the 7th century. See Phillipson, Mär Jacob, 1864.

have proclaimed the protest of Kenite tradition against all outward sacrifices. Yet it is recorded of all these, except Asaph, that they themselves sacrificed. If they did so, then, like Hezekiah and Josiah, from motives of policy, on exceptional occasions, they acted contrary to the express command of Joshua, that there should be but one altar, and that the same should not be for burnt offering or sacrifice. Either God did not command, what is recorded to have been ordered by Joshua, in the name of the Lord, or God commanded not the record transmitted to us about the sacrifice of David, through which God was 'intreated for the land, and the plague was stayed from Israel.' As it is certain, that the books of Chronicles were not finished till long after the captivity, and that the entire collection of Scriptures was revised under Sadducean, that is, anti-Kenite influences, in the time of Ezra, we have here one of those instances, where the word of God was made of none effect by the commandment of men, by human tradition as recorded under priestly rule. Thus a belief was ingrafted on the Jews, and through them on Christians, which has been the cause of the most dangerous idolatry, sanctioned, as the same was declared to be, by the oracles of God.

Although Jeremiah had declared, that God commanded 'nothing' to the fathers concerning sacrifices, and in spite of Ezekiel's assertion, that statutes that are 'not good' had been given to Israel in the name of the Lord, the final revisers of Scripture, under Ezra, did not remove all those wicked statutes from the Scriptures. Even the command of human sacrifice continued to form part of God's word written. Jewish tradition had been vitiated by the interests of parties opposed to each other. Five centuries of Sadducean rule, after the captivity, sufficed to discountenance, if not to quench any tradition which had not been recorded by Ezra. The new school of tradition, the Masora, had not to watch over the interpretation of Scripture by the light of ancestorial tradition unrecorded, but to preserve the stereotype cast of holy writ, as finally accomplished, and as decreed for all future ages, under the presidency of Ezra, the Sadducean priest and scribe. Every letter was counted, and the interpretation was stereotyped, as the letter had been. Thus crystallisation became the forerunner of stagnation. What was not written, was forbidden to be written, and was heresy. It was under these circumstances, that the greatest importance was attributed to the recorded propitiatory sacrifice of David, on Mount Moriah, whereon the temple had been built and rebuilt. According to the Sadducean tradition, which was now registered in the Chronicles, Solomon had built 'the house of Jehovah in Jerusalem, on Mount Moriah, where he appeared to David his father, in a place which David prepared in the threshing-floor of Araunah the Jebusite.'[1] It was important to establish a Divine authority for sacrifices; accordingly, in both accounts it is recorded, that the angel of the Lord, in whom is the name or spirit of God, and who therefore was believed to be the manifester of Divine presence, appeared to David on the threshing-floor of Araunah. Thus the sacrifices which were then offered at Jerusalem were directly connected with those recorded to have been offered by David on the same spot, and with those which Moses was recorded to have commanded.[2]

The evil did not stop here. Not enough, to have laid the foundation of an idolatry of the most serious nature; to have counteracted the words of the prophets against all sacrifices, words which were spoken publicly, and had been so ingrafted on the memory of living generations, as to exclude the possibility of their being falsified or suppressed; not satisfied with having laid down indestructible rules of worship, to be enforced by fire and sword; the stiffnecked Sadducean rulers of the Jews, 'uncircumcised in heart and ears,' unable to hearken to the voice of

---

[1] 2 Chr. iii. 1.     [2] Ezra iii. 2-4; Exod. xxix. 38-41.

the Lord, which is better than sacrifice; those among the Jewish 'fathers' that 'resisted the Holy Ghost, now proceeded to vitiate even the Messianic' expectations of the Jews. The expected deliverer was to be connected with a propitiatory sacrifice. To accomplish this end, the tradition was ingrafted and promulgated, that the propitiatory sacrifices of Abraham and of David, were made on the same place. So universally was this tradition believed six hundred years later, in the time of Josephus, that the historian, although a Pharisee, and as such upholding the anti-Sadducean, or Kenite tradition, recorded in these words the above tradition about Mount Moriah: 'God being desirous to make an experiment of Abraham's religious disposition towards himself, appeared to him,' and said that he required Isaac 'as a sacrifice and holy oblation. Accordingly he commanded him, to carry him to the Mountain Moriah, and to build an altar, and offer him for a burnt offering upon it.' Abraham 'concealed this command of God, and his own intentions about the slaughter of his son, from his wife, as also from every one of his servants; otherwise he would have been hindered from his obedience to God, . . and having his son alone with him, he came to the mountain. It was that mountain upon which king David (Solomon) 'built the temple.'[1]

It was not at once, that such a tradition would take root, in the face of Kenite opposition to Hebrew tyranny. The written interpretation, or Targum, called after Onkelos, proves, that between the promulgation of the same, and the later recorded tradition in the Jerusalem Targum, the flow of tradition had been gradually checked by official crystallisation. The more ancient Targum having called the land of Moriah the 'land of worship,' thus paraphrases the passage in Genesis,[2] without referring to sacrifice: 'And Abraham sacrificed and prayed in that place, and he said before Jehovah: In this place shall

---

[1] Ant. i. 13, 1, 2; comp. vii. 13, 4.    [2] Gen. xxii. 14.

generations worship, because it shall be said in that day: In this mountain did Abraham worship before Jehovah.' The later interpretation of this passage runs thus: 'Because in generations to come it shall be said: In the mount of the house of the sanctuary of Jehovah, did Abraham offer up Isaac his son, and in this mountain, which is the house of the sanctuary, was the glory of Jehovah much manifest.'[1] Unless all and every connection between the Targums and the Scriptures, revised by Ezra, can be disproved, we must insist on the writers, or final framers of both having derived their information from the same, or a similar source, that is, from Sadducean, anti-Kenite and anti-Davidic tradition. This was the origin of the recorded identity of the place, where Abraham and David offered propitiatory sacrifices. That place, Zebus, had been a non-Hebrew possession. It belonged to the descendants from the Amorites and the Hittites, that is, to Kenites. This explains why Araunah was 'a particular friend' of David. To the Kenite origin of Jerusalem, Ezekiel refers, when he writes: ' Cause Jerusalem to know her abominations, and say: Thus saith the Lord unto Jerusalem: Thy birth and thy nativity is out of the land of the Kenaanites, thy father the Amorite, and thy mother a Hittite.[2] Assuming that Jeremiah was authorised to say, that no sacrifices were ever sanctioned by God, we can comprehend why no reference to Abraham's sacrifice is made, either in the detailed account of David's dedication of the threshing-floor of Araunah; or of Solomon's building, of Nehemiah's rebuilding,[3] of the restorations and purification by the Maccabees, in the record of Stephen's address, and in the description of the symbolism of sacrificial ritual, which is so fully interpreted by the author of the Epistle to the Hebrews. There is no authority, older than the time of Ezra, for any connection of Abraham with Jerusalem, if Salem, or Shaveh, where

---

[1] Comp. Beer, 'Leben Abraham's nach jüdischer Sage,' pp. 57–71.
[2] Ezek. xvi. 3–5. [3] Comp. Neh. ix. 7.

Melchizedec offered bread and wine, is proved to be Mount Gerizim, where, according to Samaritan tradition, the sacrifice of Abraham took place, of which the earliest Targum knows nothing.

It is generally acknowledged that there are weighty reasons for identifying Gerizim with the place where Melchizedec, and also Abraham, communed with God. The tradition of the Samaritans, or Kenites, cannot be discredited, seeing that it is confirmed, by their almost uninterrupted custom, of worshipping on this mountain. Hebrew tradition was always opposed to the Samaritans, and cannot, therefore, be trusted. Even Josephus, who certainly was not the representative of anti-Kenite principles, describes the Samaritans as 'apostates of the Jewish nation.'[1] Because they caused the Purim massacre, and encouraged Herod's persecution of the Sadducees, whilst being 'a colony of Medes and Persians,'[2] the Jews had no dealings with the Samaritans. They always were not only enemies, but rivals, of the Hebrews, supporting the Kenites in Israel. According to the Samaritan Pentateuch,[3] known by the fathers of the second and later centuries, even their Messianic hopes point to an enemy of the Mosaic law, such as they still suppose (we think rightly) Solomon to have been. It was in the plain of Moreh, near Sichem, the present Neapolis, where the remnant of the Samaritans live, that God first appeared to Abraham, and that the first altar was erected. About the base of Mount Gerizim, Jacob built his altar, as the Samaritans always believed; here was his well, and Joseph's tomb. To oppose the Samaritan tradition, which connects Moriah, or Moreh, with Shechem, the Hebrew chronicler, whose interest it was to have Abraham's sanction for the so-called Mosaic sacrifices, assumes that God appeared to Abraham, as in the plains of Moreh, so on the supposed Mount Moriah, on the threshing-floor of Araunah. As no

---

[1] Ant. xi. 8, 6.    [2] Ibid. xii. 5, 5.    [3] Gen. xlix. 10.

appearance of Jehovah is recorded in the two narratives about David's purchase of this place; as it is allowed, on all hands, that the Chronicles were completed long after the captivity; as the temple-mount could not have been seen when Abraham was 'afar off,' we have sufficient evidence for entirely discrediting the connection of Mount Moriah with Jerusalem, which is recorded in the second book of Chronicles. Equally unhistorical and absurd is the later assumed identity of the supposed Mount Moriah, at Jerusalem, where the temple was built, and the place outside the city, called Golgotha, and, according to tradition, Calvary. In both cases, the palpable error was caused by the desire to establish types and anti-types for a propitiatory sacrifice.

Great as was the danger to spiritual religion, when the brazen and fiery serpent had ceased to be a symbol, and was worshipped as an idol, a far greater danger arose from the idolatry of sacrifice. Every non-spiritual sacrifice removes the sublime significance of the symbol set up by Moses in the wilderness. It symbolised life, not death; God's love, not his curse. Calvary pointed, as the Apostle tells us, to the wilderness of Egypt, and not to the real or the false Moriah. Yet the brazen serpent was interpreted, not as a symbol of the ever present healing power of the Saviour of all ages, of the eternal Christ, but as the type of a human, nay, of a Divine sacrifice. The scapegoat in the wilderness was insisted upon, as a Divinely instituted type, requiring its anti-type. The incarnate Christ, the God with us, God's Spirit personified, was not to heal like the symbol of that Saviour in the wilderness. He was to save mankind from a curse by God imposed. Man had sinned in Eden, and God could not and did not forgive without a propitiatory sacrifice. The curse of God must be removed from the sinful, and the sinless must bear the load of that curse, must be forsaken by his God. It was asserted that Divine justice required blood, and since 'blood maketh an atonement for the soul,' the cross, originally connected with the symbol of fire, was connected with a bloody sacrifice. Forgetting that blood is the emblem of human life, that man's spiritual dedication must be an overcoming of flesh and blood, bloodshedding was regarded, at once, as a sign of God's wrath and of his forgiveness.

Burnt offerings and sacrifices, which the Kenite tradition condemned, could have no other effect upon a nation steeped in idolatry, that is, in misunderstood and wrongly applied symbolism, than to encourage and perpetuate merely outward religion. Solomon's toleration of any kind of symbolism, was a dangerous experiment, though it led to peace, power and glory. The time was not come, when catholicity could be established on the basis of unity without uniformity. Solomon's high priest, Zadok, was the declared enemy of Kenite tradition, and of the universality which formed the corner-stone of it. With him the line of Eleazar, the line of the Sadducees, was restored to power. His rival, the Kenite Abiathar, was separated from the priesthood, and the persecution of the Kenites recommenced. But the tribe to which Caleb and David had belonged, the tribe of Judah, kept faithful to the Kenite house, and after Solomon's reign, was given to Rehoboam, son of Solomon, by Naamah, the Ammonite princess, for the sake of David the servant of God. It would have been well for Israel, if a Kenite king had followed Solomon in the rule of the united kingdom. But whilst Jeroboam was in Egypt, probably planning with his father-in-law, Shishak, the introduction of Egyptian imagery into Israel, the ten tribes revolted and separated from Judah and Rehoboam, as the prophet Ahijah of Shiloh had announced to Solomon.[1] At Dan and at Bethel, Jeroboam set up the Egyptian image of the golden calf, and he 'made priests of the lowest of the people, which were not of the sons of Levi.'[2]

Although the son of an Ephraimite, to which tribe Joshua the Kenite had belonged, and though raised by the second

---

[1] 1 Kings xi. 29–40.  [2] Ibid. xii. 31.

Kenite king, Jeroboam feared lest the kingdom should return to Rehoboam, of the house of David. The idolatry which he had introduced in Israel was the cause of his fear; and if so, it follows, that Judah was then free of that idolatry. The Levites 'left their suburbs and their possession, and came to Judah and Jerusalem, for Jeroboam and his sons had cast them off from executing the priest's office unto the Lord.'[1] As Benjamin, Simeon and Dan were added to the Southern kingdom, we can assert that all the families of the Aaronites recognised the son of Solomon. A prophet of Shiloh had announced Jeroboam's rebellion, and a prophet of Judah, whom Josephus identifies with Iddo, or Jadôn, the seer, foretold the fact, that Josiah would sacrifice on that very altar the priests of the high places.[2] The idolatry of future kings of Israel hastened the fulfilment of this prophecy. In the time of Ahab and Jezebel, daughter of the king of the Zidonians, Baal was worshipped at Bethel.[3] And yet 'sons of the prophets' resided there, when Elijah, the Kenite, visited the place, previous to his destruction of Baal worship in all the land. The reformatory work of Elijah, who called fire from heaven, was of short duration. For although Jehu 'destroyed Baal out of Israel,' yet he again reintroduced the golden calves of Jeroboam, who 'made Israel to sin.'[4] Soon after this, Bethel became a royal residence, other altars were in that place erected to other gods, and sacrifices were offered, against which the prophet Amos raised his warning voice.[5]

Whilst idolatry never ceased to spread in the kingdom of Israel, the kingdom of Judah and Benjamin, for a time, preserved the traditions of David, under its Kenite kings. Faithful to those traditions, as represented by its priestly and high priestly organs, the Southern kingdom followed an absolutely independent course. The idol shrine at Bethel, in Benjamin, remained separated from the kingdom

[1] 2 Chr. xi. 14.   [2] 1 Kings xiii. 1-3.   [3] Ibid. xvi. 31.
[4] 2 Kings x. 28, 29.   [5] Amos vii. 13; iii. 14; v. 21, 22.

where idolatry was excluded, and it was owing to the efforts of enemies of idolatry, of the kings Abijah and Asa, Rehoboam's successors, that Bethel and other cities, from which the idol shrines must have been removed, were added, for a time, to the Southern kingdom.[1] Even the pillage of Jerusalem by Shishak, did not prevent Judah's triumphs, marked by the victories of its kings, and by a numerous migration from Israel into Judah. The common danger to both kingdoms, arising from the ascendancy of Damascus, led to an alliance, of eighty years' duration, between Israel and Judah. The seeds of apostacy from the Kenite faith, seem to have been sown, during this time, by the North in the South. In vain were the efforts of Jehoshaphat, and especially of Hezekiah, and of Josiah, permanently to establish, by force, throughout Judah, the worship of One God, without any symbol which might lead to idolatry. Essentially, outward religion cannot be re-formed by outward means. Idolatry was also re-established in Judah, and after having lost their independence, the inhabitants of Judah were, like those of Israel, scattered among the Assyrians, in literal fulfilment of the prophecy of Moses, recorded in Deuteronomy.[2] Thus symbols had become idols in Israel.

The Chaldean idolatry, which had been, probably, caused by the substitution of terrestrial for heavenly bodies, and of images of man's creation, for the symbol of fire, was put down, soon after the accession of Cyrus, whom a prophet in Israel called the Anointed, or Christ, of the Lord, and 'the Shepherd' who carries out the Divine decrees.'[3] For according to the Behistun, or Babylonian inscription, Darius 'rebuilt the temples which Gomates, the Magian, had destroyed, and restored to the people the religious chants, and the worship, of which Gomates, the Magian, had deprived them.'[4] We may

---

[1] 2 Chr. xiii. 19; xv. 8; xvii. 2.     [2] Deut. vi. 5.
[3] Isa. xliv. 28.     [4] Beh. inscr. col. i. part 14.

now assert that African imagery vitiated Asiatic symbolism. No trace of bloody sacrifices can be found in the most ancient records of Eastern tradition. The doctrines therein contained exclude all outward sacrifices. They declare purity in thought, word and deed, to be the only remedy against evil; proclaim obedience to 'the spiritual power,' as the only means to 'distinguish right from wrong;' and promise that the good law of God 'entirely cuts off all punishment.[1] This pure law of God was, no doubt, introduced into Babylon by Darius. Babylon formed the connecting link between the East and the West.

[1] Hidden Wisdom of Christ, i. 27.

## CHAPTER VIII.

### JOSHUA THE KENITE HIGH PRIEST.

THE jealousy and hostility between Kenites and Hebrews explains the use of certain terms, which have hitherto not been satisfactorily interpreted. We first refer to 'Sons of Belial.' This composite word has at different times received different meanings. In Deuteronomy, where it is applied to an animal, it clearly means 'common,' in the sense of 'low descent,' or literally, 'without ascent.'[1] But the Vulgate has connected the second part of the word with 'yoke.' Taken in the sense of 'without yoke,' that is, without law, the word Belial may be identified with 'the lawless' and 'the transgressors,' to which the books of the Maccabees refer.[2] We shall prove, that 'sons of Belial' was the name given, in the earliest times, to the Kenites by the Hebrews, and to the Hebrews by the Kenites; that it was applied very much like the word infidels in later times. This interpretation will enable us to explain the passage in the book of Judges, where the term 'sons of Belial' first occurs after Deuteronomy.[3] A Levite, that is, a Hebrew, from Mount Ephraim, where Phinehas the high priest is recorded to have had a possession, is represented as having taken a concubine out of Bethlehem Judah, the ancestral home of the Kenites, ever since the time of Joshua and Caleb. As the matrimonial metaphor is so constantly used, we may assume, that by this allegorical story, the hostile feelings between Kenites and Hebrews are to be described. A fusion between equals is recorded,

---
[1] Deut. xiii. 13.
[2] 1 Macc. iii. 6; ix. 23; i. 11; iii. 8, &c.    [3] Judg. xix. 22.

for the concubine was free before her marriage. Still it
was a fusion between hostile, though cognate elements.
The annihilation of the Shechemites had shown, how such
a fusion was abhorred in those times to which the book
of Genesis refers. A similar fusion was now attempted,
in the time of the Judges, but it did not last. The Kenite
returned to Bethlehem, followed by the Levite. Either
peace was restored between the parties, or the one took
the other with him by force. On their return to Mount
Ephraim, they were received by an old man in Gibeah,
who was also of Mount Ephraim, though the inhabitants
were Benjamites, among whom were 'sons of Belial.' On
their return, 'the servant said unto his master: Come, I
pray thee, and let us turn in into this city of the Jebusites, and lodge in it. And his master said unto him:
We will not turn aside hither into the city of a stranger,
that is not of the children of Israel; we will pass over to
Gibeah.' As the Jebusites were a cognate nation with
the Kenites, and as these lived as strangers among the
Hebrews, it is quite evident. that the servant, whether he
was a Kenite or not, is shown to have proposed a dwelling together, if not a fusion, of Hebrews and non-Hebrews
in the future city of the Kenite king, and that the Levite,
the Hebrew, objected to this scheme. Nothing is more
probable, than that, after their arrival at Gibeah, the Benjamites, at least those who are called 'sons of Belial,' sided
with the Hebrew, as if determined to uphold the principles of the separatists, and to prevent a fusion between
Hebrews and Kenites. They clamoured for the extradition of the Levite, apparently because he had joined
himself to a Kenite. But at the request of the old
Ephraimite, the people were satisfied with the extradition
of the Kenite concubine, whom they killed. Hereupon
the Levite divided her flesh and bones into twelve parts,
and sent one to each tribe, including Benjamin, unless
Manasseh, divided by the Jordan, received two.

This outrage led to the battle of Gibeah, and thus to

the destruction of Benjamin, and to the substitution of the Kenite for the Hebrew line of Aaron. The figurative meaning of the above recorded introduction of Kenite remains into every part of Israel, we may now declare to be self-evident. Because Kenites were in every tribe of Israel, their anger was kindled, and led to the annihilation of Benjamin at the battle of Gibeah. As even Phinehas, the representative of the Hebrew line, was forced to fight against Benjamin, which was in a peculiar sense his brother-tribe, it follows, that the cause, or the strength of the Kenites, forced the Hebrews of the eleven tribes to follow the leadership of Judah, the Kenite tribe, and to destroy the power of Benjamin, the Hebrew tribe. In both accounts the Hebrew is shown to have been the offender, and the Kenite the offended party. The Levite had been constrained, by the worthless Benjamites, the allies of the Hebrew Aaronites, to deliver up the Kenite, whom he found dead before his door. Instead of returning with her to her kindred, he sent her remains to the eleven tribes, who were thus roused to revenge the outrage of the Benjamite separatists.

Like the Hebrews, the Kenites had good reasons to consider their rivals and adversaries as of lower descent, in comparison with themselves. On the one side it could be pleaded, that the Kenites were earlier mixed with the African, or dark-coloured race, than the Hebrews, who first met the adversary in the land of Kenaan, where both Kenites and Hebrews had to contend with the black-skinned man, later called Chedorlaomer. But though the Hebrews certainly were a pure white race, when they crossed the Tigris and Euphrates, as the Kenites were when they crossed the Indus, in the time to which the name of Cain refers; and though the Hebrew tradition was represented by Eleazar, the eldest son of Aaron; yet the Kenites were, as we shall see, connected with the descendants from the eldest son of Levi, with the Gershonites; whilst Aaron was a descendant from Kohath, Levi's younger son. If we accept the other interpretation of the word Belial, it can be shown, that either party had reason to consider the other as 'without a yoke,' that is, 'without a law.' It cannot be asserted, and it is highly improbable, at the outset, that the Kenites accepted the Mosaic law, as gradually settled by the Levites, to be the sole and binding standard of the faith. We have seen, that the Kenite tradition, so faithfully preserved and acted upon by the Kenites, at all times, was directly opposed to all sacrificial ordinances, to the statutes that were not good, and yet had been promulgated in the name of God. The Kenites, we may conclude, did not accept the written law of Moses, as it was finally settled, in the time immediately preceding the Babylonian captivity, and on the return from the same, under the presidency of Ezra, the great enemy of the Kenites. They represented the covenant made with Abraham 430 years before that of Moses, which, in the form in which it was finally revised, had the tendency of making the former of none effect. The Kenites considered the Hebrews to be without a law, because these forsook the covenant of Abraham, and thus also that which Moses had really made known, having gone 'backward and not forward' since the exodus. The Hebrews considered the Kenites as being without a law, because they opposed the gradual crystallisation of Levitical doctrines and rites. The only remaining interpretation of sons of Belial, in the sense of worthless, good for nothing, is rather too vague; but if accepted, is open to the same historical explanation. We hope to have proved, that 'sons of Belial' was a degrading epithet, expressing the hostile feeling between Hebrews and Kenites, who both used it against their respective adversaries.

Although the first recorded application of this term refers to the Levites, or Hebrews, whom the Kenite scribe in the time of Joshua, the Kenite, would naturally designate as such; yet, not many years later, the same term was applied to the other branch of the Aaronites. The reason given for the sons of Eli being called 'sons of Belial' is, that they 'regarded not the Lord,' and 'abhorred the offering of Jehovah;' therefore was their sin 'very great before the Lord.'[1] Priests of the house of Eli opposed the custom, which is sanctioned by the ceremonial law as transmitted to us, according to which meat offerings were allowed, and were given to the Lévites. In the days of Eli the priests demanded that meat, instead of being offered, should be roasted for the priests, although the sons of Aaron were, by the written law of the Hebrews, commanded to eat boiled meat.[2] By taking for themselves what the Israelites offered to the Lord, the Hebrews said of the Kenites, that they 'regarded not the Lord,' and 'abhorred the offering of Jehovah.' Eli himself is recorded to have disapproved of their conduct, but we are not told that he did not likewise oppose the meat offerings. He was grieved that his sons robbed the Israelites of the meat which they thought was due to the Lord. In this they had been misguided by Eli's predecessors, according to the Kenite tradition against sacrifices. Under these circumstances, the record about the sons of Eli must be received with caution.

The sin which the sons of Eli committed, is recorded to have been the ruin of Eli's descendants, although Abiathar's separation from the priesthood was caused by a personal act of his own, which, if it had succeeded, would have probably kept his descendants in office. We do not know, that the 'evil dealings' for which Eli reproved his sons, were any other than their taking and roasting for themselves the meat which Israelites brought for offerings. For in the most ancient manuscript, nothing is said about 'women that assembled at the door of the tabernacle.' This passage is of great value, although an interpretation very late introduced into the text, because

---

[1] 1 Sam. ii. 12–17.   [2] Lev. viii. 31.

it proves, that tradition continued to be recorded in the figurative form of the past, even after the fourth century. Without charging the sons of Eli with profligacy, we may assume, at the outset, that they mixed themselves up, and perhaps identified themselves with the Gershonites, who had charge of the outer fabrics of the sanctuary, and were placed under the superintendence of the Kenite house of Ithamar, to which Eli belonged.

Eli, the Kenite high priest, was special overseer of the Gershonites, or Kenites, who were confined to the inferior services of the tabernacle, ever since the days of Moses, according to the Pentateuch. From this it follows, that it was not only Eli's interest, but also his duty, to bring forward, as David did after him, the descendants of the senior son of Levi, who had been so long eclipsed by the descendants from the second son of Levi, by the Kohathites. We have seen, that the separatist Hebrews regarded as their adversaries the Kenites, whose tradition was against all sacrifices. It was in the spirit of Kenite tradition, that the sons of Eli, probably all his spiritual sons, all the Kenite priests and Levites, tried to put an end to the abomination of sacrifices, by publicly preparing the meat, contrary to the Hebrew law, and by eating it themselves. Such offence would naturally be severely censured by the Hebrew chronicler of later times. Accordingly the loss of the ark is recorded to have been a direct consequence of the iniquity of the sins of Eli. A battle against the Philistines having been lost, the people are recorded to have fetched the ark from Shiloh, believing that the Holy Presence was really and exclusively therein confined. The same idolatrous view was taken by the Philistines, who dreaded the presence of the ark in the camp, as a thing which had not occurred before. That ark, they knew, contained the God who had smitten the Egyptians 'with all the plagues in the wilderness.' So the Philistines were urged to establish their independence of the Hebrews, who had been the servants of the Philistines.

In the ensuing battle 30,000 Israelites were slain. This would not have happened, as the Hebrew chronicler implies, if the ark had not been taken by the enemy. For whosoever possessed the ark, possessed the God of battles. As the two sons of Eli, Hophni and Phinehas, were slain, it was their iniquity which was thus punished. 'A man of Benjamin' came from the camp to announce the flight of the Israelites, the slaughter among the people, and the death of Eli's sons. So entirely, it is implied, did Eli unite in the feeling, that with the ark, God had left Israel, that the old high priest and judge fell from his chair and died. Even the wife of Phinehas confirmed these views, by calling her son Ichabod, because, with the ark, 'the glory,' the Holy Presence, had departed from Israel.

We have shown, that the Kenites were the first proclaimers of Jehovah in Israel; that two Kenites were, by God's voice, marked out as having alone entirely followed Jehovah; that the first seers in Israel were Kenites; that the disappearance of the Urim and Thummim, as means for discerning God's will, and the proclamation of oracles by prophets, as well as the introduction of the schools of prophets, must be connected with the accession of the high priestly line of Ithamar, in the person of Eli; and that the opposition of David and Asaph, the Kenites, to all sacrifices, stands in direct connection with the word of God as proclaimed by Kenite seers. If we have succeeded in proving these positions, we are entitled to the assertion, that the record in the book of Samuel, about the sons of Eli, is a party-statement, composed in that spirit of hostility, and with that view to party interests, of which the books of the Old and of the New Testament afford such ample proofs to the unprejudiced reader. It is impossible to believe, that Eli could have idolised the ark, as Micah idolised the images, which the Danites had stolen, the loss of which was to him the loss of the Holy Presence, which he had thought to possess. Equally unhistorical is the charge of profligacy against the sons of

Eli, which has been added after the fourth century of the
Christian era. Although the Kenites believed in the one
God Jehovah, and the Hebrews in many gods, Elohim,
the Hebrew chronicler accused the sons and followers of
Eli, of having followed other gods than Jehovah, and this
iniquity was described, before and after the time of Eli,
by the matrimonial metaphor, as profligacy.

The song of praise of Hannah, mother of Samuel, who
was brought up for the priesthood in the sanctuary, under
the guidance of Eli, confirms the view we have suggested
about the use of the word 'sons of Belial,' whilst it
confirms the Kenite and Levite descent of Samuel. Elkanah, direct descendant from Korah the Kenite, was
married to Hannah, whose song of thanksgiving proves
that she rejoiced in the accession of the Kenite line of
Ithamar, to which Eli belonged. Hannah's 'horn' was
'exalted by the Lord.' Her horn is the tribe of Ephraim;
for Moses had compared Ephraim, Joseph's first-born, to
'a majestic bullock,' whose horns are like those of the
buffalo,[1] with which he pushes down the people, both the
ends of the earth. God is called 'the rock,'[2] and a God
of 'knowledge' or 'wisdom.' 'The mighty' stand with
a 'broken bow,' and the weak, or 'the stumbling,' are
'girded with strength.' Those who 'were full,' hire themselves out for bread,' and those 'who suffered hunger,' rest
from their labour, by which they earned their sustenance.
'Whilst the barren gives birth to seven, she that is
rich with children withers away. The Lord killeth and
maketh alive, and bringeth down to the grave, and
bringeth up. The Lord maketh poor and maketh rich,
he bringeth low and lifteth up. He raiseth up the poor
out of the dust, and lifteth up the beggar from the dung-
hill, to make him throne by the side of the mighty, to
make them inherit the throne of glory. For the pillars
of the earth are the Lord's, and he hath set the world

---

[1] Comp. Job xxxix. 9.     [2] Comp. Deut. xxxii. 18.

upon them. The feet of his saints he keepeth, but the godless must perish in the darkness. For not through strength does man conquer. The Lord breaketh to pieces his adversaries, he thunders over them in heaven. The Lord judgeth the ends of the earth. But may he give strength to his king, and exalt the horn of his anointed.'[1]

We derive the following conclusions from this important document, of which we shall afterwards show the direct connection with Mary's song of thanksgiving, recorded by St. Luke. The mighty, those who were full, who hire themselves out for bread, and wither away, being made poor, are the representatives of the senior line of Eleazar, who, in consequence of the annihilation of Benjamin at Gibeah, lost their exclusive right to the high priesthood. A striking confirmation of this interpretation is the recorded fact, that the rivals hired themselves out for bread. This is what Uzzi, the grandson of Abishua, the last high priest of the senior line before Eli, is reported to have done, according to historical tradition. He went to Mount Gerizim, and there deposited, among the Samaritan priesthood, the secret tradition of Aaron.[2]

Further confirmation of the above interpretation of Hannah's song, is contained in the reference to the poor, who is made to throne by the side of the mighty. Benjamin the wolf had during its early history devoured the prey, the Aaronic inheritance, and in the time of Eli was obliged to divide the spoils with Ephraim, that is with the tribe to which Joshua, the Kenite, had belonged, and which after the battle of Gibeah, and the marriage of the Benjamites with Ephraimite women, became amalgamated with Benjamin. The horn of Ephraim was suddenly exalted over that of Benjamin, the chief support of the senior Aaronite line of Eleazar. Thus the Kenites, 'the

[1] 1 Sam. ii. 1–10.
[2] In the record of this tradition by Josephus, Uzzi must be read for Moses. This is confirmed by another tradition of the Samaritans, according to which the Samaritan Pentateuch is identical with that which Abishua used.

strangers,' inherited the throne of glory, and became 'pillars of the earth,' on which the Lord had set the world. Here we have an historical interpretation of the hidden wisdom expressed in some of the enigmatical sayings which form the book of Proverbs. 'Wisdom hath builded her house, she hath hewn out her seven pillars.'[1] 'The secret' of the Lord is 'with the righteous,' that is, with 'the wise,' who shall inherit glory.'[2] The book of Genesis shows, that Adam, Methuselah, Shem, Isaac, Levi, Amram and Moses, formed the seven pillars of oral tradition. For according to the chronology there recorded, Shem was for 150 years the contemporary of Abraham, and for 50 years he lived with Isaac, before whose death his grandson Levi reached his 34th year, whose grandson Amram was the father of Moses.

According to the song of Hannah, the line of Ithamar began to share the dignity of the high priesthood in her time. History shows that this cannot be interpreted to mean, that two high priests were set up in the time of Eli. This was the case in the time of David, when both the Kenite and the Hebrew line were represented in distinct sanctuaries. Already in the time of Solomon, Abiathar, the representative of the junior line, was 'thrust out from being priest unto the Lord,' and in course of time, the sons of Ithamar, the Kenite priests and scribes, who continued for a long time to be separated from the sons of Zadok, from the Hebrew secession, were called, and we suggest for this reason, the separated, the Pharisees.

Other terms, which, in the most important passages, may be interpreted by the hostility between Kenites and Hebrews, are the words 'saints' and 'adversary,' or Satan. As regards the former, it can be shown that both parties considered their respective members as 'saints' or Chasidim. Thus in Asaph's 79th Psalm the Kenites are

---

[1] Prov. ix. 1.     [2] Ibid. iii. 32–35.

referred to as the saints, whose flesh has been given to the beasts of the land.[1] And yet, in the first book of the Maccabees, this passage is quoted as an authority for regarding the Maccabees, that is, the Sadducees, as saints, who are recorded to have been treacherously slain by 'a priest of the seed of Aaron,' probably by 'that wicked Alcimus,' made high priest about the year 163 B.C.[2] The word 'adversary' occurs, without the article, in many places. Thus we find it in the 109th Psalm. We suggest, that the same was written by David, after the massacre of the priests of Ithamar at Nob, and whilst Abiathar, the only one who escaped, had taken refuge in his hiding-place. 'The wicked' are the families of the high priestly line of Eleazar, whose chief, Zadok, the ally of Saul, fought against David, 'without a cause.' They have become 'adversaries' of David, although his love was extended towards them. They rewarded him 'evil for good,' and hatred for his love. He showed his impartiality and love for that branch of the Aaronites, even after the defeat of his enemies, by acknowledging Zadok as high priest in Gibeon. The chief of these adversaries of David is now singled out by the Psalmist. God is asked to set over 'him,' that is, over Zadok, 'a wicked man,' and 'an adversary,' a Satan, an accuser, 'at his right hand.' His days are to be few, and his priestly, if not high priestly 'office' is to be received by 'another.' He is no longer to be a spiritual 'father' over his children, nor a husband to his wife, a Lord of his congregation. His priests, his children, are to be 'continually vagabonds, and beg,' and 'seek their bread far away from their ruins.' The 'office' which Zadok occupied during the latter years of Saul's reign, was more than that of a priest. After his victory over the Philistines, Saul vainly consulted the oracle, through Ahijah, at the ark, or at the altar, which Saul had built.[3] Ahijah seems to have

---

[1] Ps. lxxix.   [2] 1 Macc. vii. 8–17.   [3] 1 Sam. xiv. 35.

invited Saul to the ark, which was under Ahijah's care, the fourth high priest of the line of Ithamar, and when the ark was probably at Kirjath-Jearim, at the border of Benjamin, or at Baale, in Judah. Yet, after this time, Saul no longer enquired at it.[1] Between that time and the massacre at Nob, the sanctuary was moved to this latter place, whilst Saul was at Gibeah, where, shortly afterwards, David established Zadok as high priest. As Zadok had become the ally of Saul, and as the tribe of Benjamin supported both, we may assume that Zadok's office in Gibeah was, already in the last days of Saul, that of a high priest.

David prays that another may receive Zadok's office. At the time when this Psalm seems to have been written, Abiathar had escaped from the massacre at Nob, and was lodging with David at Keilah, and in the wilderness of Ziph, whilst Zadok was officiating at Gibeah. Abiathar, therefore, had been the substitute for Zadok's office, whom he had in view when there was, perhaps, no high priest in Israel, unless Zadok was in that position at Gibeah, after the all but complete annihilation of the line of Ithamar. If Zadok, like an extortioner, or usurer, has caught, has drawn to himself, or amassed all that he now holds, that is, the highest dignity in the church, then may 'strangers plunder his labour.' These 'strangers' are the Kenites, to whom, like David, Abiathar belonged, and who always lived as 'strangers' in Israel. No one is to love him, nor to have mercy on his fatherless children. 'His' posterity is to be cut off, and 'their' name, the name of the line to whom Zadok belongs, is to be blotted out in the next generation. Instead of being continually before the Lord in the sanctuary, according to the promise recorded to have been made to Zadok's ancestor Phinehas, the families forming that line are to stand continually before the Lord, so 'that he may cut off the memory of them from

---

[1] 1 Chr. xiii. 3.

the earth, because that he remembered not to show mercy, but persecuted the poor and needy man, that he might even slay the broken in heart.' We shall see, that in the song of Hannah, which refers to the downfall of Eleazar's line, and the raising up of Ithamar's line, the representatives of the latter are called 'the poor' and the 'beggar.' Thus interpreted, the above passage refers to the persecution of the priests of Ithamar, which ended with the massacre at Nob. The expression, 'the broken in heart,' refers to those of a broken and contrite heart, whom God will not despise. The adversary is referred to as continually girding himself. As the Hebrews did not gird themselves continually, and as the priests did, we may see here another reference to Zadok. David says that he is 'poor and needy,' and thin with fasting, traits which all point to his Kenite descent.[1] The Lord is asked to stand at the right hand of the poor, of the persecuted only representative of the Aaronic line of Ithamar.

The 109th Psalm confirms our assertion, that the word adversary, or Satan, refers to a human foe, and that it is made to refer to the hostility between the Kenites and the Hebrews. The same can be proved in the three passages where the word adversary occurs with the article.

We have seen that, in the book of Job, the adversary, or the Satan, is a human being, and that he represents the African, or dark-coloured race, which, in the time of Abraham, or at a still earlier period, insisted upon dwelling together with the white race, in the land between the Euphrates and the Nile, and upon worshipping the same God, possibly in the same sanctuary. The second place where the adversary is mentioned, in the Old Testament, refers to the numbering of the people by David, as recorded in the Chronicles.[2] From combining the accounts, we gather that 'the anger of the Lord was kindled against

Israel.' For what reason is not stated. As God's anger was not supposed to be kindled against Judah, it is probable that Judah was by David regarded as the instrument through which Israel was to be punished. The readiness of Judah to fight Israel would confirm him in this view. To ascertain the respective numbers of fighting men in Israel and in Judah was David's first object. The writer, who states that the anger of the Lord was kindled against Israel, adds, that God moved David to number Israel and Judah. But in Chronicles it is recorded that the adversary, or the Satan, stood up against Israel, and provoked 'David to number Israel.' That the adversary is here identified with Judah seems to be implied by two facts. The adversary does not provoke David to number Judah, and Joab, who had vainly pleaded for Israel, not for Judah, does not number the fighting men in Benjamin or Levi, 'for the king's word was abominable to Joab.' Joab was determined to prevent the war, if possible; but, at all events, it was not to be a renewal of the feud between the Aaronic lines, each of which was now represented by a high priest, the one residing in Benjamin, the other in Judah. Contrary to the orders received, Joab counted not Benjamin and Levi among those that drew the sword. The Levites were scattered among all tribes in Israel and Judah, whilst Zadok, of the house of Eleazar, had received the support of Benjamin in the fight of Saul against David. Although Israel and Judah, that is, all the twelve tribes, were united under David's rule, yet it seems that the enmity between Benjamin and Judah, and their respective allies, had not ceased, and was centered in Zadok and Abiathar, whose cause these tribes had respectively sustained. It is to be remarked, that in both records Israel is distinguished from Judah, although we are at a loss to understand how such a distinction could have existed in the time of David, unless we assume that the two Aaronites, Zadok and Abiathar, were the cause of it. And yet the separation of the ten tribes was not sanctioned by the Aaronites or by the Levites, both of whom sided with the Southern kingdom. We therefore suggest that it was Abiathar, Zadok's adversary, who provoked David to number Israel, and that, humanly speaking, it was Joab, who caused David's heart to feel that he had sinned, and to confess his sin to God. As in the book of Job, so in the book of Chronicles, the adversary, or the Satan, is a human foe.

The third passage where the word 'the Satan' occurs in the Old Testament, can likewise be explained by the hostility between the Aaronites, as the respective representatives of Hebrews and Kenites. In order to prove our assertion, we must first refer to the family descent of Joshua, and then to the vision of Zechariah, the prophet, who saw Joshua and the adversary standing before the angel of the Lord.

Joshua, the high priest, was son of Jehozadak, and son of Seraiah, who must not be identified with Seraiah or Azariah (Eliezer), from whom Ezra descended. The name Seraiah, or Saraiah, occurs as the name of the son of Kenaz, brother of Othniel, and father of Joab.[1] Again, the name of Kenaz occurs as the name of the son of Eliphaz, the son of Esau,[2] from whom Caleb and Othniel, the Kennezites, or Kenites, were descended. From this it follows, that Seraiah or Azariah was a Kenite name at a very early date. It is a compound word, the first word, Azar, meaning help. To be helped by God was considered to be essential to all rulers. By compounding Azar with El, or with Hadad, the name of a Phœnician Deity, the names Eleazar, or Eliezer, and Hadadezer were formed. And when all original distinction between El and Jehovah was to be obliterated, the name Ezra was formed, which was occasionally written Azariah,[3] the meaning of which is the same as Eleazar.

It can be rendered highly probable, by circumstantial evidence, that Joshua's ancestor was either the martyr of Riblah, the high priest of Zedekiah, or Seraiah, the son of Neraiah and brother of Baruch 'the blessed,' who received from Jeremiah[1] a book of prophecies, which he was to take with him to Babylon. He is called 'the prince of the rest,' that is, we suggest, the prince of the Shechina, the prince of prophecy. The Vulgate's rendering of 'the prince of prophecy' would thus be explained. As this Seraiah was Baruch's brother, who, according to Josephus, was 'of a very eminent family,' and as Seraiah, the high priest, was an Aaronite by birth, these two Seraiahs were probably connected by family ties. Jehozadak, the son of Seraiah, was taken captive to Babylon, where his son Joshua was probably born; the connection between Joshua the high priest, and Seraiah the martyr at Riblah, becomes, therefore, increasingly probable.

'Sirach, or Seraiah, of Jerusalem,' is referred to in the book of Ecclesiasticus, written by Jesus, or Joshua, after his father's, or ancestor's Hebrew original, called the Wisdom of Sirach. That the great high priest and martyr was the writer of this Apocrypha, we hope to have proved. Here we have only to remark, that the probable connection between Seraiah or Sira, the high priest, and Baruch, confirms the supposed Kenite origin of the former. For Baruch was the friend, amanuensis, and attendant of Jeremiah, who was 'the son of Hilkiah, of the priests that were in Anathoth.'[2] As the 'fields' of Abiathar, the Aaronite of the Kenite house of Ithamar, were in Anathoth, and as the rivalry and enmity between the two lines, which never ceased, renders it impossible to assume that the fields of the antagonistic Aaronites were contiguous, it is reasonable to suppose that Jeremiah was of Kenite descent. This is rendered well nigh certain by his connection with the Rechabites, of whom one bore

[1] Jer. li. 59–61.   [2] Ibid. i. 1.

his name. As a Kenite, Jeremiah would choose an amanuensis from the Kenite families of Scribes. And if Baruch was a Kenite, his probable connection with the family of the high priest Seraiah, goes far in proving the Kenite descent of the martyr of Riblah. This will be proved as a fact, when we have interpreted from our Kenite point of view, the vision of Zechariah about Joshua the high priest.

The high priest Joshua, whose name like that of the son of Nun, points to Shuah the Kenite, and who had laid the foundation, finished and consecrated the temple, in 516 B.C., is seen in a vision, by his contemporary, the prophet Zechariah, as standing before 'the angel of the Lord, and the adversary standing to his right hand, that he might be adverse to him. And the Lord said unto the adversary: The Lord rebuke thee, thou adversary, yea, may the Lord rebuke thee, who hath chosen Jerusalem. Is not this man a brand saved from the fire?'[1] The mention of the angel of the Lord, as representative of Divine Presence, as the manifester of his name or spirit,[2] points to the apparition of the angel of the Lord unto Moses, in a flame of fire, out of a thorny bush, which 'burned with fire, and yet was not consumed.' Joshua stood before the sacred fire on the altar, which symbolised the Divine Presence, as Moses had stood before the burning bush, from which the Lord spoke unto him through an angel. Like Moses, whom God made 'the shepherd of his flock,' by putting the Divine Spirit 'within him,'[3] so Joshua was a shepherd of God's flock. As the fire was manifested through the instrumentality of the bush, which burned, and yet was not consumed, so by Joshua, as by Moses, was manifested the spirit of God, which enlightened without consuming. In this sense the high priest Joshua, we would suggest, is called a brand saved from the fire. He was not, like Rezin,

---

[1] Zech. iii.  [2] Ex. xxiii. 21.  [3] Is. lxiii. 11.

king of Syria (Aram), and Pekah, son of Remaliah, king of Israel, who attacked Jerusalem in the time of Ahaz, and whom Isaiah had compared to the ends of two smoking, or extinguishing firebrands.[1] As Tiglath Pilesar, king of Assyria, became the ally of Ahaz, and destroyed his enemies, so Darius Hystaspes, then ruling in Babylon, the intimate friend of Zerubbabel, had proved himself the friend of the Jews in Jerusalem, by the renewal of the decree, and by his subsidies for the building of the temple.

The connection between these two passages in Exodus and in the book of Zechariah, can also be traced in the latter part of the vision. Moses was commanded not to draw nigh to the burning bush, before he had put off his shoes from off his feet, because that the ground on which he stood, was holy ground. Likewise Joshua is not to stand before the presence of the Lord in the 'filthy garments' in which he was clothed. The Angel of the Lord commanded those that stood before him, either inferior angels, or inferior priests, to take them away from Joshua, and he said unto him: 'Behold, I take away from thee thine iniquity, and clothe thee with festive garments.' And the prophet (according to some, the Angel) said: 'Set a pure mitre upon his head.' The filthy garments, and the impure covering of the head, are signs of repentance for sin committed. Of this sin Joshua had been accused by the adversary, who occupied the more honourable place on the right hand in the sanctuary.

It is evident, that, in the vision, Joshua is represented as one who has been only just admitted to share in the privilege of the high priesthood. For the promise is made conditionally: 'If thou walk in my ways, and keep my charge,' that is, the charge of the sanctuary, which was committed to the Levites in the time of

---

[1] Is. vii.: comp. 2 Kings xvi.; 2 Chr. xxviii.

Moses,[1] 'then thou also shalt judge my house, and thou also shalt keep my courts, and I will give thee free access among those that stand here.' Among those that stand before the sanctuary, a privilege which still during the captivity had belonged exclusively to the 'sons of Zadok,'[2] Joshua is promised permission to go in and out. The promise about the Messiah, the Zemah, or Branch, about the servant of God, is made exclusively to Joshua and to his 'friends,' that sat before him. For these are 'men of signs and wonders,'[3] 'diviners' according to the Septuagint, they are organs of tradition, who being witnesses of the promise, of the sign, shall be, through their successors, witnesses of the wonderful fulfilment.

When Ezekiel declared, during the captivity, which the Kenites shared with the Hebrews, that 'the charge' of the sanctuary was only to be kept by 'the sons of Zadok,' that these rivals, or adversaries of the sons of Ithamar, were alone to stand before God in 'the most holy place,' at that comparatively recent time, the children of the captivity had brought 'strangers' in the sanctuary, who are recorded to have been stigmatised, by the Hebrew prophet Ezekiel, as 'uncircumcised in heart and uncircumcised in flesh.' No 'stranger' whatever was to be admitted, and such of the Levites as went astray after their idols, were to bear their iniquity, although they might be 'ministers' in the sanctuary, keeping charge of the gates of the house, as the Gershonites, with whom the Kenites were connected, had done in the time of Eli. From this it follows, that the non-Hebrew priests and Levites, who had been introduced into the sanctuary during the captivity, and whose admission Ezekiel condemned, were those of the Kenite or Rechabite families, the adversaries or rivals of 'the sons of Zadok,' who dwelt as 'strangers' among the Israelites. Again, it follows, that Joshua, the high priest, who is addressed as

---

[1] Comp. Lev. viii 35; Num. i. 53.
[2] Ezek. xliv. 15.          [3] Comp. Is. viii. 18.

a new comer in the sanctuary, and whose name, like that of the son of Nun, points to Kenite descent, is in the vision of Zechariah described as one to whom the joint privilege of standing before the Lord is to be granted, as a fulfilment of Jeremiah's promise, that, like the sons of Phinehas, or Zadok, 'Jonadab, the son of Rechab, shall not want a man to stand' before God 'for ever.' If this be sufficiently proved, then we may assert, that 'the adversary' or Satan, who is described as standing at the right hand of Joshua in the sanctuary, is a representative of the rival Hebrew line of Zadok, and that the Kenite line of Ithamar was after the captivity admitted to share with the Hebrew line of Zadok the privilege of the high priesthood.

The history of the Kenites is the history of Cain, whose sacrifice in Eden was not well-pleasing to Jehovah, who went out from the presence of the Lord, accompanied by a sign unto life. Although sin was lurking at the door, desirous to possess Cain, he was to become ruler over the same, by faith in the symbol of that Divine Presence, which went with him. Before the time of Melchizedec, Cain had found, had believed in the One Most High God, had come before his presence, before which Kenite priests ministered in the sanctuary. The Hebrews regarded them as strangers, and their priests as adversaries. Yet to the Kenites as well as to the Hebrews an everlasting priesthood was promised. The two brothers, who had separated in the sanctuary in Eden, met again, and ministered together in the sanctuary at Jerusalem. Cain had lived in far countries, going to and fro on the earth, but he returned to his father's home. The son who had been lost, was found.

We shall later point out a striking confirmation of this assertion, contained in one of the parables of the New Testament. We now refer to some passages in the Psalms, which, from this point of view, seem to admit of a new interpretation. This leads us to consider which of the Psalms may be regarded as Kenite Psalms.

## CHAPTER IX.

### KENITES AND PSALMS.

THE history of Israel is the history of Kenites and Hebrews, of the descendants from Cain and from Seth, from Melchizedec and from Abraham, from Jethro and from Moses. If this has been proved, the Psalms must show traces of a double stream. Again, if the Kenites were separated from the Hebrews, ever since the great separation in Eden; if the tradition of the former, as promulgated by them, was essentially different from the tradition of the latter; if the Pharisees, the separated, always belonged to the Kenites, and the Sadducees to the Hebrews, it may be possible to distinguish Kenite Psalms from Hebrew Psalms. Assuming as proved, the Kenite descent of the house of David, of Asaph, and of the sons of Korah, we have above seventy Psalms, which, by the traditional superscriptions, in the Hebrew Canon, are attributed to David, twelve of Asaph and ten of Korah. Many others can, by their contents, or by the superscriptions in the Septuagint, be referred to Kenite authors, with more or less probability. It is not our object, minutely to examine these Psalms, but to suggest a few rules for testing their Kenite, or their Hebrew origin. It will be found, that only very few are clearly anti-Kenite.[1]

1. All Psalms are written by Kenites which refer to David or his house.
2. The principle of universality, the doctrines about the invisibility of God, about the Word of God, about

---

[1] Ps. xxix., xxx., lxxxviii., &c.

angels and spirits, righteousness not by deeds only, atonement by righteousness, and not by sacrifice, the injunctions to prayer, must all be regarded as indicating Kenite authorship.

3. Less certain, but sometimes reliable, are the indirect references to Kenites as 'strangers,'[1] or the 'rebellious;'[2] the injunction to 'fools' to be 'wise,'[3] to learn the wisdom the hiding of which the Sadducees, that is, the Hebrews, enforced; the reference to shepherds;[4] to 'the destitute,' that is, the poor,[5] whose cause the Kenites always served, and to 'the secret council of the upright,' which a Sadducee would hardly have directly connected with 'the congregation.'[6] The 'presence of the God of Jacob;' Judah as God's 'sanctuary;'[7] the complaint against the 'plowers,' or agriculturists by the shepherds; these, among other traits, may be mentioned as suggestive of Kenite authorship.

'The sweet Psalmist of Israel,' the Kenite king, was the first who popularised the principles of Kenite tradition, by the composition of poems adapted to the purposes of devotion. Before his time the sanctuary was the house of oracles, but David made it the house of prayer. Israel had been taught to do certain things, and to leave others undone; but even Moses had not ventured to command, or even to invite the ignorant and Egyptianized Hebrews, to pray, either in private, or in public. David, the king after God's own heart, the first opposer of image worship, as the cause of idolatry, proclaimed the necessity of direct individual communion between man and his God, and he taught the people how to pray. Prayer had been his soul's desire, his comfort in adversity, the hallowed means of obtaining the assurance of pardon for his sins, the invisible ladder of his father Jacob, which connected earth with heaven. Moved by the Spirit of God, he prayed in the Spirit, he wrote in the Spirit, and he saw in the Spirit things to come. His Kenite ancestors, though they had not ploughed the land, nor sown seed thereon, had been sowers of a spiritual seed, and ploughers of the hearts of men. The Kenites had not dwelt in houses, but they knew that their hearts were intended to be, what the holy of holies foreshadowed, dwelling-places of the Most High God. Thus the creature communed with the Creator. Men of high degree and men of low degree were equally privileged. But although, in a measure, every Kenite may have been taught that every man ought to be his own sanctuary, his own priest, all Israel was now to be brought together, a national sanctuary was to be built, and public services established, to meet the exigencies of the times.

We have seen with what difficulties David had to contend. He laid the basis of a future peace, by admitting both Aaronic lines to the high priesthood. But sacerdotal succession was not his only difficulty. Partizanship among the Aaronites encouraged rivalry and opposition among David's sons. Even his faithful friend and supporter, the sharer of his trials, the high priest Abiathar, fanned, if he did not kindle, the fire of rebellion in the king's household. David had seen his beloved Jonathan perish with Saul, and he had to see Abiathar join Adonijah, the heir to the throne. But Solomon had been brought up by Nathan the prophet, and he promised to excel all the men of the East in that Wisdom, which had had been the heir-loom of the Kenites. Attended by the beautiful Kenite shepherdess, Abishag the Shulamite, he closed his eyes, whilst the son of his hopes already was established as king of all Israel. To that son he left the building of the temple. But what David had done, paved the way for it. Acknowledging their common origin, the Phœnicians allied themselves with Israel. Had Tyre been, like the Philistines, steeped in idolatry, Hiram would not have been ' ever a lover of

David,'[1] nor would the latter have accepted Hiram's alliance and his gifts; and still less would Solomon have corresponded with him on the wisdom hidden in enigmatical sayings, and also about the building of the temple. Hiram sent 'a man of understanding and knowledge' to consult with the initiated of Solomon and of David.[2] We may assume, that a consultation, between men of wisdom, on traditional symbolism is implied. This view is confirmed by the facts, that by his mother, a Danite, Hiram was connected with Aholiab, the artist in the wilderness, whose tabernacle became the model of Solomon's temple,[3] whilst Hiram furnished the principal architect for the building of the same.[4] The symbolical meaning of the temple cannot, therefore, have been unknown to the king of Tyre.[5] The Philistines were also a cognate race with the Israelites, especially with the Kenite part of their community. But they were idolaters in the eyes of David. Jealous of David's possession of Mount Zion, they attacked him, but were repulsed, and their gods were burnt with fire.[6] Then the ark was solemnly removed to Jerusalem, and a council, or assembly, consisting of priests and Levites, was formed.[7] To another kind of council, the members of which must have been initiated in secret tradition, the Psalmist refers, when he says, according to the version of the Vulgate: 'I will give thanks unto the Lord with my whole heart, secretly among the faithful, and (openly?) in the congregation.'[8] As the Scribes, or learned in Scripture, can be traced up to the time of David, and as they often were priests, if not exclusively priests or Levites, it is highly probable that this council which David formed, was chosen from among the Scribal corporation, the later existence of which is certain. David himself, or Gad, or Nathan his

[1] 1 Kings v. 1.
[2] 2 Chr. ii. 13, 14.
[3] Wisd. ix. 8.
[4] 1 Kings vii. 13, 40.
[5] Comp. Ps. lxxxvii. 4.
[6] 2 Sam. v. 17; 1 Chr. xiv. 12.
[7] 1 Chr. xv. 2-27.
[8] Ps. cxi. 1.

adviser,[1] may have presided over the consultations of these councillors. He himself was dressed, occasionally, in priestly garments, and his sons were priests,[2] whilst he, and even Benaiah, the captain of his guard, took part in the musical performances in the sanctuary, and gave the benediction. Brought up in the prophetic schools, which Samuel the Kenite seems to have been the first to establish, David made over to Asaph, the Kenite seer, and to his brother, some of his writings, which were later worked up into Psalms, and otherwise promulgated.

We now consider the principal doctrines enunciated by the Psalms. They will be found to form part of those Psalms, the Kenite authorship of which is more or less certain. As it can be proved, that very few Psalms express anti-Kenite doctrines, we may say, that the doctrines of the Kenites are to be found almost in the entire collection of Psalms. We shall confine our extracts, which we quote from the Prayer-book version, that is from the Latin Vulgate, and thus essentially from the Greek Septuagint, principally to the first fifty Psalms. What only a few knew, David thus made known to the people, applying this knowledge to devotional exercises, and illustrating the same by an honest endeavour to live in accordance with this wisdom.

### 1. *God is One and invisible.*

'The Lord is in his holy temple,' and yet 'The Lord's seat is in heaven.' 'The fool hath said in his heart, there is no God.' 'God is in the generation of the righteous.'[3] 'I have set God always before me; for he is on my right hand; therefore I shall not fall.'[4] 'There went a smoke out of his presence, and a consuming fire out of his mouth, so that coals were kindled at it; he bowed the heavens also and came down, and it was dark under his feet. He rode upon the Cherubims, and did

---

[1] 2 Sam. vii. 3. [2] 2 Sam. viii. 18. [3] Ps. xi. 4; xiv. 1, 9. [4] Ibid. xvi. 9.

fly; he came flying upon the wings of the wind. He made darkness his secret place, his pavilion round about him with dark water, and thick clouds to cover him. At the brightness of his presence his clouds removed (as well as) hailstones and coals of fire. The Lord also thundered out of heaven, and the Highest gave his thunder, hailstones and coals of fire. He sent out his arrows and scattered them, he cast forth lightnings, and destroyed them. The springs of waters were seen, and the foundations of the round world were discovered, at thy chiding, O Lord, at the blasting of the breath of thy displeasure.'[1] 'The heavens are telling the glory of God.... In them hath he set a tabernacle for the sun, which cometh forth as a bridegroom out of his chamber, and rejoiceth as a giant to run his course. It goeth forth from the uttermost part of the heaven, and runneth about unto the end of it again, and there is nothing hid from the heat thereof.'[2] 'Thou continuest holy, O thou worship of Israel,' or 'Thou art the holy one, throning amidst Israel's songs of praise.'[3] 'Thou shalt hide them privily by thine own presence, from the provoking of all men; thou shalt keep them secretly in thy tabernacle from the strife of tongues.'[4] 'Thou deckest thyself with light as it were with a garment, and spreadest out the heavens like a curtain. Who layeth the beams of his chambers in the waters, and maketh the clouds his chariot, and walketh upon the wings of the wind. He maketh his angels spirits, and his ministers a flaming fire.'[5]

Light, or fire, is the most perfect emblem of God's presence, but it is not in reality that presence. It is but a garment. In these and other passages, are clearly described the unity, spirituality and invisibility of God; his throne in heaven; the power which proceeds from the place where God is, like the rays from the sun, and lightnings from the cloud; and the mission of that Divine power, to establish the holy presence on the earth.

2. *The firstborn among all Creatures is the Divine Spirit, Wisdom or Word, the Mediator between the Creature and the Creator, the organ of sanctification and immortality. The Saviour of mankind.*

'O Lord, thy word endureth for ever in heaven.'[1] 'By the word of the Lord were the heavens made, and all the hosts of them by the breath of his mouth.'[2] 'He spake the word, and they were made, he commanded, and they were created' (or renewed).[3] 'When thou lettest thy breath go forth, they shall be made, and thou shalt renew the face of the earth.'[4] 'His word runneth very swiftly; he giveth snow like wool, and scattereth the hoar frost like ashes; he casteth forth his ice like morsels; who is able to abide his frost? He sendeth out his word and melteth them, he bloweth with his wind, and the waters flow.'[5] 'Fire and hail, snow and vapours, wind and storm, fulfil his word.'[6]

From these passages it follows that the Word of God was conceived by the Psalmists, as the uncreated light, symbolised by the sun and its rays, and by the fire from the cloud. The connecting links between the sun and the earth, as well as between the cloud and the earth, the solar rays, and lightnings, or the fire from the Lord, were messengers, or angels from God. But in the higher sense, the Divine Word, the uncreated light, and the uncreated fire, was the Mediator between the Creature and the Creator, who is encompassed with light, the intermediate intelligence between earth and heaven, the enlightening medium, the teacher of mankind. Thus the Word of God became the Wisdom of God, and was identified with the same.

'By his excellent wisdom' God 'made the heavens.'[1] 'Thou requirest truth in the inward parts, and shalt make me to understand wisdom secretly.'[2] God made Joseph 'lord of his house,' that 'he might inform his princes after his will, and teach his senators wisdom.'[3] 'The law of the Lord is an undefiled law, converting the soul, the testimony of the Lord is sure, and giveth wisdom unto the simple.'[4] 'The mouth of the righteous is exercised in wisdom, and his tongue will be talking of judgment.'[5] 'Wherewithal shall a young man cleanse his way? Even by ruling himself after thy word.' 'Thy words have I hid within my heart, that I should not sin against thee.' 'I will not forget thy word.' 'That I may live and keep Thy word.' 'Thy salvation according to Thy word.' 'Thy word is a lantern unto my feet, and light unto my paths.' 'Thy word is tried to the uttermost, and Thy servant loveth it.' 'Thy word is true from everlasting.'[6] 'O send out thy light and thy truth, that they may lead me.'[7] 'He that speaketh the truth from his heart, shall dwell in the tabernacle' of the Lord, that is, in his presence.[8] 'God shall send forth his mercy and truth.'[9] 'Mercy and truth shall go before thy face.'[10] 'Thy law is the truth.'[11] 'Hear me in the truth of thy salvation.'[12] 'Lead me forth in thy truth, and learn (teach) me; for thou art the God of my salvation.'[13] 'The Lord gave the word; great was the company of the preachers.'[14] 'He sent his word and healed them, and they were saved from their destruction.'[15] 'O quicken thou me, according to thy word.'[16] 'I will worship towards thy holy temple, and praise thy name, because of thy loving-kindness and truth; for thou hast magnified thy name and thy word above all things.'[17]

The Divine Teacher is not any written word, of which no mention is here made, and which, whatsoever may have been at that time recorded of Divine mysteries, could only have been regarded as the record of what had been taught by the word ingrafted on the heart. The witness which man has in himself, the Divine word or wisdom, is further identified in the Psalms with the breath or spirit, or presence of God.

'Make me a clean heart, O God, and renew a right spirit within me. Cast me not away from thy presence, and take not thy holy spirit from me. O, give me the comfort of thy help again, and establish me with thy free spirit. Then shall I teach thy ways unto the wicked, and sinners shall be converted unto thee.'[1] 'They provoked his spirit.'[2] 'Whither shall I go from thy spirit, or whither shall I go from thy presence?'[3] This indwelling presence of God, the holy name, which was in the angel or messenger of God's presence, is described as the organ of sanctification and of light. 'Preserve thou my soul, for I am holy.'[4] 'My heart hath talked of thee: Seek ye my face. Thy face, Lord, will I seek.'[5] 'Light is sprung up (or, is sown) for the righteous.'[6] 'The Lord hath showed us light,'[7] 'When thy word goeth forth, it giveth light and understanding unto the simple.'[8] 'The Lord is my light and my salvation.'[9] 'Lord, lift thou up the light of thy countenance upon us.'[10] Finally, immortality is a gift of the holy presence. 'Lighten mine eyes, that I sleep not in death.'[11] 'My flesh also shall rest in hope. For why? Thou shalt not leave my soul in hell, neither shalt thou suffer thy holy one to see corruption.'[12] 'When I awake after thy likeness, I shall be satisfied with it.'[13] 'He asked life of thee, and thou gavest him a long life, even for ever and ever.

For thou shalt give him everlasting felicity (or, make him a blessing for ever and ever), and make him glad with joy (or, in the presence) of thy countenance.'[1] 'The eye of the Lord is upon them that fear him, . . to deliver their soul from death.'[2]

It is through the Divine presence which went with the Israelites, that God manifested himself as 'the Saviour' of his people in Egypt.[3] 'He sent his word and healed them, and they were saved from their destruction.' That word was known to the Psalmist, to have been symbolised by the fiery and brazen serpent. The same tradition we have pointed out in the Apocrypha and in the Targums. The holy presence in the heart saves the soul.[4] For God saves by his name, by his right hand, by his finger.[5] He sends from heaven, to save man.[6] God causes his face, the light of his countenance, to shine, and man is healed and saved, if he will.[7]

This is the mission of the Word of God, of the wisdom of God, of the Holy Spirit, of the Holy Name, of the Holy Presence.

### 3. *Righteousness by Faith.*

The mission of the Divine Mediator and Saviour cannot be accomplished without man's co-operation. He is at liberty to invite the blessed of the Lord to enter into the tabernacle of his soul, or to let him stand without, asking for admission. If man will not be brought near to God, not even the Creator can do it. Dedication of the will, obedience, is therefore the road to heaven. The obedient, the righteous, are those who strive to follow the inward monitor, desiring by him to be led to purity in thought, word and deed. Because 'the Lord is righteous in all his ways, and holy in all his works,'[8] therefore man, created in the Divine image, is destined to become righteous and holy, like God Himself. The reward of the righteous is, that his inner light, the reflex of uncreated light, leads him from one glory to another. Like Job, man may 'put on righteousness, and be 'clothed' with the same.[1] His mouth shall speak wisdom,'[2] he will speak righteousness, that is, truth, instead of lying,[3] he will not hide God's righteousness within his heart,[4] but will show forth God's righteousness,[5] he will give thanks to the name, that is, to the holy presence of God,[6] for 'the salvation of the righteous cometh of the Lord.'[7]

Because salvation is a gift of God, bestowed on those who desire it, and in the measure they desire it, therefore the righteous man prays to God, who 'trieth the very hearts and reins:' 'Lead me, O Lord, in thy righteousness.' He knows, by experience, that his help comes of God, who 'preserveth them that are true of heart.'[8] He thinks not 'of his own heart's desire,' but desires God to be 'in all his thoughts,' that his Maker may 'prepare' his heart, and enable his ear to hearken unto his voice,[9] so that he may behold God's presence in (or through) righteousness,[10] and that God may convert his soul.[11]

### 4. *Atonement by righteousness.*

Sin is disobedience to the indwelling Spirit of God, to the law of God written within the heart. Therefore, all sin is selfishness, preponderance of man's will over God's will. Following his own way, man goes astray, and becomes estranged from God. Disobedience, or wickedness in thought, word and works, necessarily separates from God, unless union and communion be re-established by obedience, by the forsaking of sin, and by repentance for sin committed. Reconciliation, or At-one-ment, is the reward of obedience, the fruit of the Spirit. The centre of man's liberty, and therefore the origin and cradle of all sin, as also of consequent separation from God, is the mind of man. Even the perfectly obedient, the sinless man, cannot deprive a man of his liberty to sin. He may show to his brethren the way to such atonement and reconciliation, and thus urge them to follow him in obtaining the prize of humanity's high calling; but he cannot remove in others the possibility of sinning, nor can he change the commandment of God, who has promised forgiveness and immortality to the sinner who turns from his ways. Atonement is the reward of righteousness, that is, of obedience and repentance.

David and all other Kenite Psalmists, could, therefore, not refer to propitiatory sacrifice. Nor do they refer to sacrifices, excepting for the purpose of putting an end to idolatrous practices, which could not but increase and perpetuate the estrangement from God. 'The sacrifices of righteousness,' man's offering his will, his heart, to God, is the atonement proclaimed by David.[1] He could say: 'My strength faileth me, because of my iniquity, but my hope hath been in thee.'[2] 'Blessed is he whose unrighteousness is forgiven, and his sin is covered. Blessed is the man unto whom the Lord imputeth no sin, and in whose spirit there is no guile.'[3] 'I waited patiently for the Lord, and he inclined unto me, and heard my calling.' 'Sacrifice and meat offering thou wouldest not, but mine ears hast thou opened. Burnt offerings and sacrifice for sin hast thou not required; then said I: Lo, I come' in order to 'fulfil thy will, O my God: I am content to do it; yea, thy law is within my heart.'[4] The ear has been opened, and the true, the only efficacious sacrifice revealed. Therefore David could hope, that God would do away his offences, duly acknowledged, that he would open a sinner's lips, so that his mouth might show forth God's praise.

[1] Ps. iv. 5.  [2] Ibid. xxxi. 12, 16.
[3] Ibid. xxxii. 1, 2.  [4] Ibid. xl. 1, 8, 9; comp. l. 8-10.

'For thou desirest no sacrifice, else would I give it thee, but thou delightest not in burnt offerings. The sacrifice of God is a troubled spirit; a broken and a contrite heart, O God, shalt thou not despise.'[1] Away, then with all other sacrifices. 'Bind (or, chain, fetter) the sacrifice with cords, yea, even unto the horns of the altar.'[2]

### 5. *Universality of God's saving love.*

The Israelites, by their mixed origin, were peculiarly qualified to become the missionaries of mankind. The entire Noachian humanity was represented by the Shemites. The high castes were Aryans, or Japhetides, the low castes were the Hamites. Asia and Africa, the two cradles of mankind, were both united by, and formed an inherent part of Israel. History has shown, that the Israelites came alternately into contact with the most civilised nations of the earth, with the Egyptians, the Assyrians, the Greeks and the Romans. And when they ceased, for a time, to form a nation, they found asylums on every part of the globe. The Israelites are even now the representatives, and ought to be the missionaries, of catholicity.

Nothing could more favour the spread of truth, than the rivalry between Hebrews and Kenites. What the one kept secret, the other made known. Thus Divine mysteries were gradually promulgated among the high and low, the rich and poor of all nations. It mattered not, whether one nation chose the sun, another the moon, another a star, for the most appropriate symbol of the uncreated light, of the invisible God, if it was the Creator who was worshipped through the image of things created. This catholicity, in principle acknowledged by David, became the policy of Solomon's reign. But Sadducean reaction turned the boon into a curse, symbolism to idolatry.

David knew and proclaimed, that 'in all the world'

---

[1] Ps. li. 16, 17.   [2] Ibid. cxviii. 27.

the Lord and governor of Israel has established his 'excellent name,' his saving presence. To 'still the enemy and the avenger,' to prevent the machinations of the adversary, that is, of the Hebrews, who insisted on the hiding of tradition about 'the matters of God,' God has 'ordained strength (or praise) out of the mouth of very babes and sucklings.' The uninitiated, those who were not supposed to be 'sons of God,' but 'sons of men,' were visited. Since the time of Eli the Kenite line, the representatives of those who had not been admitted to power, the poor, had been made rich. The 'son of man' had been made lower than 'the angels,' that is, than the ministers of God, who approached his presence, but he was raised to a participation in that privilege, the son of man was 'crowned with glory and worship,' the dominion of the despised Kenites extended to all parts of the earth. Therefore David said, that he would give thanks unto the Lord 'among the Gentiles.'[1] 'The Lord looked down, and beheld all the children of men; from the habitation of his dwelling he considereth all them that dwell on the earth. He fashioneth all the hearts of men, and understandeth all their works.'[2] 'All they that put their trust in him, shall not be destitute.'[3] 'God reigneth over the heathen; God sitteth upon his holy seat; the princes of the people are joined unto the people of the God of Abraham.'[4] 'God be merciful unto us, and bless us, and show us the light of his countenance, and be merciful unto us; that thy way may be known upon earth, thy saving health among all nations.'[5]

Although these and other passages in the Psalms acknowledge the principle of catholicity, and notwithstanding the bold experiment of Solomon, to make the same the corner-stone of his polity, that principle and that polity never took root, or became indigenous in the land of Israel. The hostility between Hebrews and Kenites

[1] Ps. xviii. 50.  [2] Ibid. xxxiii. 13, 14.  [3] Ibid. xxxiv. 22.
[4] Ibid. xlvii. 8, 9.  [5] Ibid. lxvii. 1, 2.

was increased by the alliance between the Kenites in Israel and the Kenites in the land of Samaria. Separation and exclusion, like tares among the wheat, checked the growth of what David and Solomon had planted. We shall see, that the prophet Jonah rebelled against the Divine command, to make known God's 'saving health among all nations.'

### 6. *Angels and Spirits.*

If there is a life beyond the grave, the human frame must be exchanged for another in other spheres. The Psalms testify to the existence of good angels, and of evil angels. 'Praise the Lord, ye angels of his, ye that excel in strength, ye that fulfil his commandment, and hearken unto the voice of his words. O praise the Lord, all ye his hosts, ye servants of his that do his pleasure.'[1] From this it follows, that good angels, like good men, hearken unto the voice of God's word, and do it. Man is able to eat 'angels' food,' that is, 'food from heaven.' Whilst 'the angel of the Lord tarrieth (or, encampeth) round about them that fear him, and delivereth them;' among the disobedient Israelites 'evil angels' are sent.[2] David prayed, that 'the angel of the Lord' might 'scatter' and 'persecute' his enemies,[3] so sure was he of doing God's work.

### 7. *Injunction to pray.*

We have already pointed out, that the object of David, in writing Psalms, and thus inciting others to do the same, was to teach the people the necessity of prayer, and how to pray rightly. All these doctrines, which we have traced in Kenite Psalms, are not to be found in the Scriptures attributed to Moses, excepting that the Angel of the Lord is referred to in a few passages.

---

[1] Ps. ciii. 20, 21.   [2] Ibid. lxxviii. 25, 26, 50.   [3] Ibid. xxxv. 5, 6.

## CHAPTER X.

### KENITES AND PROPHETS.

The Prophetic institution in Israel was of Kenite origin. The Kenites had a prophet in the time of Moses, when the Hebrews had none. The Hebrew leader, allied with, and probably a pupil of, the Kenite priest, implored the Kenites, not to separate from them, but to be their seers and guides. Whatsoever Jethro advised, Moses carried out. Judah, the tribe with which the Kenites were incorporated, formed the vanguard of Israel, and two Kenites, because they had alone entirely followed Jehovah, by Divine command were pointed out and rewarded as patterns of obedience. Hebron, and Bethlehem, and Zion became Kenite possessions. The Kenite high priestly line of Ithamar having superseded the Hebrew line of Eleazar, prophetic schools were established, and prophets soon became a power in the State, giving out the oracles of God, without the symbolical Urim and Thummim. Thus Kenite tradition was engrafted on Hebrew tradition.

We have seen, that both traditions were of Eastern origin, and that they were essentially the same, in the time of Melchizedec and of Abraham. The Hebrews having been entirely Egyptianised, the Kenites, through Moses the Hebrew, commenced that restoration of patriarchal tradition among the Hebrews, which was always opposed by the Egyptian priests of the latter, who headed the party of zealots, later called Sadducees, the enemies of tradition and of catholicity. The fundamental principle of this Hebrew party in Israel, was secrecy and caste privilege, consequently, exclusion of the lower classes, and separation from other nations. Thus tyranny led to ignorance, and ignorance to the degradation of symbolism into idolatry. The importance attached to the prophetic office in Israel, ever since the accession of the Kenites to power, would be quite inexplicable, had they not been the representatives of the people, the exposers of its wrongs, the vindicators of its rights. As seers, as leading organs of tradition, the prophets could not have had so lasting and so reforming an influence with the people and the kings.

Prophets took the place of seers. We have the authority of Isaiah for asserting, that prophets were teachers of secret tradition, interpreters of the enigmatical sayings of the wise. 'The Lord hath poured upon you the spirit of deep sleep, and hath closed your eyes (the seers), and covered the chiefs, or rabbis, and thus each vision is become unto you as the words of a book that is sealed, which men deliver to one learned in Scripture, saying: Read this, I pray thee; but he saith: I cannot, I have no knowledge of Scripture.'[1] As the rabbis had scholars, it follows, that, already in the time of Isaiah, the threefold division existed of rabbonis, rabbis, and rabs, of doctors of secret tradition, of teachers and of scholars, forming an exact parallel with the ancient classification of the Magi, into 'destur-mobeds, mobeds, and harbeds.' In the time of Isaiah prophets took the place of the doctors of tradition, later called rabbonis.

The prophets represented the non-priestly, or popular element. Prophetic schools, or colleges, were established, under Kenite rule, in order to teach to people of all classes, what had exclusively been taught among the members of the Scribal corporation. This was done in the spirit of Moses, the prophet, who wished, that the gift of prophecy might not be confined to the corporation of

[1] Is. xxix. 10-12.

seventy elders, but might extend to the whole camp of Israel. It is for this reason, that Samuel is, in Holy Writ, classed with Moses,[1] and even pointed out, in some sense,[2] as the first of the prophets in Israel, although Abraham, and possibly the patriarchs generally are designated as prophets.[3] By the establishment of these lay-seminaries, or national colleges of theology, the right of the people was recognised to possess the key of knowledge, and to participate in the government of Church and State. Thus freed from priestly dominion, the people clamoured for a lay ruler. The demand was at first refused by the Kenite judge, who remembered, how the government of Moses was threatened to be undermined by the rebellion of Korah. Moreover Samuel's desire was, to establish a hereditary judgeship in his family. But his sons shewed themselves unworthy of this privilege, and ready to receive popular bribes. Then the elders of Israel demanded a king from Samuel. The prophet, priest, and judge had become old; with advancing age his vision seems to have failed him. He prayed unto the Lord. At first Samuel interpreted the Divine voice to discourage the clamour of the people. God was understood to say, that the lay ruler would be a greater tyrant than the priestly ruler had been. But having 'rehearsed all the words of the people in the ears of the Lord,' he received the command to 'hearken unto their voice,' and to 'make them a king.' The people were told, to go 'every man unto his city,' which they must have understood as the announcement of a popular election.

Before the tribe, and the family and the man were chosen by lot, the anointed and the anointer were by visions brought together. As in the case of Saul of Tarsus, and Ananias of Damascus, Saul, the son of Kish, was by revelation sent to Samuel, and Samuel was told of

---

[1] Jer. xv. 1; Ps. xcix. 6; Acts iii. 24.   [2] Comp. Num. xii. 6.
[3] Gen. xx. 7; Ps. cv. 15.

Saul's coming. Before Saul was anointed with oil, and received from Samuel the holy kiss of brotherhood, Saul was, at a feast, introduced by Samuel to thirty, according to the Septuagint and Josephus, to seventy Israelites. Nothing is said about the rank and office of these guests. But it is not improbable, that they formed a secret council of tradition, like that of the seventy elders, which Moses had instituted. According to the Vulgate version the Psalmist refers to the existence of a secret council, by the words 'secretly in the council.'[1] This hypothesis is confirmed by the recorded fact, that Samuel, while he was alone with Saul, bade him stand still that he might communicate to him the word of God. It cannot refer to what God had spoken to Samuel, respecting Saul's election; for the prophet had already acquainted him with this, and Saul had expressed his surprise that he should be the chosen one. If Samuel introduced Saul to a council of initiated, to men of wisdom, to the guardians of hereditary and secret tradition, then there can be no doubt, that the first chosen man of Israel was, before his anointing, initiated in all the mysteries of tradition. This was a compromise probably with the priests and Levites, and shows, that the lay, national colleges of prophets, were but elementary establishments, in which the greater mysteries were not taught. The council of elders, which later was probably merged into the Sanhedrim, or council of state, was to be consulted by Saul, which, however, he seems never to have done.

The feud between the Aaronites, which had brought so much misery on Israel, was intended to be ended by placing a layman above the priestly rulers. But it was soon found that Saul could not do without the support of one of the contending parties. His own tribe, and Zadok the Benjamite, pushed him on to renew the feud, whereby he lost his throne and his life. He was the last who seems to have consulted the Urim and Thummim. With the

[1] Ps. cxi. 1.

accession of the Kenite king of Judah, prophets were raised to the highest dignities, and the third king was a pupil of a prophet. But Nathan the prophet was also a priest. If he drew up the consecration prayer, nothing can be more certain, than that Nathan was not, like Zadok, the high priest, an enemy of the promulgation of secret tradition. Zadok's influence would be counterbalanced by Nathan, as long he lived. Beyond the inauguration of the temple, we cannot, however, trace him. He probably died shortly after that event. Then Zadok's influence must have become great. If so, prophets cannot have had the same share in Solomon's government, which they had in that of his father. Indeed, Solomon is not reported to have had any intercourse with prophets after the inauguration of the temple. But once a prophet, Ahijah, of Shiloh, addresses him, and it is for the purpose of announcing the division of the kingdom after his death. But we may connect this fact with Zadok's ascendancy. The priestly element overpowered once more the newly introduced lay element; tradition was again concealed, and the rise of prophetic power prevented.

Among the successors of Zadok, the Sadducees, Kenite influence was, as a matter of course, kept down, and the word of the Lord once more became scarce. The Sadducees never willingly suffered any prophets. But a compromise between the Hebrew and the Kenite sacerdotal and scribal line became necessary, after the separation of the ten tribes under Jeroboam. Both lines of the Aaronites, together with the priests and Levites, must have joined Rehoboam, as a non-Levitical priesthood is recorded to have been set up in the northern kingdom.[1] Because of this compromise, or in spite of the same, Sadducean influence prevailed, and during upwards of 200 years, between the reign of Solomon and that of Hezekiah, the voice of prophecy was silent. The silence of prophets, or the not recording and publishing of their

[1] 1 Kings xii. 31.

prophecies, may well have been caused, to some extent, by the tyranny of the Sadducees, then in power. At all events, it is a remarkable fact that the first attempt to put down idolatry coincides with the rise of prophets. The importance of this coincidence is heightened by the fact, that before the commencement of the captivity, the Kenite sacerdotal line of Ithamar was restored to power. We have seen that Seraiah, the martyr of Riblah, and ancestor of Joshua the high priest under Zerubbabel, belonged to that line, and that the uprooting of idolatry was always the mission of prophets. These rose and fell with the fall and with the rise of the Sadducees, the enemies of tradition, of which prophets were the most enlightened propounders.

We may connect the destruction of the brazen serpent by Hezekiah, with the influence of Isaiah, and also with the renewed acknowledgment of Kenite tradition. We have seen that David regarded the brazen or fiery serpent as the symbol of the Divine Word, of the Holy Presence. Moreover, Hezekiah was the first king who, after David, was not faulty, or 'failed not,' in the opinion of the Kenite high priest Seraiah, the contemporary of Josiah, the second and last king who was placed on a par with David.[1] And it is especially recorded that Hezekiah 'did that which was right in the sight of the Lord, according to all that David his father did.'[2] Another fact, which proves the revival of Kenite tradition in the time of Hezekiah, is his re-opening and purifying the sanctuary, that is, David's and Solomon's house of prayer, which had been closed to the people, and that Hezekiah 'set in order' the 'service' of the house of the Lord.[3] Again, it was Hezekiah's object, to re-unite the two kingdoms. To do this, he first communicated with Ephraim and Manasseh, the leading tribes of the Northern kingdom, with the inheritance of Joseph, of Caleb and other Kenite ancestors, inviting them to the house of the Lord at Jerusalem. As a

---

[1] Ecclus. xlix. 4.   [2] 2 Kings xviii. 3.   [3] 2 Chr. xxix. 35.

pledge of this intended union, Hezekiah married Hephzi-bah,[1] sister of Isaiah. According to traditional interpretation of Scripture, the prophet interpreted her name as a type of the 'delightful' union of Judah and Israel,[2] and the son of this marriage was called Manasseh.

Before the death of Hezekiah, Isaiah prophesied that a great change would soon take place among the rulers of God's house, that the then ruling high priest, the proud, idolatrous and despotic Shebna, the 'shame of the Lord's house,' was to be followed by the son of Hilkiah, by Eliakim, 'the servant of Jehovah.' Thus spoke the Lord through Isaiah. 'And it shall come to pass in that day, that I will call my servant Eliakim, the son of Hilkiah, and clothe him with thy robe and surround him with thy girdle, and commit thy government into his hand, and he shall be a father to the inhabitants of Jerusalem, and to the house of Judah, and the key of the house of David will I lay upon his shoulders, so that what he openeth none shall shut (or, seal), and that when he shuts, none shall open. Then shall I fasten him as a nail in a sure place, and he shall be for a glorious throne to his father's house. And on him hangs all the glory of his father's house.'[3]

We have the authority of the Septuagint, the latest pre-Christian authorised record of ancestorial Israelitic tradition, and likewise the authority of the learned St. Jerome, of Nicephorus and others, for thus interpreting the office of Eliakim and of Shebna. According to St. Jerome, the 'treasurer' means the overseer of the temple, he who is placed before it, who stands and ministers before the house of God, the person who 'inhabits the tabernacle.' This tradition of the Church is entirely confirmed by Scripture. For the high priest was always the treasurer, that is, the receiver of offerings in the temple,[4] and Josephus states that, in the time of Ezra, 'the treasurers were

[1] 2 Kings xxi. 1.     [2] Is. lxii. 4, 5.     [3] Ibid. xxii. 18–24.
[4] 2 Chr. xxxi. 10; xxv. 6, 8, 11; 2 Kings xxii. 4.; comp. Mark xii. 41.

of the families of the priests.'[1] The priest, or high priest Shebna seems to have introduced into, or suffered in the temple, chariots dedicated to the sun, such as were later destroyed by Josiah. For, of the latter it is recorded that he destroyed with fire 'the chariots of the sun,' and 'the horses, which the kings of Judah had given to the sun.' Because of these idols, Shebna was to be sent to 'a distant land, and there,' so prophesied Josiah, 'the chariots of thy glory shall be, thou shame of thy Lord's house. Thus do I drive thee from thy station, and from thy state shall he pull thee down.'[2] We suggest that this banishment and degradation of the high priest Shebna, took place at the time of Manasseh's return to Jerusalem, after his enlightenment and repentance in Babylon, in the year 676 or 673 B.C. For these reasons we assert, that the priestly 'robe,' and the priestly 'girdle' of Shebna, was to be transferred to Eliakim, and that 'the key of the house of David,'[3] which was to be committed to Shebna's successor, was 'the key of knowledge,' the key of tradition, to unseal and to seal, to bind and to loose,[4] to hide and to reveal.

This suggestion is confirmed by Isaiah's prophecy about Eliakim. 'On him hangs all the glory of his father's house, the offspring and the issue.'[5] As there is no doubt about Eliakim's 'father's house' referring to the Kenite house, and to the Kenite branch of the Aaronites, no interpretation of 'the offspring and the issue' can be correct, which does not connect the latter with the Messianic expectations of the Kenites. These hopes centered in Isaiah's prophecy about the 'rod' which shall come forth, spring up, or arise, 'out of the stem of Jesse,' and the 'branch' that 'shall grow out of his roots.'[6] The expectation about the offspring and the issue, that is, the

[1] Ant. xi. 5, 2.     [2] Is. xxii. 18, 19.
[3] Is. xxii. 22; comp. Rev. iii. 7; i. 13-18.     [4] Comp. Matt. xvi. 19.
[5] The keys 'were long, and made like a hook, and then laid upon the shoulder and worn there as the badge of an office.'—Lowth.
[6] Is. xi. 1.

rod and the branch, or according to the Septuagint, the
blossom, is to hang on Eliakim, as the key of David
hangs upon his shoulder.[1] A blooming rod of Aaron,[2]
an Aaronite yielding fruit, tradition not stagnating, but
fructifying, this promise was to be connected with Eliakim.
The 'rod and staff' which comforted David,[3] were emblems of the Holy Presence, proofs that God was with
him. The stock of tradition cannot bring fruit, without
the direct influence of God's Spirit. In the spirit of
David, a 'God with us' was promised and expected, a man
of wisdom, whose words were to be 'as nails fastened
by the master of assemblies, that are set up' by 'One
Shepherd.'[4] The key of David was to be restored.

Political events helped to accomplish, what Isaiah foretold about the change in the hierarchy. Between the
time of Moses and that of Solomon, who married an
Egyptian princess, Egypt is not referred to in Holy Writ.
But once this mysterious silence, of about four centuries,
is broken. In the war which Saul and Zadok carried on,
against David and Abiathar, it was an Egyptian who
assisted David in recovering what the Amalekites had
carried away. This incident is important, as it shows,
that the enemies of the Kenite king, and of the Kenite
priests, were supported by Egyptians. Shishak, or
Sheshonk I. had restored the empire, and attacked
Judah; probably at the instigation of Jeroboam. An
Ethiopian ruler in Egypt had allied himself with Hoshea,
the last king of Israel, and in the time of Manasseh,
Psammetichus I. (B.C. 664) took Ashdod, which was
probably held by the Assyrians. After this success, the
Egyptian king was supposed to be the best ally of Judah.
As in the time of Jeroboam and of Hoshea, the Egyptian
alliance was dreaded by the Eastern branch of Israel, by
the Kenites and their prophets. These observed with
horror, that Manasseh's son and successor was called

---

[1] Is. xxii. 24.    [2] Num. xvii. 8.    [3] Ps. xxiii.
[4] Eccl. xii. 11.; comp. 'the Preacher.'

Amon after the Sun-God of Egypt, that chariots and horses were dedicated to the sun, and that men of Judah were exported to Egypt, to serve in the army, or to be sold as slaves.[1] The Egyptian party, represented by Shebna, and by the high priestly line of Zadok, rose in power. In harmony with the principles of the Sadducees, prophets and their allies were killed, daily executions took place,[2] and no prophecies were recorded, during the longest reign of the kings of Judah. And yet Manasseh could hear Isaiah, Habakkuk, Jeremiah and Zephaniah.

But the Egyptian ascendancy was of short duration. Although the Assyrian invasion under Sennacherib (714 B.C.) had failed, Hezekiah's Babylonian ally, Merodoch-Baladan was subjected to Assyrian rule, Judea was attacked, Jerusalem probably taken, and Manasseh, we may assume with Shebna, was made a prisoner. Eastern influence was instrumental in opening the eyes of the idolatrous king. He believed no more in the carved images which he had made; but turned his heart unto Jehovah. On his return to Jerusalem, he put away the strange gods, and destroyed the idols and idolatrous altars he had set up. It was under these circumstances, we submit, that Eliakim was raised to the high priesthood.

We have seen that there are strong reasons for assuming, that the Hebrew, or Sadducean party in Israel, to which the high priestly line of Eleazar belonged, always had a leaning to Egyptian tradition, if not to Egyptian alliance; whilst the Kenites, headed by the Pharisees, and by the line of Ithamar, were orientalists by descent, tradition and association. Once more the line of Eleazar had to make room for the line of Ithamar. This assertion is, at the outset, confirmed by the recorded fact, that, in the beginning of Hezekiah's reign, about the time when Isaiah prophesied against Shebna, the high priest was Azariah, 'of the house of Zadok,' that is, of the line of Eleazar. Azariah's successor seems to have been

[1] Deut. xxviii. 68; Jer. ii. 14, 16.   [2] Ant. x. 3, 1.

Shebna, who is mentioned by Church authorities, as a high priest in the reign of Hezekiah ; and as the predecessor of Eliakim. Isaiah points to the change as one of policy, of principle. He announces the Assyrian, as a punishment for the treacherous alliance of Israel and Rezin, king of Damascus, against Judah, that is, against the Kenite house of David. Now, as the line of Ithamar was always allied with the house of David, it is certain, that Eliakim, the son of Hilkiah, belonged to the Kenite line of the Aaronites.

According to Nicephorus, and to the author of the Alexandrian Chronicle, Eliakim was a high priest, and the latter authority calls him Eliakim-Muselum, or Meshullum, and points him out, as the immediate successor of the 'impious' and 'lost' son, Somnas (Sobnas, or Shebna), whom he designates as high priest during the reign of Hezekiah. As the name Meshullam, or Shallum, was very common, it is probable, that Eliakim was the honorary name of Shebna's successor. This Shallum, called Eliakim, cannot have been a descendant from the high priest Shallum, son of Zadok, and ancestor of Ezra.[1] Eliakim was the ancestor, and thus one of the spiritual fathers, of Seraiah, the martyr of Riblah, whose Kenite descent we have proved, and who was, as we hope to render probable, the author of the Wisdom of Sira, of which the book called Jesus-Sirach, or Ecclesiasticus, is a Greek translation.

Isaiah, whose Messianic hopes were so directly connected with the Eastern branch of the Aaronites, must have been himself a Kenite. The deliverer whom he repeatedly foretells, was to be a Son of David; a Kenite, a man from the East, and not from the West. Under the rule of Shebna, who sided with the Egyptian or Western party, the land was darkened, but, as Isaiah prophesied, this darkness was to pass away in his time. Thus spoke the prophet, clearly pointing to Shebna, the 'shame' of

---

[1] 1 Chr. vi. 12, 13; Ezra vii. 2.

the Lord's house: 'As the earlier time has brought shame on the land of Zebulon and the land of Naphtali, so the later time shall raise to honour the land on the sea-coast, beyond Jordan and the gentile border of Galilee. The people that walketh in darkness, seeth a great light: upon them that dwell in the land of the shadow of death, light doth shine.' All war is to be at an end. 'For unto us a child is born, unto us a Son is given, and the government rests upon his shoulder. And he is called: Wonderful-Counsellor, the Mighty one of God, and the Father from everlasting (or from the beginning), the Prince of peace.'[1]

We suggest, that this child,—already then born, was not the son of Ahaz, Hezekiah, supposed to have been about ten years old, when Isaiah proclaimed this prophecy; nor, as might be conjectured, Manasseh, the son of Hezekiah, whose marriage with Hephzibah seems to have been connected by Isaiah with the realisation of Messianic hopes. The child of the prophet's hopes was Eliakim, son of Hilkiah, into whose hands was to be committed the government of the house of God, and on whose shoulder should be laid ' the key of the house of David.' As the son of a priest, if not of an Aaronite descendant, as a Kenite he would be called a Father from everlasting, or from the beginning, because of his connection with Melchizedec. Eliakim, the son of Hilkiah, was to be 'a father, to the inhabitants of Jerusalem' not only, but also to the whole Kenite 'house of Judah.' Or, if we accept another reading, Eliakim would be called the 'divider of the spoil.' For, by the substitution of the line of Ithamar, of Judah, for the line of Eleazar, of Benjamin, the spoils of the hierarchy were to be divided, as they had been divided, in the time of Eli, according to the prophecy on Benjamin, recorded in Genesis. Again, the expected Branch of the house of David would be called a mighty man of God, because God would be in him, and he would be the promised 'God with us.' By making peace be-

[1] Is. ix. 1-6.

tween the hostile parties in the Church, he would become the Prince of Peace.

It was in the spirit of Isaiah, that Origen interpreted the name of Eliakim, as meaning 'My God is risen,' and that St. Jerome explained the hidden meaning of Eliakim's name, as 'the rising God,' or 'the resurrection of God.' These interpretations, especially the former, were confirmed by the announcement of 'the day-spring from on high,' a word which points to the rising of the 'branch,' and of the sun from the East. So directly was the Messiah connected with the East, and with the Kenites, also in the next generations after Isaiah, that to the son of Hilkiah, one of the priests of Anathoth, the name of Jeremiah was given, which, we venture to suggest, has exactly the same meaning as the name Eliakim, given to the son of another Hilkiah. What Eliakim could not accomplish was to be fulfilled by Jeremiah, whose name implies that God has set up, has issued forth, has sprung up, has risen in man.[1] Once more this expectation was premature. But the great unknown prophet of the captivity could point to Jeremiah as a type of the Messiah.

This wonderful prophecy is divided into five parts, of which each has three verses, the prophet speaking alternately in the name of the Lord, in his own name, or in that of all other prophets, and in the name of the people. The first division describes, in general terms, the contrast of exaltation and debasement; the second pictures the low estate in its living reality; the third, the perfected servant of the Lord, as the sin offering for the people that had erred and transgressed; the fourth describes his shameful death, and his degrading grave; the fifth announces, that, 'although his life is offered as a sin offering, yet that he shall see seed, and continue to live, and the pleasure (purpose) of the Lord shall prosper through his hand; freed from the travail of his soul, he will satisfy his eyes; by his wisdom, he, my servant, the righteous

[1] Thus rose Heremias, or Sárameya, the dawn's son.

one, justifies many, and he bears their iniquities; therefore will I give him his portion (of the spoils) in a great multitude, and he shall divide the spoil with the mighty because he hath given his life unto death, and was numbered with the transgressors, though he bore the sin of many, and made intercession for the transgressors.'[1]

Isaiah died, and so did Eliakim, and yet the promise was not fulfilled. But the Messianic hopes were transmitted from father to son, from one high priest to another. Even after the captivity one of the sacerdotal houses or courses, was that of Jakim, which in some manuscripts is called Eliakim, thus showing, that the name underwent the same change which is marked by the names Eleazar and Azariah. The house of Jakim is in Chronicles implied to have been the sixth house of the line of Ithamar.[2] Among the successors of Eliakim was Seraiah, the high priest of Zedekiah. He was a contemporary, and possibly the son of Hilkiah, the high priest of Josiah, who found and presented to the king the hidden book of the law of Moses, in the time of Jeremiah the prophet. Thus a Kenite king, who lived after David's pattern, a Kenite prophet, and a Kenite high priest of great wisdom, co-operated in the restoration and fulfilment of Kenite tradition. This significant combination must be borne in mind, when we try to explain the mysterious revelation, in that time, of a Mosaic law, unknown to Josiah and to his high priest. It has been rendered highly probable, that, through the instrumentality of Jeremiah, a second law of Moses, a Deuteronomy was suddenly revealed, acknowledged and promulgated. In a certain sense at least, Jeremiah was the prophet 'like Moses.' But whether the written Mosaic law required amendment or enlargement, or both, it certainly was not closed at that time. The revelation made in the seventh century before Christ, may have contained more than what we find in Deuteronomy. The oral law of Moses was not

---

[1] Is. lii. 13-15; liii. Bunsen's 'Bibelwerk,' ii.   [2] 1 Chr. xxiv. 12, 4.

at once fully revealed. If Seraiah was the author of the Wisdom of Sirach, the book of Ecclesiasticus proves, and yet more so 'the Wisdom of Solomon,' how much still belonged to the hidden wisdom. The mysteries of secret tradition were gradually recorded, in accordance with the increased capabilities of the people, to understand and apply them.

To regulate the gradual crystallisation of tradition, to make known 'the good deposit' of the stream of tradition, was the office of prophets. After a long period of forced silence, this prophetic activity would lead to startling results. By the concealment of tradition, and by its non-application, the same had been lost, during the 200 years of Sadducean rule. But the Kenites, or Rechabites, with whom Jeremiah was connected, were by him held up as patterns of obedience to the people of Israel. If any persons had faithfully transmitted the secret tradition of Melchizedec, of Jethro and of Moses, this conservative party in Israel had done so. And as it gained in power, its leaders, the prophets, the possessors of Divine light, would promulgate what had been revealed to them by the light of truth, connecting it with what had been kept hidden from the people, and had been lost by the privileged classes, by the wise. The key of knowledge was gradually given to the unlearned, to the people, by the prophets. For this object they lived and died.

Josiah having put down idolatry, carrying out the injunctions of Jeremiah, the newly found law of Moses, based upon the verbal tradition of the lawgiver, was engrafted on the old. Either it formed the whole, or part of Deuteronomy, the language of which book is as different from that of the first four books of Moses, as it is like that of Jeremiah's prophecies. If the book of Ecclesiasticus can be shown to be a late Greek compilation and translation, by a Sadducee, of the Wisdom of Sirach or Seraiah, of Jerusalem, the contemporary of Josiah and Jeremiah, the Apocrypha of the Greek Canon is a valuable commentary on the events of this portentous period. In conjunction with the book of Jeremiah, it helps us to realise by what means the great pre-Babylonian reformation among the Israelites was accomplished, how the Hebrew or Sadducean power fell, and the Kenite or Pharisean power rose in its stead.

This reformation, the work of prophets, laid the foundation of the gradual annihilation of idolatry, during the Babylonian captivity. The first of the great prophets, Isaiah, already condemned the dedication of chariots and of horses to the sun, a practice which was common among the Persians soon after the time of the Jewish captivity in Babylon.[1] The name of Eliakim, in whom Isaiah's Messianic prophecies centred, proves, that the expected deliverer was conceived as a spiritual sun, as the rising of Divine light, which comes from above, as a 'dayspring from on high.' Not the symbol of that uncreated light of the soul, not the sun was to be worshipped, or introduced, as a symbol of Divine presence, into the temple; but the source of spiritual enlightenment, the tradition about which had originated, had issued forth, had risen, like the sun, in the East. For this reason the house of tradition was called the house of the chariot, the house of Rechab, over which high priests and prophets presided. The unknown prophet of the captivity whose prophecies are recorded in the last twenty-seven chapters of the book of Isaiah, raises his voice against the continuance of idolatry, whilst Ezekiel, in the spirit of Jeremiah, protests against the acknowledgment of 'statutes that are not good,' though promulgated in the name of God. It was under the influence of the Kenite high priest Joshua, that the new temple was built without any outward symbol. Had the Kenites remained in power, the idolatry of sacrifices would not have been re-introduced, and the house of prayer would not have been desecrated into a den of thieves.

[1] Xen. Cyrop. viii. 3-12; see the book of Esther.

Whenever the Sadducees, that is, the representatives of Egyptianised Mosaism, were in office, and ruled over God's heritage, the voice of prophecy was hushed, ignorance prevailed, and symbols became idols. But the stranger living within the gates of the Hebrews, the Orientalist, forming an inherent part of Israel, though despised, persecuted, and crushed, could not be annihilated and for ever silenced. During the last two centuries before the captivity, the Kenites gradually gained the ascendancy, prophets rose and idols fell. Egyptian influence became supplanted by Assyrian influence, and thus paved the way for the acknowledgment of the great Aryan ruler, called Cyrus, Koresh, or 'the Sun,' as 'the Anointed' or Christ of the Lord. Under his auspices, and those of his successors, the theocracy in the holy land was re-established, first under Kenite, and then under Hebrew or Sadducean rule. Vain attempts were made to undermine this anti-traditional and anti-catholic power. The Maccabees, identical with the Assideans of the captivity, maintained themselves in their position, and the Sadducean rule extended over five centuries. This long period commenced, as we shall see, with the final composition and revision of holy writ, and no further record of tradition was sanctioned by the spiritual rulers of Israel.

But the successors of Joshua and his contemporaries never forgot the promised deliverer, the servant of the Lord, 'the man whose name is the Branch.' The faith of Isaiah was engrafted on the guardians of Kenite tradition, with which we have connected the names of Melchizedec, of Jethro, of Samuel, of David, of Solomon, of Eliakim, of Jeremiah, and of Joshua the high priest. The fulness of time, which the son of Hilkiah, probably Isaiah's pupil, was destined to usher in, had been more clearly discerned by later prophets. What Isaiah had considered to be so near its fulfilment, though unfulfilled in the days of Joshua, was newly announced by Zechariah, after the rising of Cyrus, the Eastern Sun. The Holy

Spirit from above was to be personified by a chosen human being, by a son of man and son of God. Thus 'the sun of righteousness' was to arise, 'with healing in his wings.'[1]

Already in the time of Hezekiah, the commonwealth of Israel, symbolised by Isaiah as the woman, was with child, and was bearing a son, whom Israel, the mother, was to call 'God with us.'[2] Believing Israel looked forward to the bringing forth of her which was then travailing, to the birth of the ruler, whose issuing forth, whose rising, whose coming, has been ever since the aboriginal days of history, to the man who was to fulfil the promise made to Cain on the heights of Eden, that he should overcome sin, to the Kenite who, like David, was to be born in Bethlehem Judah,[3] and who was to be, what the names of Eliakim and Jeremiah foreshadowed, 'the dayspring from on high.'

[1] Mal. iv. 2.     [2] Is. vii. 14.     [3] Mic. v. 2, 3.

## CHAPTER XI.

### PARTIES IN THE JEWISH CHURCH.

THE high priestly or Aaronic lines of Eleazar and of Ithamar, since the settlement at Shiloh, respectively formed part of the tribes of Benjamin, Simeon, and Judah. We have traced the history of these tribes, from the time of Canaan's conquest to the captivity. Then the tribal organisation must have been nearly, if not entirely dissolved. All the greater was consequently the importance attached during that time to genealogies. The Aaronites must have known, that though Israel had to be, for a long time, without any national or theocratic organisation, yet that the national and theocratic spirit was so deeply rooted among the scattered Israelites, as to make them look to the time when they would be restored to independence. Whenever that time arrived, the Aaronic families would be prepared to gather the remnants of their two tribes, and these would establish a new theocracy in the land of promise. After fifty years, Cyrus, the Anointed of the Lord, permitted the return to Judea of those Israelites who wished to do so. Before we consider this great movement, the question arises, whether, during the captivity, distinct parties were formed within the scattered remnants of Israel.

The tribal and family distinction cannot have suddenly subsided. It had caused the two rival tribes, to which the Aaronites respectively belonged, to form opposite camps, bent upon the annihilation of the one by the other.

If the past of Israel's history had shown the alternate ascendancy of Benjamin and of Judah, the hope of such future ascendancy must have formed the object of a well-founded emulation during the captivity, among the descendants of Eleazar and of Ithamar. The Aaronic families would be carefully separated from the rest, and the representatives of the senior, and of the junior high priestly lines, would continue to form an hereditary aristocracy, whose heirloom was the tradition of the past, and the promised instrumentality in the fulfilment of the future. But herein lay the germ of schism. Tradition had been, for centuries, more or less exclusively verbal. Mosaic writings existed, but an important part of Mosaic tradition had not been recorded till the time of Josiah. The reformation, caused by the Apocalypse of Mosaic Apocrypha, had led to the abolishment of imagery, and had popularised the principles of secret tradition, which had been confided to the guardianship of the few initiated, among whom the representatives of the high priestly lines, and prophets took the foremost place. More than one copy of the hidden book of Moses may have been taken, and it is probable that, during the captivity, meeting houses or Synagogues were organised; also that the written law of Moses was there publicly read, and publicly interpreted.

But how much was to be read, and how was it to be interpreted? This could only be finally decided by the principal organs of tradition, that is, by the members of the high priestly aristocracy. The latter was represented by two rival lines. The separation of the ten tribes had caused all priests and Levites to side with the Southern kingdom. This was practically a compromise between the Aaronites, which was followed by the re-admission of Abiathar's successors to the high priesthood, in the person of Seraiah, the martyr of Riblah. The aristocratic and hierarchical organs of tradition would be led to a closer alliance, during the years of the scattering. They would agree, as much as possible, with regard to the amount of tradition which was to be promulgated. But an entire agreement of this kind was impossible. We know, that some time after the captivity, if not during the same, a party of Zadokites or Sadducees was opposed to the party of Pharisees or Separatists, the former being adverse to all verbal tradition, the latter favourable to the promulgation of the same.

If we have succeeded in showing that Zadok the high priest of the line of Eleazar, in the time of Solomon, belonged to the tribe of Benjamin, then we may safely assert that the Zadokites or Sadducees were originally separated by family, if not by tribal distinctions, from the descendants of Ithamar, who before the captivity had exclusively belonged to the tribe of Judah. As the return of Benjaminites and Judahites proves the existence of clans, of which the Aaronites were chiefs, we should be obliged to assume, if it could not be proved, that the Sadducees continued, after the return, to represent the principles of Zadok, the descendant from Eleazar, that is, the principles of the Hebrews, as opposed to those of the Kenites, represented by the line of Ithamar. We have reasons to believe, that during and after the days of Ezra, the tribal organisations, though not family distinctions, were discontinued. Yet party spirit, and party organisations, were at their height. We shall show, that the narrower views of some were opposed by wider views of others in the time of Ezra and Nehemiah; and that these governors of Judea were appointed by the Jewish Prime-minister, Mordecai the Benjaminite, and the Zadok, under circumstances which were adverse to the spread of tradition and catholicity. The Purim massacre, as we hope to prove, led to the ascendancy of those zealous defenders of narrow literalism and rigid formalism, who were represented by the Assideans during the captivity, and by the Maccabees after the return to Palestine. The further record of written tradition, and thus the gradual promulgation of verbal tradition, was once and for ever checked. With this stagnation, the Masoretic, or traditional, school is directly connected, and its memorial is the blank occasioned in holy writ, by the exclusion of all Scriptures referring to that period of nearly 500 years, which elapsed before Scriptures of 'the New Covenant,' were added to those which had been acknowledged as constituting 'the Old Covenant.'

Josephus mentions three parties among the Jews: the Sadducees, the Pharisees, and the Essenes. The Jewish historian gives no clue as to the causes of their origin, but he speaks of the two former parties having existed about a century and a half before the beginning of the Christian era, in the days of Jonathan the Maccabee (B.C. 143). At that time the Pharisees, opposed by the Sadducees, already formed a mighty party.[1] We hope we have proved the existence, in Israel, of a Hebrew, and of a non-Hebrew, Kenite or Rechabite stream of tradition, ever since the time of Abraham, and to have connected with the former the Sadducees, and with the latter the Pharisees. It cannot be determined at what time these two parties in Israel were distinguished by these names. But, as the Sadducees are called Tsedûkim, from Tsâdôk, the just, in the Mishna, and as Zadok belonged to the senior Aaronic line of Eleazar, to the Hebrew line, as distinguished from the Kenite line, we may assume as proved, that the Sadducees were the descendants of Zadok.

The Sadducees were members of the Council, and formed a kind of hereditary sacerdotal aristocracy. Josephus informs us, that, if they accepted office, which they did unwillingly, they were obliged to yield to the opinions of the Pharisees, as otherwise they could not have been suffered by the people.[2] Although both parties must have acknowledged, by compulsion or otherwise, the collection of Scriptures which Ezra and his associates revised, and partly composed, yet we shall see that the mode of inter-

[1] Ant. xiii. 5, 10.     [2] Ibid. xviii. 1-4.

preting holy writ was different, and that the verbal interpretation of the recognised text harmonised the same with the tenets of each party. For it is certain that the Pharisees admitted allegory, which the Sadducees rigidly excluded.

The Sadducees taught, that the free actions of men depend upon their will only, and that God exerts no influence on the latter, so that every individual is the sole originator of his destiny. They held, that the soul of man dies with the body, and that consequently there is no recompense or punishment after death, no continuity of individual existence, no life beyond the grave. Consequently they did not believe in other spheres and forms of individual life. According to their creed, there were neither 'angels nor spirits.' Josephus writes: 'The Sadducees take away fate entirely, and suppose that God is not concerned in our doing and not doing what is evil. And they say, that, to act what is good, or what is evil, is at men's own choice, and that the one or the other belongs so to every one, that they may act as they please. They also take away the belief in the immortal duration of the soul, and the punishments and rewards in Hades.'[1] 'The doctrine of the Sadducees is this: that the souls die with the bodies, nor do they regard the observation of anything besides what the law enjoins them, for they think it an instance of virtue to dispute with those teachers of philosophy whom (whose meetings) they frequent.'[2]

But the Pharisees believed, that the free actions and destinies of men are the united result of human liberty and Divine intervention. God himself has fixed every man's destiny, and man can no more evade the same, than he can interrupt the Divine plan of the world. Yet within the limits of this predestined fate, man moves and acts in the consciousness of his liberty, and his virtue is his merit. They believed in the existence of higher spirits; in the immortality of the human soul, and in the

[1] De Bell. ii. 8.  [2] Ant. xviii. 1, 5.

doctrine of future reward. Josephus writes, that when the Pharisees 'determine, that all things are done by fate (or providence), they do not take away the freedom from men, of acting as they think fit, since their notion is, that it hath pleased God to make a temperament, whereby what he wills is done, but so that the wills of men can act virtuously or viciously. They also believe, that souls have an immortal vigour in them, and that, under the earth, there will be rewards or punishments, according as they have lived virtuously or viciously in this life; and the latter are to be detained in an everlasting prison, but that the former shall have power to revive and live again; because of these views, and their conduct, they were popular.'[1]

The derivation of the name of the Pharisees, from *Perîshîn*, the Aramaic form of the Hebrew word *Perûshîm*, 'separated,' seems to denote that they were the dissenters in the Jewish Church, at some time or other. For but few of them led a retired life, whilst as the most numerous and influential sect, they came into so close a contact with the people, that it is not possible to explain this name as the designation of their separation from the rest of the community. On the other hand, the fact, that the Sadducees excluded all doctrines which were not actually inculcated by the writings attributed to Moses, goes far to sanction the supposition that they represented the, incorrectly so-called, conservative party among the Israelites. Josephus informs us,[2] that the SaddUcees rejected all those precepts, which were not contained in the laws of Moses, and which were only derived from tradition. This assertion is strikingly confirmed by the bringing to light, under non-Sadducean influence, of the hidden book of Moses, in the time of Josiah. The Jewish historian writes: 'The Pharisees have delivered to the people a great many observances by succession from their fathers, which are not written in the laws of Moses. And for

---

[1] Ant. xviii. 1, 3.   [2] Ibid. xiii. 10, 6.

that reason it is, that the Sadducees reject them, and say, that we are to esteem those observances to be obligatory, which are in the written Word, but are not to observe what are derived from the traditions of our forefathers.' In the same passage Josephus declares, that the notions of the Sadducees were 'quite contrary to those of the Pharisees.' Ancestorial tradition was the cause of schism. From this it clearly follows, that the Pharisees believed in the principles of a verbal tradition, transmitted to them 'by succession of their forefathers,' and that the Sadducees regarded the teachers of this verbal tradition as 'teachers of philosophy.' This the Pharisees, the believers in tradition, certainly were in a certain sense; for Josephus states, that the party of the Pharisees was 'of kin' to that of 'the Stoics,' as the Greeks call them.'[1] But nevertheless, and because of this, the Pharisees were 'supposed to excel others in the accurate knowledge of the laws of their country.[2]

We may here mention, that also among the Mahometans the acceptation or rejection of tradition or 'Sunna,' as the supplement of the Koran, became the distinguishing feature of the Sunnites and the Sheites. Yet even the latter believe so far in tradition, that they recognise a continued revelation. They believe, that as the Scribes and Pharisees, organs of tradition, sat in the seat of Moses, so the Jmams, the successors of the great prophet, are God's representatives on earth. During the first three centuries of Mahometanism, there existed the mystic sects of the Karmathi, who, by allegorical interpretation of the Koran, taught the hidden wisdom.

By the side of the Pharisees and Sadducees, Josephus mentions but one other party in the Jewish Church, that of the Essenes. All we know about this mysterious sect, tends to show, that they were the true guardians of secret tradition. Whilst the Sadducees, and among them particularly 'the teachers of the law,' rejected this tra-

[1] Vita, 2.      [2] Ibid. 38.

dition altogether, and the Pharisees, especially the Scribes, or rather 'the learned in Scripture,' admitted only so much of tradition as they considered compatible with their selfish and absolute rule, the Essenes formed a chosen band, or brotherhood, the recognised members of which strove to realise the grand object of their society, to carry out in their life and conversation the principles which they professed. The mysterious fact that they are not mentioned at all in Scripture is best explained by the assumption, that the Essenes were identical with the disciples of John the Baptist. They called themselves Essenes, and 'healers,' a name which well characterises the spiritual nature of their mission, and which may even directly refer to the Divine Word that 'healeth all things.'[1] Philo calls them 'physicians,' because they applied themselves to the cure of souls. They were organs of 'the holy Word,' which Divine power is already in the Zend-Avesta called the healer or Saviour of men.[2] Theirs was the religion of the heart, and therefore essentially a spiritual religion. It was mainly directed against the materialistic tendencies of the age. To be in a spiritual frame of mind, in a mould well suited to the influences of God's Holy Spirit from above; and to regulate one's thoughts, words and deeds, in accordance with this Divine visitor,—these were the leading principles of their faith and practice.[3] To be zealous in works of charity, and thus to manifest their love to God and to their fellow-creatures; not to despise poverty, but even to seek it, by the free distribution of their property; to abstain from bloody sacrifices; not to swear; not to keep slaves;[4] to teach by parables; to exemplify the doctrine of universal priesthood, and universal brotherhood,—these are Essenian principles, which were destined to receive the

---

[1] Wis. xvi. 12, 7.     [2] Vend. vii. 118-120.
[3] Comp. 1 Pet. ii. 5; Heb. iii. 6; 1 Tim. iii. 15; 1 Cor. iii. 9 f.; 2 Cor. vi. 16; Eph. ii. 19 f.
[4] Jos. Ant. xviii. 1-5; Philo ix. Op. 1. 457.

highest degree of Divine sanction in and through the
author of the Christian religion, who was, and was called
a 'Physician,' but whom few Essenes acknowledged.

The Essenes seem to have been famous for the healing
and also for the prophesying qualities of some of their
members. Without belonging to the Jewish Church, from
which they had separated, perhaps as the original Pharisees, they would be highly esteemed, and readily received
among the Jews of all classes and parties. Thus they
would convert some to their knowledge and to the
strangely materialistic practice [1] of their high spiritual
principles. Their reforming mission would be facilitated
by the liberal organisation of the synagogue, according
to which any gifted person might be called upon by the
ruler, or president, to interpret holy writ. In their own
meetings they even went so far, as to give leave to every
member of their higher classes of the initiated, to speak
in his turn. Sometimes the Essenic teacher withdrew
himself to secluded districts, where the people followed
him, to hear the word of God. Such a prophet would
strive to fulfil prophecy, by preparing in the wilderness
the ways of the Lord. The earliest Essene, whom we
know by name is Judas, of whom Josephus reports, that
he never failed in his predictions, and that many 'attended
upon him as scholars.' [2]

He writes, that Herod held the Essenes in special
honour, 'and thought higher of them than their mortal
nature required.' He adds the following anecdote:
'There was one of these Essenes, whose name was Manahem, who had this testimony, that he not only conducted
his life after an excellent manner, but had the foreknow-
ledge of future events given him by God also. This man
once saw Herod when he was a child and going to school,
and saluted him as King of the Jews.[3] But he, thinking
that either he did not know him, or that he was in jest,

---

[1] So opposed to Mark vii. 14 f.     [2] De Bell. i. 3; ii. 8.
[3] Comp. 1 Kings xi. 29-39.

put him in mind, that he was but a private man. But Manahem smiled to himself, and clapped him on his back with his hand, and said : "However that be, thou wilt be king, and wilt begin thy reign happily, for God finds thee worthy of it. And do thou remember the blows that Manahem hath given thee, as being a signal of the change of thy fortune. And truly this will be the best reasoning for thee, that thou love justice (towards men), and piety towards God, and clemency towards thy citizens. Yet do I know, how thy whole conduct will be, that thou wilt not be such an one; for thou wilt excel all men in happiness, and obtain an everlasting reputation, but wilt forget piety and righteousness; and these crimes will not be concealed from God, at the conclusion of thy life, when thou wilt find, that he will be mindful of them, and punish thee for them." Now, at that time Herod did not at all attend to what Manahem said, as having no hope of such advancement. But a little afterward, when he was so fortunate as to be advanced to the dignity of king, and was in the height of his dominion, he sent for Manahem, and asked him, how long he should reign. Manahem did not tell him the full length of his reign; wherefore upon that silence of his, he asked him further, whether he should reign ten years or not. He replied, "Yes, twenty, nay thirty years," but did not assign the just determinate limit of his reign. Herod was satisfied with these replies, and gave Manahem his hand, and dismissed him; and from that time he continued to honour all Essenes.'[1] This Manahem, or Manaen, may be connected with the person bearing the same name, who was brought up with Herod the tetrarch.[2] For the son of the Essenic prophet, or his grandson, or both, would naturally be highly favoured by him who continued to honour all Essenes.[3]

The Essenes lived principally in the region of the Dead

---

[1] Ant. xv. 10, 5.   [2] Acts xiii. 1.   [3] Comp. 2 Sam. xix. 37, 38.

Sea, where the absence of a rigidly enforced church government, favoured the gradual development of a more spiritual religion. Some members, probably a separate and more rigorous branch of the order, objected to matrimony. In the time of Josephus they numbered 4,000, and formed a religious society, the members of which belonged to one of three orders; the third was alone admitted to their religious meals and meetings. The property of every individual belonged to the society, which was highly respected because of the simplicity, soberness, and useful, as well as harmless, activity of its members. The Essenes were of opinion that the sacred records of the law cannot be understood without Divine inspiration. By means of an allegorical interpretation, they strove to harmonise the written law with their mystic or secret tradition, the general principles of which were known to all members. Like the Therapeuts they probably had books of their own. They studied and inculcated a hidden wisdom. Josephus writes, that before sunrise 'they put up certain prayers, which they had received from their forefathers;' and that 'they also take great pains in studying the writings of the ancients, and choose out of them what is most for the advantage of their soul and body.'

The Essenes formed a secret society. Josephus writes: 'If any one hath a mind to come over to their sect, he is not immediately admitted, but he is prescribed the same method of living which they use, for a year, whilst he continues excluded; and they give him a small hatchet, and the girdle and the white garment. And when he hath given evidence, during the time, that he can observe their continence, he approaches nearer to their way of living, and is made a partaker of the waters of purification; yet is he not even now admitted to live with them, for after this demonstration of his fortitude, his temper is tried two more years, and if he appear to be worthy, they then admit him into their society. And before he is allowed to touch their common food, he is obliged to take tremendous oaths; that, in the first place, he will exercise piety towards God, and then, that he will observe justice towards men, and that he will do no harm to any one, either of his own accord or by command of others ; that he will always hate the wicked, and be assistant to the religious ; that he will ever show fidelity to all men, and especially to those in authority ; because no one obtains the government without God's assistance—and that if he be in authority, he will at no time whatever abuse his authority, nor endeavour to outstrive his subjects, either in his garments or any other finery ; that he will be perpetually a lover of truth, and propose to himself to reprove those that tell lies ; that he will keep his hands clear from theft, and his soul from unlawful gains ; and that he will neither conceal anything from those of his own sect, nor discover any of their doctrines to others, no, not though any one should compel him so to do at the hazard of his life. Moreover, he swears to communicate their doctrines to no one, any otherwise than he has received them himself; that he will abstain from robbery, and will equally preserve the books belonging to their sect, and the names of the angels. These are the oaths by which they secure their proselytes to themselves.'[1] Oaths were forbidden only to the unlearned.

We are led to assume, that the doctrine of angels, which, as we shall show, had been more fully developed by the Jews during the captivity, formed a distinguishing characteristic of Essenic doctrine. Since the Sadducees did not believe in angels or spirits, this doctrine, and that about the Divine Word and Spirit, must have belonged to the hidden wisdom of Palestine.

Another marked peculiarity in the doctrine of the Essenes, was the doctrine about the pre-existence of the souls. The souls pre-exist in the purest ether, which is their celestial home. By a natural affection they are drawn towards the earth, and they are enclosed in the human bodies as in a prison. The death of the body causes the return of the soul to its heavenly abode. Then souls partake more directly of the Divine essence, that is, of the Divine Spirit. Since the latter was conceived as symbolised by fire, the souls of the righteous are represented in the Apocrypha as shining like fire-flies in the stubble;[1] as not yet having put on immortality, but as being transformed, as it were, from one glory to another. The Essenes can, therefore, not have believed in the resurrection of the body, but of the soul only; or, as St. Paul says, of the 'spiritual body.' This is positively asserted by Josephus. 'Their doctrine is, that bodies are corruptible, and that the matter they are made of is not permanent; but that the souls are immortal, and continue for ever.' Eternal happiness is the lot of good souls, and 'never ceasing punishments' of bad souls.[2] We find the same doctrine about the pre-existence and immortality of the soul in the Apocrypha of the Septuagint, and in later writings of that kind, all of which point, as we shall show, to a tradition of Eastern origin. These supposed relations between the spiritual and the natural led the Essenes to regard the flesh as a necessary evil, and consequently rather to discourage matrimony. But what is infinitely more important, these views about what is temporal, and what is eternal in man, seem to have been one of the causes, which led the Essenes to detest bloody sacrifices, and therefore to abstain from them altogether.[3] This also is a doctrine of the hidden wisdom, the origin and importance of which we have pointed out.

In conclusion, we give the remarkable passage in which Philo, who seems to have visited Palestine, refers to the Essenic principles of life and doctrine. 'The following three things regulate all they learn and do : love to God, love of virtue, love to man. A proof of their love to

---

[1] Wis. iii. 7; comp. Enoch i. 8.  [2] De Bell. ii. 11.
[3] Philo Mang. ii. 457.

God is the matchless sanctity of their entire life, their fear of oaths and of lies, and the conviction that God is only the originator of good, never of evil. They show their love of virtue by indifference to gain, glory, pleasure; by temperance and perseverance, and also by simplicity, absence of wants, humility, faithfulness, and straightforwardness. Their love to their fellow-creatures, they exemplified by kindness, absence of pretensions, and finally by the community of goods.'[1]

Such were the principal doctrines of the Essenes. They can hardly be regarded as having at any time formed a part of the Jewish Church, so opposed was their doctrine, and still more the practice of their religion, to the life and doctrine of the recognised spiritual rulers of the Jews. Josephus states expressly,[2] that they were 'Jews by birth' as if wishing to describe them as a dissenting party in Palestine. They do not appear ever to have joined in the temple service; and although they sent sacrifices to the temple, which they were most probably obliged to do by the Jewish Church authorities, yet Josephus expressly states,[3] that they themselves did not offer up any sacrifices in the temple, inasmuch as they considered more holy their own rites. The following passage from Josephus throws much light on their public life:—'They have no one certain city, but many of them dwell in every city; and if any of them come from other places, what they have lies open for them, just as if it were their own; and they go into such as they never knew before, as if they had been ever so long acquainted with them; for which reason they carry nothing at all with them, when they travel into remote parts, though still they take their weapons with them for fear of thieves. Accordingly, there is in every city where they live, one appointed particularly to take care of strangers, and to provide garments and other necessaries for them. . . .

[1] Mang. ii. 458.   [2] De Bell. ii. 8, 2.   [3] Ant. xviii.

They do not allow of the change of garments or of shoes till they be first entirely torn to pieces, or worn out by time. Nor do they either buy or sell anything to one another, but every one of them gives what he hath to him that wanteth it, and receives of him again, in its stead, what may be convenient for himself; and although there be no requital made, they are fully allowed to take what they want of whomsoever they please.'[1]

A party similar to the Essenes in Palestine, were the Therapeuts in Egypt. It has been supposed that the former were a branch of the latter society; but if we succeed in showing that the leading principles of both were developed from an early tradition, the connection between these sects, and likewise the difference in their habits, will be better explained. Our knowledge about the doctrinal principles and the rites of both these sects, particularly about those of the Essenes, is very incomplete; but it is probable that it was the main object of the Essenes to carry out their spiritualising doctrines in the performance of the daily duties of an active life; whilst contemplation and monastic seclusion constituted the principal characteristics of the Therapeut. About these Philo writes [2] substantially as follows :[3]—

Having given over their property to others, they left parents, brothers and sisters, wife and child, and retired from the turmoil of public life, into solitary places, principally to a gently rising ground, of healthy and secure situation, above the Lake Moeris. Each dwelling-house had a sanctuary, which they called 'semneion,' or 'monasterion,' where in solitude they gave themselves up to the mysteries of a life of dedication, and occupied themselves with laws, prophetic oracles, hymns, and other practices, which furthered knowledge and piety. Their

[1] De Bell. ii. 4; comp. Luke x. 4; iii. 11; Mat. x. 10; Mark vi. 9; Acts ii. 44 f.; iv. 32.
[2] Mang. ii. 474 f.
[3] Hilger's 'Geschichte der Häresien;' comp. Gfrörer's 'Urchristenthum,' ii. 280 f, &c.

morning prayer, which they offered up at the time of the sun rising, expressed the desire, that their souls might be filled with heavenly light; whilst, with the setting sun, they prayed that their soul, 'freed from the burthens of our senses and of the outward world, and entering into the depths of her innermost sanctuary, might behold the truth.' Occupied with the Holy Scriptures, they search wisdom, whilst applying a deeper sense to the holy records; for they believe that the words are symbols of a more deeply seated truth, which is only suggested, and not expressed. They also possess scriptures of wise men of old, of the founders of their sect, who have left behind many allegorical memorials. Led by these, they search after the hidden wisdom. Philo writes: 'The entire law is in their eyes a living organism, whose body is the letter, whose soul is (the receptacle of) a deeper meaning. As through a mirror, the reasonable soul sees, through the words of the law, the most hidden and the most extraordinary things.'[1]

'In the study of the holy books, they treat the national philosophy by allegories, and by the interpretation of the symbols, they guess the secrets of nature.' 'There are some who discover by dreams, during their sleep, by visions, the venerable doctrines of sacred philosophy.' 'Our souls owe above all, and almost exclusively, to the providence of God, that they are not without direction, and that they have an irreproachable and perfectly good Shepherd, who prevents our thoughts from going astray. It is necessary, that one and the same direction should guide us to one sole aim and end. Nothing is more insupportable, than to obey different orders. Such is the excellence of the pastoral functions, that they are justly attributed, not only to the kings, the wise, and to the souls that have been purified by initiation, but to God himself. He who affirms this (David), is not the first who came, he is a prophet whom it is well to believe, he

---

[1] De Vita cont. ii. Mang. 475. The same simile is in the Zohar, iii. 152.

who has written the hymns. This is what he says: "The Lord is my shepherd, I shall not want." Let every one say the same for himself, for this chant must be meditated upon by all the friends of God.'[1] This doctrine of the two natures of man, is thus farther defined by Philo in another passage: God 'deems it good, that the directing faculty of the soul shall be the work of the Master, and that what is to obey, shall be the work of his subjects.'

The same view is expressed in a work, probably written by a Therapeut of Egypt, who attributed it to the mythological Hermes Trismegist, the Greek name for Thot, the personification, the symbol of Egyptian priesthood, and therefore of their secret tradition. It is entitled: 'the Shepherd of Man' or Poimandres.[2] The author begins by stating: 'The sleep of the body produced the lucidity of the intelligence, my closed eyes saw the truth.' 'I thy God, the intelligence, am this light, anterior to the moist nature, which issues forth from the darknesses. And the enlightening Word of intelligence is the Son of God. They are not separated, for their union is their life. The Word of God lifted itself up from the inferior elements to the pure creation of nature, and united itself to the creating intelligence, for it is of the same essence. In life and light consists the Father of all things. A holy Word came down from the light to nature, and a pure fire extended itself from the moist nature to the heights. That which in thee doth see and hear, is the Word of the Lord: the intelligence is the God-Father. I believe in thee, and testify of thee: I walk in life and in light. O Father, be thou blessed. The man who belongeth to thee, desires to participate in thy holiness, as thou hast given him power to do so.'

On the days of the week the Therapeuts led an active and extremely simple and abstemious life. Before the setting of the sun, they partook of neither food nor drink,

---

[1] 'De Agricultura.'
[2] Parthey, 'Hermetis Trismegisti Poemander,' 1854.

but they postponed till the night the satisfaction of their corporeal wants, because they considered this gratification as a work of darkness, regarding only the occupation with wisdom as a performance worthy of the light. Every Sabbath they attended, festively attired, the Synagogue, when one among them read in the holy books. The interpretation is given by 'one of the most experienced,' and he 'passes over what is not (generally) known; for the principal parts are with them taught ' through symbols, with time-honoured zeal.'[1] The social meals they solemnised on every seventh Sabbath, as on the evening preceding the jubilee or high feast of the fifty, the Pentecost; because the number seven was by them held to be peculiarly holy. Women also took part in the festivity, principally elderly and spiritually-minded virgins, striving after the new birth, that is, to be born by the union between a god-loving soul and wisdom. Or, in the very words of Philo: 'They have chosen wisdom as their companion, ... and long not for mortal, but immortal progeny, to which only a god-loving soul can give birth, when the Father of the world pours out upon them his spiritual rays, and with them the knowledge of higher wisdom.' Some of the Therapeuts 'have so entirely given themselves over to the depths of wisdom, which richly nurtures their souls,' that they abstain from food for more than three days, and do not break the fast before the sixth day. The seventh day they regarded as the holiest feast, which they highly celebrated. 'Next to the soul, they allow also to the body a better care.' Their fundamental doctrine was, that 'from the lie issued forth the manifold kinds of evil, but from the truth the riches of heavenly and of earthly treasure.'[2] Therefore, Philo writes of the true Therapeuts, that 'they have devoted their whole life to wisdom and to the searching (thereof), according to the holy rules of the Prophet Moses.'[3]

[1] Philo ix. Op. 1. 12, 458.  [2] Mang. ii. 474 f.  [3] Ibid. 481.

Having prayed to God, that their meal may be well pleasing, they laid themselves round the table. In the beginning the most solemn silence prevailed, till at last one from among the meeting raised a question on any passage of Holy Scripture, and at once tried to answer the same, whilst all the rest listened with the greatest attention, manifesting with outward signs their approval, and also their doubts; at the close of this address, all clapped their hands as a proof of their satisfaction. Then all, one after another in due order, sang a hymn, and only hereupon was carried in, by the principal young men of the society, the table covered with the holy food, consisting of bread, salt, and hyssop; the drink was water.[1] After the meal followed the holy solemnity of the night; it consisted in a continuous singing of hymns, alternately performed by the choir of the men and of the women, and ending in a joint chorus of men and women, probably after the type of that melodious shout, which was performed at the Red Sea, by Moses and the prophetess Miriam, in order to thank God the Deliverer. At the break of morning dawn, they stood turned to the east, and on the rising of the sun they raised their hands towards heaven, and prayed for the bright shining of the inner sun, and of truth, and for sharpness of the spiritual eye; after this prayer, they retired again to their solitude and to their usual occupation.

There can be no doubt, but that the Pentecostal feast of the Therapeuts corresponded with the paschal feast of the Israelites,[2] as solemnised by Josiah. Not only the letter, but also the rites of the law, were regarded as the hieroglyphics of hidden mysteries. The true meaning of the paschal rite had therefore to be found out, by a spiritual interpretation of the same. It seems to have

---

[1] Recognising no other altar than the heart of man, and believing that through Divine enlightenment every man is capable of being his own priest, and to offer up his will unto the Father, these spiritual sects spiritualised the paschal rite which the written law prescribed.

[2] See Gfrörer, 'Urchristenthum,' ii. 294.

been this. Egypt, the house of bondage, was but a type of the body, the house of sin; the deliverance from the bondage of Egypt was, therefore, but a type of the deliverance from the bondage of sin and death. The terrestrial Shilo is but a symbol of the heavenly Shilo, the eternal haven of the soul, the rest which remaineth for the people of God. And as the Israelites were led, by the outstretched arm of Jehovah, through the Red Sea, in the face of their persecutors, so the soul of man is led, through the changes and chances of this life, to the paradise of God in heaven, by the Divine Spirit or Word, of which the cloudy and the fiery pillar, and the Shechina, were the type, and of which the soul is the predestinated dwelling-place. The rite of the passover would, therefore, be regarded by the Therapeuts as a typical memorial of the soul's deliverance from the prison-house of sin to the glorious liberty of God's children. Regarding as an abomination all bloody sacrifices, they did not acknowledge the elements of the Hebrew paschal rite, and instead of the lamb, they regarded bread and water as the proper elements of this mystic rite. Water having been substituted for the wine, which seems originally to have been used on such occasions by the adherents of secret tradition, and which beverage the Therapeuts despised, the new elements of the 'holy food' were no doubt regarded as typifying the 'bread' and the 'wine,' which were offered by Melchizedec, and which the Divine Wisdom, Word or Spirit 'mingles'[1] in the sanctuary of the soul.

To these earliest testimonies of Josephus and of Philo, about the Essenes and the Therapeuts, we add the after-apostolic notices of Epiphanius. 'The Essenes, who do all according to the law, make use also of other Scriptures by the side of (or 'later than') the law; but they discard most of the later prophets.'[2] Again, 'the heresy of the Essenes follows the policy of the Jews with respect to the

---

[1] Prov. ix. 5.    [2] Ep. ad. Ae. and Paul.

keeping of the Sabbath, and the circumcision, and the keeping of the whole law, but they condemn the books in like manner as do the Nazarenes.'[1] What books these were, and in what sense they were condemned by the Essenes in the fourth century, we may gather from the following passage, which we find in the writings of Epiphanius, and which refers to the Nazarenes:—'The patriarchs in the Pentateuch from Adam till Moses, who distinguished themselves by piety, they do accept as divinely inspired men, particularly Adam, Seth, Enoch, Methuselah, Noah, Abraham, Isaac, Jacob, Levi, Aaron, and Joshua the Son of Nun; but they discard the Pentateuch, not as if they denied Moses, or as if they did not believe that the law had been given to him, but they merely assert, that the (identical) law, which really had been given to him, is another than that which is generally used.'[2] The 'other' law of Moses can only have been the oral law, and we shall prove, that the former being partly ingrafted on the most ancient Mosaic records, after the finding of the hidden book in the temple, led to the composition or the revision of Deuteronomy the 'other' or second law. This tends to show, that the Essenes in Palestine, and the Therapeuts in Egypt, were acquainted with the principles of a secret tradition, which they believed to have originated with Adam, and of which Moses was the last revealer. The same view is developed in that remarkable work of the first, second and later centuries, A.C., which was originally entitled 'The Preaching of Peter.'

What Josephus thought of the Therapeuts, may be inferred from the manner in which he refers to the mode in which Moses communicated the revelations with which he had been favoured. Moses only recognised such an observance of the laws which he had given them 'by Divine suggestion,' as was supported by meditation 'upon

[1] Haer. i. 19.  [2] Ibid. i. 18.

the wisdom that is in them.'[1] Even Moses saw 'through a glass darkly,' or, more literally, he saw enigmatically in a mirror. What he saw enigmatically, he recorded, or he orally transmitted symbolically. The Mosaic writings are therefore the hieroglyphics of the hidden wisdom. 'Everything is adapted to the nature of the whole, whilst the lawgiver most adroitly suggests some things as in a riddle, and represents some things with solemnity, as in an allegory; but whenever it may be expedient to make a straightforward statement, he expresses things clearly and definitely. Those, however, who desire to dive into the causes of each of these things, will have to use much and deep philosophical speculation.'[2]

It is highly probable that the doctrine of the Essenes and of the Therapeuts was identical. Both despised bloody sacrifices. The house of God had, by the priestly caste, been turned into a revenue-office and a slaughter-house. The representatives of the universal priesthood, of worship in spirit and in truth, therefore absented themselves altogether from the temple, and were, what we should now call, dissenters. In both sects, community of goods was the established rule. Marriage seems to have been discouraged, if not actually forbidden. Slaves were not suffered. The members of both orders wore the same, or at least a similar kind of white garment,[3] during summer, and one of a coarser and warmer substance during winter. They abstained from meat, and they ranged in the society according to the time of membership. Overseers rigidly maintained discipline and order. Prayers were regularly held in the morning and in the evening, the faces turned towards the sun. The Sabbath was more strictly observed than among the Jews; and, finally, both

[1] Ex. xxxiii. 12.   [2] Ant. iv. 8, 2; Pref. to Ant.
[3] According to Clement of Alexandria, Christians were ordered to wear 'simple garments of white colour' (Paed. iii. 11). Josephus records (Ant. iv. 8, 11) that Moses forbade garments 'made of woollen and linen,' which were appointed for priests only. The white garments of the Essenes therefore typify the universal priesthood.

orders had mystical meals. It cannot be proved when either of these brotherhoods was first organised. Nor is this important, if their common origin is certain. Eusebius [1] identifies the Therapeuts with the Christians. We may here briefly refer to the probable identity of the Essenes and Therapeuts with the Elkoshites of Galilee, to whom the prophet Nahum belonged. The name Essenes is derived from *Chasah*, to see, from which Chosim, seers. The Elkoshites may be derived from *Elxai*, which means, 'the magician,' that is, the man of (spiritual) power, or 'maga.'

Already, in the time of Jeroboam, the two sacerdotal lines, respectively connected, as they probably were, with the Sadducees and with the Pharisees, that is, with Hebrews and Kenites, had so far made a compromise, that they both sided with the Southern kingdom. Some time after the return from Babylon the Sadducees and Pharisees are first mentioned. Both filled the high priestly office, though we have shown that this depended on the rule of the one or of the other party. But a compromise had been made. Both parties agreed to accept the text of Scriptures, as finally settled by Ezra, and not to acknowledge the authority of anything that might be said or written in future. This compromise would force the Essenes to separate themselves from the Jewish Church. How early this was done, cannot be determined. They were theoretically the true guardians of Davidic tradition. Their regard for prophecies, their culture of the prophetic element, can only be thus explained; for the prophetic office was a Kenite institution. But their rites were, in part, contrary to the spirit of Christianity.[2] The Essenes became Christians, but Jesus was not an Essene.

---

[1] H. E. ii. 17.   [2] Comp. Mark vii. 15, 23; Matt. xi. 19.

## CHAPTER XII.

### SECRET TRADITION.

WHATEVER may have been the origin of the secret or hereditary tradition among the Jews, its early existence cannot be doubted. Yet it has hitherto been treated merely as a theory, and not even the Jews have done more than to establish a not-proven probability. It is true, that Josephus refers only to the 'observances' which were 'not written in the laws of Moses,' and which had been transmitted to the Pharisees 'by succession from their forefathers.' But such succession necessarily implies an organisation for the preservation of a verbal tradition. To an unwritten tradition Josephus directly refers, when he states, in one passage already quoted, that Moses has in his writings suggested some things as in a riddle, and represented others in an allegorical form, for the purpose of hiding from the multitude the 'philosophy' of his teaching. Again, we are expressly told, that the Sadducees objected to allegory, and regarded the Pharisees as 'teachers of philosophy,' whilst the Essenes and Therapeuts were seeking after the hidden wisdom. Again, Philo states, that the Jews were instructed in their synagogues at Rome, in the philosophy of the Fathers, that is, in the verbal tradition.[1] For, in another work he shows, that the secret tradition was the standard for the interpretation of holy writ. 'Having learned also these things from the sacred books, . . . and from some of the

[1] Leg. at Caj. 1001, 4.

elders of the nation. For they interwove that which was said, with that which was read.'¹

Whether or not we assume, that Moses formed an organisation, that of the seventy elders, for the restricted transmission of the 'traditions of the elders,' of the oral law, in contradistinction to the written law, we may safely conjecture, that the peculiar manner in which God revealed himself to Moses, led to an exceptional mode of transmitting some of those mysteries which were revealed by him to the Hebrews. It was a distinction, that God did not reveal himself to Moses in ' riddles,' or dark speeches;² and the lawgiver may have been compelled, as Josephus implies, to hide many things, which the Israelites could not then bear. 'Dark sayings of old,' and 'dark sayings of the wise,' are specially referred to in the books of Job and Proverbs, as also in the book of Psalms.³ One of the Psalmists who does so, Asaph, 'the seer,' is pointed out in the Gospel as a 'prophet,' because he referred to the revelation by Jesus Christ of those things which had been kept secret or rather 'in silence,' since the world began.

Here we may also refer to the book of Jesus Sirach, called Ecclesiasticus, where the fathers of the Jews are praised, for having been inspired by God's great power from the beginning; for having 'declared through prophecies,' for having been leaders of the people by their counsels and by 'intelligent Scripture interpretation for the people;' and finally for the 'wise doctrines,' which their instruction contained.⁴ Interpretations of Scripture for the people, are especially referred to in the book of Nehemiah, where it is stated, that the interpreters (targumists) 'gave (or pointed out) the sense,' and 'interpreted' the book of the law, whilst reading it.⁵ Such interpreters were the Scribes, or the learned in Scripture, the Soferim, some of whom are supposed to have formed the great

---

[1] De Vitâ Mos. i. 2; Mang. 81.  [2] Num. xii. 8.
[3] Prov. i. 6; Ps. xl. 4; lxxviii. 2.  [4] Ecclus. xliv. 1-4.
[5] Neh. viii. 8.

synagogue, of which Ezra was the president, whilst Daniel, Haggai, Zechariah, Malachi, Nehemiah, and Mordecai, according to Jewish tradition, were among its members. It is very probable, that originally the Scribes were only chosen among the priests and Levites. For the prophet Malachi declares, that 'the priest's lips shall preserve knowledge, and teaching shall be sought from his mouth, for he is a messenger (apostle) of the Lord of hosts.'[1] At all events, this passage refers to the priests, as appointed guardians of secret tradition. As it is certain that the oral law was the interpreter of the written law, the Scribes, or rather, 'the learned in Scripture,' who had to investigate, to search, to dive into the hidden mysteries of the written law, can hardly have been laymen. It is only in the last centuries before the Christian era, that we hear of priests and laymen being sent as interpreters of holy writ to Alexandria. Yet, from the earliest times, the lay or popular element was represented by Kenites. Both Hebrews and Kenites had Scribes, or men learned in Scripture. To be, like Ezra, 'a ready Scribe in the law of Moses,'[2] was to 'seek,' to investigate 'the law of the Lord, and to do it, and to teach in Israel statutes and judgments.'[3] Already in the time of David and Solomon, Scribes are mentioned,[4] and we shall show, that they were men who interpreted the law, according to the principles of verbal tradition. 'The interpretation (midrash) of the prophet of Iddo,' which is referred to in the second book of Chronicles,[5] has not been transmitted to us; but it furnishes a proof of the early existence of Scripture interpreters or targumists. The Scribes of Hezekiah committed to writing those proverbs, that is, dark sayings, with which the name of Solomon was associated. Whether or not they all originated with him, they were known, or supposed to have been known, in the time of the son of David. If so, and as we are not told that

---

[1] Mal. ii. 7.     [2] Ezra vii. 6.     [3] Ibid. vii. 10.
[4] 2 Sam. viii. 17; xx. 25; 1 Kings iv. 3.     [5] 2 Chr. xiii. 22.

the Scribes 'copied,' but that they wrote them, these short sententious maxims must have been transmitted by verbal tradition, at least from the time of Solomon.

The Scribes, at least those among the Hebrews, formed a secret society, the brotherhood of Chaberim or associates. Having passed their novitiate, and having by an examination proved themselves sufficiently instructed in the tradition of their forefathers, they were called 'chosen ones.' The same name of associates was given to all those 'who were initiated in the mysteries of the hidden wisdom.'[1] The Scribes correspond to the privileged class of the Ukala, or initiated, among the Druses in our days. Their importance must always have been considerable, especially in those early times, when there were few Scriptures, and when those which did exist, were confided to the guardianship of a few privileged persons, in whose power it lay to hide them from the public as much and as long as they thought fit to do so. Like a prophet, 'a teaching priest' was an exception. We have no proof of Scriptures having, before the captivity, been publicly read at regular intervals. And when they were read to the people, the interpreters were, next to the prophets, the persons most esteemed. Already in the time of Ezra, 'the words of the Scribes' were honoured above the law, and even Jesus himself, whilst excluding the Sadducees, who rejected tradition, ascribed to the Scribes and Pharisees the honoured mission of sitting in the seat or pulpit of Moses. Organs of tradition were alone regarded as authorities in matters of doctrine.

A regular organisation for the oral transmission, and thus for the preservation, of secret tradition, must have existed before the times when Scriptures were first composed. Like Eliphaz in the book of Job,[2] Asaph, the prophet, refers in the plainest terms to an unbroken succession of organs of tradition, dating from the Patriarchal and earlier times. The 'dark sayings of old,' the pro-

[1] Zohar iii. 157, 158, &c.     [2] Job xv. 17, 18.

verbs, which he utters in his sublime Psalm,[1] constitute
that which he and others had 'heard and known.' Their
fathers had told them, so that their ears would hear, in
what words their ancestors did proclaim 'the praises of
the Lord, and his strength, and his wonderful works that
he hath done.' What had been confided to the ears of
Asaph and his associates, they have fixed in their memory,
so that they knew what they had heard. If this knowledge
had not been confided, under restricting obligations,
to a selected few, to a privileged class, to a corporation,
then there would have been nothing to hide from the
public. Yet, before the time of David, edifying knowledge
was hidden from the people.

The senior brother of Aaron's ancestor, Gershom, represented
in the time of David by Asaph the seer, authorises
us to assert, that the 'law' of God, transmitted from
father to son, was, partly at least, a verbal law. God
'gave statutes in Jacob, and judgments in Israel, which
he commanded our fathers, that they should make them
known to their children; that the generation to come
might know them, the sons which should be born, that they
might grow up and might narrate them to their children;
that they might set their hope in God, and not forget the
works of God, and keep his commandments, and might
not be as their fathers, a stubborn and disobedient generation,
a generation that did not direct its heart (to God),
and whose inward parts were not faithful towards God.'

Not a word is said, in this passage, about Scriptures.
The tradition is to be narrated, recounted, related by
word of mouth. Therefore Asaph says, about the tradition
of the fathers, in his name and in that of his associates:
'We will not hide them from their children,
proclaiming (by word of mouth) to the coming generation
the praises of the Lord, and his strength, and his
wonderful works that he hath done.' The knowledge of
God's ways and acts is necessary to a true worship of God.

[1] Ps. lxxviii.

If the people had known the former, they might have known the latter. But the 'ways' of God had only been made known to Moses, and the acts of the Lord, though known to the people, were not rightly understood. Therefore the prophet calls upon them to incline their ears to the words of his mouth. What he knows they do not know. At this time the people cannot have known, that which was unknown to Hilkiah the high priest, that is, the Mosaic book of the law, then found in that temple, the building of which Asaph may have lived to see. But, whatever Scriptures were known to the people in the time of David, they required to be interpreted by the light of secret tradition.

Without the renewing activity of the prophets, tradition must have been more or less vitiated. The prophets' office was, as we have seen, to restore, to interpret and to apply the principles of oral tradition, and thus to prepare the people for the acceptation of new revelations, from that God who alone knows the future. God spoke in all ages through the mouth of his prophets, and yet certain things had been kept in silence since the world began. The prophets alone had a full and clear knowledge of the things kept hidden from the people. What the fathers had orally, or partly by writing or symbolic signs, transmitted from one generation to another, and what the prophets had revealed,—this constituted the most precious inheritance of Israel, that is, the secret tradition, the source of all knowledge about heavenly things. The family and the tribe became the cradle of that tradition. In every generation some men were specially revered as conveyancers, if not as revealers of Divine mysteries. These chosen ones, perhaps at times also the chiefs of the fathers, and often the chiefs of the tribes, were considered as landmarks of the past, as new starting points, as epochs of tradition. The representatives of hereditary tradition formed the generations of the elect, ' the princes of God.'

The initiated must have understood in this sense, what is recorded in Genesis about the 'generations,' the 'tholedoth.' The names which are enumerated as generations, and to which we have referred, mark the successive organs of tradition, whether these names are regarded as referring merely to individuals, or to tribes also. Among the Israelites, as among the Egyptians, the Arabs, the Greeks, and other nations, it was considered essential to preserve exact lists of generations, in the form of genealogies. Not the direct sonship, but the general descent, was to be pointed out, with a view to political events, especially to tribal migrations, and to territorial divisions, which were the necessary consequence of such migrations. Thus the principal migrations of the organs of tradition were fixed in the memory of the initiated, and engraven on blocks of wood, on stones, on leaves and skins, in order to direct the attention of future generations to their descent from a common ancestor, to the origin of their tradition. Herein, and not in chronology, lies the value of genealogies. The doubtful genealogy of Benjamin, and whether Ephraim and Manasseh are in Genesis enumerated as sons instead of grandsons of Jacob, is unimportant. Jacob was the founder of the nation. He represented the promise, connected with the name of Abraham, that in his seed all the nations of the earth were to be blessed, and that his seed should possess the land. It was Jacob in and by whom these two promises, marking the distinct mission of Israel, as the people of catholicity, were typically fulfilled. He had twelve sons, and these became the chiefs of tribes, the patriarchs of Israel. At the time of the migration of Jacob's family into Egypt, the importance of genealogical descent was heightened, by the unavoidable contact of the sons of Jacob and their families, with a powerful and highly cultivated nation. Let the Israelites preserve the ancestorial institution of tribes, brotherhoods, and families. Not that such divisions were peculiar to them, but they were the necessary framework of the transmission of tradition.

From the days of Abraham, if not before, the generations of tradition had transmitted their hereditary knowledge about the creation, that is the renewing, the 'bará,'[1] of the heavens and of the earth. The records of this traditional succession were likewise called generations, the design was connected with the designer. But the earliest genealogies of the Israelites were lists not only of lineal, but also of collateral descendants from an aboriginal ancestor. These lists were local, if not personal centres for the transmission of tradition. In some instances a name, like that of Shem, represents an astronomical period.[2] During the long interval of 500 years Shem lived, according to recorded tradition, as the founder of a locally circumscribed corporation, the chosen members of which transmitted the tradition of their forefathers, in an unbroken succession, from one generation to another. As one day tells its tale to another, and as one night certifieth it to another, so the generations of tradition were like rocks surrounded by the storms of ages. They represented the crystallised deposit of tradition. Exposed though they were to the influences of time, buried as they had been in the alluvial soil of an ever-varying surface, they survived, like the granite, the action of all the powers of the elements. They engrafted on the minds, if not in the hearts of their generations, a good deposit, and what they committed to their successors was faithfully kept by them, sufficiently pure in substance to be understood, interpreted and applied by the spirit of prophecy in future ages.

The genealogical records in the book of Genesis can, even now, be shown to have had in view tribal migrations, and not the mere descent of the Sons from the Fathers.

[1] Comp. Ps. civ. 30, where the same word refers to the renewing of the face of the earth.
[2] Bunsen's 'Ægypten's Stelle in der Weltgeschichte,' last vol., p. 305.

Thus the sons or generations of Shem are geographical names, marking the successive settlements from Elam, on the Persian gulf, to Aram, on the Mediterranean. And it is more than probable, that the names Adam and Enos were originally generic terms, that Noah refers to the period of the Flood, and that Shem, Ham and Japhet point, not only to astronomical periods, but to contemporaneous settlements after the Flood. So strong was the belief, that the tradition of the fathers was divided from their antediluvian ancestors, that these and other names, were in after times regarded as having belonged to individuals only. The chiefs of the fathers, in every generation, were not solely remembered for their personal deeds, but for the mysteries of which they were, by descent or by election, the living stewards. They were messengers, apostles of the ever renewing and revealing Spirit of God. It was the sublime mission of the stewards of tradition, not only to protect, but to trade with the treasure entrusted to them. Their calling was Divine. They were the fathers of the faithful, and the friends of God.

We cannot prove, how early the hereditary members of the Scribal corporation were divided into scholars, teachers and masters, or chiefs of verbal tradition. The existence of such an organisation, during, if not before the Babylonian captivity,[1] is implied by the distinction of the 'rab,' the 'rabbi' and the 'rabboni' or 'rabban,' which offers, as already observed, an exact parallel to the organisation of the wise men, or Magi, of the East, among whom there were 'harbeds,' and 'mobeds' and 'desturmobeds.' Those who were especially gifted with the prophetic power, would be naturally chosen as chiefs or fathers of the tribes. These chiefs may already, in earlier times, have formed a college under the presidency of one or two superiors, whose names would be recorded in the genealogies of tradition. It is an historical fact, that,

---

[1] Is. xxix. 10-12; comp. Matt. xxiii. 34.

more than one century before the commencement of the Christian era, the Scribal succession was marked by two names, which designated the Scribal 'pairs,' of which five are recorded by trustworthy tradition. These pairs of Scribal succession are supposed to have been formed by the Nasi, or President, of the Sanhedrim, that is, by the high priest, or by the rector of the Great College, and by the Vice-president the 'father of the House of Judgment,' the Ab-beth-din, for the time being. Although in the time of the Maccabees, the high priest was the Nasi or president, since both titles are given to Judas Maccabee,[1] yet we cannot be sure that this was always necessarily the case. We have stated, on what grounds we base our hypothesis, that the Scribal pairs represented the separate Scribal organisations of the Kenites and of the Hebrews. The first pair whose names have been transmitted to us was formed by Joses ben-Joezer, a priest, and Joses ben-Jochanan, who held this position from about 140 to 130 B.C. Among the later representatives of Scribal tradition were Shemaiah, Abtalion and Hillel, whose grandson and successor was Gamaliel. Of this remarkable man it is here sufficient to state, that he stood in the same relation to St. Paul, as Aquila stood to Apollos.

We hope to prove, by unassailable documentary evidence, that the Scribal pairs were the recognised supreme organs of a secret tradition, which can be traced back to the commencement of the Babylonian captivity, and to the days of Solomon, thus rendering it certain, that the Jewish theory about a secret tradition from the days of Moses, was based upon this fact.

The verbal tradition in Israel, in later times called 'Cabbala,' that is, what was received, comprised till towards the time of Mahomed, in its general sense, everything that was not contained in the written law. It originally constituted the oral law, which was received in course of time by the Pharisees and the Essenes, and rejected by the

---

[1] 1 Macc. xv. 2.

Sadducees. We have seen, and shall fully establish, that, on the return from the captivity, the Jewish Church was divided into Traditionalists and Anti-traditionalists. The statement of St. Irenæus, preserved to us by Eusebius, shows, that few, if any authoritative Scriptures had been preserved, in their original form, at the time of the return to the Holy Land. He draws a parallel between the revising activity of Ezra, and that of the Seventy, the latter being, as we shall see, the representatives of Scribal tradition. St. Irenæus writes: 'And there is nothing wonderful in God having worked this (the Greek Version of the Hebrew Canon); for even when, during the captivity of the people under Nebuchadnezzar, the Scriptures had gone to ruin (perished); and when, after seventy years, the Jews returned into their own country, then, in the time of Artaxerxes, king of the Persians, did he (God) inspire (breathe upon) Esdras the priest, of the tribe of Levi, again to go regularly through the words (written and orally transmitted) of the Prophets, that had gone before, and to re-establish (restore) among the people the legislation of Moses.'[1]

It is customary, entirely to discredit this positive statement of St. Irenæus, uncontradicted though it be by any of the Fathers of the Church. No reason is given, why an assembly of Scribes and others, forming what was afterwards called 'the great synagogue' in the time of Ezra, may not have been instituted, for the purpose of revising the text of the Scriptures, according to the principles of oral tradition. Whether all the Scriptures had been destroyed during the Babylonian captivity, which we consider absolutely incredible; whether they had till then been preserved only in the form of the Samaritan Pentateuch; or whether the tradition was preserved chiefly by the memory of the initiated;—in either case, the fact remains, that a new composition, a new version, was edited by Ezra. The

---

[1] H. E. v. 8.

above assertion of St. Irenæus, with which the statement in the second book of Esdras coincides, is supported by the authority of Clement of Alexandria, and of Tertullian. We may even assume, that the assertion just quoted, was made in answer to the positive charge, so often referred to in the so-called Clementine Recognitions, and Homilies, that the Scriptures of the Jews were not genuine, having been to some extent adapted to, what were supposed to be, the opinions of later ages. We know, that such an accusation was actually raised by Celsus, the probable contemporary of St. Irenæus; and that the same charge was made, according to Epiphanius,[1] by the Nazarenes, who were closely allied to the Essenes. St. Irenæus had, therefore, every reason to make the most of the supposed record of Mosaic tradition, which was assumed to have guided Ezra, in the performance of his important undertaking. Instead of doing so, he establishes a parallel, between the implied infallibility of the Seventy, in their secluded cells, and between the individual Divine inspiration of Ezra. The difficulty, which thus presents itself, must be fully admitted. Yet the statement of St. Irenæus is easily explained, if the early existence of an oral law can be established. Then the great synagogue would cease to be a mystery.

Ever since the return from Babylon, synagogues were established in every part of the land. They had probably originated in Babylon, under 'the heads of the captivity.' About this time, as we have seen, the Dibrê Sôfĕrim, or words of the Scribes, were of more authority than the words of the written law. No wonder, then, that the chiefs of the fathers of all the people, the priests and the Levites, were gathered together unto Ezra the Scribe, even to understand the words of the law.'[2] It is highly probable, that 'the chiefs of the fathers' were delegates from the synagogues; for it is not likely that a great college existed already at that time in Jerusalem. By the intro-

[1] Haer. 18.  [2] Neh. viii. 13.

duction of the vowel points, which were then added to the sacred text, and tended to fix its real meaning, the written law was harmonised with the oral law, as far as it was, at that time, considered expedient to do so. If secret tradition led to the assembly of the great synagogue, to which Nehemiah directly refers, then the silence of Philo, or of Josephus, cannot be insisted upon as a proof of its mythical origin. In course of time, perhaps already under Ezra, the sanhedrim seems to have taken the place of the great synagogue. As under David and Solomon, and as under Constantine, so also, soon after the captivity, the civil power became more or less united with the spiritual power. This fact throws much light on the final fixing of the Canon of the Old, and of the New Testament.

So long as the tradition remained a verbal one only, it was quite possible for the Sadducees and the Pharisees, to agree in the recognition of the law and the prophets, as composed and compiled by Ezra. It would be left to the mode of interpretation to harmonise the sacred text with the peculiar tenets of each party. And this seems to have been the practice in the Jewish Church after the return from the captivity. For we know that the letter of Scripture was by the Pharisees not deemed sufficient for the right understanding of the ancient records of the faith. Josephus writes: 'The Pharisees ... follow the conduct of reason, and what that prescribes to them as good for them, they do; and they think they ought earnestly to strive to observe reason's dictates for practice.'[1] Now, if we remember that the Pharisees and Essenes are stated to have admitted the allegorical form of interpretation, which the Sadducees excluded, it will be sufficiently obvious, that the authority of private judgment was gradually acknowledged by the side of Scriptural authority, in the literal sense of the word. Thus originated two totally distinct systems of doctrine with

[1] Ant. xviii. 1.

regard to the nature of revelation. To the Sadducees, the Hebrews, the very letter of the sacred text, would be regarded as absolutely binding on the conscience; but to the Essenes and Pharisees, to the Kenites, the written word was binding only in so far as it could, by interpretation, be brought in harmony with 'the dictates of reason,' and, above all, with authoritative tradition. Thus the domain of verbal tradition enclosed the domain of Scripture, the source of both being regarded as Divine. The Spirit of God testified to the spirit of man, if the latter, and as far as the latter, was willing to be led by the former. Even a Hebrew ought to have known, as every Kenite did know, that God had in all ages spoken 'in' the prophets.

Moreover, by the partial recognition of the principle of private judgment, and by the acceptation of the standard of oral tradition in the synagogues, a new element had been introduced, which was dangerous to the authority of those to whom the government of the Church had been confided. Reason and conscience and faith, are essentially individual, therefore the interpretation of Scripture by the aid of progressive and individual enlightenment must be subversive of any authority which disregards the claims of individual consciousness. The traditional practice of the Scribes and Pharisees has not lost sight of a circumstance so likely to endanger the continuance of their absolute rule. To erect a hedge round the written law,[1] as edited by Ezra, and as rigidly preserved by the later Masoretic school, this was the imperative injunction of Sadducean tradition in Palestine.[2] Philo writes, that 'after a lapse of more than two thousand years (the Jews in Palestine) had not changed a single word, of what had been written (by Moses), but would sooner endure to die a thousand times, than consent to violate his laws and customs.[3] Of course this refers to the finally revised Pentateuch under Ezra. And yet so

[1] 'Facite sepem præ lege.'   [2] Pirke Abóth i. 1.   [3] Pr. Ev. viii. 6.

little did Philo agree with this restriction, that he regarded the systematically amended later Septuagint as the pure Mosaic code. The conservative and exclusive principle of the Masoretic or traditional institution, was followed up by the strictly enforced practice not to teach the secret tradition in the schools.

Whilst, then, the written law was in Palestine carefully preserved, as it had been settled, after the return from the captivity, the verbal law, the standard of interpretation, was known but to few. The Scribes and Pharisees strove to preserve their caste privileges, not only by shutting out the sources of light, that is, the received standard of Scriptural interpretation, the key of knowledge, but also by trying to prevent the promulgation of copies of the Scriptures among the people. These were allowed to hear, at least after the captivity, but not early encouraged, if permitted to possess the archives of revelation. Having closed the Canon, and thus excluded all further ingrafting of tradition, the Anti-traditionalists, the Sadducees in later times, mockingly accused the Pharisees of keeping the (oral) law 'in a corner,' whilst the (written) law was ' in the hands of every man.'[1]

In Egypt the case was widely different. The Jews in Alexandria imported to the former country of bondage the traditions transmitted by succession of their forefathers. There they were not restrained by any severe church-government, and accordingly the habit of interpreting the sacred records by tradition, soon led to a revision and reformation of holy writ. The Alexandrian Jew would not revere the letter of Scripture as the conveyancer of its plain meaning, as the stereotype expression of an unvarying truth; but as the mysterious hieroglyphic of a truth to be spiritually discerned, as an outward sign of a hidden mystery. Seen in this light, the letter would lose its for-ever-binding authority, and it would be

[1] Jost. Judenthum i. 235.

totally disregarded, whenever it was irredeemably opposed to the principles of secret tradition, which were always intended to complete and interpret the written law. The right of private judgment having thus, to a certain extent, been admitted, the individual, to whom the oral tradition had been confided, had thereby become, in a fuller sense of the word, a responsible agent. The honest enquirer after truth could not but perceive, that in various instances it was impossible to harmonise, by any ideological process, the literal meaning of the sacred text, with the exigencies of an advanced age, that is, with the ever-revealing 'still small voice' of conscience, the indwelling witness of the Most High, through the instrumentality of which, the hidden things of God gradually were revealed to the people.

The Mishnah or the second law refers in these words to the origin of that verbal law, which, ever since Moses, had been orally transmitted: 'Moses received the (verbal) law from Sinai, and delivered it to Joshua, and Joshua to the elders, and the elders to the prophets, and the prophets to the men of the great synagogue.'[1] This statement is corroborated by the very remarkable passage from Josephus, to which we have referred, and in which he insists on Moses having known more than he dared to disclose to the people. And in the Epistle of St. Peter to St. James, prefixed to the so-called Clementine homilies, as well as in the latter themselves, Moses is shown to have given over the tradition 'to the seventy men who took his seat after him;' and these were the forerunners of the Pharisees, whom Jesus acknowledged as sitting in the seat of Moses. Yet nowhere is it said or implied, that the secret tradition was altogether originally revealed on Mount Sinai to Moses. So great was the respect which, according to the Mishnah, had to be paid to every Scribe, or authorised interpreter of the written law, that to say

[1] Pirke Aboth 1.

anything against any of them, was specified as an offence twice as great as any directed against the letter of the law.¹

By the application of verbal tradition to the written law, a reformation was effected, similar to the transformation of water into wine. For, according to the pre-Christian Apocrypha, the Divine Word 'maketh all things new.'² Such renovation of doctrine would lead to a reformation of Scripture. The first step in this direction would be, to record the principles of verbal tradition, where such records were not forbidden, and to confide such new Scriptures exclusively to the stewards of the mysteries. Such Scriptures for the initiated only, we know to have existed in the pre-Christian period. In the second book of Esdras, which we shall later consider, it is written, that the same God who had appeared to Moses in the bush, inspired Ezra and other Scribes (as if referring to the great synagogue) to write books, some of which he was to 'publish openly, that the worthy and the unworthy may read it,' but others he was to 'keep and deliver only to such as be wise among the people: for in them is the spring of understanding, the fountain of wisdom, and the stream of knowledge.'³

Further proofs of the early existence of a secret tradition may be found in the essentially different narrative of the exodus, as contained in the book of Wisdom.⁴ Again, in the life of Moses as recorded in the Acts and also by Josephus; in the facts mentioned in the speech of St. Stephen; in Jude's reference to the book of Enoch, and to the disputes between Michael and the devil; in St. Paul's allusion to the rock which accompanied the Israelites, and to Jannes and Jambres. The latter circumstance is all the more curious, as the same names are mentioned in the Targum or Paraphrase called after Jonathan. We may also here observe that Jannes, who 'withstood Moses,' and 'resisted the truth,' is by Pliny referred to, as one of

¹ Mish. Sor. xi. 3.  ² Wis. vii. 27.  ³ 2 Esdr. xiv. 45-47.  ⁴ Wis. xvi.-xix.

those Jews, who, like Moses, founded 'another kind' of Wisdom or Magic, than that which, 'many thousand years before,' had been founded by Zoroaster. That Moses transmitted a verbal tradition is also confirmed by the assertion of St. Stephen, that Moses (not the fathers) received on Sinai living oracles, or rather, living words, which were to be given to Israel, but which did not prevent the fathers from thrusting him 'from them,' and turning back in their hearts unto Egypt.[1] For, although the living words of Moses might possibly be identified with the ten commandments written on stone, yet the finding of the hidden book of the law of Moses proves that he had transmitted a fuller tradition, which was kept secret till the reign of Josiah, when it was unknown even to the high priest.

If, by connecting the fact of a written Apocrypha or hidden Wisdom, with the theory of a verbal Apocrypha, we succeed in proving the undoubted existence of a secret tradition, dating, at least, from the time of Solomon, then the supposition will gain in force, that the same tradition was represented by Moses. The origin of secret tradition we have not here to discuss.[2] God has spoken in all ages through the mouth of his holy prophets, and yet, ever since the beginning, certain things have been kept 'in silence,' that is, hidden from the unlearned. It is our object to prove, by the most trustworthy documentary evidence, that the Apocrypha, those hidden books which, as the Hebrew name Genûsim implies, were kept from view, contain the interpretations of holy writ, as they were gradually recorded in the course of ages, not excluding the important period of five centuries, during which the Hebrew Canon was closed.

[1] Acts viii. 38, 39.
[2] The Eastern origin and Western development of tradition, has been sketched out in 'The Hidden Wisdom of Christ.'

# CHAPTER XIII.

### APOCRYPHA.

WE purpose to give a brief epitome of our investigations of those Scriptures which we comprise under the name Apocrypha, or Genûsim, that is, things hidden, later records of earlier tradition.[1]

The book of Job belongs to the pre-Mosaic period, and forms the most ancient part of the Bible. Uz lay in that part of North-Western Arabia, which formed the Kenite possession, later called Edom proper. The contents bear a striking resemblance to the Proverbs of Solomon. The Kenite doctrines, which we have traced in the Psalms, are more or less developed; but we find no trace of immortality. The Proverbs of Solomon are dark sayings or parables of old, first recorded by the men of Hezekiah, and intended 'to give intelligence unto babes,' that is, 'words of the wise and their enigmatical sayings.' As Hezekiah was the first good king after David,[2] he would cause the Solomonian tradition to be written down. 'The Song of Songs' has no dogmatic importance, though it may be numbered among the thousand and five songs attributed to Solomon. He may have had a hunting-place on the slopes of Lebanon, where the scene is laid. The heroine is Abishag, the 'very fair' Shunamite, or Shulamite, of Shunem, who attended upon David during the last days of his life, and who, by exciting Solomon's jealousy, caused Adonijah's death. The poem shows how Solomon vainly tries to gain the affections of his beloved one, and it displays the victory of

---

[1] The subject demands a separate work.
[2] Ecclus. xlix. 4.

humble and constant love over the temptations of wealth and royalty. The 'daughters of Jerusalem' are the ladies of Solomon's court, to whose charge the shepherdess, probably a Kenite, is committed. Already in the first section, the king approaches her.[1] The shepherdess then explains, that the cruelty of her brothers is the cause of her separation from her beloved.[2] Then is described the entry of the Royal train into Jerusalem, how the shepherd follows the shepherdess, and proposes to rescue her,[3] how she relates her dream, and gains the sympathy of her companions,[4] and how the shepherd takes her back in triumph.[5]

The book called 'the Preacher,' or 'Ecclesiastes,' although it points, in the form transmitted to us, to the time of Ezra, was originally a collection of ancient proverbs, strung together at different times, but principally, if not solely, by a contemporary of Saul, of David, and of Solomon. 'Better a poor, but wise young man, than an old and foolish king, who knows no longer how to let himself be warned. For, from the house of the slaves he issued forth, in order to be king, though he was born poor in his kingdom. I saw all the living under the sun, who walked with the other young man, who entered into the place of the former. There was no end of all the people, of all over whom he ruled. Nevertheless those that come, will not rejoice over him. For even that is vain and windy endeavour.'[6] We suggest that this passage refers to the first three kings of Israel. The doctrines are Sadducean. Such a man as Heman, contemporary of Zadok, and author of the 88th Psalm, may have written the book, in which traces can be discovered of the existing jealousy between the two Aaronic lines.[7]

'The Wisdom of Solomon' is the fullest compendium of Kenite tradition. It refers fully to the doctrine of

---

[1] Song i., ii. 7.  [2] Ibid. ii. 8; iii. 5.  [3] Ibid. iii. 6; v. i.
[4] Ibid. v. 2; viii. 4.  [5] Ibid. viii. 5-14. See Smith's Dictionary.
[6] Eccl. iv. 13-16.  [7] Ibid. iv. 4, 9, 12; v. 1; comp. vi. 8; ii. 18-21; x. 6, 7.

immortality, which is excluded in 'the Wisdom of Sirach.' From this it does not necessarily follow, that the latter was written before the former. Well-accredited tradition considered the Wisdom of Solomon as the most ancient. It may have been written, in Greek, during the reigns of Hezekiah or of Josiah, when, with the fall of the Sadducees, prophets again rose, and Kenite tradition could be recorded. The condemnation of idolatry, including that of 'beasts that were most hateful,' may possibly refer also to the brazen serpent, which Hezekiah destroyed.[1] If the writer lived in Egypt, which is probable, as St. Jerome identifies him with Philo, the connection between the Therapeuts, whose rites are here indirectly referred to, would account for the title. It was in the time of Kenite reformation, during the reign of Josiah, that a book was brought to light, which was unknown to the high priest and to the king, and which yet both publicly acknowledged to be 'the book of the law of Jehovah through Moses.' Something was added to the then existing written law. It can only have been Mosaic verbal tradition, and probably was divulged by Jeremiah the Kenite prophet. The Apocrypha of Moses, the hidden book, was added to holy writ, and has been transmitted to us as the second law, or Deuteronomy, the language of which is as different from the preceding books, as it is similar to the writings of Jeremiah.[2] The national development of Jewish doctrines was chiefly caused and regulated by the gradual revelation of true Mosaism, as transmitted by verbal tradition, and by successive records of the same.

'The Wisdom of Sirach,' or 'Ecclesiasticus,' originally written in Hebrew and in Palestine, was written by Sirach or Seirah, 'son of Eleazar,' or Azariah, that is, we suggest, by Seraiah, son of Azariah, high priest at Jerusalem, beheaded at Riblah by Nebuchadnezzar. The final compiler or reviser was a Sadducee, for the doctrine of immortality

---

[1] Wisd. xv. 14-19.
[2] Proofs of this in Colenso's Pentateuch.

is excluded, the Korahites (Kenites) are called 'strangers,' and no high priest of the Kenite line is mentioned. The book of Daniel, like other Scriptures composed during and after the captivity, is a book of chronicles, and extends to a longer period than the life of the prophet. It is a record of the hidden wisdom, therefore not classed among the prophets. The identity of Daniel the prophet and Daniel the priest of the line of Ithamar is probable, if the mission of Ezra can be proved to have taken place in the seventh year of Darius Hystaspes, that is, fifty-nine years earlier than has been hitherto assumed. He was probably present at the consecration of the temple, and at the great synagogue in 516, and if so he witnessed, though he may not have survived, the Purim massacre in 515. The books of Ezra, Nehemiah and Esther may be ranged among the Apocrypha, because the continuous history which they contain has been obscured by the titles of the rulers in Babylon, which have been wrongly interpreted as distinctive names. These we here explain:

1. Darius, Darayawush, Tariyavaus in inscriptions. Already Herodotus derives the name from the Sanscrit word *dhâri*, 'firmly holding,' which must be connected with the idea of rule. Darius means the ruler.

2. Xerxes is the Greek form for *kshérshé*, king.

3. Artaxerxes, Artachshasta, is by Herodotus explained as a compound of *arta*, great, and *kshérshé*, king; but may be connected with the Arya, the Arii, whom Herodotus calls Artaioi, and which is the name of the ancestors of the Persians. Artaxerxes means king of the Aryans.

4. Ahasuerus, Achashverosh, is identical with the Sanscrit *kshatra*, which appears as *kshérshé* in the arrow-headed inscriptions, and therefore means king.

It can be shown, that the Ahasuerus to whom the Samaritans complained, after the edict of Cyrus had been promulgated, refers to Cyrus; that the temple was consecrated in the sixth year of Darius Hystaspes, and that in the seventh year of that king of the Aryans, or Artaxerxes, Ezra was sent as governor to Jerusalem. The entire book of Esther must be placed between the sixth and the seventh chapter of Ezra. We will here confine ourselves to the proof, that Darius is the king of Esther. He is called Ahasuerus, or king, in the Hebrew Canon, and Artaxerxes, or king of the Aryans, in the Greek Canon. Josephus indirectly confirms our view by stating, that the king who married 'a Jewish wife, who was herself of the Royal family also,' was called by the Greeks Artaxerxes. The blunder which the historian commits is, that he regards him to have been the son and successor of Xerxes, whom he calls Cyrus.[1] We may assume, that his information went to show, that Cyrus was called by the Greeks Artaxerxes, or king of the Aryans. For the successor of Xerxes was Artaxerxes Longimanus, and not Cyrus.

On the etymology of Hystaspos, or Vistâspa, a high authority writes as follows:[2] 'The long â in the middle of the word is evidently formed by the union of two short ones, and the word must be thus divided: *vista-aspa*. *Aspa* signifies horse, in Zend; it is the Sanscrit *aswa*, and the Latin *equa* (equus). As to *vista*, this Zend word presents an *s* in consequence only of a rule of euphony, which at the same time lengthens the *i* which precedes it. It is, therefore, the Sanscrit *vitta*, of the root *vid*, or *vind*, which is the *finden* of the Germans. The entire name signifies, the possessor of the horse.'

That Darius Vistâspa is the Ahasuerus, or king of the book of Esther, is confirmed by the name Vistâspa, thus interpreted. We know from Josephus, that there was a council of state in the time of Darius, and this council of state, to which the king referred in his letter to Ezra, consisted of 'seven counsellors.' According to the well-known legend, Vistâspa was one of the seven Persian nobles, who

---

[1] Ant. xi. 6.  [2] Mons. Burnouf, in a letter, 1866.

made a conspiracy against the life of the false Smerdis, who had usurped the throne after the murder of Cambyses. Nothing is more probable, than that these seven noblemen, after the nomination of a substitute for Vistâspa, formed the council of state to which the king refers. These seven noblemen correspond, perhaps, with the seven 'chiefs of the Persians and Medes,' who are mentioned by their names in the book of Esther, as having 'served in the presence of Ahasuerus the king.' The omission of the name Vistâspa would be thus explained.

It is the above-traced meaning of the successful conspirator's name, 'the possessor of the horse,' which probably originated the unhistorical legend about his horse winning the throne for him by neighing at the rising sun. The framers of that legend must have understood its hidden significance. The horse was connected with the rising sun, as the symbol is connected with that which it represents. It is known that the horse was a symbol of the sun, and the sacrifices of chariots and horses to the sun must be thus interpreted. The 'sacrifice of the horse,' the *aswamêdha*, is the subject of many hymns of the Vedas.[1] If in the time of Darius, a woman, called Atossa,[2] held so high and influential a position at his court, that the great poet of his time coupled her with the glories of Persian rule; if even the popular legend recorded the name Atossa as that of the most influential woman at the court of Darius; if by internal evidence the Purim massacre can be proved to have taken place during the reign of Darius; if the name of Vistâspa was connected with the sun, then the heroine of Israel, Hadassah, the daughter of Abihail, the son of Shimei, the son of Kish, would naturally receive the honourable epithet of Esther or Astar, the planet Venus. Darius and Esther were both

---

[1] The translation and interpretation of these hymns ('the oldest collection of religious poetry'), by Professor Max Müller, is announced.

[2] Comp. Virgil's Elissa, who is the Sidonian, or Phœnician, that is, the Semitic Dido.

connected with enlightenment, symbolised by the light of heavenly bodies.

We venture to assert, that a full investigation of the books of Ezra, Esther, and Nehemiah, will establish as an indisputable fact, that the Purim massacre took place between the years 516 and 515 B.C., and that its result, directly caused by the change in the ministry at Babylon, led to the mission of Ezra to Jerusalem. Haman had sided with the Samaritan or Kenite party, and Mordecai, the Sadducee, sided with the Hebrew party. But Ezra, the Sadducee, could not maintain himself beyond six or seven months. The abrupt conclusion of his diary is explained by a sudden attack of Jerusalem by the Samaritans and their allies under Bagoses, when the Hebrews were obliged, for seven years, to pay tribute to their enemies. Even twelve years after Ezra's mission, Hanani referred to the partial destruction of Jerusalem and the 'great affliction and reproach' of his countrymen. Nehemiah assisted Ezra in establishing a government in Palestine on Sadducean principles. After Ezra, the descendants from Zadok, the Sadducees, the leaders of the Hebrew party, as opposed to the Kenite party in Israel, ruled for about five hundred years, and even after that long period of stagnation, the policy of Ezra and Nehemiah turned the scales of Jewish history.

The book of Tobit refers to the Purim massacre as having taken place when Nineveh was still the capital of Assyria. 'Remember, my son, how Aman (Haman) handled Achiacharus that raised him up; how out of light he brought him into darkness, and how he rewarded him again. Yet Achiacharus was saved, but the other had his reward, for he went into darkness. Manasseh gave alms and escaped the snares of death, which they had set for him, but Aman fell into the snare and perished.'[1] The Babylonian censorship cannot have allowed, for a

[1] Tob. xiv. 10; comp. Jud. viii.

considerable time, any direct reference to an event which had so greatly increased the hostility between the Samaritan and the Hebrew party. Even the book of Esther, no doubt published long after the event, refers to it in such a manner that, up to this day, the year of the Purim massacre cannot be even approximately fixed. Even Jeremiah had reasons to mystify his prophecy against Babylon, by turning the name of that city into Shishak,[1] according to the well-known Atbash alphabet. The initiated would understand, that Achiacharus refers to Achashverosh, though the same name is given to the royal cupbearer and keeper of the signet. The name Manasseh would not only point to Mordecai by its initial letter, but we may assume, that Mordecai, or Merodach, like Daniel, had a Chaldean and a Hebrew name, and that the latter was Manasseh. This name had a peculiar significance when Mordecai was born. At the approach of Cyrus, the unknown prophet of the captivity had spoken 'comfortably' to Jerusalem, announcing the end of her bondage; Cyrus had given permission to return and to build the temple, and God had caused the Jews to forget their sorrow. They that had sown with tears, hoped to reap with joy. As the birth of Manasseh was given to the son of Joseph during the banishment from Canaan, because God had made him forget all his toil and (that of) all his father's house, so that name was in itself an amnesty during the Babylonian captivity. Since Manasseh is clearly referred to, in the book of Tobit, as the antagonist of Haman, no doubt can exist as to Manasseh being the Hebrew name of Mordecai.

This helps us to explain the book of Judith as an allegory of the events recorded in the book of Esther. We suggest, that it was the earliest Scripture which referred to the days of Purim. An allegory could be published when no historical account would have been suffered. For the same reasons the writers of the Assumption of

---

[1] Jer. xi. 41.

Moses, and of the Apocalypse of Esdras and St. John, could not directly refer to the events of the past and present. The name Holofernes, which, like that of Judith, is not mentioned in any historical narrative, literally means, 'the licker of the serpent.' The serpent was the symbol of Median power, and as even Cyrus was called 'the Mede,' Vistâspa was still more entitled to be regarded as the representative of Median power, after that Arphaxad had been beaten and slain, and when the Median territories may have been, at least partly, annexed to those of Babylon. Although an Amalekite, Haman had gained the favour of Vistâspa, probably by an abject submission to the will of the Asiatic despot. Judith, or the Jewess, is Esther, the representative of the Hebrews, who is born in Bethuliah, which name means 'the virgin of Jehovah,' and symbolises the relations between God and Israel. The person who threatened to destroy her country, or in the language of the allegorist, the besieger of Bethuliah, is Haman, or Holofernes, who is called, in the book of Esther, 'the man-Satan.'[1] Manasseh is stated to have been of Judith's tribe and kindred, just as Mordecai is described in the book of Esther as the heroine's nearest of kin, being, like her, a descendant from Kish. Manasseh is called the husband of Judith. It is stated, that she went to Bethuliah, that is to Judea, 'and remained in her own possession.' She may have bought some land with the presents which the people had made to her, including all the property of Holofernes. A similar incident is recorded about Esther, who received the house of Haman, over which she set Mordecai. Having thus become master over Esther's house, Mordecai could be called her husband by the allegorist, and we need not assume that the king liberated her from a not enviable position, and that she married her next of kin, the partner in her glory.

---

[1] Esth. vii. 6.

## Principal Events from 536 to 490 b.c.

### First Caravan, 536.

536—First year of Cyrus, the Artaxerxes. Zerubbabel is sent as governor. Joshua. Foundations of the temple and the walls laid about 534. Nehemiah, but not Ezra, present. Works soon stopped.

### Second Caravan, 520-516.

520—Renewal of edict. Temple consecrated 516. Public reading of the law by Ezra. Great synagogue under Ezra. Covenant sealed with Nehemiah.
516-515—Purim massacre.

### Third Caravan.

515—Ezra sent as governor. Nehemiah not at Jerusalem. After six or seven months, Ezra's return, caused by Samaritan attack.

### Fourth Caravan.

502—Nehemiah's first mission to Jerusalem. Appoints Hanani and Hananiah, and returns to Babylon.
490—Last mission of Nehemiah. He punishes the leaders of the anti-Sadducean party.

The records of the Maccabean or Asmonean period consist of four books, which form part of the Septuagint, under the title of Maccabees. The Hebrew and Greek writers of these books have treated historical events with the freedom with which a targumist would enlarge upon the sayings of the Fathers. The first two books of the Maccabees oppose the principles contained in the book of Enoch, written soon after the latter, between 130 and 100 b.c. The first book was written in Palestine. The third book forms part of the Septuagint, and refers to the end of the third pre-Christian century, but it may not have been written before the second book. The fourth book is not, like the former, of Alexandrian, but of Palestinian origin, and refers to the first Christian century, though it is not written by Josephus, as Eusebius asserts. The latter part is a later addition.

The Maccabees are identified with 'the Jews that be called Assideans,' whose captain was Judas Maccabeus.[1] Assideans means the pious, the puritans, 'all such as were voluntarily devoted unto the law.'[2] Zeal for the written law, as sanctioned by Ezra the Sadducee, was the chief characteristic of the party of Modin, and we have seen, that Zadok, 'the master' of the Sadducees, in whose doctrines, according to Epiphanius, his descendants did not continue,[3] belonged to the Hebrew Aaronic line of Eleazar, and was the enemy of tradition and catholicity. The identity of the Maccabees and of the Sadducees, is confirmed by the siding of the Nabathæans, or Kenites, with the enemies of Jonathan, though he had regarded them as 'his friends.' 'The children of Ambri came out of Medaba, and took John and all that he had, and went their way with it.' Soon after, they 'made a great marriage, and were bringing the bride from Nadabatha (Medaba) with great train, as being the daughter of one of the great princes of the Kenaanites.'[4]

The Sibylline Oracles were in part (third book) written in the time of the Ptolemies, about the middle of the second century B.C. The prophecy of Isaiah is interpreted as referring to a woman 'in whom God will dwell, to whom he grants immortal light.' This cannot have been added by a Christian, as Virgil expresses a similar expectation It is the Kenite tradition about 'the man the Branch.'

The book of Enoch was written during the Maccabean or Sadducean rule, by a Palestinian, who need not have

[1] 2 Macc. xiv. 6.  
[2] 1 Macc. ii. 42.  
[3] Haer. i. 4.  
[4] 1 Macc. ix. 35-37.

belonged even to the Essenic party, but who represented the principles of Kenite tradition. On these grounds alone, it could not then have been received into the Hebrew Canon, even if the same had not been closed. The fully developed doctrine about angels shows, that the writer, if he was an Essene, was not bound, as the later Essenes were, to conceal the names of angels. He mentions four by name, one of whom, 'the merciful and long-suffering, the holy Michael,' also called 'the angel of peace,' who went with Enoch, showed 'all that is hidden.' This Apocalypse of the Apocrypha is described as a heavenly mystery, and opposed to 'an unworthy mystery,' which 'in the hardness of their hearts,' men had made known, and thus caused 'much evil on the earth.' The writer could not have expected Judas Maccabeus as 'the great horn' that would precede the coming of the Messiah. Every Kenite must have expected the Messiah as the Son of God; we need not, therefore, be surprised to meet here with the expression of such an expectation.

The so-called Psalm-book of Solomon, could no more have been written by the Son of David than the canonical book called Ecclesiastes. Both have been written by Sadducees. The principles of the anti-catholic party in the time of Solomon are directly connected with those of the Maccabees in the time of Antigonus, their last ruler, who made way for the triumphant entry into Jerusalem of Herod Antipas, to whom Pompey himself opened the gates of the holy city. To this historical incident of the year 63 B.C., the Psalm-book of Solomon clearly refers. Even the death of Pompey is described in an allegorical form. The writer may himself have witnessed the accession of Herod in 48 B.C. The Messiah will be preceded by the rule of a stranger; then the second David, born in Bethlehem, will rule over Israel. The Messianic expectations have reached their highest point. We suggest that the passage where Herod is described as 'the man of strange lineage,' may be explained by a reference to 'the

Assumption of Moses,' which was written between the years 44 and 45 A.C., and where it is said of Herod the Great, that he was not of sacerdotal lineage.[1]

The examination of the Apocrypha, that is, of the Scriptures referring to the hidden wisdom, and extending, by their traditional contents, over a period of at least two thousand years, will confirm the existence of two separate camps in Israel, from the earliest times, and will prove that, at all times, an organisation for the conveyance of tradition has existed. The word ' apocryphal ' in the sense of not genuine, cannot be traced before, if as early as, the end of the second century A.C. Like householders, the organs of tradition were entrusted with the responsible office of bringing forth ' old things and new.' The memory of the chief representatives of the Church was gradually engrafted on all its members by the Apocalypse of the Apocrypha. Because these Scriptures prove, in an especial manner, how the Kenites always were in favour of tradition and catholicity, and how the Hebrews always opposed these principles, therefore the successors of St. Peter, to whom the keys of tradition were confided, have always fully recognised the inspiration of the Apocrypha of the Old Testament, in the same sense, as the Hebrew Canon was regarded as inspired, though without them. The whole Bible without tradition is a lock without a key, and the Hebrew Canon without the Apocrypha is a sealed book. The New Testament cannot be regarded as the sole key to the Old Testament, so long as the proof is wanting, that the Gospels are identical with the Keys of St. Peter.

[1] For 'ἡριτῶν' read 'ἱερ῾ων.'

## CHAPTER XIV.

### TARGUMS OR PARAPHRASES.

PARTS of the law and the prophets were read every Sabbath in the synagogues, at least after the captivity;[1] the book of the law was publicly read on the Feast of Tabernacles of every Sabbatical year, in much earlier times.[2] To render this possible, a translation into the Hebrew-Aramean dialect must have become necessary soon, if not immediately after the Babylonian captivity. Not only a translation, but an interpretation of holy writ had become necessary. Both translation and interpretation were designated by the term Targum. In one sense, no part of the Scriptures was composed, after the captivity, in the same manner as before that period. The addition of the vowel points, to which we shall presently refer, fixed the interpretation of the word. Till then, words had been, more or less, hieroglyphics, mystical signs, which only the wise, the learned, the initiated could interpret. Every Scripture became a Targum. But as the Scriptures were not, and could not be, in the hands of every man, or even of every father of a family, or chief of a tribe; and as the temple services did not include even the reading of Scripture, the reading of the commandments excepted, the synagogues became the centres of Scriptural knowledge. The words of the interpreter, meturgeman,[3]

---

[1] Acts xv. 21 ; comp. Luke iv. 16.   [2] Deut. xxxi. 10-13.
[3] Turcimanno, truchement, dragoman.

became now, as they had already been during the captivity, equally important, and even more so, than the words recorded in holy writ.

The principal Targum to the Pentateuch is ascribed to 'Onkelos,' and it may be assumed, that this word is a corruption of the name Aquila, the author of the Greek version of that paraphrase.[1] Although Aquila of Sinope, a convert to Judaism, was a contemporary of the Apostles, yet it is generally acknowledged, that the Targum called after Onkelos and Aquila is a record of a more ancient tradition. For the general, and often the literal harmony between it and the Samaritan Pentateuch, can only be explained by the age of the tradition which is recorded in both. The importance of Aquila's Paraphrase can hardly be over-estimated. For although this collection of interpretations was not closed till after the Apostolic age, the work could not have received the name of Aquila, unless that remarkable man had given the weight of his authority to these views. Were it not for the identity of Aquila and Onkelos, we should know nothing about the doctrinal views of the former, as Aquila the targumist, and Aquila the friend of St. Paul, were both natives of Pontus; and as we have no trustworthy information about the time when the former lived, we may identify him with the latter, who, together with Priscilla, took Apollos of Alexandria unto themselves, and expounded unto him 'the way of God more perfectly,' or rather 'more accurately.'[2] Accepting this identity, we should know that Aquila was a targumist, and that the additional knowledge which he taught Apollos, was targumistic lore, developed and applied. The doctrine of Aquila was, according to the above hypothesis, what Apollos, in the Epistle to the

---

[1] Mr. Deutsch on 'Versions (Targum)' in Smith's Dictionary, from which the following quotations are taken. A scientific work on the Targums is greatly needed, and would lead to critical editions of the Samaritan Pentateuch, and the Septuagint, and the writings of Flavius Josephus.

[2] Acts xviii. 26.

Hebrews, calls 'the more perfect' doctrine of Christ, as going beyond his 'elementary' doctrine.

All Targums were interpretations of the written law by the oral law, by the Apocrypha or hidden wisdom. If we succeed in explaining the relation between the Samaritan, the Hebrew and the Greek Canon, by the more or less exclusion or admission of secret tradition, then we shall be enabled to assign to the Targums their place in history. It has been well said, that so far from the written Targum superseding the oral Targum at once, the former 'was, on the contrary, strictly forbidden to be read in public. Nor was there any uniformity in the version. Down to the middle of the second century we find the masters mostly differing materially with each other with respect to the Targum of certain passages, or we find translations quoted, which are not to be found in any of our Targums. The necessity must thus have pressed itself upon the attention of the spiritual leaders of the people, to put a stop to the fluctuating state of a version, which, in the course of time, must needs have become surrounded with a halo of authority, little short of that of the original itself. We shall thus not be far wrong in placing the work of collecting the different fragments with their variants, and reducing them into one finally authorised version, about the end of the third and the beginning of the fourth century, and in assigning Babylon to it as its birth-place. It was at Babylon that about this time the light of learning, extinguished in the blood-stained fields of Palestine, shone with threefold vigour. The academy at Nahardea, founded, according to legend, during the Babylonian exile itself, had gathered strength in the same degree, as the numerous Palestinian schools began to decline. And when, in 259 A.C., that most ancient school was destroyed, there were three others simultaneously flourishing in its stead,—Tiberias, whither the college of Palestinian Jabneh had been transferred in the time of Gamaliel III. (200) : Sora, founded by Chasda of Kafri (293); and Pumbadita, founded by Rabbi Jehuda ben Jecheskeel (297). In Babylon, for well nigh a thousand years, "the crown of the law" remained, and to Babylon, the seat of the "Head of the Golah" (Dispersion), all Israel, scattered to the ends of the earth, looked for its spiritual guidance.'

The oral tradition, as embodied in the Targum, forms an important link between the Old and the New Testament. The law recorded in Scripture, was only a partial annotation of 'the law that is upon the lip,' of the 'Torah shebeal Peh,' which contained 'precepts of Moses from Sinai,' the 'halacoth le Mosheh me Sinai.' Hillel is the first who is mentioned in connection with a classified compendium of Targums. A complete record of the principles of verbal tradition, based upon the six orders, or 'Sedarim,' which Hillel has laid down, was not composed before the very end of the second century, at the time of Rabbi Jehuda, called 'the Holy,' or the Prince, being one of the teachers at the High school of Tiberias. He wrote the 'Mishna,' or 'the second law' (Deuteronomy), or, as i is especially called, 'the verbal law,' which, with its later supplement, the 'Gemara,' or 'complement,' formed the 'Talmud,' that is, 'instruction' (from 'lomad') or 'science properly so called.'[1] The Talmud is essentially a compendium of the oral law, as partly preserved in secret rolls, 'megillath setharim,' and was finally published in the end of the fifth century. By the same, the Israelitic faith and constitution were for ever regulated. The gradual publication of this verbal tradition, or at least the gradually general acceptation of the same, is proved by the fact, that there existed, previously to the publication of the Talmud, a double Gemara, or complete compendium of the principles of tradition. That neither in the Mishna nor in the Gemaras any reference can be found to one or more authors of the written Apocrypha in the Septuagint, will be fully explained by the fact, that

---

[1] Comp. 1 Tim. vi. 20.

these books were not authorised to be read in Palestine. Thus we can likewise explain, why the Talmud does not refer to the Essenes. They were not members of the Scribal corporation, and therefore unauthorised guardians and interpreters of tradition. Of the so-called Jerusalemitic Gemara, of Galilean origin, only some extracts have been transmitted to us, all of which probably point to the early fourth and the preceding centuries; whilst the Babylonian Gemara, which was composed in Sura of Babylon, and completed about the year 500 A.C., is regarded up to the present day by the Jews as the sublimest exponent of their faith.

Every page of the Talmud of Babylon and of Jerusalem shows, and this has not been contradicted, that it is a late record of a much earlier tradition. The most ancient part of the Talmud, or collection of oral Laws, the Mishna, or 'learning,' contains the expounding of Scripture for legal purposes, or the Halâchah, which, together with the expounding for homiletic or popular purposes, the Haggâdah, was comprised under the general term of Midrash, a word derived from 'darash,' which means to 'search,' and was the name of the interpreter, also called 'darshan.' Whilst the Halâchah, to be such, required reference to traditional authority, the Haggâdah did not claim for itself any authority at all. Both centred in Scripture. But the former would only be proclaimed by recognised organs of tradition, and therefore implied and constituted the privilege of a scholar, whilst the other was, or was intended to be, the common birthright of every Israelite. The universality of the office of teachers is strikingly expressed in a passage of the Mishna, to which we shall presently refer. Accordingly, any gifted person might be called upon, by the president of the synagogue, to interpret the Scriptures. The synagogal institution was intended to be, and was in fact, a protest against all caste privileges, against the Scribal corporation, against the non-proclamation of the hidden wisdom, against the taking away of the Key of Knowledge. We have already pointed out, and hope to prove conclusively, that the increase of Sadducean or Maccabean, that is, of anti-traditional and anti-catholic influence after the captivity, checked, for a time, that development of Scripture, of which the long silence of the Hebrew Canon, the exclusion of the written Apocrypha, and the rejection of Christianity by the Jewish nation, are the indelible memorials.

The different branches of interpretation, marked by the names Halâchah and Haggâdah, are not distinguished from each other, either in the earliest or in the latest parts of the Talmud. Although at all times Scripture formed the centre of tradition, yet the horizon of Scriptural interpretation gradually became more extended. Thus stagnation was prevented by the traditional teaching. The synagogues, which were open also to those who were not Jews, became the centres of religious life. They constituted the common basis for the crystallisation and application of those forms and precepts, which had been transmitted from times of old. At the same time, they gave birth to that development of form, and to that fuller revelation and application of precept, of which the dark sayings of old, the proverbs confided to the memory of the wise, seemed capable. This secret tradition was gradually engrafted on holy writ. The revered hieroglyphics of religious thought were encompassed with a glory, which had not been seen in times past, except by the prophets, nor even fathomed, except by those who were initiated in the mysteries of the hidden wisdom. Every century drew its own circle around the immovable centre of divine revelation. Through the spirit of prophecy, barrier after barrier was removed, and thus man was gradually led to a truer conception of God's attributes, and of God's revelation to man.

The necessary consequence of this expanding system of Scripture interpretation was, that, in the same degree as the oral law was engrafted on the written law, traditional authority took the place of Scriptural authority. The spirit of interpretation, and not the mere knowledge of the letter, was acknowledged as essential. Scripture was no longer exclusively regarded as a code of laws, but as a mine of hidden treasures. In course of time the expounders of Scripture, the targumists, ceased to refer even to traditional authorities. They developed and established canons of interpretation from the letter of Scripture, according to the secret tradition, the standard of targumistic expansion, and in the form best adapted to the exigencies and capabilities of the time. The dark sayings of old could not at once be interpreted to an ignorant multitude, which had been deprived of the Key of Knowledge. The uninitiated could no more have borne the sudden revelation of the glorious mysteries of tradition, than the Israelites could bear the unveiled manifestation of the glory which Moses had seen. In the time of the Exodus the Israelites were in such a state of ignorance, and consequent hardness of heart, that to see that glory was regarded as the cause of instant death. Even the great lawgiver, who had received Divine revelations, through the medium of fire, on the Sinaitic rocks, may have been struck to the ground, like Daniel, like the three disciples on the mount of the transfiguration, like St. Paul on his way to Damascus, like St. John at Patmos. At all times, those who knew how to interpret what God had spoken in all ages, through the mouth of his holy prophets; those who knew the fact, that from the beginning certain things had been purposely kept hidden from the multitude; the men of wisdom and understanding, the apostles of light and truth, had many things to say which their contemporaries could not then bear. It might have been said, at every phase of Jewish history, that 'every scribe which is instructed unto the kingdom of heaven, is like unto a man that is an householder, which bringeth forth out of his treasure things new and old.'[1]

[1] Matt. xiii. 52.

The development, application and record of tradition, the gradual engrafting of the word heard on the word written, accounts for the entire development which we can trace in the Bible. And yet this is not the only cause. The interpreters of Scripture, the composers and revisers of the same, became umpires between contending parties. Concord was necessary, and concord required compromise. The history of the Church, written from this point of view, without regard to party prejudice, that is, neither in the interest of corporations, nor in the interest of their blind antagonists, would throw much light on the causes of schisms, and on the means adopted for putting an end to them. It would confirm the view we try to establish, that the Apocrypha, the records of the hidden wisdom, form the missing link between the Old and the New Testament, the coveted bridge over the chasm which separates the churches, and thus over the gulf which divides the heavens above from the earth below.

This scriptural development, caused by the elasticity of the allegorical garment, in which ideas had been clothed, and caused likewise by the perfectability of the human mind, and its desire for progress, can also be traced in the Targums and in the Talmud. Thus in the ethical part of the Mishna, in the 'Pirke Abôth,' or isolated sententious maxims, proverbs of the Fathers, we only meet with the kernel of normal interpretations, with the Halâchah, from which the teachers would develope their popular addresses, the Haggâdah. As there was a wisdom of the few, and a wisdom of the many, so there were Scriptures for the initiated, for the learned, 'the wise and intelligent,' and others for 'the unlearned,'[1] for 'babes,' who were gradually taught what was hidden even from the privileged classes. These sententious maxims of the Jewish Fathers, although not recorded before, but after the apostolic age, confessedly refer to the pre-Christian period.

[1] 1 Cor. xiv. 16, 23.

They are of high interest, inasmuch as they help to confirm the intimate connection between Christianity and that Kenite Judaism, the main principles of which we find recorded in the Palestinian and in the Alexandrian Apocrypha. We therefore give the following extracts from the Pirke Abôth.

'Upon three things stands the world: upon the law, upon works, and upon charity; or, according to another authority, "on right, on truth, and on peace."'[1] 'Be not like unto servants who serve their master with the view of receiving a reward, but like unto those servants who serve their master without any view of receiving a reward, and let the fear of heaven (God) be over you.'[2] 'Let thy house be a meeting-house for the wise, be dusted with the dust of their feet, and drink their words with avidity.'[3] 'Judge every man according to the scale of equity.'[4] 'Ye wise give heed to your words, that ye may not pay the penalty of the captivity, and be led away to a place where there is foul water, so that the disciples who come after you, drink thereof and die, and thus the name of heaven (God) be desecrated.'[5] 'He who does not attend (to his knowledge), the same will lose (what he has learnt); he who will not learn at all, is guilty of death.'[6] 'Make thy will as his (God's) will, so that he may also make his will as thy will. Break thy will because of his will, so he will also break and destroy the will of others because of thy will. Say nothing which cannot be understood, with a view to its being understood in the end. Say not, when I shall have leisure, I will study; perhaps thou mayest not have leisure.'[7] 'He who has earned a good name, has earned it for himself, but he who has earned the words of the law, has earned life eternal.'[8] 'Which is the right way for man to follow?.. a good heart; the evil way, which man must avoid, is...

---

[1] Mish. i. 2, 18.    [2] Ibid. 3.    [3] Ibid. 4.    [4] Ibid. 6.
[5] Ibid. 11.    [6] Ibid. 13.    [7] Ibid. ii. 4.    [8] Ibid. 7.

a bad heart.'[1] 'Let the honour of thy neighbour be as dear to thee as thine own honour, and be easily made angry and repent a day before thy death' (therefore to-day.)[2] 'An evil eye, evil desires, and misanthropy (a want of love to man) take men out of the world.'[3] 'Let the property of thy neighbour be as dear to thee as thine own; put yourself to learn the law, for it is not come as an heirloom to thee. And all thy works shall be done for the sake (name) of heaven (God).'[4] 'When thou prayest, let thy prayer not be an imposed act of duty, but let it be a prayer of lovingkindness and mercy before him (God.)'[5] 'It is not (laid) upon thee to finish the work, but it is likewise not left to thy choice to leave it entirely undone.'[6] 'Consider three things, and thou shalt not fall into the hands of sin. Consider whence thou comest, whither thou goest, and before whom thou must one day give an account.'[7] 'When two sit together and talk about the law, then the Shechina is in the midst of them. . . But that God hath also fixed a reward for a single person who sits and studies in the law, is evident from Lamentations iii. 28 : " he shall sit alone and be silent, for he has taken it (the burden of the law) upon him." '[8] 'He who learneth the law with the intention to teach, to him power will be given to learn and to teach; but he who learns with the intention to do (to act), to him it will be given to learn, teach, to keep, and to do.'[9] 'Say not, "accept my opinion," for the majority of votes is with them, and not with thee." '[10]

'Be humble (poor) in spirit towards all men.'[11] 'All meetings which take place in the name (spirit) of God, will stand in the end, but those which do not take place in the name of God, will not stand.'[12] 'This world is an entrance-hall to the world to come; prepare thyself therefore in the entrance-hall, that thou mayest enter into

[1] Mish. ii. 9.   [2] Ibid. 10.   [3] Ibid. 11.   [4] Ibid. 12.
[5] Ibid. 13.   [6] Ibid. 16.   [7] Ibid. iii. 1.   [8] Ibid. 2.
[9] Ibid. iv. 5.   [10] Ibid. 8.   [11] Ibid. 10.   [12] Ibid. 11.

the dining-hall; (the supper-hall, the triclinium).'[1] 'An hour of spiritual joy in the world to come, is better than all the life in this world.'[2] 'Look not at the vessel (symbol) but at that which is in it. There are new vessels full of wine, and old vessels in which there is not even new wine.'[3] 'Turn about and about in the law, for everything is in it. Therein thou wilt see, and in doing that become old and gray. Do not turn away from it, for there is no greater privilege than this.'[4]

By engrafting the idea on the form, the targumists restored symbols to their aboriginal meaning. The targumists abolished idolatry. By interpreting the allegorical form, they sufficiently removed, without setting it aside, the alluvial soil of ages, which had covered the rocks of pre-historic times. The mission of the targumist was to pave the way for the prophets, and the mission of the prophets to prepare the way of God. Few targumists were prophets, but every prophet was in fact a targumist, whether he belonged to the Scribal corporation or not. Every prophet had 'the fan in his hand,' his office was 'thoroughly to purge the floor, and gather his wheat into the garner,' but to 'burn up the chaff' with unquenchable fire.' The smoking flax was not to be quenched by the prophet, but all was to be removed which might cause the lamp to go out in the sanctuary of the soul. In the midst of an ignorant and fallen world, God raised as prophets such men as strove to be obedient to the voice of the Spirit, who gradually became convinced that God is not in the wind, nor in the earthquake, nor in the fire, but in the still small voice, which speaks in the heart of man. During the last 500 years of the pre-Christian era no prophets arose in Israel. This was the period, when, as we shall show, some of the first records of the verbal tradition, some of the earliest written Targums, or interpretations of the hidden wisdom, were composed,

---

[1] Mish. iv. 16.   [2] Ibid. 17.   [3] Ibid. 20.   [4] Ibid. v. 22.

partly in Palestine, partly in Babylon, and partly in Egypt. But even the prophets who were dead, continued to speak through the organs of hereditary tradition. The seer had been enabled to throw light on the present and on the future. In the prophetic schools or colleges, men were brought up in the knowledge and in the spirit of their predecessors, and especially of those great lights who had shone like beacons in the darkness of the night. To connect the present with the dim outline of the future, which prophets had traced, was the high mission of the hereditary or otherwise chosen guardians of tradition. Thus faith in prophecy, belief in its future fulfilment, was preserved and kindled anew. This would necessarily lead, as it has always led, to wrong interpretations and expectations. But, in course of time, a concatenation of events would become, by irresistible logic, the interpreter of what had really been seen in visions, and what had been described, not without alloy, but with sufficient accuracy to deserve the name of a prophecy.

During the five hundred years, when the voice of prophets was silent in Israel, when Confucius arose in China, Budda in India, and Heraclitus in Asia Minor, the targumists, the interpreters of secret tradition, were revered above all other teachers. They were regarded as having succeeded to the place which Moses had occupied. After having been the means of revising the text of holy writ, Jewish tradition was then lost in the barren soil of Palestine. But it continued to flow, as a fertilising stream, in Babylon and in Egypt. Even in Palestine, 'a hedge' could not be erected around the written law, as finally revised by Ezra. Men of Babylon, of Alexandria, of 'Galilee of the Gentiles,' began to teach the hidden wisdom to some of the 'unlearned,' and thus prepared the multitude, even in Judea, for going out into the wilderness, to hear the words of a prophet who prepared the ways of the Lord.[1]

[1] In China, Christianity was opposed by the initiated, partly on the ground,

The Apocrypha of the Septuagint proves, as we hope we have established, that these records of the hidden wisdom were composed from the days of the high priest Seraiah, the son of Azariah (or Eleazer, before 586), to the two last centuries of the pre-Christian dispensation, during which the book of Enoch was written in Palestine. The development of doctrine, which they attest, is confirmed by a similar development in the prophecies, contained in the last twenty chapters of Isaiah, in those of Jeremiah, Ezekiel and Daniel. To the connection between these prophecies and Rechabite tradition we have referred. When the Jewish nation came into nearer contact with the Chaldeans, the principles of secret tradition, the Eastern origin of which can be proved,[1] and which may during the captivity have been further developed, ceased to be altogether confided to the few, and gradually formed part of the national faith. The verbal law was added to the written law, not only as a supplementary charter, but as the standard of interpretation, for the records of the past. These were revised, and finally edited in the form we possess them, at a time when it had become advisable, if not necessary, to harmonise the verbal with the written law. The second law, or Deuteronomy, was clearly composed, at least in part, at an earlier period, after the finding of the hidden book of the law, which became the Targum or interpretation for all earlier Scriptures. It is, in the highest sense of the word, the book of Moses. Only the record, and not the contents were new. The development in the Pentateuch must be explained by the gradual engrafting of the verbal law on the written law. Deuteronomy is the Targum of Moses, and the prophet like Moses is the Targum of Deuteronomy. According

---

that they declared it to be inexpedient, that the unlearned multitude, whose idolatry they despised, should be taught to worship, through the established symbols, the One God, the knowledge and worship of whom was regarded as a caste privilege. What were symbols to the wise were idols to the people. Note in Milman's History of Christianity, p. 15.

[1] The Hidden Wisdom of Christ, i. 1-30.

to the tradition recorded in Rome in the year 96 A.C., God said unto Moses: 'These words shalt thou declare, and these shalt thou hide.'[1] Until the destruction of Jerusalem the Jewish doctors of the law taught the things which were not written, in spite of the Sadducees, who wished to keep the law 'in a corner.'[2] What the Israelites could not have borne in the days of Moses, what the great prophet and lawgiver had secretly revealed to the chosen few, what the faithful guardians of secret tradition had transmitted ever since the days of Moses, of Abraham, and of Adam, was gradually proclaimed to the people, from the days of Josiah to the days of Daniel and of Christ.

[1] 2 Esdr. xiv. 6.     [2] Jost. Judenth. i. 97, 235, 367.

## CHAPTER XV.

### THE SEPTUAGINT.

THE Greek version of the Old Testament, the Septuagint, may be called the Canon of the Apocrypha, or hidden wisdom. The inestimable value of the Alexandrian Canon is, that it contains, in addition to the books forming the Hebrew Canon, the 'Genûsim,' that is, 'the books hidden.' Thus the Greek Canon interprets the mysterious period of nearly five hundred years, during which the Palestinian Church, under Sadducean dominion and censorship, admitted no Scriptures into the Canon, which had been finally revised by Ezra. Because the Septuagint contains the Apocrypha, it forms the link between the Old and the New Testament. What Deuteronomy is to the other books of the Pentateuch, the Septuagint is to the Hebrew Canon. If the Alexandrian version of holy writ was preeminently, if not exclusively, the Canon of the Apostles and of their Divine Master, the targumistic development, the gradual proclamation of the hidden wisdom, has been sanctioned and individually applied by the highest authority.

The composition of the Greek version of the Old Testament is attributed by such men as Josephus, Justin Martyr, and St. Irenæus, to 70 or 72 Jews, or elders, who, as the latter informs us, were 'best skilled in the Scriptures, and in both languages.' He adds, that as Ptolemy, the son of Lagus, 'wished them to make the attempt separately, and apprehensive lest by concert they might conceal the truth of the Scriptures by their interpretation; therefore separating them from one another, he commanded all to write the same translation. And this he did in all the books. Assembling therefore in the same place, in the presence of Ptolemy, and each of them comparing their respective versions, God was glorified, and the Scriptures were recognised as truly Divine, as all of them rendered the same things in the very same expressions, and the same words from the beginning to the end. So that the Gentiles present knew that the Scriptures were translated by a Divine inspiration.'

Discarding this legend, the historical fact remains, that, about the year 285 B.C., the first complete, though rectified and augmented, version of the Hebrew Canon was commenced in Egypt. Although but the five books attributed to Moses seem to have been written in the third century before Christ, yet all other Scriptures which form part of the Alexandrian collection, were in circulation in the second pre-Christian century. Now, we must bear in mind that no Jewish colony had settled in Egypt before the foundation of Alexandria (332 B.C.), except the Jewish refugees, who after the murder of Gedaliah took refuge there, and were carried captive to Babylon by Nebuchadnezzar. The Jews who settled in Alexandria in the time of its founder, and under the Ptolemies, were, therefore, the descendants of those who had returned from Babylon, or who had remained among the Chaldeans. If, then, it can be proved that the Jewish colony in Egypt introduced new doctrines into the Greek version of the Hebrew Canon, the supposition will gain ground that these new doctrines were deduced from the principles of the oral or Scribal tradition.

The first question we have to consider is, why, if the miraculous origin of the Septuagint must be discredited, the Seventy were connected with the Greek Canon. We are told, that the elders who, by Ptolemy, were assembled on the island of Pharos, near Alexandria, consisted of six delegates from every one of the twelve tribes. Whether the 'interpreters' or targumists, as Josephus calls them, whom the high priest Eleazer sent, and who 'carried the law,' were 70 or 72, they formed a convocation of authorised interpreters of the law. They had been summoned for a purpose similar to that which caused 'the chiefs of the fathers' to be gathered together unto 'Ezra the Scribe.' The object was not only the translation, but the interpretation of the law, and the latter implied knowledge of the hidden wisdom. In both cases the fathers, or representatives of the people, were targumists, or guardians of secret tradition. Although the organisation of twelve tribes in Judea, at this time, cannot be credited, yet it is highly probable, that the seventy elders, to whom Moses is supposed to have confided the verbal law, constituted that council, that 'holy congregation at Jerusalem,'[1] which represented the twelve tribes in earlier times, perhaps already in that of David. The Scribes who watched over the traditions of their forefathers, and who, therefore, sat in the seat or pulpit of Moses, must have desired to perpetuate the Mosaic institution of the seventy elders, by the corporation of 'associates,' or members of a secret society. The same need not have been limited in numbers, but since the Sanhedrim consisted of 70 members, and as it may have stood in some connection with the great synagogue, it is almost certain, that the latter consisted of 70 fathers, at that time, all chosen from priests and Levites, and over whom Ezra the priest and scribe presided. The direct connection in which the work of the Palestinian interpreters must be assumed to have stood with the work of the great synagogue, renders it extremely probable, that their version was called that of the Seventy on this account, if not, because the seventy elders whom Eleazer sent to Ptolemy were the actual members taken from among the Scribal corporation, who formed the Sanhedrim in Judea.

[1] Berachot, 9. See Gelinek's note to Frank's 'Cabbala,' p. 199.

Josephus gives a full account of the circumstances, under which the Palestinian interpreters of the law were sent to Egypt, and back again to their own country.[1] The second successor of Alexander, Ptolemy Philadelphus, was urged by his intimate friend Aristeus, 'to set all the captives in his kingdom free,' which were 'a few more than ten times ten thousand.' The king having referred to the greatness of the request, one of the captains of the king's guards, Sosibus, 'and the rest that stood by, said, that he ought to offer such a thank-offering as was worthy of his greatness of soul, to that God who had given him his kingdom.' The king 'promised to publish a magnificent decree about what they requested, which should confirm what Aristeus had proposed, and especially what God willed should be done.' In the decree it was stated: 'Out of regard to justice, and out of pity to those that have been tyrannised over, contrary to equity, I enjoin those that have such Jews in their service, to set them at liberty.' This having been promptly done, the king ordered Demetrius Phalerius, his librarian, 'to give him in writing his sentiments concerning the transcribing of the Jewish books.' Demetrius then wrote: 'I let you know, that we want the books of the Jewish legislation, with some others, for they are written in Hebrew characters, and being in the language of that nation, are to us unknown. It hath also happened to them, that they have been transscribed more carelessly than they should have been, because they have not had hitherto royal care taken about them. Now it is necessary, that thou shouldest have accurate copies of them. And indeed the law is full of hidden wisdom, and entirely blameless, as being the law of God, for which cause it is, as Hecateus of Abdera says, that the poets and historians make no mention of it, not of those men who lead their lives according to it, since it is a holy law, and ought not to be published by profane

---

[1] Ant. xii. 2.

mouths. If then it please thee, O king, thou mayest write to the high priest of the Jews, to send six of the elders out of every tribe, or those such as are most skilful of the laws, that by their means we may learn the clear and agreeing sense of these books, and may obtain an accurate interpretation of their contents, and so may have such a collection of these, as may be suitable to thy desire.'

In his reply to the king's letter, Eleazer wrote : ' When we received thy epistle, we greatly rejoiced at thy intentions, and when the multitude were gathered together, we read it to them, and thereby made them sensible of the piety thou hast towards God. Know then, that we will gratify thee in what is for thy advantage, though we do what we used not to do before; for we ought to make a return for the numerous acts of kindness which thou hast done to our countrymen.' The deputation having arrived, Josephus states, that ' as the old men came in with the presents, which the high priest had given them to bring to the king, and with the membranes upon which they had their laws written in golden letters, he put questions to them concerning those books ; and when they had taken off the covers wherein they were wrapped up, they showed him the membranes.' Having been taken to the island ' they made an accurate interpretation with great zeal and great pains.' Hereupon ' all, both the priests and the ancientest of the elders, and the principal men of their commonwealth, made it their request, that since the interpretation was happily finished, it might continue in the state it now was, and might not be altered. And when they all commended that determination of theirs, they enjoined, that if any one observed either anything superfluous, or anything omitted, that he would take a view of it (revise it) again, and have it laid before them, and corrected ; which was a wise action of theirs, that when the thing was judged to have been well done, it might continue for ever. So the king was chiefly delighted with hearing the laws read to him, and was astonished at the deep meaning and wisdom of the legislator. And when the king had received these books, he adored them, and gave order that great care should be taken of them, that they might remain uncorrupted. He also desired, that the interpreters would come often to him out of Judea, because he highly valued a conversation with men of such learning, and should be very willing to lay out his wealth upon such men.'

From these statements we derive the following conclusions:—

1. Ptolemy regarded the God who had given him his kingdom, and who was in Egypt called 'the giver of life,' as the same God whom the Jews worshipped.

2. The divulging of the secret interpretation of the law is expressly pointed out as an exceptional favour, and we may assume that Ptolemy's request would not have been complied with, had he not promised the liberation of the Jewish slaves.

3. What the Alexandrians coveted was not merely a copy and the interpretation of the books of the Jewish law, but also some other books. These must have been the prophetical writings, and possibly also the Genûsim or Apocrypha; for of some of these we know that they were inserted in the Greek version. Even the Scriptures containing the law were considered as replete with hidden wisdom, which ought not to be proclaimed by the uninitiated. The difference was, that in Egypt more hidden wisdom was promulgated among the unlearned, than in Palestine.

4. The Palestinian interpreters were priests, elders, and some of the principal men of the Jewish commonwealth. This threefold division is similar to the three classes among the Jews in the time of Nehemiah.

5. The members of the targumistic convocation, in the spirit of their predecessors, that is, of the members of the great synagogue, enjoin the unaltered preservation of the interpretation of Scripture, as agreed upon between

themselves. That which distinguishes the Septuagint from the Hebrew Canon, had the sanction of the Seventy.

6. A re-consideration and revision is determined upon, for the elimination of possible errors. No infallibility is claimed, but the further record of tradition is to be prevented, as this was done in Palestine in the time of Ezra, by the introduction of the vowel points, and probably also by the establishment of the Masoretic school.

It can be fully established, that in the Septuagint the text of the Hebrew Canon has been, to some extent systematically altered. The general tendency of this reformation of Scripture, was one analogous to that which was effected in the time of Josiah, when the hidden book of the law of Moses was incorporated with Deuteronomy, or led to the entire composition of the same. The new cast of Scripture was made in accordance with certain clearly defined principles. Thus, the idea of God, as formed after the analogy of the human form, that is, anthropomorphism, was abolished, and the eternal Word was to be substituted for the angel of the Lord, as the eternal and invisible, instead of the temporary and visible revealer of the ways of God.

God did not 'repent' that he had made man, but the Lord 'reflected,' or meditated, because he had made man. It was not 'the God of Israel' who was seen by Moses, Aaron, Nadab and Abihu, with the seventy elders;[1] they only 'saw the place where the God of Israel stood'—not 'the similitude,' or rather 'the shape' of the Lord,[2] but 'the glory' of the Lord was seen by Moses. Job says: 'I know that he is eternal, who is about to deliver me, and to raise up upon the earth my skin that endures these sufferings; for these things have been accomplished to me of the Lord, which I am conscious of in myself, which mine eye has seen, and not another, but all have been fulfilled to me in my bosom.'[3] 'The Lord[4] wills not to behold vanity, for he is the almighty beholder of those

[1] Ex. xxiv. 9-11. [2] Num. xii. 8. [3] Job xix. 25-27. [4] Ibid. xxxv. 13.

who accomplish iniquity, and he will save me. Judge, then, thyself in his sight, if thou canst praise him as he is.' Isaiah did not see the Lord and 'his train,' but 'the glory of the Lord.'[1] Again, in Palestine Isaiah was recorded to have said: 'I said, I shall not see the Lord, even the Lord in the land of the living;'[2] but in Egypt the Jews read this passage as follows: 'I shall never again behold the salvation of the Lord.' Not 'the God of hosts,' but the 'God of powers' is a man of war.[3] It is not Moses who will give rain to the Israelites, and who will be with Joshua, but it is God who will do so. Thus in various passages the Septuagint changes 'I' into 'He.'[4] Instead of saying with the Psalmist, that the dew issues forth from morning dawn,[5] the Septuagint has it, that the Word has been born out of God's bosom before the creation of the morning star. When God created man, he did not create a 'male' and a 'female,'[6] but he made him (the spiritual man) male and female. Not 'I am' but 'The Being' sent Moses to the Hebrews.[7] 'I appeared to Abraham and Isaac and Jacob, being their God, but I did not manifest to them my name Lord.'[8] Moses does not declare in his song that he will prepare God 'an habitation,' but that he will glorify him.[9] God has not 'sworn' that he will have war with Amalek, but 'with a secret hand God wages war against him.[10] It is God himself who will 'pass before' Moses 'with his glory.'[11] Not 'the bread,' but 'the gifts' of God are to be offered.[12] Not the 'blaspheming,' but the 'naming the name of the Lord' was to be punished by stoning.[13]

It is evident that such systematic alterations, involving principles, could not have been sanctioned by the highest Jewish authorities, unless they knew that these alterations of the Hebrew text were in harmony with the tradition

---

[1] Is. vi. 1.    [2] Ibid. xxxviii. 11.    [3] Ibid. xlii. 13.
[4] Deut. ix. 13–15; xxix. 2, 5, 6; xxxi. 22, 23.    [5] Ps. cx. 3.
[6] Gen. i. 27.    [7] Ex. iii. 14.    [8] Ibid. vi. 3.
[9] Ex. xv. 2.    [10] Ibid. xvii. 16.    [11] Ibid. xxiii. 19.
[12] Lev. xxi. 17.    [13] Ibid. xxiv. 15, 16.

of which they were the guardians. What was not agreed to by the great synagogue under Ezra, was passed as authoritative by the seventy Palestinian interpreters in the time of the Ptolemies. Essentially the same Jewish tradition was deposited in the written Targums, of which that called after Onkelos was written in the first Christian century, and later in the Talmud. Whilst we read in Genesis: 'Unto Adam also and to his wife did the Lord God make coats of skins, and clothed them,'[1] it is written in the Targum, that called after Onkelos (Aquila): 'And Jehovah Elohim made unto Adam and his wife garments of glory, on the skin of their flesh, and clothed them.' In the second recension of the Targum Jerushalmi, these garments are called 'garments of honour from the skin of the serpent,' which God had cast out, 'on the skin of their flesh, instead of their beauty which they had cast off, and he clothed them.' Again, in a Midrash, or interpretation of the Mishna, or oldest part of the Talmud, it is stated that 'God did not reveal himself unto Adam until he had made himself a covering,'[2] that is, a 'garment of glory.' In this spiritual sense must we interpret the record in Genesis about Adam and Eve being ashamed of their nakedness. They had lost the covering of God's glory. In the Apocrypha, to 'make garments for men' is interpreted to mean to 'bring glory to men.'[3] Therefore it is written, that God put upon Moses 'a robe of glory,' so that 'in glory there was none like unto him.'[4] According to the Zohar, or book on 'glory,' the garments of the flesh hide 'the deep secret of the heavenly man,' of the Divine Word, through whom, as in a chariot, God descends to man, and makes him the mediator of his presence.[5]

That these and similar passages point not to the

[1] Gen. iii. 21.
[2] Mish. iv. 18; comp. Rev. i. 13; iii. 4; xvi. 15; John xxi. 7.
[3] 1 Esdr. iv. 17.   [4] Ecclus. xxvii. 8; xliv. 19.
[5] Zohar ii. 76, *a*; 42, *b*; 43, *a*; comp. Ps. civ. 2; Matt. xvii. 2.

physical creation of the first man, but to a creation in the literal sense of the Hebrew word, to a renewing, and that they refer to a spiritual clothing, symbolically expressed, is also confirmed by an otherwise inexplicable passage in the book of Ezekiel. 'Thou wast a perfect ring to seal with, full of wisdom, and perfect in beauty. In Eden, the garden of God, thou wast covered with every kind of precious stones, . . . and of gold were the works of art of thy sealing, and of the ring-caskets about thee; on the day when thou wast created, they were prepared.'[1] The knowledge of casting precious metals can be asserted to have existed before the migration of Cain to Nod, if we assume as proved, the suggested identity of the separation of the sons of Adam in Eden, and of the great Aryan separation in Central Asia, in a place likewise called Eden.[2] This identity is confirmed by the above passage, unless we conjecture that before the birth of Adam's third son, the Adamites were able to work in metals.

The importance of the book called the Zohar cannot be altogether denied, because of the acknowledged fact, that the records of tradition, like many of the holy Scriptures, have been chronicled at different times by different hands. If we have succeeded in proving the existence of secret tradition before the final revision by Ezra, and before the original composition of the most ancient Scriptures forming the Hebrew Canon, then a late record may contain ancient tradition. The Zohar, or book on 'glory,' cannot be traced, in the form transmitted to us, beyond the thirteenth century, A.C. When this compendium of traditional lore was commenced, and when it was concluded, the organisations for the conveyance of secret tradition had not ceased to exist. From Spiritual Father to Spiritual Son, tradition was transmitted, by other than generally recognised organs, with a faithfulness which even the unscrupulous would have regarded as necessary for

---

[1] Ezek. xxviii. 12, 13.   [2] Hidden Wisdom, i. chap. i.

the attainment of private ends. Although the Christian organisation for the secret transmission of ancient tradition had taken the place of the Jewish organisation, independent organisations may well have continued to exist. Thus we may account for the late and unauthorised publication of hereditary tradition.

One of the principal parts of the Zohar is entitled 'the book of the mystery;' another, 'the great congregation.' The latter part refers to Simon ben Jochai, the father of Gamaliel, and represents him as in the midst of his disciples. Another division bears the title 'the small congregation,' and here the dying Simon is described as communicating his last instructions to a smaller number of his disciples, that is, as we may infer, to the initiated, to those to whom the deeper mysteries could be revealed. The book confessedly refers to the mystery of God's glory, name or presence, that is, to the indwelling of the same, to the Shechina of the Most High. Here it is shown, in literal harmony with the earliest known records of the hidden Wisdom or Apocrypha, that the Divine Wisdom or Word, has created all things, and supports all things. It is defined as the source of all life, as the true Eden, the upper, or heavenly Eden. By this power of God, by this heavenly light, Adam was enlightened and sanctified to such a degree that even the highest angels were jealous of him.[1] 'Before that Adam had sinned, he heard only that wisdom, the light of which comes from above, he had not yet separated himself from the tree of life. But having yielded to the longing to know the earthly things, and to descend unto them, he was attracted by them, he knew the evil and forgot the good, he separated himself from the tree of life. Before men had committed this sin, they heard the voice from above, they possessed the heavenly wisdom, they preserved their glorious and high nature. After their sin, however, they did not even

---

[1] Zohar i. 65, a.

understand the voice from below.'¹ 'When Adam, our first (spiritual?) father, inhabited the garden of Eden, he was clothed as man is clothed in heaven, with a garment of heavenly light. . . . That light serves him as a garment, on his entering the other world, and on his appearing before the Holy One. . . . The soul, therefore, has a different garment for each of the two worlds which she shall inhabit, one for the terrestrial, and another for the celestial world.'²

We have seen that, in the Septuagint, Adam is recorded to have been made male and female. We find the same view fully developed in the Zohar. 'Every form in which is not found the male and the female principle, is no higher, no heavenly, no perfect form. The Holy One does not set up his dwelling, except where these two principles are found perfectly united. The blessing can only be there, where this union exists. So the word tells us: " He blessed *them*, and called *their* name Adam, on the day when *they* were created. For even the name Adam (man) can only be given to a man, and to a woman, who are united to one being."'³ This view corresponds well with the word bàrà in the first verse of Genesis, which does not mean created, but renewed. The above doctrine may be connected with that of the 'syzigia,' or pair, which was taught by Simon Magus.

The traditional interpretations above referred to, receive an authoritative confirmation from the Apocrypha of the Septuagint, from the Targums, the Talmud,⁴ and also from Philo. He writes: 'The name Mother we attribute to the highest Wisdom. God has united himself with the same in a mysterious manner, in order to cause the generation of things. It is she, who, fructified by the Divine germ, hath with pains and in the appointed time, given birth to the only and much-beloved Son, whom we call

---

¹ Zohar ii. 163, *a* and *b*.      ² Ibid. 229, *b*.
³ Ibid. i. 55, *b*; comp. iii. 290, *a*, and Frank's 'Cabbala.'
⁴ Jora Sutra, ad fin.

the world. Therefore a holy writer presents unto us Wisdom in the following words, speaking about herself: "Among all the works of God I was formed the first; time did not yet exist when already I was. For it is natural, that all that is born must be younger than the mother and nurse of the world."'[1] In another passage Philo calls the Divine Wisdom, or Word, 'the mother of all beings.'[2] He explains, that the image of God, in which, or to which, man was created, is nothing else than 'the eternal Word,'[3] that is, a power beyond all heavenly powers, separated from God, and yet at one with him,[4] 'the source which revives the whole earth, and which pours the nectar into the souls, being himself this nectar.'[5] Although Philo borrows most of the terms he uses from Greek philosophy, yet Jewish tradition is his source.

[1] De Temul.  [2] De Somn. i. 1; Mang. 653.
[3] Deling. conf. i.; Mang. 427.  [4] Leg. alleg. ii.  [5] De Somn. ii.

## CHAPTER XVI.

### MESSIANIC EXPECTATIONS.

The great separation in the family of Adam was caused by jealousy. In the words of the Septuagint: 'God looked upon Abel and his gifts, but Cain and his sacrifices he regarded not. And Cain was exceedingly sorrowful and his countenance fell. And the Lord God said to Cain: Why art thou become very sorrowful, and why is thy countenance fallen? Hast thou not sinned, if thou hast brought it rightly, but not rightly divided it? Be still, unto thee shall be his submission, and thou shalt rule over him.' The descendants from Cain, who left Eden for the East, were to rule over those who remained in Eden and did not go to the East. But was not Eden the place where God had exclusively manifested his presence to man? Therefore Cain said: 'If thou castest me out this day from the face of the earth, then shall I be hidden from thy presence, and I shall be groaning and trembling upon the earth; then it will be that anyone that finds me shall slay me. And the Lord God said unto him: Not so; anyone that slays Cain shall suffer sevenfold vengeance; and the Lord God set a mark upon Cain that no one that found him might slay him.' The Divine presence went with him to the East, and Cain, that is, the Kenite, never died. The Kenite was to rule over his brethren.

The record of Rebekah's twins seems to contradict this. The greater 'nation' shall serve the less. But this refers to the rule of high caste over low caste. Jacob represents the ruling high caste, which was of the same Eastern origin among Hebrews and Kenites, and he connected his son Judah with the Davidic or Kenite rule, which centred in that tribe. 'A ruler shall not fail from Judah, nor a prince from his loins, until there come the things stored up for him, and (until) he is the expectation of nations.' Thus the catholicity of the house of David is connected, by the writers of the Septuagint, with the hope of the last of the patriarchs. The mystery of Shiloh was unveiled, and the interpretation of Balaam's prophecy rendered possible. 'Balaam, the son of Beor, says, the man who sees truly says, he says, who hears the oracles of the Mighty One, who saw a vision of God in sleep; his eyes were unveiled. . . There shall come a man out of his seed, and he shall rule over many nations, and the kingdom of Gog shall be exalted, and his kingdom shall be increased. God led him out of Egypt, he has, as it were, the glory of a unicorn. . . I will point to him, but not now; I bless him, but he draws not near; a star shall rise out of Jacob, a man shall spring out of Israel, and shall crush the princes of Moab, and shall spoil (Targum: rule over) all the sons of Seth. And Edom shall be an inheritance, and Esau, his enemy, shall be an inheritance.' We have seen that this prophecy can only refer to David, and was literally fulfilled by him. Here again the Kenite, the Eastern branch, rules over the Western branch, Cain over Seth. And yet even 'the Kenite,' whose 'dwelling-place is strong,' and who lives in caves, having put his rest 'in a rock,' even the Kenite, among whom Beor, that is, Balaam, has 'a skilfully contrived hiding place,' shall be carried away captive by the Assyrians.

Not even this passage can be referred to a personal Messiah, who was still expected in the time of the Ptolemies, when Jewish tradition, the standard of interpretation, was engrafted on the Hebrew Canon. Isaiah was aware, that Balaam had not seen beyond the time of David. But the hopes of the Kenite seer lived in the Kenite prophet. The traditions of the first Kenite king, the keys of David, were destined to open what was shut, to reveal what was hidden, to loose what was bound. But not all stewards of Divine mysteries were desirous to fulfil this high destiny. What one party was determined to hide, another was resolved to bring to light. The Apocalypse of the Apocrypha constituted, at once, the fear of the Hebrew leaders, and the hope of the Kenite leaders in Israel. In the time of Isaiah a change in the high priesthood was promised by the man of God. The Hebrew high priest and treasurer Shebna was to be succeeded by Eliakim the Kenite. Once more the line of Ithamar was to rule. The writers of the Septuagint knew well, that the hopes of Isaiah were not then realised. Shebna, here called Somnas, who lives in 'the chamber' of the temple, has nothing to do there. 'Behold now, the Lord of hosts casts forth, and will utterly destroy such a man, and will take away thy robe, and thy glorious crown, and will cast thee into a great and unmeasured land, and there thou shalt die; and he will bring thy fair chariot to shame, and the house of thy prince (Zadok, or Eleazer) to be trodden down; and thou shalt be removed from thy stewardship, and from thy place.' In recording the promises made to his successor Eliakim, who is to possess 'the key of the house of David,' the Greek version has it, that 'there shall be none to shut' when 'he shall open,' and adds, that 'there shall be none to speak against him,' no adversary or rival to accuse him. Again, if Eliakim shall shut, 'there shall be none to open.' The dark passage about Eliakim being fastened 'as a nail in a sure place,' and about cutting off 'the burden' of Shebna is thus rendered: 'And I will make him a ruler in a sure place, and he shall be for a glorious throne of his father's house; and every one that is glorious in the house of his father shall trust in him, from the least to

the greatest, and they shall depend upon him in that day.
Thus saith the Lord of Hosts, the man that is fastened in
the sure place shall be removed, and be taken away and fall,
and the glory that is upon him shall be utterly destroyed.'[1]

Isaiah centred his hopes in a high priest of the Kenite
Aaronic line, whose birth his prophetic spirit had enabled
him to connect with the then expected realisation of
Kenite hopes. These expectations of Isaiah are thus interpreted in the Greek version: 'For a child is born to
us, and a son is given to us, whose government is upon
his shoulder, and his name is called the Messenger of
great counsel; for I will bring peace upon the princes,
and health to him. His government shall be great, and
of his peace there is no end: it shall be upon the throne
of David, and upon his kingdom, to establish it, and to
support it with judgment and with righteousness, from
henceforth and for ever. The zeal of the Lord of hosts
shall perform this.' Again, the writers of the Septuagint
knew, that even Isaiah had not referred to a future
individual, who should realise his hopes. Isaiah had not
regarded Eliakim as a type of a future deliverer, of a
future possessor of the key of David. The Messianic
future, foreshadowed in Eden, was to be known by the
victory of Kenite principles over Hebrew principles. In
vain had David protested against sacrifices. The Egyptianised Hebrews still maintained, that blood was necessary
'to make an atonement for the soul.' But thus spoke
Isaiah, according to the Septuagint interpretation: 'Of
what value to me is the abundance of your sacrifices,
says the Lord; I am full of whole-burnt-offerings of
rams, and I delight not in the fat of lambs, and the blood
of bulls and goats; neither shall ye come with these to
appear before me; for who hath required these things at
your hands? Ye shall no more tread my court. Your
hands are full of blood.'[2] The sanctuary is to be cleansed,

[1] Brenton's Septuagint Version.     [2] Is. i. 11-15.

by the abolition of such sacrificial rites. 'And in that day God shall shine gloriously in counsel on the earth, to exalt and glorify the remnant of Israel. All that are appointed to life in Jerusalem shall be called holy; for the Lord shall wash away the filth of the sons and daughters of Sion, and shall purge out the blood from the midst of them, with the spirit of judgment, and the spirit of burning. And he shall come. And it shall be with regard to every place of Mount Zion, yea, all the region round about it shall a cloud overshadow by day, and there shall be as it were the smoke and light of fire burning by night, and upon all the glory shall be a defence.'[1] The interpreters avoid the interpretation of 'the Branch,' and omit the word. But they give the prophecy of Zechariah about God's 'servant the Branch.' Perhaps they feared that the Hebrew version might be understood to refer, like the other prophecies of Isaiah, to Eliakim, a contemporary of his.

The 'priests' are commanded by the unknown prophet of the captivity, to comfort God's people, announcing the accomplishment of Israel's 'humiliation,' the forgiveness of its sin, which had caused the Babylonian bondage.[2] Israel's sin has been borne by the servant of God, who 'shall understand, and be exalted, and glorified exceedingly.' Though many shall be 'amazed' at him, yet his face shall be 'inglorious among men,' and his 'glory' shall not be honoured. But 'many nations' shall wonder at him, and 'kings shall keep their mouths shut, for they to whom no report was brought concerning him, shall see, and they who have not heard shall consider.' This servant of God is clearly interpreted to mean a person known to the generation then living. It might be Jeremiah the Kenite prophet, who 'was dishonoured and not esteemed.' He did undergo imprisonment and hardships, such as are here described. 'He was wounded on

[1] Is. iv. 3-5.    [2] Ibid. xi. 1, 2.

account of our sins, and bruised because of our iniquities; the chastisement of our peace was upon him, and by his bruises we were healed. His life is taken away from the earth, because of the iniquities of my people, he was led to death. If ye can give an offering for sin, your soul shall see a long-lived seed. The Lord also is pleased to take away from the travail of his soul, to show him light, and to form him with understanding, to justify the just one, who serves many well, and he shall bear their sins. Therefore he shall inherit many, and he shall divide the spoils of the mighty, because his soul was delivered to death, and he was numbered among the transgressors, and he bore the sins of many, and was delivered because of their iniquities.'[1]

These passages, without exception, do not refer to a future Messiah. Yet the seventy authorised interpreters of the law believed in a future Messiah. Not only is Micah's prophecy about 'a ruler in Israel' literally rendered, but the prophet Zechariah had clearly described God's 'servant the Branch,' or 'the man whose name is the Branch.'[2] We have seen, that all Kenite expectations centred in this prophecy, and are now in a position to assert, that all the Messianic expectations were Kenite expectations.

These are fully expressed in the book of Enoch. The Messiah is described as standing by the side of the 'Ancient of days,' also called 'the Lord of Spirits;' and 'the Son of Man's' countenance was 'as the appearance of a man, and full of grace, like one of the angels,' who reveals 'all the treasures of that which is concealed.' He himself was 'chosen and hidden in the sight of God before the world was created,' and God revealed him to the 'elect.'

---

[1] Is. lii. 13–15.

[2] Zech. iii. 8; vi. 12. In Hebrew *zemah*, but in Is. xi. i. *netser*. To this passage the prophecy about 'a Nazarene' refers. St. Jerome suggests it, knowing that it did not point to Judg. xiii. 5, where, according to the Vatican Codex, the word means a Nazarite. The Alexandrian Codex has Nazeiraion.

He is 'the son of a woman,' and 'the Son of God;' other men are also called 'the children of God.' When the Messianic kingdom comes, there will be an inexhaustible 'fountain of righteousness,' surrounded by 'many fountains of wisdom,' from which all the thirsty will drink, and be filled with wisdom, and dwell with the holy and the elect. There will be a new heaven, angels will descend and live with men, 'and the chosen One shall dwell among his chosen people.' Going beyond the interpretation recorded in the Septuagint, the Targum called after Onkelos, written probably in the first half of the first century, connects Shiloh not only with Judah, but with the 'Messiah, whose is the kingdom, and the gathering of the nations.' Whilst the Septuagint interprets Balaam's prophecy as referring to 'a man,' he is here called 'a Messiah anointed from Israel.' Similar interpretations are in the Targum called after Jonathan, probably written in a still later period.

The Hebrews, that is, the Sadducees, expected likewise a deliverer, but this expectation was moulded after the Maccabean type. They expected a prophet 'with the Urim and Thummim.' The beggarly elements which were laid aside soon after, if not during the reigns of David and Solomon, were to be re-introduced. The Sadducean Messiah was to be a seer according to Egyptian fashion. The formalists looked for one who should decide, what was to be done with stones which had been used for an altar. The ritualists looked to regulations, the spiritualists to a renewing of the mind. The Hebrews kept to their sacrificial rites and separatist customs, the Kenites continued to protest against them. Righteousness solely by the performance of rites, was preached by the one, righteousness by the forsaking of sin, was the standard of the other party. The Kenite writer of the Psalm-book of Solomon, who had witnessed the fall of the Sadducees, after Pompey's capture of Jerusalem, 63 B.C., and also the accession of Herod the Idumean, the friend of the

Kenites, announces the Messiah as a man 'free from sin,' as 'an anointed Lord,' as a Christ, who 'shall not be very weak,' but receive his strength from God. 'Happy are those who are born in his days, to see the blessings of Israel, which God shall bring to pass in the congregation of the tribes.'

That congregation of Israel was a mixed one, consisting at all times of Kenites and of Hebrews. The Kenites, descendants from Cain, to whom the promise was made in Eden, and later by prophets, that they should rule over their brethren, were represented by the Essenes only. For the Pharisees, although originally belonging to them, had made a compromise with the Sadducees, and ventured not to oppose them. Even the Essenes were lost in formalism, and as a secret society they could not spread the principles of tradition and catholicity. Yet their great prophet, who preached not only 'the law and the prophets,' but the kingdom of heaven, to all who would press into it, was declared to be the greatest man living, and yet not so great as 'the least in the kingdom of heaven.' He expected a terrestrial Messiah, and did not, therefore, regard Jesus as him that should come. He kept strictly to the Nazarite regulations, which included the abstinence from bread and wine, whilst 'the Son of man came eating and drinking,' notwithstanding his Kenite descent. Wisdom 'was' not 'justified by all her works,'[1] but 'wisdom is,' at all times, 'justified by her children.'[2] Not even the Essenes, the most spiritual party in Israel, could understand, as a body, the liberty from dead formalism which became the pillar of the Christian Church.

And yet the Christian Church grew out of the Jewish Church. Its founder was a descendant from David, the first disciples were Kenites, and thus Israelites, whether they inhabited Judea, Samaria, or Galilee. Christianity is the revelation of Kenite tradition, which had been 'kept

---

[1] Matt. xi. 19; Cod. Sin.     [2] Luke vii. 35.

in silence since the world began,' and the spirituality and catholicity of which the Hebrews had always opposed. What Isaiah had vainly expected from the child who was born in Jerusalem, was accomplished by the Son who was born in Bethlehem. The promise made in Eden to Cain, his ancestor, was fulfilled, by the man who became the ruler over sin, and thus overcame the world.

In the Septuagint Eve is called 'life.' This expression stands in direct connection with the view which Philo expresses, in the passage we have quoted, where he declares, that the world is the only much beloved son, the fruit of a mystic union between spirit and matter, the Creator and creation, the invisible and the visible. Life, and therefore blood, is necessary for incarnation. Philo did not, perhaps, go beyond the conception, that God is manifested in the world. The Divine manifestation in the flesh may have been, in his time, no more than a theory. But it is important to know, that the belief of some of the leading spirits among the Jews centred in this theory — that there was a preparation, a demand for the supply which God was then about to grant, in accordance with his eternal laws of cause and effect.

We must connect this preparation and expectation with Isaiah's announcement of the Divine incarnation. As already observed, the virgin, or rather, the woman, is by high authorities, among modern commentators, interpreted as the symbol, not as the type, of the commonwealth of Israel, the people of catholicity. This explanation is confirmed, in the most direct manner, by the Apocalypse of the seer at Patmos.[1] Israel, that is, humanity, was being prepared, before the captivity, for the unspotted reflection of God's glory, in the face of one of David's descendants. The shining face of Moses, which the Israelites could not then bear to behold, was a type of the shining face of the prophet like Moses. Both cases refer to the indwelling

---

[1] Rev. xii.

of the Divine Word, Wisdom, Spirit or Glory, which, in all ages, God has poured on all flesh. In both cases human obedience to Divine instruction was necessary. What had been typified in Israel, was being fulfilled in Israel. 'Behold, the Virgin is with child, and is bearing a Son, and thou (the mother,[1] that is, Israel) shalt call his name Immanuel.'[2] But the mystery of the kingdom of heaven, the indwelling of the Spirit of God, was not known to the people, from whom the key of knowledge had been taken away. And the spiritual rulers of Israel believed in, but trembled at this doctrine, the tendency of which necessarily was, to undermine all the exclusive privileges of the hierarchy. They had, therefore, put a stop to the further engrafting of the oral law on the written law. The people were forcibly kept in ignorance by Sadducean influence, and gross darkness covered the people.

History is thus shown to have been, not only the record of the past, but the revealer of the future. Historical records are witnesses of God in the universe. It is by his Spirit, Wisdom, or Word, that God is present in the world. This Divine Mediator was known as the 'Saviour of all,' and as having been symbolised by the brazen and fiery serpent. Because this Saviour dwells in the hearts of men, because Israel represented all the races of mankind, therefore Israel, the symbol of catholicity, was by Israel's prophets connected with, and in a certain sense, identified with the Divine Saviour. The time came, when the birth, the life, the death of an anointed man, could lead to the anointing of mankind. The world was to become 'the only and much beloved Son' of God, by the mystical union of God with this man-indwelling Wisdom, and thus by the union between the Creator and the creature. Philo called the Divine wisdom the mother, in order to distinguish the same from the son, that is, from

---

[1] Comp. Gen. xvi. 11.     [2] Is. vii. 14.

humanity. Because and inasmuch as the former dwells in the latter, because God's Spirit is in the soul of man, Israel, the representative of mankind, is by the prophet called the virgin, or woman, bearing the Son, the God-with-us.

## CHAPTER XVII.

### THE SON OF DAVID.

THE Anointed One, the Messiah, the God-with-us, had been, by prophets, promised to David, to the town of David's birth, and to the Kenite branch of Israel, to which the house of David belonged. The prophet Zechariah saw in a vision, that the men who, with the Kenite high priest Joshua, ministered before the altar, were men of typical significance.[1] They were emblems and hostages of the Messianic future, proofs, that Israel was then travailing, that the Israelite servant of God, 'the Branch' was soon to be born. Zechariah the prophet, or one of the two prophets of that name, spoke plainly about 'the man whose name is the Branch.'[2] Thus it became evident, to all who knew how to interpret prophecies and visions, that the Branch was a term applied to the 'ruler in Israel,' who was to be born in Bethlehem-Ephrata, and whose 'origins' have been 'ever of old, since the aboriginal days.'[3] Some of the initiated may have connected with these Messianic prophecies, the passage recorded in the Psalm of Asaph, that 'the Branch' would be a man whom God made strong for himself.[4] To this would be added one of the figurative sentences of old, 'that the righteous shall flourish as the branch.'[5] For already Jeremiah had announced, that God would raise unto David 'a righteous Branch,' who should wisely rule as king, and execute right and righteousness on earth,' and whose name should

---

[1] Zech. iii. 8; comp. Is. viii. 18.     [2] Zech. vi. 12.
[3] Micah v. 2.     [4] Ps. lxxx. 15.     [5] Prov. xi. 28.

be, 'The Lord our righteousness.'[1] The rising of ' the Sun of righteousness, with healing in his wings,' was promised to those that fear the ' name,' that is, the Spirit of God.[2]

The Branch is connected with righteousness, that is, according to the principles laid down by Kenite Psalmists and prophets, with obedience to the indwelling Spirit of God, the healer and Saviour of all. As sin is disobedience to God's voice, and therefore opposed to righteousness, it necessarily follows, that perfect righteousness, or perfect obedience, is sinlessness. The Branch was foretold by prophets, as a man who should be in all things like his brethren, yet without sin. The overcoming of sin, the dominion over sin, was held out and promised to Cain, when he went out from the presence of the Lord in Eden. Though sin is lurking at the door, desiring to have him, yet Cain shall gain dominion over her. This prophecy was to be fulfilled by the descendants from Cain, by the Kenites, and it was fulfilled by a descendant from David the Kenite. The records of the Kenite wanderings, from Eden to Jerusalem, are the history of Paradise lost, and Paradise regained. Man goes out from the presence of the Lord, and returns to the same. His sacrifice is not pleasing to God, whatever be the outward gifts which he offers. The dedication of the will, the sacrifice of obedience unto death, is alone graciously accepted.

Ever since the days of Isaiah and Eliakim, the Kenites, and especially the Kenite priesthood, looked forward to the birth of David's Son. His forerunner was born in the family of Zechariah, a priest of the Kenite course of Abiah. The prayerful expectation, that it was the high destiny of the Kenites, to fulfil the Messianic prophecies, led to the birth of John. It is recorded of him, that he was ' filled with the Holy Ghost, even from his mother's womb,' in order to go before the Lord, ' in the spirit and power

[1] Jer. xxiii. 5, 6.  [2] Mal. iv. 2.

of Elijah,' the Kenite prophet. As God's message was conveyed to Zacharias by an angel, so likewise is God recorded to have spoken to Mary through the same medium. She was to give birth to the man whose name is the Branch, to the God-with-us, to the 'Son of the highest,' to whom would be given 'the throne of his father David,' who should rule over 'the house of Jacob' for ever, and of whose kingdom there should be no end. The 'performance' of those things which were told Mary from the Lord, was to be accomplished through the instrumentality of the Holy Ghost. In like manner God's promise to Elizabeth had been performed. For John was filled with the Holy Ghost, before he saw the light of day. The records of the hidden wisdom prove, that the belief in such an effectual operation of the Divine Spirit, was very general among those, to whom the mystery, which had been kept in silence since the world began, had been even partly revealed. The wife and the relative of a Kenite priest would both belong to the narrow circle of initiated, at a time when the birth of the promised deliverer was expected, and when even heathen philosophers could consider the world sufficiently prepared, so that 'the Christ might be born.'

The universal expectation of a Christ in the flesh, was to be fulfilled by the birth, the life, the death, of a universal Saviour, in the midst of a people, which represented the catholicity of mankind. Both genealogies transmitted to us, agree in the Davidic, that is, in the non-Hebrew, in the Kenite, or Rechabite, descent of Jesus. But the first Gospel, where the account about the faith of the Kenite woman, coming from the district of Tyre and Sidon, is given without the interpretation, which we find in the second Gospel, that she was 'a Gentile, a Syrophœnician by birth,' contains a genealogy which connects David, and therefore also the Son of David, only with Abraham, the ancestor of the Hebrews, whilst that in St. Luke connects the Kenite king, and his Kenite descendant, not only with

Abraham, but also with Adam 'the son of God.' Thus the spiritual birth of Adam, and the spiritual birth of Jesus, are connected by human links, the human descent is connected with the Divine descent, and the principle of universality is laid down. The canon of catholicity, the pearl of Kenite tradition, the doctrine which was strenuously opposed by the guardians of Hebrew tradition, is expressed by the words of Simeon, perhaps Simon ben Jochai, the renowned targumist. His eyes, according to a previous revelation, saw the salvation, which God had prepared 'before the face of all people' : a light to lighten the Gentiles, and the glory of God's people Israel.

Whatever traces of Sadducean, or Hebrew, influence, may be found in the records of the New Testament, the new covenant is anti-Sadducean, and anti-Hebrew; it is the covenant and tradition of the Kenites, of the men from the East, who formed an inherent part of Israel's commonwealth. Thus much can be positively asserted, in the face of foregoing investigations, that the Sadducees, if they countenanced any Messianic expectations at all, believed only in a man of terrestrial descent, and of terrestrial glory. The Sadducees can never have believed in the Spirit of God. Least of all would they assist in the fulfilment of Kenite hopes, and in the establishment of Kenite principles. The rival stranger, by his enemies called the man of low degree, the descendant from Cain, was to be kept down by force, and the enlightenment of the people, which the Kenites coveted, was to be prevented by all means. The inheritance of Benjamin was not to be, once more, shared with the men of Judah.

Similar aspirations had been thwarted in the time of Eli, and in the time of Joshua the high priest. The first division of the spoils of 'God's heritage,' between the rival Aaronic lines, had led to the introduction of prophetic schools, to the recognition of Jehovah as the national God of Israel, and to the setting up of the Kenite house of David. Through his Psalms, and the

Psalms of other sons of Rechab, the key of knowledge had been given to the people. The leaven of knowledge concerning 'matters of God,' permeated the entire Israelitic community. After the captivity, synagogues took the place of the temple. A Kenite high priest had rebuilt the same, excluding all imagery, and with it the idolatry which had been Israel's ruin. But the adversary, the rival Hebrew Aaronite, stood on the right hand of Joshua, in order to bring adversity on the high priestly line which was connected with the house of David. He succeeded, and the Sadducee ruled for five centuries over the Lord's vineyard.

But as, in the days of Eli, Hannah, the handmaid of the Lord, prayed that she might give birth to a son, whom she would dedicate to God, so Mary, the handmaid of the Lord, the highly favoured, the God-with-her, must have prayed for the Son, who was afterwards promised and granted to the 'blessed among women.' Whether or not, in those days, as in the days of Eli, the Kenite high priestly line of Ithamar had been raised to power, Mary knew that her Son, like the son of Elizabeth, would be of Davidic descent, and that he would rule over the house of Jacob, that is, over the Kenite branch of Israel. Once more the Lord had sent a 'word unto Jacob, and it had lighted upon Israel.'[1] The 'little child' was to be born, who should rule over adverse parties, inaugurating the period when all persecution should end, and when the earth should be full of the knowledge of the Lord, as the depths of the sea are covered by the waters.[2] As in the days of Hannah, so in the days of Mary, God had scattered the proud, had put down the mighty, and 'exalted them of low degree;' the poor, the hungry had been fed, and the rich had been sent empty away. The Lord had entered into judgment, as Isaiah had announced, 'with the ancients (elders) of his people, and the princes (spiritual

---

[1] Is. ix. 8.   [2] Ibid. xi. 6-9.

rulers) thereof, who had eaten up, or burnt, 'the vineyard,' and in whose houses was 'the spoil of the poor,' that part of the priestly inheritance which Benjamin, the wolf, had devoured.[1] The evening of Benjamin's rule had again set in, when it was to divide the spoil.

Josephus informs us, that when Herod was made king by the Romans, in the year 37 B.C., he 'did no longer appoint high priests out of the family of Asmoneus,' that is, of the descendants from Chasmon, son of Joarib, and, therefore, of the house of Eleazar,[2] to which the Sadducees belonged; 'but made certain men to be so, that were of no eminent families, but barely of those that were priests.' Excepting the short interval of the high priesthood of Aristobulus, this policy was pursued during the entire reign of Herod, and of Archelaus, his son, 'although, after their death, the government became an aristocracy, and the high priests were entrusted with a dominion over the nation.'[3] We have seen that, whenever the Sadducees fell, prophets arose. Such a period of reformation was the reign of Herod. Whatever truth there may be in the assertion of later Jewish tradition, respecting Herod's having sided alternately with the Asmoneans, that is, with the Sadducees, and with the Romans, and those that went with them, Josephus clearly establishes the facts, that the Sadducees lost their hereditary sacerdotal dignity, and that, from the very commencement of his reign, 'he promoted such of the private men in the city as had been of his party; but never left off avenging and punishing every day those that had chosen to be of the party of his enemies.' Who these enemies were, is not here stated, but it is certain that they were the Sadducees. For the historian continues: 'But Pollio, the Pharisee, and Sameas, a disciple of his, were honoured by him above all the rest; for, when Jerusalem was besieged, they advised the citizens to receive Herod, for which advice they were well re-

---

[1] Is. iii. 14.   [2] 1 Chr. xxiv. 7.   [3] Ant. xx. 10.

quited.'[1] Moreover, Herod was appointed king of Judea by the Roman senate, to the exclusion of the Asmoneans, with whom the Sadducees were connected, and whose cause had been taken up by Antigonus and the Parthians.

Josephus enables us to assert, that 'men of low degree' took the place of 'men of high degree,' that the poor took the place of the rich, in the time when Jesus was born. The same change had occurred in the time of Hannah, when Eli, of the Kenite line of Ithamar, had become high priest. Thus, the remarkable parallel between the songs of Hannah and of Mary, is explained in all its points. We need not assume, that the line of Ithamar was raised to the high priesthood during the reigns of Herod and of Archelaus. For a descendant from Joshua, the high priest, would hardly have been classed, by Josephus, himself a Pharisee and a priest, with men that were 'of no eminent families, but barely of those that were priests.' Hereditary sacerdotalism had been put down by Herod, the Aaronites ceased to rule. The popular and foreign element, if not the lay element, was encouraged by the Idumean ruler of the Jews. As these principles were always supported by the Kenites, their accession, at all events, the influence of Kenite, or anti-Sadducean tradition, in the time of Herod the Great, is highly probable at the outset. The connection between the Kenites and the Idumeans, and the history of Edom, removes all doubt on this point. For we have pointed out, that the Nabathæans were a cognate race with the Kenites, who took Edom proper, or Mount Seir, during the Babylonian captivity, left off their nomadic habits, and founded the kingdom of Arabia Petræa, some of whose monarchs took the name of Aretas. Again, Herod was an Arabian by birth, and he married a Samaritan, that is, a Kenite. His enemies, the Asmoneans, had captured part of Idumea, and forced the Edomites to conform to Jewish law,[2] and Herod had to abandon his kingdom, because of the attack of the

---

[1] Ant. xv. 1, &c. [2] Ibid. xii. 8, &c.

Parthians, the allies of the Asmoneans. The reign of Herod completely undermined the long-established Sadducean rule.

The Herods were not Hebrews, either by descent or in their faith. Their connection with the Kenites, and therefore with the Pharisees, enabled them to identify themselves with Israel. We hope to have proved that religion in Israel was never separated from party interests, that, to a certain extent, it was always a policy. Exclusion was the leading principle of one party, universality of the other. Since the days of Solomon, so catholic a ruler as Herod had not ruled over Israel. The means employed for undoing what the Maccabees had done, were not more cruel, nor were they more enlightened, than those which were sanctioned by the standard of Modin. Sadducean, or Hebrew, principles having been enforced, in Southern Idumea, by John Hyrcanus (about 130 B.C.), Pharisean, or Kenite, principles were enforced in Judea by Herod the Idumean. To speak of conversion, under such circumstances, would be to degrade the meaning of that word. But there was an essential difference between the policy pursued in Idumea by the Maccabees, and in Judea by the Herodian rulers. We cannot assert, that any party welcomed the Maccabean conquerors in Idumea, whilst the Herods had, in Judea, the sympathetic support of the most enlightened party in Israel's commonwealth. The Kenites, represented by the Pharisees, prepared the way for Herod's rule. This led, as Josephus informs us, to the elevation of that party.

The Idumean policy was essentially identical with the Samaritan policy, in the time which preceded the Purim massacre. The object was, in both cases, to put down Sadducean rule, and to establish an independent state on the more enlightened Kenite principles, which the Samaritans and the Idumeans fully recognised. Such a policy was necessarily dependent on foreign recognition and support. A neutral state would have been impossible in those days; and nothing short of the necessity of establishing the true principles of catholicity, would render the formation of a neutral state in those regions possible, in our days. The dissolution of all the bonds, which had made Israel's commonwealth the type of the world's catholicity, the degradation of Israel, was not caused by the prevalence of Kenite, Samaritan and Idumean principles, but by the Hebrew, or Sadducean negation of the same. Israel fell because the Hebrews opposed the Kenites, because Christianity was rejected.

The Messianic expectation was by some so directly connected with the East, that several of the Herods—Antipas, Herod the Great, and Agrippa, were each regarded as the promised Messiah, by the party of the Herodians.[1] The East had been the birthplace and cradle of those traditions which were gradually to mould the religious convictions of the world. As in Eden, so in Palestine, a tree of life was planted. Life was symbolised by different trees in different countries.[2] The sacred tree of the Hebrew patriarchs was the oak; in Eden, because among the Assyrians and Persians, it was probably the palm, and so it was among the early Egyptians, till the sycamore fig-tree took its place. Israel's tree, the symbol of its national and of its spiritual life, was cut down to the root,[3] but the prophet who announces this calamity, foretold the branch which should grow out of its roots.[4] As the man whose name is the Branch, as the Messiah, was to be a descendant from David, so the tree which was cut down, and from the roots of which the branch should grow, was the tree of life which David, the Kenite king, had planted. As the Kenites, the descendants from Cain, came from the East, so the Davidic tree was of Eastern origin, and 'the man whose name is the Branch,' the Son

---

[1] Vict. Ant. ap. Cram. Cat. in Mart. p. 400; Philastrius Haer. xxviii.; Epiph. Haer. xix.

[2] See Barlow's Essays on Symbolism, 1866.

[3] Is. ix. 14, where the 'branch' ought to be the 'palm-branch.'

[4] Ibid. xi. 1.

of David, like his forerunner John, was an impersonification of the healing Spirit or Word of God, of 'the sun of righteousness,' of the ' dayspring from on high,' that is, of the rising sun, coming from the East.

The Son of David, nevertheless, warned his disciples, that they should ' beware of the leaven of the Pharisees, and of the leaven of Herod.'[1] At the time when St. Luke recorded the different traditions about ' the eyewitnesses and ministers of the word,' all knowledge about the party of the Herodians seems to have been lost, for he does not refer to them. They are never mentioned together with the Sadducees, whilst their acting in concert with the Pharisees is specially mentioned in St. Matthew and St. Mark.[2] Thus the testimony of Josephus is directly confirmed by the Gospels. We may assume, therefore, that ' the leaven of the Pharisees' was identical with ' the leaven of Herod.' Of the former St. Luke informs us, that the Son of David stigmatised it as ' hypocrisy.'[3] They knew the truth, but they did not apply it, nor promulgate it; they were like those who ' say and do not ;'[4] like ' the chief priests and elders' of Israel, compared with the son who was asked to work in the vineyard of his father. and who said : ' I go, sir, and went not.'[5] At that time, and ever since the time when ' the child grew, and waxed strong, becoming filled with wisdom,'[6] the Sadducees had returned to power. Under their influence the chief priests and elders were appointed, of whom the Son of David said, that ' the publicans and the harlots' went into the kingdom of God before them.

By this Sadducean reaction, the immediate fulfilment of the Messianic hopes was frustrated. The Hebrew adversary, represented by the Sadducean high priest, did not only stand at the right hand of his Kenite rival, but the high priesthood seems to have been exclusively held by the Sadducees, up to the time of Jerusalem's destruction, unless we except the high priesthood of Ishmael, the

---

[1] Mark viii. 15.   [2] Matt. xxii. 16; Mark xii. 13.   [3] Luke xii. 1.
[4] Matt. xii. 3.   [5] Ibid. xxi. 30.   [6] Luke ii. 40.

son of Phabi. Cowed down by Sadducean tyranny, by a want of faith in the final victory of truth, the Pharisees, and the Herodians, withheld their support from the Son of David. All influential parties seem then to have agreed, that the knowledge of the wise must not become the knowledge of the people. This restriction was necessary, to keep up the hierarchy, as then constituted. But the Essenes dissented from this policy. So powerful had the influence of their leader, John the Baptist, become, that Herod, 'who feared, lest the great influence John had over the people, might put it into his power and inclination to raise apostacy, thought it best, by putting him to death, to prevent any renovation (or, reform) he might cause, and not bring himself into difficulties, by sparing a man, who might make him repent of it, when it should be too late.'[1] The chief priests and the elders feared the people, because 'all the people held John as a prophet.'[2] Yet he declared, that he was not the Christ.

The cause of the Baptist's death, which Josephus has transmitted, is not recorded in the first three Gospels, whilst the fourth does not refer to his death at all. For this a reason may be suggested. If John had been put to death, because of his anti-hierarchical and anti-Sadducean doctrines, thus creating what was regarded as an apostacy and reform ; moreover, if his Essenic doctrines contained the elements of the hidden wisdom, the promulgation of which was strictly forbidden in Palestine, then the first Evangelist, the Apostle St. Matthew, writing, as we shall prove, under Sadducean restriction and compulsion, would see the necessity of avoiding all reference to the real cause of the Baptist's martyrdom, which was closely connected with that of Jesus and of St. Stephen. At the time when the Gospel after St. John was published, the earlier recorded conflicting traditions on the cause of the Baptist's persecution and death, led to the omission of all reference to these events, in this last Apostolic Gospel.

---

[1] Ant. xviii. 5, 2.  [2] Matt. xxi. 26.

In the Gospel records, the baptism of the Son of David marks the time, when he began to show himself unto Israel. St. Matthew's record has for its object, to show that, what Isaiah had foretold about the Branch, was fulfilled at the baptism of Jesus. 'And the Spirit of the Lord shall rest upon him, a spirit of wisdom and understanding, a spirit of counsel and might, a spirit of knowledge and of the fear of the Lord.'[1] Because John knew him, as the mighty One who was to baptize 'with the Holy Ghost and with fire,' therefore he is recorded to have hesitated to perform on Jesus the rite of water-baptism, which John had announced as a preparation for the baptism by fire, that is, by the Holy Ghost. Jesus having insisted on its performance, for the purpose of fulfilling 'all righteousness,' he himself 'saw the Spirit of God descending like a dove, and lighting upon him.' Jesus alone heard a voice from heaven, saying: 'This is my beloved Son, in whom I am well pleased.' In Justin's 'Memoirs of the Apostles,' probably identical with the Gospel of the Hebrews, the original version which St. Matthew wrote in Hebrew, and which existed at the end of the fourth century, the voice is recorded to have said: 'My Son thou art, I have begotten thee to-day.' According to the Greek version transmitted to us, it is left an open question, whether or not the Messiah received the Holy Ghost at a specified time, that is, on the day of his baptism, and whether it could be said of Jesus, at any time, that he waxed strong, and was becoming filled with wisdom, the grace of God being upon him.

Very different from this is St. Luke's record. Not the Messiah was to be prepared for his office, but 'a people' was to be prepared for the Lord. The Messiah could not, at any time of his life on earth, require anything which he did not possess ever since his birth. For even John was filled with the Holy Ghost from his mother's

---

[1] Is. xi. 2.

womb. Yet, like the son of Elizabeth, the Son of Mary 'waxed strong in the spirit,' and 'increased in wisdom and stature (or age), and in favour with God and man.' Even as a child he 'knew his Father's business.' Although Jesus was 'also' baptized, yet all direct reference to the ceremony is omitted. This feature well accords with the mysterious fact, that, in the Gospel of St. Luke, water-baptism is never recorded to have been sanctioned by Jesus. Again, the heavens were not opened for him, but, like the sepulchre of Lazarus, they opened in consequence of the prayer of Jesus, and for the sake of the people. Not he alone sees the Spirit descending, nor does he alone hear the voice, but these signs were done, because of the people, who required to be prepared for the Lord.

According to the account in the fourth Gospel, John did not know Jesus, nor is it here said, that he baptized him, still less is it stated or implied, that he hesitated to do so. But it had been revealed to him, that he would see the Spirit descending and remaining on 'a man,' who was to be preferred before him, and who would baptize with the Holy Ghost. Not even Jesus, still less all the people, saw the vision, and heard the voice; but John saw the former, though he did not hear the latter. Having seen the descending and remaining of the Holy Ghost, John knew, and bare record, 'that this is the Son of God,' that is, the Christ. It is not, that Jesus then received the Spirit of God, nor even, that he received the same without measure, at the time when he began his Messianic office. But this unlimited and lasting possession of the heavenly treasure, was, for the sake of men, outwardly manifested on this occasion. In like manner, the invisible Divine presence, the Shechina in the holy of holies, was first visibly manifested in the wilderness. In this Gospel only is it stated, that the dove remained on Jesus. This may, perhaps, be explained by the fact, recorded in the Gospel of the Hebrews, as attested by St. Jerome, that the dove did not simply alight on Jesus, but went into him. Before entering Jesus, thus making him, like Moses, the shepherd of God's flock, 'the entire source of the Holy Ghost descended and remained on him, and said unto him: "My Son, in all prophets I expected thee, that thou mightest come, and I might rest upon thee; for thou art my rest, and thou art my first-begotten Son, who rulest for ever."'[1] In this particular, the Gospel of St. John takes an intermediate position between the Hebrew and the Greek versions of St. Matthew.

No voice is by St. John recorded to have been heard, either by Jesus alone, or by all the people present. We suggest, that this omission was caused by the various readings in the Hebrew and Greek texts of the first Gospel, with reference to the words pronounced by the heavenly voice. It seems, as if in the second century, when the fourth Gospel was published, it was deemed necessary to set aside this much-debated question. At that very time, different opinions on this point were held by the disciples of Valentine, who, with Marcion, exercised so much influence on the Roman Church. The Italian school of Valentine, probably supported by the Roman Church, sided with those who believed the voice to have declared Jesus as begotten on the day of his baptism. It is important to observe, that, about the year 150 A.C., the Roman Church, which Ignatius had declared, not many years before, as 'entirely cleansed from the stain of any false doctrine,' protested, indirectly at least, against the doctrine of the Eastern docetics, who maintained that the Holy Ghost had descended upon Mary.[2]

St. John, or the final revisers of the fourth Gospel, intended, by the account of Jesus' baptism, to exemplify the doctrine, that 'a man can receive nothing, except it be given him from heaven.' The reason, why Jesus must increase, and John must decrease, is clearly stated: 'For God giveth not the Spirit by measure unto him,' whom he

---

[1] Hier. Com. in Is. xv. 1. Opp. iv. 156.
[2] Comp. Hidden Wisdom i. 418.

'hath sent,' and who 'speaketh the words of God.' By this explanation, the above indicated view is confirmed, that, according to the tradition of the early Roman Church, the voice had said: 'This day have I begotten thee.' The begetting of the Son of God and Son of Mary did not consist in Jesus receiving the Holy Ghost, nor in his 'becoming filled' with the same, but in his having received the Spirit without measure, in all its fulness. The bearing of these passages on the event we are considering, is equally direct, whether we assume, that, before his baptism, Jesus had not received the Spirit of God without measure, or, that it was from that time only, that the people were to know, that in him dwelt, or was to dwell, 'the fulness of the Godhead bodily.' The Divine Word from the beginning, by the perfect obedience of Jesus, has become perfectly identified with his Spirit; the Word has 'become' flesh. Because of this identity of cause and effect, what could hitherto only be said of the Spirit of God, of the eternal Christ, must now be said of the Christ in the flesh, of Christ Jesus. The bride has been united, and has become at one with the bridegroom; the Divine Spirit has found his man; the anointing agency 'from above,' has been concentrated in the chosen human agency, in Jesus, the Christ. Henceforth it is no more the Spirit of God, no more Christ, who 'cometh from above,' and who is 'above all,' but it is Jesus. Therefore, the man Jesus is not only 'of the earth, earthy,' but likewise 'from above,' because of his spiritual nature. He is not only Jesus, but Christ; not only Christ, but Jesus; he is he, 'whom the Father hath sanctified' because of his own merit; he is Jesus the Christ.

At last, the Holy Ghost could accomplish his mission. As the perfect instrument of the Spirit of God, Jesus testified, 'what he had seen and heard.' Thus it is explained, that, 'he whom God hath sent, speaketh the words of God,' and that 'the Father loveth the Son, and hath given all things into his hand.' Because 'it is the Spirit that

quickeneth,' therefore the words of Jesus were and are
spirit and life. Apart from that spiritual influence, of his
own self, Jesus could 'do nothing.' He has been taught
by God in the same manner, as every other man whom
God taught and teaches. The prophets had said, that
'all' shall be 'taught of God.' Confirming this, Jesus
said: 'Therefore, every man that hath heard, and hath
learned of the Father cometh unto me.' Those who
'were' the Father's, were given over to the Son, although
they had not yet fully believed in the Son, as they believed in the Father. Without this knowledge about the
Spirit or Word of God, as the Saviour of all, men cannot
come to the Father. And since he has created them as free
creatures, God cannot, and will not force them to come.
He cannot 'draw' men by his Spirit, unless they will be
led by the same. Without man's co-operation, God is not,
because he willed it not, omnipotent to save. Yet many,
by far the majority of the Jews, had not even heard, that
there was a Holy Ghost. The promulgation of this doctrine, and that of others, constituting the hidden wisdom,
had been forbidden by those, whom Jesus charged with
having 'taken away the key of knowledge.'

Under these circumstances, the Son of David, and the
Son of God, could not fulfil his mission in any other way,
than by speaking in parables to the people, interpreting
them to his disciples, 'when they were alone.' Those who
watched him, could not find any fault with him, so long
as his disciples obeyed faithfully his command, not to tell
any man that he was the Christ, and to proclaim, at some
future time, and in light, what he had been obliged to
whisper into their ear. It is in the fourth Gospel, that
we see best, how necessary such caution was. And yet
this is the only Gospel where no direct reference is made
to his teaching in secret. In the very beginning of
St. John's Gospel it is shown, that, although many in
Jerusalem believed in the name, or Spirit, of Jesus, 'when
they saw the miracles which he did,' yet that this kind of

belief was not such as to lead him to 'entrust himself unto them.' 'He knew what was in man,' and was aware, that in the people was not that light which is the life of men. '*But* there was a man of the Pharisees, a ruler of the Jews,' who formed an exception. He likewise had seen the works which Jesus did, but he, among others, knew well, that no man can do those miracles, 'except God be with him.' This knowledge about the indwelling Saviour, was the key to the mysteries. To him, therefore, Jesus did entrust himself, and he explained to him the mysteries of the kingdom of heaven. Some time after this intercourse with Nicodemus, John the Baptist was cast into prison, and put to death. We have seen, that this persecution stood in some connection with Herod's fear, that John might bring about a religious and political change. Jesus had to expect, that the same course would be adopted against him. For he had begun to draw the multitude after him. The Evangelist informs us, that even before John was imprisoned, some of his disciples complained, that 'all men' came to him. Knowing that the Pharisees had heard of this, Jesus 'left Judea, and departed again into Galilee,' passing through Samaria, where many believed in him, as 'the Saviour of the world.'

Returned to Jerusalem, the Jews sought to kill him, because he had broken the Sabbath, and had declared God to be his Father, 'making himself equal with God.' He was followed by 'a great multitude' to Galilee. Having openly proclaimed the heavenly mysteries at the synagogue of Capernaum, many of his disciples went back, and would no longer 'walk with him.' Jesus even doubted, whether the Twelve would not likewise go. Simon Peter having testified to their belief in Jesus, as 'the Holy One of God,' the Master is urged by 'his (unbelieving) brethren,' to face the danger of the Jews seeking to kill him, for that no one, who desires to be acknowledged openly, does things secretly. He was not only to manifest himself to them, and to a few believers, but 'to the world.' Although the Twelve believed in his power as the Son of God, yet they expected him to set up the promised kingdom at Jerusalem. Jesus declared, that his time had 'not yet come,' when he could openly manifest himself in that city. Therefore he went up to the feast 'not openly, but as it were in secret.' When it was about the midst of the feast, the Jews having vainly sought him, and no one speaking 'openly of him, for fear of the Jews,' Jesus went up to the temple and taught, speaking 'boldly.' And some of the Jews 'were minded to take him, but no man laid hands on him.' Again, teaching in the temple-schools before 'all the people,' many Jews believed on him. The same is recorded on the occasion of his raising Lazarus. This having been reported to the Pharisees, they and the chief priests assembled in council, to consider what they should do. 'If we leave him thus alone, all men will believe on him.' Having taken counsel together, for putting him to death, and Jesus. with his disciples, having retired to the wilderness of Ephraim, the chief priests and Pharisees ordered, that his hiding-place should be made known, that they might take him.

It clearly follows from this account, that when his time had fully come, Jesus spoke 'plainly,' not only to his disciples, but also to the people, who could not understand the deep meaning of his parables. It was the keeping back of the hidden wisdom by the rulers, which caused the persecution of Jesus, and it was his defying them which led to the crucifixion.

The chief witness for the prosecution was Judas. If he was from Kerioth in Judah, he was the only non-Galilean among the Twelve. From this it does not follow, though it is not improbable, that Judas was a Hebrew, and all the others were Kenites. We assert, that he betrayed to the rulers the fact. that Jesus had spoken of himself as the Christ. and that he had taught in secret. Because Judas gave that coveted information. and because the rulers were determined to put him to death, they changed their resolution, not to bring him to judgment during the feast. The record of the betrayal of the Son of Man by a kiss, whilst referring to the scene in the garden, would seem likewise to point to 'the holy kiss' of brotherhood, which Judas, as well as the other disciples, probably received, on being admitted into the narrow circle of what, in fact, was a secret society. The holy kiss was the seal of a sacred trust.

Unless we accept the supposition, that the betrayal of Judas, the only Jewish apostle, was connected with the secret instruction of Jesus, it is inexplicable, how Judas could have been bribed by the Jewish rulers to 'betray' the places to which his Master retired, well known to all in Jerusalem. It cannot be imagined, that he who 'could not be hid' in the Gentile border of Tyre and Sidon though 'he would have no man know' that he was there, could have been hid within the precincts of Jerusalem. After his triumphant entry, how could Jesus have hidden himself on the Mount of Olives, as he did hide himself in the wilderness of Ephraim? To that mount 'all the people came early in the morning to him, for to hear him.' The information which Judas is supposed to have given, was not worth thirty pieces of silver. The rulers had been 'laying wait' for Jesus, 'to catch something out of his mouth.' They failed, for they were not present when he was 'alone' with his disciples, interpreting the parables, and proclaiming himself as the Christ. Judas supplied the missing link. Thus the Sadducean high priest Annas was enabled to ask Jesus, 'about his disciples and about his doctrine,' about the doctrine preached to his disciples when they were alone. The reply of Jesus is directly pointed against this hidden accusation. 'I spake openly to the world, I ever taught in the synagogue and in (the schools and precincts of) the temple, whither the Jews always resort, and in secret have I said nothing, or rather, 'nothing further.'[1] He did not deny, he could not have done so, that he had spoken in secret, and commanded secrecy, at some time or other. But he denied, that his private doctrine had been different from what he had ended by proclaiming publicly. Judas betrayed the confidence placed in him, and yet his accusation was in so far not founded on fact, as Jesus had said nothing in public, which excluded his private teaching, and as he had said nothing in secret, which he had not fully proclaimed in public, before the accusation and betrayal. Judas had betrayed innocent blood, he had, under the most aggravating circumstances, sinned against the Holy Ghost, and nailed to the cross 'the prince of life.' As Moses lifted up, in the wilderness, the brazen and fiery serpent, the witnessing symbol of the Word and Wisdom of God, of the ever-present 'Saviour of all,' and as the foretelling type of salvation to be realised, so the Son of Man and Son of God, the incarnate Word from the beginning, the personified Wisdom of God, was lifted up as the Lord, who is the Spirit, as the Man who was at One with his God, and made the great At-one-ment, as the God-Man, as Christ Jesus.

Divine enlightenment, symbolised by the sun, had been standing still in the time of Joshua; it was first advanced by David and Solomon, then by Hezekiah, when the shadow went ten degrees backward, at Isaiah's request. Then the people that walked in darkness saw a great light; light from heaven did shine upon those that dwelt in the land of the shadow of death. Another advance was made in the time of Josiah, when the hidden wisdom of Moses was brought to light. Again, during the captivity, idolatry ceased. But the enemies of light continued to delight in 'shameful concealment.'[2] The seed which was sown in parables, the blade which sprung up, under the genial influence of enlightening interpretation by the

[1] John xviii. 19, 20.     [2] 2 Cor. iv. 2 (Greek text).

Word, and of illustrating manifestation by the life and death of the 'sower;' the full corn in the ear, ready for harvest, was taken away, trodden under foot, cut down and withered. Tares were sown by an adversary, they hid the sun from the growing wheat, and choked it. The sower was not the reaper.

But the grain of wheat had fallen into the ground and died; it did not abide alone, but brought forth much fruit. A long night came, when no man could work. The dayspring from on high, the sun of righteousness had risen, was darkened, and went down. There was a darkness over all the earth. But the sun rose again. It shines on the evil and on the good, even on those who like darkness better than light, who hate the light, and whose deeds are evil. The true light, the Word which was in the beginning, which lighteth every man, still comes into the world. The light that dwelt *with* men, is dwelling *in* them. The light of ages is the light of our time. To do the truth, is to come to the light. The truth alone does save, and the Word of God is the spirit of truth. He that follows the light of the world, has the light of life. The life is the light of men. 'This gospel shall be preached in all the world, for a witness unto all nations, and then shall the end come,' that is, the night shall depart for ever. 'There shall be no more curse,' for the fruit of the tree of knowledge and of the tree of life shall be no longer forbidden. There shall be 'no night,' and yet neither candle, nor light of the sun, for the Lord will give light. That light of God is the light of his Son, of the Son of man. 'As the lightning cometh out of the East, and shineth even unto the West, so shall also the coming of the Son of man be.' And 'then shall the righteous shine forth, as the sun in the kingdom of their Father.'

## CHAPTER XVIII.

#### THE CONVERSION OF ST. PETER.

'THE father of the spirits of all flesh' knows 'them that are his.' The Son of David, and the Son of God, said that his disciples, those who had 'followed him in the regeneration,' were given him by the Father. 'Thine they were, and thou gavest them unto me,' and 'they have kept thy word.' Before, as after, 'the days of Christ in the flesh,' it was God the Father who directed the hearts of men 'into the love of God,' stablishing them 'unblameable in holiness before God.'[1] Thus directed by the Divine Spirit, all children of God looked for the promised Son of God, for the Anointed, the Christ. What flesh and blood could not have revealed, was revealed by the Spirit of God in man. The first among the children of God, who was inspired to see Christ in Jesus, to have the Son of God revealed in his own heart, was Simon, the son of Jonas. The former name means 'hearing,' the latter 'dove.' Hearing comes by the Word or Spirit of God, which was then symbolised by a dove. He received the name of St. Peter, the rock, because, by his confession of 'Christ, the Son of the living God,' he laid the first stone for the Divine building of the Church, for the house of tradition, the house of wisdom.[2]

In all ages, and in spite of the hiding of Divine wisdom, God had spoken 'in manifold measures and in manifold

---

[1] 2 Thess. iii. 5; 1 Thess. iii. 12, 13.    [2] Is. li. 1.

fashions' in the prophets. St. Peter was the first among the twelve Apostles to believe that God then spoke 'in a Son,' and that he revealed that Son in him, through the same agency. It was 'the power of God and the wisdom of God' which, through Jesus, its perfect advocate, spoke unto 'babes,' and not unto the wise and intelligent. That same Divine wisdom had inspired Solomon to say: 'Turn ye at my direction. Behold, I will pour out my Spirit unto you. I will make known to you my words,' so as 'to give intelligence unto babes.'[1] One of these babes, one of the 'unlearned,' was St. Peter.[2] Together with his brother St. Andrew, and their partners, St. James and St. John, these fishermen of Galilee were disciples of John the Baptist, the Kenite and Essenic prophet. Called by St. Andrew, Simon went to Jesus.

It was near Capernaum, on the sea of Galilee, that St. Peter and St. Andrew were called to the discipleship. 'Follow me, and I will make you fishers of men,' or 'make you to become fishers of men.'[3] They were to follow him in the regeneration. That fire was to be lighted in them, and through them, which Jesus had come on earth to kindle. Although St. Peter left his nets and at once followed Jesus, he was not at once converted. Even he could not bear to hear all that Jesus had to say to them. Although he was declared to be clean, yet, even a few days before the Master's death, a necessary outward rite was performed on him, the symbolical meaning of which he was to understand hereafter. He was among those who believed that Jesus would have set up the promised terrestrial kingdom. He denied him, forsook him, and fled.

St. Paul's preaching of the Gospel among the Gentiles may have been concerted between him and St. Peter, to meet whom St. Paul first went to Jerusalem. To the circumstances which led to this mysterious meeting, we

---

[1] Prov. i. 22-24.   [2] Acts iv. 13.   [3] Matt. iv. 18-20; Mark i. 17.

shall fully refer in another chapter. Here we consider some of the effects produced in St. Peter by the storm which arose, partly in consequence of St. Paul's conversion. We submit that St. Luke, St. Paul's fellow-worker, has purposely enlarged the record of St. Matthew and of St. Mark about certain scenes which occurred on the sea of Galilee; and that it was the Evangelist's object to suggest to the initiated what were the ways and means of St. Peter's gradual conversion, of making him and his companions fishers of men. As the great Master had spoken in parables, so St. Luke wrote allegories.

According to his statement, Jesus said to St. Peter: 'Launch out into the deep, and let down your nets for a draught.'[1] In order to follow Jesus, to become fishers of men, the disciples must boldly face the deep mysteries of the kingdom of heaven. The proclamation of these had become even more dangerous after the crucifixion of Jesus, after the martyrdom of St. Stephen and St. James, and after the conversion of St. Paul, who boldly preached 'the hidden wisdom,' although 'in a mystery.' St. Peter had made a near approach to St. Paul, possibly first at Jerusalem in private, and then at Antioch in public. But he had considered it right to yield to St. James, the brother of the Lord. Under the restriction which, as we shall prove, the latter imposed, it might well be said of St. Peter and his associates, that they had 'toiled all the night' and had 'taken nothing.' They could not make conversions during the night of which the Master had spoken, wherein no one would be able to work.

But in the summons of St. Paul, not to fear the depth of the knowledge of Christ, they recognised the 'word' of the risen Lord. They let down the net in the deep waters, for a draught of men. The immediate success was miraculous. They could not do the work alone, and had to ask for the assistance of their partners 'in the

[1] Luke v. 1-11.

other ship.' Christ had first taught the people from St. Peter's ship, and it was after that 'he had left speaking,' we suggest, after his death, that St. Paul, in the name, or spirit of Christ, had invited St. Peter to turn to the Gentile world. The tree of life was to be transplanted into the sea. Seeing their success, they invited the 'other' ship, that of St. James and St. John, to join them, whilst St. Peter dreaded the presence of the Lord, because of his sinfulness. 'Fear not,' was the Divine answer, 'from henceforth thou shalt catch men.' And when they had landed, they forsook all, and followed the Lord. The sons of Zebedee left their father and his 'hired servants,' and followed St. Peter and St. Paul. It was through the instrumentality of St. Paul, that St. Peter, St. James and St. John understood the parable about the casting net, which 'gathered of every kind,' till it was 'full,' when the good were separated from the bad.[1] Like the bottles containing the new wine, their vessels were in danger of losing their contents. Yet nothing was lost, although a separation was effected.

Allegorically interpreted, the record in the fourth Gospel about the conversations of the risen Jesus with his disciples, on the sea of Tiberias, refers likewise to St. Peter's first success in the Gentile world.[2] The companions of St. Peter are no longer the sons of Zebedee, and St. Andrew St. Peter's brother, but, instead of the latter, St. Thomas, called Didymus, and Nathanael of Cana in Galilee, and 'other disciples,' declare themselves willing to go with Peter a-fishing. They enter into one ship, but 'that night they caught nothing.' With the morning, Jesus stood on the shore, but they knew him not as such. Hearing that they had no meat, or rather, nothing beyond, or to add to the common food, he told them, to 'cast the net on the right side of the ship.' Having done this, they found according to promise, and were not able to draw the net, 'for the multitude of fishes,' whilst, notwithstanding these, the net 'was not rent.' Because of this marvellous suc-

---

[1] Matt. xiii. 47, 48.   [2] John xxi.

cess, 'the disciple whom Jesus loved,' said to St. Peter:
'it is the Lord.' Like Adam in Eden, St. Peter is ashamed
of his nakedness, girds himself with his fisher's coat, and
throws himself into the sea, whilst the other disciples,
who had kept close to the land, dragged the net, which,
when St. Peter drew it to land, was found to contain 153
fishes.[1] Not until St. Peter had clothed himself with the
righteousness of Christ, which is without the deeds of the
law ; not until the morning after the night; not until St.
Paul had spoken in the spirit of Jesus, as the 'other'
comforter, or advocate, of the spirit of truth, did St. Peter
become a fisher of men. He was himself caught in the
net of Christ.[2]

It is immaterial, whether the event here recorded, like
the transfiguration, was a vision, or whether the symbolical
form has been chosen, for the purpose of explaining to
the unlearned the mysteries of the kingdom of heaven.
We now consider, what was the nature of the means
employed for the conversion of the chosen Apostles, and,
through them, of men of every town and nation. The
question asked by the Lord is not, 'Do ye now believe,
ye of little faith?' Nor, 'Are you now converted, so
as to be able to strengthen the brethren?' Nor again:
'Have ye now become fishers of men?' But he asks:
Have ye nothing to feed upon which is beyond the common
bread? Have ye the bread of life, the heavenly
manna? No answer is given. Meanwhile Christ, the
pilot, is guiding the ship to the land. 'As soon, then, as
they were come to land, they saw a fire of coals there,
and fish laid thereon, and bread.' Beyond the common
food, the bread, there was another kind of food, which in
the fourth Gospel alone is called 'opsarion,' that is, something
to be eaten with bread. This additional food was
alone laid on the fiery coals. In the same manner the

---

[1] According to the numerical value of the Hebrew letters, the name 'Semon Jona' gives the sum 153.

[2] Comp. Tertull. de Baptismo, 1.

manna in the wilderness was prepared for food. It was baked, and ground, and made into wafers. By this connection the symbolical meaning of a dark passage can be discovered. The above interpretation is confirmed by the sixth chapter in St. John's Gospel.

The Evangelist's object is to show, that Christ, the power of God, works like a leaven in all that he pervades. The feeding of the five thousand men, with five loaves and two fishes, is recorded to have taken place at the time immediately preceding the Jewish passover. Thereby St. John gives a significant hint, that, in the Lord's opinion, that rite must be performed in a manner more adapted to its spiritual significance. 'As much as they would,' is given to the people, of the bread and the fishes, and yet twelve baskets of fragments remain. Hereby it is shown, that Christ's food is inexhaustible. Yet even St. Andrew did not understand what the few loaves and fishes could do among so many. So little had the people understood the true nature of the food of Christ, that they sought for Jesus, not because they 'saw' and understood the miracle, but because they misunderstood it. They followed Jesus, because they 'did eat of the loaves and were filled.' Therefore Jesus said to them: 'Labour not for the meat (or food) which perisheth, but for that meat which endureth unto everlasting life, which the Son of man shall give unto you; for him hath God the Father sealed.' They are to labour for the fruit of the Spirit, to be made 'partakers of spiritual things,' and thus to be 'sealed,'[1] by receiving 'the earnest of the Spirit' in their hearts.[2] Because the law of Moses is devoid of 'grace and truth,' Jesus said to the people: 'Moses gave you not this bread from heaven, but my Father giveth you the true bread from heaven,' the fruit of the tree of life.

Christ Jesus is the incarnate Word or Wisdom of God, which in all ages seeking rest abides in the tabernacle of the chosen, enters 'into the soul of the servant of the

---

[1] Rom. xv. 27, 28.   [2] 2 Cor. i. 22; comp. Eph. i. 13; iv. 30.

Lord,' and says: 'Come unto me all ye that be desirous of me, and fill yourselves with my fruits.'[1] The loaves, and the leavened meal are types of the heavenly manna of the Spirit of God, of which God has, in all ages, offered unto men 'as much as they would.' Already in the book of Wisdom the 'bread from heaven,' the 'angels' food,' which was sent to the Israelites in the wilderness, is interpreted as having been 'adapted to every taste, and thus transformed' or transubstantiated, 'according to the will of every man.' It is described as having been 'obedient' to God's grace, 'that nourisheth all things according to the desire of them that had need; so that thy sons, O Lord, whom thou lovest, might learn that it is not (only) the growing of fruits that nourisheth man, but that it is thy Word, which preserveth them that put their trust in thee.'[2] Solomon knew, that wisdom is 'a tree of life.'

It is in this sense that Jesus said: 'Man liveth not by bread alone, but by every word that proceedeth out of the mouth of God.'[3] Because he has the Spirit of God without measure, which proceedeth out of the mouth of God, therefore he hears God's words and sees his works, he is 'the bread of life,' and 'came down from heaven.' And as it is written in the book of Proverbs, in the name of the wisdom of God: 'Come, eat my bread, and drink of the wine which I have mingled;'[4] so Christ, 'the Wisdom of God,' the manifestation in flesh and blood of the Divine Word, says that whosoever shall at any time spiritually partake of the bread and wine which he has mingled, and of which his flesh and blood is the sacred symbol, dwells in that Divine Wisdom, dwells in Christ, and Christ in him. Without the Spirit, even the flesh 'profiteth nothing,' how much less the symbol which represents it to the carnal eye. The heavenly manna, the 'opsariom,' is to be added to the flour as a leaven, and as the manna in the wilderness was added to the honey.

[1] Wis. x. 16; Ecclus. xxiv. 7, 19.
[2] Wis. xvi. 20-26.
[3] Matt. iv. 4.
[4] Prov. ix. 5; iii. 18.

The wafer of the Israelites in the wilderness is a type of the wafer of the Eucharist, of the Christian's thanksgiving. As the Apostles prayed, 'Ever give us of this bread,' so Jesus has taught his followers to pray: 'Give us this day to-morrow's bread,' the food which regards the future. Like Job, Christians must esteem the Word of God more highly than their 'necessary food' for the body's sustenance. As of old, the heavenly manna, the super-substantial food, symbolised by the wafer, is 'transformed' or transubstantiated 'according to the will of every man.' To the worthy recipient, the wafer, the symbol, is transsubstantiated into the Divine reality, into 'Christ, the Wisdom of God.'

It was not till 'after that Jesus was risen from the dead,' that even St. Peter was fully instructed in these mysteries. The 'unlearned' and lay Apostle could say to the unlearned multitude, that they, as also their rulers, had 'from ignorance' delivered up Jesus and 'denied him in the presence of Pilate,' although the same judged that he should be set at liberty.[1] The narrative about Jesus stilling the tempest likewise admits of allegorical interpretation, and refers to the relations between Jesus and his disciples. The fathers of the Church have interpreted the ship tossed about by the waves as a symbol of the Church and of the dangers to which she is exposed.[2] Twice a storm is recorded to have arisen on the sea of Galilee. On the first occasion,[3] it was Jesus who 'entered into a ship,' whilst 'his disciples followed him.' Jesus was asleep when the great tempest arose. The disciples having called him, he reprimanded them because of their want of faith, and by rebuking the winds and the sea he caused 'a great calm.' The account in St. Luke of the stilling of the tempest exhibits this more strikingly than that in St. Matthew. In the former Christ says: 'Let us pass over to the other side of the lake,' that is, from the Galilean to

---

[1] Acts iii. 13–17.     [2] Com. Ps. cvii. 25, 28–30.
[3] Matt. viii. 23–27; Mark iv. 36–40; Luke viii. 22–25.

the Gentile side. In the latter, the disciples are 'afraid,' as well as astonished: in the former they are only said to be 'astonished' at their safe transit over the deep and stormy sea.

On the second occasion,[1] the disciples went into a ship without Jesus, and in the evening encountered a storm caused by a contrary or hostile wind. For some time the storm raged in the darkness of the night, and Jesus did not come to them. When he did draw nigh unto the ship, 'walking on the sea,' they did not at once see him. But towards morning, 'about the fourth watch of the night,' they recognised him who, though he had left them, promised to be with them to the end of the world. When they had received the Master into their ship, they thought he was 'a spirit,' such as the disciples of Emmaus must have thought when their eyes were opened and he 'vanished out of their sight.' He had come unto them as 'the Lord which maketh a way into the sea, and a path in the mighty waters.'[2] It was not St. Peter who first recognised him.[3] For he said: 'Lord, if it be thou, bid me come unto thee on the water. And he said: Come. And when St. Peter was come down out of the ship, he walked on the water to go to Jesus.' Being afraid of the boisterous wind, and having cried: 'Lord save me.' Jesus 'stretched forth his hand and caught him, and said unto him: O thou of little faith, wherefore didst thou doubt? And when they were come into the ship the wind ceased. Then they that were in the ship came and worshipped him, saying: Of a truth thou art the Son of God.' What is here said in plain words, that Jesus caught St. Peter in the water, is implied in the account in the fourth Gospel, where the number of the fishes implies that St. Peter was caught in the net of Christ. Here again, it was not St. Peter, but St. John, who first recognised the Lord. Thus the Apostles were gradually, and after the

---

[1] John vi. 16-21; Matt. xiv. 22-33; Mark vi. 45-52.
[2] Is. xliii. 16; comp. Ps. lxxvii. 20; Job ix. 8.     [3] John xxi. 7.

resurrection of Jesus, brought to 'the unity of the faith, and of the knowledge of the Son of God.'[1]

To St. Peter were confided 'the keys of the kingdom of heaven,' with power to bind and to loose.

Before we interpret, we establish the fact, by facing all the difficulties that stand in its way. It is only in St. Matthew's Gospel, that the words attributed to Jesus about the rock and about the keys are recorded. St. Mark, the interpreter of St. Peter, cannot have had any conceivable reason for appearing to lower the authority of the founder of the Roman Church, for the members of which he wrote his Gospel. Again, St. Luke, if we assume him to have had any bias, would have preferred to exalt St. Peter at the expense of St. James, the ruler at Jerusalem, between whom and St. Paul, St. Luke's guiding star, there was no excess of attachment. But for the very reason, that St. James was the overseer of the Apostles at Jerusalem, under circumstances which we shall minutely consider; because St. Peter, unquestionably the first leader of the Apostles, had been apparently superseded, the peace of the Church required, that the Divinely authorised primacy of Simon Jonah should be suppressed for a time. We firmly maintain, on historical grounds, that, if there is one fact more certain than another, it is this, that 'the keys of the kingdom' of heaven were delivered to St. Peter by the Divine founder of the Church.

The Palestinian Gospel is just the one, where we might have expected the omission of this fact. For it has never been even surmised, that St. Matthew may have written his collection of the Lord's sayings before the accession of St. James, 'the brother of the Lord.' As we cannot assert, that St. Matthew survived the destruction of Jerusalem, and as his Gospel is referred to as Scripture, before the end of the first century, the first record of

[1] Eph. iv. 13.

words of Jesus must have been composed during the
episcopate of St. James, who, as we shall prove, could
never have suffered the insertion of a passage which
would have undermined his authority. It may be objected that this is a later interpolation. The above
reasons lead us to assume this. But if the insertion had
been effected contrary to living tradition, it would have
been made rather in any other place than in Jerusalem.
Even fiction, to be acknowledged, must be based on an
historical incident, particularly if the former is introduced
soon after the latter. The silence of St. Mark and of St.
Luke proves nothing against the record in the first Gospel,
which is confirmed by a passage in the last. St. Mark
more than compensates for his silence, by his version
about the ambitious demand of St. James and St. John.

St. Peter's two rival Apostles, who with him formed the
Apostolic Trio, the secret council of tradition, St. James
and St. John, themselves asked, and not their mother,
that an exceptional privilege might be granted to them.
Setting St. Peter aside, the two sons of Zebedee asked
Jesus, that they might sit on the right hand and on the
left hand of him, at the time of the setting up of the
glorious kingdom. The 'sons of thunder,' who knew
not what spirit was in them, boasted that they knew
what they asked, that they were able to drink of the cup
that Jesus drank of, and to be baptized with the baptism
that he was baptized with. But Jesus did not, and
declared that he could not grant their request, that the
places of honour would be given by God to them 'for
whom it is prepared.' When the ten heard this, that is,
St. Peter and the rest of the Apostles, they were 'much
displeased' with St. James and St. John. The warning
which follows may refer to the sons of Zebedee, or to St.
James the brother of the Lord, who subsequently occupied the place of his namesake, but it did not refer to St.
Peter. Jesus spoke against those who are acknowledged
as princes among the Gentiles, and who 'exercise lordship

over them,' against 'the great ones among them,' who 'exercise violence over them.' The same warning is given by St. Peter in his catholic epistle. The 'oversight' over the flock is to be exercised, 'not by constraint, but willingly, not for filthy lucre, but of a ready mind.'[1] It was not St. Peter who asked 'to be great' among the Apostles. And though he was, at that time, and again before his death, acknowledged as 'the chiefest,' it may be said of the writer of the great catholic epistle, that he lived in accordance with the principles which he announced to 'the strangers,' to 'the elect,' who were scattered 'throughout Pontus, Galatia, Cappadocia, Asia, and Bithynia.' St. Peter fed 'the flock of God,' not as the sole privileged steward, but as one among the elders and witnesses of 'the sufferings of Christ,' as 'a partaker of the glory that shall be revealed,' as one to whom it was given to know 'the mysteries of the kingdom of heaven;' to whom it was promised that he should know more after the departure of his Master; as the one, to whom, with 'the keys of the kingdom of heaven,' power was given to bind and to loose, to seal and unseal, to hide and to reveal. Of no other Apostle can it more truly be said, than of St. Peter, that he was 'the servant of all,' giving to every man his due 'in due season.'

No interpretation of the keys can be correct, which does not connect them with the building of the Church on the rock, that is, St. Peter, and with 'the key of the house of David,' promised to the Messiah.[2] We have proved that 'the house of Wisdom,' which we identify with 'the house of Rechab,' or house of tradition, was originally built on 'seven pillars,' represented by seven links of tradition from Adam to Moses. As St. Peter is the first of the three 'pillars' of the Church, we are, at the outset, led to assume, that the Church of Christ was built on that rock or stone of tradition, of which St. Peter

---

[1] 1 Peter v. 2.    [2] Is. xxii. 22.

was the principal guardian. This is confirmed by the parable of the talents.

According to St. Matthew's Gospel, a sacred trust was confided to three of the Lord's servants. We shall try to prove that St. Peter, St. John, and St. James, were meant thereby. The same Evangelist and Apostle informs us, that these three disciples were the most intimate associates of Jesus. They alone saw the raising of the daughter of Jairus, and the vision of the transfiguration of their Master; also they were nearer to him on the Mount of Olives than the rest of the disciples. If, then, it was a privilege of the Apostles, that they were made to know the mysteries of the kingdom of heaven, this privilege would belong in a higher degree to the Apostolic Trio. Clement of Alexandria has recorded an ancient tradition, according to which, Jesus, 'after the resurrection,' exclusively 'imparted the gift of knowledge' to these three Apostles, who communicated it to the rest of the Apostles, and they to the Seventy.'[1] We shall see, that after the martyrdom of St. James the son of Zebedee, St. James, the so-called 'brother of the Lord,' took not only his place, but was made the Primate of the Apostles, although he had not been a disciple, nor even a believer, before the resurrection. In the form transmitted to us, the parable of the talents refers, as the tradition of Clement does likewise, to St. Peter, St. John and St. James. In the latter, however, St. James is named first, and St. Peter last.

According to their several ability, the three chosen Apostles received respectively five, two and one talent, this being the largest measure for gold or other metal. The 'Man,' that is, 'the Son of Man,' on his departure gave 'his goods,' his possessions, to three stewards. These goods are called in the parable 'the Lord's money.' He that had received the most, made the most of it, by trading, whilst he that had received but one talent,

[1] Euseb. H. E. ii.1.

'digged in the earth, and hid his Lord's money.' Now, the account about the first answers to what we know about St. Peter, the founder of the Catholic Church; and the servant who, for a time, hid the talent confided to him, and checked the promulgation of tradition, may be identified with St. James, the brother of the Lord, who, as we shall prove, belonged to the Sadducean party, was an unbeliever, shortly before the crucifixion, and was a fool and slow of heart, when the risen Lord appeared to him and to his father Cleophas. St. John may be identified with the servant who had received two talents. It corresponds well with this assumption, that St. John was the constant companion of St. Peter, and that 'the boldness' of St. Peter and St. John is especially recorded.[1]

The reference in the parable to St. Peter, St. John and St. James, is confirmed by the fact, that St. Luke enumerates the pillars of the Church in the same order, when he refers to their astonishment at the draught of the fishes.[2] Again, although in St. Luke's version of the parable there are ten instead of three servants, yet but three are asked to give an account of their stewardship. Among these, the one (St. Peter), who made the most of what he had received, is called 'the first,' and the next, in the order above referred to (St. John), is called 'the second.' The last named of the three who were called upon to declare what use they had made of the treasure confided to them, (St. James), is clearly implied to have been the unprofitable servant, who had hid the Lord's money because he was 'afraid.' Every disciple of St. Paul must have been ready to admit, that St. James, at first, did hide the mysteries of the kingdom of heaven, and checked, for a time, even St. Peter and St. Barnabas, in their zeal to proclaim on the housetops what had been whispered into their ear. St. James was the cause of what St. Paul censured as St. Peter's blamable conduct. That same Sadducean over-

---

[1] Acts iv. 14.    [2] Luke v. 8-10; comp. Gal. ii. 9.

seer of the Apostles, as we have seen, is by St. Luke implied to have been one of the two 'disciples' of Emmaus, who had not profited by the Lord's sayings, by the treasure confided to their care. The defence of St. James against the accusation of having hidden the full light of the Gospel, would be like that of the unprofitable servant, that the Lord could not take up what he had not laid down, nor reap that he did not sow.

Yet the Epistle of St. James proves, that some time before his death, probably not before the year 62 to 63 A.C., when he wrote his Epistle, St. James proved openly to the world, that he had 'become,' as Hegesippus records, 'a faithful witness, both to Jews and Greeks, that Jesus is the Christ.' The Epistle confirms the tradition which Eusebius has recorded, that the cause of St. James's death was his being supposed to have secretly sided with St. Paul. Although he opposes the principle proclaimed by the latter, that righteousness is without the works of the law, and although his Epistle may be termed an exposition of the Sermon on the Mount as recorded by St. Matthew, yet the doctrine of the indwelling Word of God, is fully and emphatically proclaimed in a country where the people did not even know that there was a Holy Ghost. Nevertheless, if the parable of the talents had been recorded, as we must assume, before the death of St. James, essentially in the form transmitted to us, though perhaps not including the passage which seems to refer to his death, those who saw St. Stephen, St. James, St. Peter, and St. Paul martyred, must have felt, that if it had not been for the more than twenty years of St. James's presidency, the enemies of truth could not have become so powerful as they then were. According to the parable, the unprofitable servant was suddenly brought low, and summoned to give an account of his stewardship. His trust, his pound, was given to him who had gained ten pounds, and whom the Lord called *the* good servant, who had been faithful. He that had what was confided to him, and had made use of it, to him more was given, and he that had not, the 'wicked and slothful servant,' from him was taken even that which he had. The one pound committed to the trust of St. James, was given to St. Peter, to the 'one faithful servant,' whom his Master set 'over all his own,' over his universal Church. Since St. Peter is always mentioned as the first of the three most intimate associates of Jesus; since to him the keys of the kingdom of heaven were confided; since on the rock of his knowledge the church was to be built; since he was commanded to feed the flock, we may assert, that, according to St. Luke's version of the parable of the ten talents, equivalent to twelve pounds, it was St. Peter, on whom the apostolic primacy of St. James devolved. Before the fall of Jerusalem, Rome was the metropolis of the Christian Church.

Both versions of the parable of the talents or the pounds, refer to the timid hesitation of one of the Apostles, in the promulgation of the things which had been kept in silence and had been revealed by Jesus to the unlearned. This interpretation receives a curious confirmation by another version of the same parable, as recorded in the Zohar, a late record of ancient traditions. 'A certain king gave a deposit to three of his servants; the first kept it, the second lost it, the third spoilt one part of it, and gave the rest to another to keep. After some time the king came, and demanded the deposit. Him who had preserved it, the king praised, and made him the governor of his house. Him who had lost it, he delivered to utter destruction, so that both his name and his possessions were blotted out. To the third, who had spoilt a part and given the rest to another to keep, the king said: Keep him, and let him not go out of my house till we see what the other shall do, to whom he has entrusted a part. If he shall make a proper use of it, this man shall be restored to liberty; if not, he also shall be punished.'[1]

[1] Zohar Chadash, fol. 47.

We suggest that this version represents the early tradition of Christians in Rome, where, according to the 'Clementines,' St. Peter was regarded as the first Apostle among the Gentiles. The Apostle and Bishop of Rome would naturally be placed above the Apostle and Bishop at Jerusalem, although in that Epistle which St. Peter is recorded to have addressed to St. James from Rome, the former calls the latter 'My Lord.' A Roman Christian, living after the destruction of Jerusalem by the Romans, would see in the death of St. James, which took place shortly before that event, a sign of God's wrath. He would say of him, as in the tradition above recorded, that, like his see, St. James was by his Master 'delivered to utter destruction, so that both his name and his possessions were blotted out.' He was cast into 'outer darkness,' as one of 'the children of the kingdom.' With him perished those, who prided themselves in having done 'all those things' which the law commands, and on the performance of which St. James had long continued to insist, in spite of the preaching of St. Peter and St. Paul. The returning Lord, the judge, will not thank them, because they did 'the things that were commanded.' They were all 'unprofitable servants.'[1] They preserved the written law, but hid its interpretation. They took away 'the key of knowledge.' The 'deposit' confided to the keeping of St. James, as 'the good deposit' was committed to Timothy,[2] had to be transmitted to St. Peter, or to St. Peter's successor, if the latter's martyrdom had taken place before the death of St. James.

Finally, the third of the king's servants, who had 'spoilt' part of his trust and given the rest to another to keep, may be identified with St. John. In his Epistles, this Apostle had referred to the doctrine of the Sonship, to the hidden Wisdom, but not yet, after the destruction of Jerusalem, had he published the words in which Jesus had taught the same. The necessarily incomplete records

---

[1] Luke xvii. 5, 10.  [2] 2 Tim. i. 12.

of St. Matthew, and even that of St. Luke, without this indispensable complement, affected the deep meaning of the Lord's mysteries. According to Jewish tradition, the Hebrew Gospel of St. John was preserved at Tiberias. As the deposit of St. James had been made over to St. Peter, we may assume that St. John made over to the Roman Church the record of his good deposit, his Gospel.[1] At the time to which the tradition refers, 'the other,' to whom St. John had entrusted a part of his treasure, had not yet publicly shown, whether or not he would make good use of the written tradition confided to his keeping. The servant was then 'kept,' that is, his liberty was restricted for a time. This may well be referred to St. John's confinement in the island of Patmos, which was caused by 'the word of God and the testimony of Jesus Christ.'[2] Like St. Paul, he was waiting for the time when the Lord would reveal, that which is hidden,' and when 'every man shall receive of God the praise which is due to him.'[3]

The most convincing proof that the parable of the talents was explained as referring to the leading Apostles, is furnished by another version, evidently written by a Hebrew, who points out St. Peter as the unprofitable servant, who was punished, not for hiding, but for bringing to light the treasures of the hidden Wisdom. 'The gospel which has come down to us in Hebrew characters, does not utter the threat against him who hid (the talent), but against him who lived riotously. For it embraces three servants: one who devoured his substance with harlots and flute-girls; another, who multiplied the talent; another, who hid it. Then, that the one was accepted, the other merely blamed, the third shut up in prison. . . . Be ye therefore approved money changers.'[4] Here we find the matrimonial metaphor used as in the

---

[1] In the 'Hidden Wisdom' the Roman editorship of St. John's Gospel is asserted.     [2] Rev. i. 9.     [3] 1 Cor. iv. 5.
[4] Hilgenfeld, Nov. Test. extra Can. rec. iv. 26.

passage about the sons of Eli, to which the parable of the prodigal son refers.

The different versions of the parable referring to Apostolic tradition, agree in the principal points, that the tradition of Jesus was confided to three of his followers, and that one of them, by disobedience, lost the treasure committed to him. In other words, Clement of Alexandria has transmitted to us the same tradition, adding that St. James, St. John, and St. Peter were the three privileged Apostles. This is confirmed by the Gospels, by the Epistles, and by Church history. Again, proofs abound that St. Peter held the first rank among the Apostles. In the eyes of many, certainly of St. Peter and of St. Paul, the Church at Rome had become more important than that at Jerusalem, many years before the destruction of the latter. Before the death of St. James, St. Peter would naturally be contrasted with the unprofitable servant, as that one 'good servant' who had been a faithful keeper of his trust, 'the faithful and wise' steward of God's mysteries. Jesus had told his disciples, that they must have their loins girded and their lights burning, in order to be ready for the coming of the Son of man. Peter asks, 'Lord, speakest thou this parable unto us, or even to all?' It was apparently addressed to all who heard it. And yet Jesus, in his reply, refers to one 'faithful and wise steward, whom his Lord shall make ruler over his servants, to give them, at the proper time, what is their due. Blessed is that servant, whom his Lord, when he cometh, shall find so doing. Of a truth I say unto you, he will make him ruler over all his own.'[1] That man will be the faithful and wise steward who does not withhold from others what is owing to them, what they have a right to demand ; that steward who, in due season, dispenses to them the legacy left to all believers. But that disciple is an unprofitable servant, who, although he knows his Lord's will, has not 'prepared, neither done

[1] Luke xii. 35–44.

according to his will.' His portion will be with 'the unbelievers,' with those who have not the necessary faith, not even so much as a grain of mustard seed, for the transplanting of the tree of knowledge and of life, from the barren soil of Palestine to the fruitful soil of the Gentile world. Peter, the rock, the possessor of the key of knowledge, or keys of tradition, is clearly implied by the parable, to have been the good and faithful servant in the Lord's vineyard. By his Divine Master, who 'hath the key of David,' to shut and to open, to seal and to unseal the mysteries, he was commanded to feed the sheep of God's pasture. He transplanted the tree of life.

In another chapter we shall prove that St. Peter went from Jerusalem to Rome in the year 41, when and where he did found the Roman Church. For some time before his glorious martyrdom he presided at Antioch over the first of the Gentile Churches,[1] and then probably after the martyrdom of St. Paul at Rome, if not of St. James at Jerusalem, he presided over the Church which he had founded, and which was destined to become the centre of Catholic Christianity. Thus St. Peter had taken possession of the post assigned to him. In a city where the overseer of the priests, the Pontifex Maximus, was appointed for life, and represented the highest spiritual authority, it is highly improbable, the promise of the keys apart, that St. Peter's powers should not have exceeded those of a president of elders. What St. James had been in Jerusalem, that, and much more, St. Peter was in Rome. Whilst St. James wrote to 'the twelve tribes,' St. Peter wrote a catholic epistle shortly before his death, and from Babylon, the name given to Rome in St. John's apocalypse. St. Peter had not assumed without authority the position of

---

[1] The ancient tradition about the Antiochian Episcopate of St. Peter, (comp. Acts xi. 27), confirmed by Origen, is corroborated by an Arabian MS. in the Bodleian Library, where Antioch is called 'the chair of Peter,' or 'the see of the great Apostle Peter.' Payne Smith, cod. 140, 5, as quoted by Overbeck in 'Die orthodoxe katholische Anschauung,' 1865.

'Lord over God's heritage.' He had taken it 'not by constraint,' as St. James did, who was set up by the Jews, 'but willingly, not for filthy lucre, but of a ready mind,' and in life and in death he was an 'ensample of the flock.'[1]

[1] 1 Pet. v. 2, 3.

## CHAPTER XIX.

### THE CONVERSION OF ST. PAUL.

THE Apostle relates himself, in what manner the principles of the Gospel which he proclaimed were revealed to him. The revealer was Jesus Christ, whom he had persecuted, 'the power of God, and the wisdom of God,' the Lord who 'is' the spirit, 'the Son of man,' whom Stephen had seen 'at the right hand of God,' when Saul was consenting unto his death. 'The Saviour of all,' by whom God had spoken in the prophets and in a Son, by whom 'the Son of the living God' was revealed to St. Peter, revealed that same Son in Saul. The difference between the means employed, for the conversion of St. Peter and of Saul, was a twofold one. In the first place, the light of the world, which had dwelt *with* St. Peter and the other disciples, in the likeness of sinful flesh, as the Word from the beginning, had been removed, after a little while, from those conditions in which human eye could see, and human hand could handle it, and the time had come, when that same light should be, should dwell and abide in the believers. In the second place, the revelation to Saul was outwardly confirmed by a miracle. He was caught up into paradise, whether in the body or out of the body, he could not tell, and he heard 'unspeakable words, which it is not lawful for man to utter.' These words, the promulgation of which was forbidden, and which referred to the spiritual world, St. Paul must have recollected, when he wrote those Divinely inspired words, about the Holy Spirit's advocating man's cause, 'with groanings which cannot be uttered.'

As a pupil of Gamaliel, Saul was brought up in the belief of God's supernatural action on the soul of man, he delighted 'in the law of God after the inward man.' Nevertheless, as a Pharisee, and as the tool of the ruling Sadducees, the law had exercised over him a kind of dominion, which brought 'fruit unto death,' through the oldness of the letter that 'killeth,' and by the consequent exclusion of the newness of that spirit which 'giveth life.' It was not till after his conversion that he read the written law by the light of the law written on the heart. Before that event, he could not experience, that what sin is to death, the written law, carnally or literally understood, is to the decaying of spiritual life. 'The sting of death is sin,' or sin is the cause of death, '*and* the strength (or power) of sin is the law.' As 'the carnal mind is death,' so the carnal view of the written law is the cause and power of sin. It draws man away from the influence of the Word which is engrafted on the heart, and able to teach him what sin is, and how to overcome the same. The symbol of the word has become an idol. Man is misled into the dangerous belief that in the letter of the law he 'has eternal life.' 'The commandment which was ordained to life' has become for him 'the cause of death.' Having served 'with the flesh the law of sin,' converted Saul was led to 'serve the law of God with the mind,' that is, with the understanding, and thus to offer 'a reasonable service' to God.

Saul knew the holy Scriptures, and he had been taught the rudiments of 'the key of knowledge,' of the traditional patristic standard of interpretation. Sitting at the feet of Gamaliel he had heard, that man's aim must be to make his will like God's will, that a good heart is the right road for a man to follow, that prayer ought not be offered in the spirit of an imposed act of duty, and that the Holy Presence is in the midst of those who are contemplating the law. But this seed had fallen on stony ground. Saul was foremost among those, whose object it was, to identify more and more the doctrines of the Pharisees with those of the Sadducees. He was a declared enemy to the proclamation of tradition, to the principle of catholicity. He had not experienced the effects of the unresisted indwelling Power of God and Wisdom of God, through which alone the mysteries of Scripture can be fully discerned, even by the learned. He read the law as he read the character of Jesus. He knew Christ only 'in the flesh,' from a material point of view, as being 'according to the flesh, made of the seed of David,' not yet as 'the Son of God.' Whether he knew him personally, as is probable, or whether he did not, he had not spiritually discerned his true character.[1] He had not learnt, what Ananias first fully taught him, that righteousness is by faith, and 'without the works of the law.' Between Saul's Judaism and Christianity there was a great gulf. Saul had not yet 'ears to hear.'

As to Abraham, so to Saul, the Word of God came in a vision. He saw the incarnate Word, Christ Jesus. It is as uncertain, as it is unimportant, whether the Divine communication was made directly through the person of the risen Jesus, or indirectly through a Divinely caused vision representing his image. In this case, as in that of St. Stephen, God may have spoken, through the mediation of Jesus 'face to face,' as he is recorded to have spoken to Moses; or he may have spoken to both in visions, as he spoke to the prophets. To see directly the reality, or to see it indirectly through the medium of vision, must be essentially the same. Thus St. Peter had seen and felt the chains falling off from his hands, and yet 'he wist not, that it was true (real), which was done by the angel, but thought he saw a vision.'[2] Again, the transfiguration of Jesus on the mount is described as 'a vision;' and it was in a vision that Saul first saw Ananias, and that the latter received the commandment, which was announced

---

[1] Rom. vii.; 2 Cor. v. 16.  [2] Acts xii. 7-9.

to Saul during the apparition. And finally, had Saul felt sure, that the latter was not a vision, he could hardly have written, that he knew not, whether he was in the body or out of the body, when caught up to the third heaven. Whether Divine communications are made to man through the medium of a vision or without it, God takes the initiative. When he reveals 'through the mediation of angels,' of individualities that are no longer in the body of the flesh, these 'flaming spirits' are sent from above, and appear to man below, but when God speaks through the medium of a vision, then the soul is no longer 'in the body,' but is translated from lower to higher spheres.

Trances and ecstacies seem often to have been the medium of revelations. Thus the 'deep sleep' which fell on Abraham when the Word of the Lord came unto him 'in a vision,' is by the Septuagint interpreted as an ecstacy. Balaam, Saul, Jeremiah and Ezekiel are described as having occasionally been in, what we may call an ecstasy. Again, the state into which Daniel fell, when the angel appeared, and into which the disciples of Jesus were thrown at the transfiguration, resembled that which Ezekiel describes. In every case, those in a trance had to be touched by the 'hand of the Lord,' the finger of Jesus or of the angel, in order to see 'the vision of God.' A state similar to a trance was produced through the medium of the Urim and Thummim. According to the Zohar, the soul leaves the body during sleep,[1] accompanied as she always is by 'the Mother,' who is 'the queen,' that is, by the indwelling Shechina, the Divine Wisdom, which is 'the mother' of all good things, and probably was symbolised by the moon, the 'queen of heaven.' Although it may be regarded as an open question, what was the state of Saul when he knew not, whether he was in the body or out of the body, and what was the nature of the apparition on the way to Damascus, the recorded fact remains, that God

---

[1] Zohar i. 83, b.

speaks to men in visions, whether or not 'through the mediation of angels.' It certainly cannot be asserted that St. Paul in his Epistles places the apostle above the prophet,[1] with a view of marking the distinction of direct apparitions to the former, and of indirect apparitions to the latter. The disciples of Emmaus, and the five hundred brethren were not apostles, and yet what they are recorded to have seen could not have been a mere vision.[2]

Thus it was that God revealed his Son in Saul, that the unconverted received the baptism of regeneration, became 'a new creature,' a follower of Jesus. This revelation to the soul, was to be confirmed by a revelation to the senses, by a vision and its fulfilment. He saw 'in a vision a man named Ananias coming in, and putting his hand on him, that he might receive his sight.' This Ananias, 'a certain disciple at Damascus,' was commanded, likewise in a vision, to ask for 'Saul of Tarsus, for behold he prayeth,' and 'he is a chosen vessel unto me, to bear my name before the Gentiles and kings, and the children of Israel.' It was through Ananias that Saul received his sight, and was filled with the Holy Ghost. Ananias is described as 'a devout man according to the law,' as having 'a good report of all the Jews which dwell at Damascus,' and yet as believing in 'the Lord Jesus,' and urging Saul to call 'on the name of the Lord,' so that he might see 'the Just One.'[3]

An incident is described by Josephus about the missionary activity of a merchant Ananias, which occurred about the same time as the meeting between Saul and Ananias of Damascus. It was about the year 44 A.C., that is, about the time of Herod Agrippa's death and of his son's succession, that 'Ananias, a certain Jewish merchant,'

---

[1] 1 Cor. xii. 28.

[2] Comp. Holsten's 'Christus-vision des Apostels Paulus,' Zeitschr. 1860, p. 223; and Beyschlag, 'Bekehrung des Apostels Paulus,' Stud und Krit. 1864, 2 Heft.

[3] Acts ix. 10-20; xxii. 12-16.

got among the women that belonged to the king of Adiabene, one of the Mesopotamian kingdoms, the richest province of Assyria, the capital of which was situated on the river Zab or Diab.[1] Ananias taught these women 'to worship God according to the Jewish religion.' Through them he became acquainted with Izates the king, 'and persuaded him in like manner to embrace that religion,' whilst his mother Helena, the widowed queen of Adiabene, 'was instructed by a certain other Jew, and went over to them.' Supposing 'that he could not be thoroughly a Jew unless he were circumcised,' Izates was by Ananias instructed 'that he might worship God without being circumcised, even though he did resolve to follow the Jewish law entirely, which worship of God was of a superior nature to circumcision.' But Izates listened to the representations of 'a certain other Jew that came out of Galilee whose name was Eleazar, who was esteemed very skilful in the learning of his country,' and who persuaded Izates to be circumcised. Josephus adds, that 'nevertheless God's providence preserved Izates from dangers, and demonstrated thereby that the fruit of piety does not perish with those who have regard to him, and fix their faith upon him only.'[2]

Soon after Saul's conversion, a Jewish merchant-missionary, such as Mahomed was, taught a superior or more spiritual Judaism than the Judaism of circumcision, in a locality where the caravans from Phœnicia and Syria probably exchanged their goods with those from Arabia Felix. Without insisting on the possible identity of the Ananias of the Acts and of Josephus, thus much may be asserted—that the Ananias of Josephus, about the time of Saul's conversion, preached a Judaism in harmony with Kenite doctrines, and that Eleazar, his rival, represented the Sadducees, and perhaps was connected with the high priestly line of Eleazar. This incident proves that others

---

[1] Amm. Marcellinus, xxiii. 20.   [2] Ant. xx. 2.

preached against circumcision before the disciple of Ananias became the apostle of the uncircumcision.

A mystery will always be connected with the 'voice' which was heard on the occasion of St. Paul's conversion. But we may assume that he who had not known 'Christ in the flesh,' and who was made to know him in the spirit, —that the spiritual ear of this great persecutor heard the voice from heaven whilst he was on his way to Damascus. He himself tells us that it was 'by the Spirit' that to him, as likewise to the 'holy apostles and prophets' of his time, was revealed the mystery which in other ages was not made known unto the sons of men,' as it was then revealed, that is, the great mystery of the indwelling word of 'Christ within.' That was one of the mysteries which had been 'kept in silence since the world began,' although God had in all ages spoken through his holy prophets. By the preaching of Jesus Christ, and by his life, this mystery had been fully manifested, 'truth and grace' had been added to the Mosaic law. Although St. Paul had been educated at Tarsus and at Jerusalem in the elementary principles of the hidden Wisdom, of which Gamaliel and Simeon, and possibly Hillel were, in his time, the most renowned teachers, yet St. Paul's conversion was a sudden one. It was not till afterwards that he could write, that what had been so long kept hidden was 'manifested, and by means of prophetic writings, according to the commandments of the everlasting God, made known to all nations.'[1] This was fully accomplished by St. Paul. He opposed to 'the shameful concealment,' to 'the deceitful handling of the word of God,' the 'manifestation of the truth,' which commends itself and its apostles, 'to every man's conscience in the sight of God.'[2] The Apocrypha, the hidden wisdom, the truth, so long shamefully concealed, at last was revealed to all, and commended itself, because it harmonised with the law written on the

---

[1] Rom. xvi. 25, 26.  [2] 2 Cor. iv. 2.

heart by the finger of God. The 'truth and grace,' which came not by Moses, but by Jesus Christ, was first fully and universally proclaimed by St. Paul.

'Mine ears hast thou opened.' These words of David explain what Saul must have felt when, on his way to Damascus, his conscience awoke and he gave himself up to the leadership of the Divine Spirit. 'My Lord and my God! I will persecute thee no longer; speak, for thy servant heareth; lo, I come; I will arise and go to my Father.' The indwelling Son of God once revealed, Saul has become conscious that he has the witness of God in himself, and that he need not 'confer with flesh and blood.' Thus led and taught by the Spirit of God, the unbelieving Pharisee has become a disciple of Jesus, he has received a foretaste of that universal teaching of the Holy Ghost, when all shall know the Lord without being taught by man. The hidden Wisdom of God was fully revealed to him and by him. The risen Jesus is the personified Power of God and Wisdom of God. That Divine power has become the ruling principle of Saul's life, for he has been taught to commune through the Spirit with the Son, and thus with 'the Father of the spirits of all flesh.' A gulf has been fixed between the Judaism of Saul, and the Christianity of St. Paul.

## CHAPTER XX.

### THE CONVERSION OF ST. JAMES.

If the Christian doctrines in themselves contained nothing essentially new, but were a confirmation, development and application of the pre-Christian hidden wisdom; if none of the Apocrypha, except the book of Job, of Proverbs, and of Jonah, ever formed part of the Hebrew Canon; if the verbal teaching of the secret tradition in Palestine was confined to a few authorised guardians of the same; if a long probation was prescribed for the teachers before they could be made acquainted, and that by word of mouth only, even with the rudiments of what was 'hidden in darkness;' if, owing to these restrictions, to the jealous watchfulness of the spiritual chiefs of the Jews, and to the consequent ignorance and hardheartedness of the people, Jesus expounded these doctrines, at first, to the disciples alone, in secret and in darkness; if, what is not improbable, their Master warned them against the universal proclamation of these mysteries immediately after his death; then we are, at the outset, led to expect that the twelve Apostles would see the wisdom, if not the necessity, of continuing the same caution which their Master had exercised, and by a temporary keeping back of his secret doctrine, to allow the development of the blade and the full corn in the ear, and thus to save the Christian Church from the persecutions of the Jewish rulers, which would otherwise certainly take place.

Here we have to refer to an accumulation of circumstantial evidence, which tends to confirm the assumed dependence of the Apostolic body on the Jewish rulers. Before we consider this evidence, let us try to realise the circumstances under which the Apostles were placed after the crucifixion. Eleven Galilean disciples[1] awoke to the fact, by painful experience, that a member of the Apostolic institution of the Twelve, that Judas from Ish-K'rioth in Judah,[2] the only Judean among them, had betrayed their Master and his cause, turning the kiss of brotherhood, 'the holy kiss,' which had made him a member of the secret society, into a mark of denunciation and treachery. Whether or not he was a spy all the time of his discipleship, he offered himself, and was paid as informant against Jesus. He betrayed innocent blood. The Hebrew denounced the Kenite, and was his 'devil' or 'accuser.' By so doing he had jeopardised the sacred cause of Jesus and his disciples, who were to proclaim, at some future time, on the housetops and in light, what their Master had whispered into their ears when they were alone. The Jewish rulers, among whom the Hebrew Sadducees took the lead, having become acquainted with the instructions of Jesus, knew well that these would gradually undermine the hierarchy, if they were carried out. They took the utmost precautions, determined to put down by force any attempt to promulgate the doctrines of the hidden wisdom. St. Stephen had proved that men were prepared to lay down their lives for the truth; and his martyrdom, which was followed by that of St. James, the son of Zebedee, was the signal of a general persecution of all Christians, from which the Apostles at Jerusalem were exempted. Something must have taken place between the time when 'the priests, the captain of the temple and the Sadducees' laid hands on the Apostles, putting them in the common prison, and the time when all disciples of Jesus, 'except the Apostles,' were scattered

---

[1] Acts ii. 7.  [2] Josh. xv. 25.

abroad. For the Apostles at Jerusalem were necessarily at the mercy of the Sadducees, and these had weighty reasons for anxiety.

Ever since the days of Cyrenius, according to Josephus, religious zealots and reformers arose in great number, threatening alike the civil and the spiritual power. Quirinus, consul in 12 B.C., may have been twice governor of Syria, from the year 6 A.C., and also some time earlier, when a census in Palestine, in connection with a general census in the empire, may well have taken place. But the attempt to fix the year 4 B.C. for the first governorship, is not conclusive, and would not remove the difficulty.[1] About the year 7, when, on the banishment of Archelaus, the census and similar measures were taken for the purpose of incorporating Judea with the Roman empire, three rioters are mentioned, one of whom, possibly Judas, whose name is not unlike Theudas, to whom Gamaliel referred, got together 'a multitude of men,' and attempted to raise himself to 'the Royal dignity.'[2] The same historian records[3] that, after the death of King Agrippa I., in 44, Theudas, 'a certain magician,' persuaded 'a great part of the people,' that he was a prophet, and caused them to follow him to the river Jordan. At this very period Ananias, the merchant, preached at Adiabene that an orthodox Jew need not be, and must not be circumcised. And we have seen that Saul, who had received 'authority from the chief priests' to bind all that called on the 'name' or Spirit of God, that is, of Jesus, was turned, probably by the same Ananias, from a persecutor to a disciple. There must have been, not only a general similarity, but a direct connection between all these attempts to undermine the essentially Sadducean rule at Jerusalem. For Gamaliel, a Pharisee, and therefore not one of 'the rulers,'[4] compares the recorded opposition of the Apostles to those set in authority over them with the

[1] Zumpt, Comm. ii. 28.
[2] Ant. xvii. 10, 5.
[3] Ibid.
[4] John vii. 48.

popular risings caused by Theudas and by Judas of Galilee, and he warns the Sadducees that the disciples of Jesus cannot be overthrown if their work be of God. These disciples of the Crucified declared that they 'ought to obey God rather than men,' and in the spirit of the Apostles, as well as of Gamaliel and of the Pharisees who 'believed,'[1] 'the Scribes that were of the Pharisees part,' later opposed the majority of the Sanhedrim, headed by the high priest. They stood up for the principle of not fighting against God. Not the Pharisees, but the Sadducees laid their hands upon the Apostles and imprisoned them.

This was the state of the parties in Judea in the time following upon the crucifixion. Before we proceed, we must consider the probable date of this event. It certainly took place before the death of Tiberius, who reigned, according to Josephus. from the 19th of August, A.D. 14, 'twenty-two years five months and three days,' that is, till January 24 in the year 37. For Pontius Pilate was sent to Rome by Vitellius, governor of Syria, in order to answer before the emperor the accusations of the Samaritans, whose rising he had put down by force. On Pilate's arrival at Rome, Tiberius had been murdered. If the rising of the Samaritans could be brought into some connection with the crucifixion of Jesus, it would become probable that this event occurred between the years 35 and 36. Josephus states that the leader of the Samaritans on this occasion persuaded the people that he would show them on Mount Gerizim 'those sacred vessels which were laid under that place, because Moses put them there.'[2] This Samaritan leader, according to a highly probable conjecture, was Simon Magus.[3] What he had in view by his causing the people to rise, was a discovery of hidden treasure, apparently like that which was made in the time of Josiah on Mount Zion. In both

---

[1] Acts xv. 5.   [2] Ant. xviii. 4, 1.   [3] Ewald, Gesch. v. 43.

cases a hidden wisdom was attributed to Moses. It is this circumstance which evidently led to the introduction of the name of Moses in this passage. For the great lawgiver never went to Mount Gerizim himself, though in that part of the Pentateuch which contains what was hidden up to the time of Josiah, he is recorded to have appointed that, on entering the land of promise, the tribes of Simeon (Levi?), Judah, Issachar, Joseph and Benjamin, should 'stand upon the (Kenite) Mount Gerizim to bless the people.'[1] It has been shown that the hidden treasures to which Simon of Samaria referred, are by early Samaritan tradition explained to have been the ark and other sacred vessels, deposited in Mount Gerizim by Uzzi, or Ozis, the grandson of Abishua, the last high priest of the line of Eleazar before the accession of the Kenite line of Ithamar. Again, in the person of Eli, the Samaritans (Kenites) insist upon their Pentateuch being the same as that which Abishua used, and they boast that they have preserved the Aaronic tradition. Nothing, indeed, is more likely than that Uzzi, the son of Bukki, the son of Abishua, being out of office, went to the Samaritans to bless the people from Mount Gerizim. And if the Aaronic descendants were the guardians of the secret tradition which Moses confided to the elders, Mount Gerizim would be from that time considered as a deposit of the hidden wisdom of Moses. If we substitute the name of Uzzi, Ozis, or Ozeos, for Moses, or Moseos, we may assert that the Aaronites deposited their tradition on Mount Gerizim.

To that secret tradition Simon Magus referred, that hidden wisdom he was determined to preach to all Samaritans, rich or poor, initiated or uninitiated, as Buddha had done in India with the secret doctrine of the Brahmins, about five hundred years before. In that same country of Samaria, where John the Baptist was imprisoned and beheaded, and where Elisha and Obadiah

---

[1] Deut. xxvii. 12.

were buried, according to the positive assertion of St. Jerome,[1] Jesus had taught with great success the doctrine of the Holy Ghost, of which the Hebrews in Judea were grossly ignorant, their spiritual rulers having taken away the key of knowledge. Some of the Jews called Jesus 'a Samaritan,' others may have called him the 'son of Joseph' because of his Kenite descent. For the Samaritans, or lowlanders, were, as we have seen, of the stock of the Perizzites, that is, descendants from the pre-Abramitic Canaanites who had migrated from the Eastern 'lowland' to the West. We have seen that Simon professed 'faith in Christ,' that he was baptized, considered as an organ or apostle of 'the great power of God,' that he proclaimed a secret doctrine, confiding the higher mysteries to the initiated, that in his writings he quotes the Gospels and the Epistles of St. Paul, and that, notwithstanding his super-spiritualism, which was developed into the heresy of doceticism, he was the great forerunner of St. Paul, and probably one of the many Samaritans who believed because of the 'own word' of Jesus.[2] We now are in a position to suggest, as a probable hypothesis, that Simon of Samaria caused the people to rise, Pilate to be deposed, and some of his decrees to be abrogated, all in consequence of Pilate's having yielded to the Sadducees, and condemned Jesus to death.

The Roman governor of Syria had taken the side of the Samaritans against Pilate. Not only did he fear the renewal of those struggles between the Samaritans and the Jews which had led to the massacre of Purim in the time of Ezra, and to the persecution of the Sadducees by Herod the Great, but he knew that Tiberius, notwithstanding his execrable conduct, had taken a peculiar interest in the person of Jesus. Eusebius affirms, on the testimony of Tertullian, who lived in Rome at the end of the second century, and who had 'made himself accurately acquainted

[1] Reland, Ant. Hebr. pp. 980, 981.  [2] John vi. 41.

with the laws of the Romans,' that Tiberius was so 'obviously pleased with the doctrine of the name, or spirit of Christ, which was then spreading throughout the world,' that he proposed to the senate that Jesus should be 'consecrated a God.' As such Jesus was regarded 'by the great mass of the people' in Judea, after his resurrection, according to the report of Pilate to the Emperor. In like manner Simon was worshipped in Samaria and in other countries. Justin Martyr writes, and Eusebius refers to this passage: 'After the ascension of our Lord into heaven, certain men were suborned by demons as their agents, who said that they were gods.' Among these was Simon 'a certain Samaritan,' whom 'nearly all the Samaritans, a few also of other nations,' worshipped, 'confessing him as the supreme God.'

It may be assumed from the accounts of Josephus, that the rising of the Samaritans under Simon occurred in the year 35. If this rebellion stood in direct connection with Pilate's vacillating, unjust, and cruel conduct towards Jesus, who counted so many followers in Samaria, then the crucifixion of Jesus can hardly have taken place before the early part of that year. We shall now show that the year 35 is the only possible year for the death of Jesus, if the positive assertion of St. Irenæus is believed, that Jesus was about fifty years old when he died. This learned father of the Church, the first who mentions the four Gospels by name, states on the authority of presbyterial, that is, apostolic tradition, that the public ministry of Jesus took place between his fortieth and fiftieth year. This tradition cannot have been contested in his time, for St. Irenæus refers to it as generally credited, when he explains that it was necessary for the Saviour to go through all the stages of human life.[1] Whilst St. Irenæus is the earliest father of the Church who refers to the age of Jesus, so is he the only one who does so previous to

---

[1] Contr. Haer. ii. 22, 4, 5.

Eusebius, who, on no other authority than a dark passage in St. Luke, directly connects the commencement of Jesus' public ministry, which according to general custom required the age of thirty years, with his baptism in Jordan during the fifteenth year of Tiberius, 28–29 A.D. Assuming this to be correct, Jesus could only have lived about five years after his baptism. There can be no doubt that, according to St. Luke, Jesus was 'at the beginning' of his ministry 'about thirty years old.' But because this information directly follows upon the record of his baptism, it does not necessarily follow, that Jesus began to teach immediately after, or even about the time of his baptism. The people of Cana are recorded to have invited Jesus and his disciples to a marriage feast. He did, therefore, publicly teach before his baptism, and the assumed commencement of his teaching in the fifteenth year of Tiberius falls to the ground.

Whilst the third Gospel does not necessitate, and the fourth excludes the chronology of Eusebius, the Gospel after St. John contains two references which indirectly confirm the tradition recorded by St. Irenæus, who knew, of course, all about secret tradition. In the last year of his ministry, which, according to this Gospel, extended over three or nearly four years, Jesus is told that he is 'not yet fifty years old;' and in the first year of his ministry, a remark is made about 'the temple of his body' having been built in forty-six years. We have no reason to assert that the priests and Levites misunderstood Jesus to refer to the stone temple. We need not, therefore, assume that he pointed to himself, when uttering the recorded words, as every man in the East would have done, and would do up to this day. All who knew anything about the future life, must necessarily have referred the 'three days' to the resurrection. Those who accused Jesus of having threatened the destruction of the stone temple were 'false witnesses.'

If we accept the age of about fifty years for the time

of Jesus' death, and assuming the crucifixion to have taken place in the year 35, certainly not later, Jesus must have been born in the year 15 before our era. In this case he would have been twelve years old in the year after Herod's death, in the fourth year before our era. The dispute in the temple has certainly not taken place earlier than the year after Herod's death. For, according to the Gospel account, Joseph and Mary with Jesus did not leave Egypt till they had heard that Herod had died, and, fearing Archelaus, they did not go at once to Jerusalem. A later date for his twelfth year would remove the date of the crucifixion beyond the year 35, which is impossible. From this it follows conclusively, that the years 4 B.C. and 35 A.C. are the only possible years respectively for the dispute in the temple, and for the crucifixion; the birth of Jesus was fixed in the seventieth year before the destruction of Jerusalem. The rising of Simon took place almost immediately after the death of Jesus.

The object of Simon must have been to undermine the power of the Sadducees at Jerusalem, and to strengthen the party of the Pharisees, although some of them had joined with the Herodians to bring about the condemnation of Jesus. It was perhaps partly due to this Samaritan demonstration, which was supported by the Roman government, that Gamaliel the Pharisee, and seventeen years later president of the Sanhedrim, was able to speak so boldly in favour of the Apostles and of the Pharisees, as he is recorded to have done shortly after the crucifixion. From the year 37 the Apostles at Jerusalem must have enjoyed a greater liberty. Having been imprisoned between the years 35 and 36, the deposition of Pilate, and the abrogation of some of his decrees at Jerusalem, which the Samaritans had brought about, was the commencement of better days. Light followed upon darkness. 'The angel of the Lord by night opened the prison doors,' brought them forth and commanded them to go boldly to the temple, and to preach to the people all the words of life which Jesus had commanded them to proclaim. Then it was, that 'Peter and the Apostles' openly defied the Jewish rulers. We shall now try to prove that, about four years later, in the year 41, with the accession of King Agrippa I., the re-establishment of unlimited Sadducean power led to portentous events.

Herod Agrippa I., son of Aristobulus, was by his Asmonean or Sadducean descent a half-Jew. Josephus writes, that he was 'very ambitious to oblige the people,' that 'he loved to live continually at Jerusalem, and was rigidly careful in the observance of the laws of his country; he therefore kept himself entirely pure, nor did any day pass over his head without its appointed sacrifice;' he 'omitted nothing which the law required.'[1] As a rigid observer of the law, he regarded St. James, the brother of St. John, as a seducer to strange worship, laid hands upon him and others, and had him beheaded. This statement, in the form transmitted to us, leads us to assume that Agrippa intended the same punishment for others. For if many were guilty of such offence, they were not to be stoned but beheaded, according to the Jewish law. The martyrdom of St. James the brother of St. John, and the setting up of St. James 'the brother of the Lord' at the head of the Apostles at Jerusalem, took place before the converted Saul's first journey to that city, when he met that same St. James. In order to ascertain the probable date of this event, we must first enquire whether the martyrdom of St. Stephen, at which Saul was present, may not have taken place very shortly before the other. According to the Acts it happened 'about that time,' and the events which occurred between the record of St. Stephen's death and that of St. James, do not require more than a few months, even if we assume that St. Peter had started for, and had returned from his journey to Cornelius before the death of St. James.

[1] Ant. xix. 7, 3; 6, 1.

Saul was probably among those Jews of Cilicia, the country of his birth, who disputed with St. Stephen. Perhaps, also, he was among those who suborned men, and stirred up the people and the elders and the Scribes, and even false witnesses, to testify against the Hellenist. He was on good terms with the high priest Annas, the Sadducee, who, apparently on his sole authority, caused St. Stephen to be brought before the judges of the Sanhedrim, and stoned to death. Saul was not a casual bystander, when 'the witnesses laid down their clothes' at his feet. In accordance with custom, Saul, a person of authority, gave his consent to the execution, by holding the clothes of the denunciators and chief executioners. As commissioner for the execution, he represented the high priest and the chief priests, who were probably the judges of the Sanhedrim. The same authorities he represented on his journey of persecution to Damascus, which was the commencement of the general persecution against all Christians, except the Apostles at Jerusalem. The dying disciple of Jesus, whom tradition numbers among the Seventy, prayed, probably within the hearing of Saul, that God would not lay the sin of his enemies to their charge. Having fallen asleep, Saul, continuing ' to breathe out threatenings and slaughter against the disciples of the Lord,' received power to persecute. Denunciation by foul means, nominal condemnation by an arbitrarily summoned tribunal, and summary execution, apparently without the consent of the Roman government,—these were the measures in which Saul took a leading part, and which led to the official murder of St. Stephen.

Under exactly similar circumstances Josephus records that St. James, the head of the Apostles, was stoned to death by order of the high priest Annas or Annanus, shortly before the destruction of Jerusalem. The Jewish historian, a contemporary of the latter event, writes, that Annas was 'a bold man in his temper, and very insolent; he was also of the sect of the Sadducees, who are very rigid in judging offenders (against the law), above all the rest of the Jews; he assembled the Sanhedrim of judges, and brought before them the brother of Jesus, who is called the Christ, whose name was James, and some others (or, some of his companions), and when he had formed an accusation against them, as breakers of the law, he delivered them to be stoned. But as for those who seemed the most equitable of the citizens, and such as were the most uneasy at the breach of the laws (by the high priest), they disliked what was done, they also sent to the king (Agrippa), desiring him to send to Ananus, that he should act so no more, for that what he had already done was not to be justified.'[1]

The passage in which St. James is called 'the brother of Jesus who is called the Christ,' is universally admitted to be a later insertion. Were we, like Eusebius, to follow this statement in the book on the antiquities, as transmitted to us, the death of St. James occurred in the interval between the death of Festus, most probably between 60 and early in 62, and the arrival of his successor Albinus in Judea. 'Festus was now dead, and Albinus but upon the road.' The latter was appointed upon the Emperor's (Nero) 'hearing the death of Festus,' and, according to Hegesippus and Eusebius,[2] 'immediately after' the death of this same St. James, Vespasian invaded and took Judea. Not till 65 did the rising of the Jews take place, which led to Vespasian's being sent to Syria in 67. It is impossible to assume, that during this long and turbulent period of five years, Judea was left without a procurator. Moreover Agrippa II., who was in the country, was not a friend of the Jews, as Agrippa I., but quarrelled with them, and joined the Roman forces in the conquest of Judea. Under these circumstances no high priest could possibly have ventured upon the 'bold and very insolent' plan, to assemble the Sanhedrim of judges on his own accord, to accuse Christians as breakers of the Jewish

[1] Ant. xx. 9. 1.   [2] H. E. ii. 23; iii. 11.

law, and forthwith to deliver them to be stoned. As this course was pursued in the year 41, with the explicit or tacit consent of Agrippa I., the friend of the Sadducees, then in power, and the zealous follower and protector of the Jewish law; as St. Stephen is in the Acts shown to have been brought before the council and stoned, in the same summary manner, without the consent of the Roman government; as 'about the same time' the Apostle St. James, the son of Zebedee, was put to death, we assert, that the above account in the words of Josephus has been displaced, and that the event recorded refers not to the time of Agrippa II. but of Agrippa I., and thus to the death of St. James the brother of St. John. The error, whenever committed, was all the more easy to fall into, inasmuch as the name of the king and of the high priest was the same in 41 and in 67 A.C.

Our assertion is confirmed by the acknowledged fact, that if the detailed account of Hegesippus, the converted Hebrew historian, is correct, that of Josephus cannot possibly be reconciled with it. If St. James and others were 'delivered over to be stoned' by the high priest, as the account in Josephus asserts, the Apostle cannot have been thrown down from a pillar, and stoned by the Scribes and Pharisees, as Hegesippus reports. Hegesippus was a contemporary of the event, for in the time of Hadrian, between 117 and 138 A.C., he held 'a distinguished rank' among the champions of the truth, and 'compiled, in five books, the plain tradition of the apostolic doctrine,' according to 'apostolic tradition.'[1] Moreover, Clement of Alexandria 'fully coincided' with the testimony of Hegesippus about the death of St. James, as Eusebius informs us.[2] But if Hegesippus could not possibly give an erroneous account of a contemporary event, equally impossible is it to assume, that Josephus, who was in Jerusalem when Vespasian attacked it, that is, immediately

---

[1] H. E. iv. 8.   [2] Ibid. ii. 23.

after the martyrdom of St. James, should himself have written a statement so absolutely irreconcilable with that of a junior contemporary. We shall show, that there were good reasons for referring to St. James, the brother of the Lord, the account which Josephus had written about the martyrdom of St. James, the brother of St. John.

In the Acts, St. James, the son of Zebedee, is stated to have been killed by the sword, and by the order of Herod Agrippa I. We have seen, that this Roman ruler was the zealous upholder of the Hebrew law and of Sadducean power. Consequently a Sadducean high priest, by nature bold and insolent, as Annas was, whom he raised to this dignity, was sure to have his tacit consent for any measures deemed necessary against refractory Jews or Christians. This may have led to the tradition, that St. James was killed according to Roman law, as according to Roman command. Moreover, according to the tradition recorded by St. Clement of Alexandria,[1] the prosecutor, probably the denunciator, moved by the last confession of St. James, and having suddenly declared himself a Christian, was likewise beheaded on this occasion. This tradition, which well accords with the summary proceedings of the Sadducean high priest Annas, has not been recorded by Josephus, who, possibly for this reason, reports the death of St. James alone, which, if it was not accompanied by that of others, would have been a death by stoning.

Unless we accept this explanation, we must assume, that the passage in the Acts, like so many others in that book, has been revised in Rome, and this feature introduced, in order to remove from Annas every suspicion of complicity. For the fabrication of history, even by such men as Eusebius, was not considered as a crime. The historian wishes to prove 'the wonderful coincidence of the history given by Josephus, with that of the sacred Scriptures,' the collection of which had been entrusted to

---

[1] Hypotyp. vii.

him by the emperor. In the Acts it is stated, that Herod was suddenly smitten by 'the angel of the Lord,' though it is not stated, that anyone saw the angel. Josephus writes, that Agrippa 'saw an owl sitting on a certain rope over his head,' and understood, 'that this bird was the messenger (or angel) of ill tidings.' But the Bishop makes the historian say, that Herod 'saw an angel sitting above his head; this he immediately perceived, was the cause of evils.'[1]

It cannot be doubted, from the account in Josephus, who had no interest in throwing unwarranted blame on a Jewish high priest, that Agrippa had kept out of the way, so as not to appear a party to the execution. For it is stated that 'king Agrippa' took the high priesthood from Annas, 'when he had ruled but three months.' Agrippa had bestowed on him the high priesthood, and we may assume, that he deposed his predecessor at the very commencement of his government. For the nomination to the high priesthood constituted one of the highest privileges of the king, who was likely to begin his reign with such an appointment. If, then, Annas was high priest only during three months, and if the martyrdoms of St. Stephen and of St. James occurred in that time, we should have fixed the year 41 for these events. If so, St. Paul's conversion did not take place before that year, his first journey to Jerusalem coincided with Agrippa's death in 44, and he was present at the Council of the Apostles in 55. It is not an insignificant confirmation of our hypothesis, placing the conversion of St. Paul in the year 41. that it supplies us with a motive for St. Paul's retirement to Arabia, and for his return to Jerusalem, three years later. It is probable, that St. Peter had not returned to Jerusalem (from Rome) before that year. The Sadducean Herod having died, the leading Apostles could return, the mysterious meeting between St. Paul and St. Peter could

---

[1] Ant. xix. 8, 2; H. E. ii. 10.

take place within the walls of Jerusalem, the persecution of Christians which followed upon the accession of Herod, and the martyrdom of St. Stephen was at an end.

After the martyrdoms of St. Stephen and of St. James, both of which Saul probably witnessed, this Pharisee and son of a Pharisee left Jerusalem on his persecuting errand, whilst St. Peter was put in prison. Having been delivered, by providential intervention, from 'the hand of Herod, and all the expectations of the Jews,' St. Peter went 'to the house of Mary the mother of John, whose surname was Mark, where many were gathered together praying.' Having 'declared unto them, how the Lord had brought him out of prison,' and desired them 'to shew these things unto James and to the brethren,' the Apostle 'departed and went into another place.' St. Peter went to Rome. On this no doubt ought any longer to exist. For Clement of Alexandria states, 'that Peter being in Rome under the emperor Claudius, had there some conference with Philo,' and he adds, that they formed a 'friendship' for each other.[1] This statement is confirmed by St. Jerome,[2] and by Eusebius, who gives his reason for not doubting that which alone seems to have been doubted in the fourth century, the friendship between St. Peter and Philo, which the bishop and historian considers 'not at all improbable.' He writes, that Philo's work, 'subsequently composed by him at a late period, evidently comprehends the regulations that are still observed among our Churches, even to the present time.' Eusebius adds, that Philo, whilst describing 'with the greatest accuracy the lives of our ascetics, evidently shows, that he not only knew, but approved, whilst he extolled and revered the apostolic men of his day, who were sprung probably from the Hebrews, and hence, still continuing to observe their most ancient customs, rather after the Jewish manner.' It appeared not in the least degree strange to Clement, that St. Peter formed a friendship with Philo.

[1] H. E. ii. 17.   [2] De Vir. 11.

Having stated, that 'Peter in his "preaching" called the Lord the law and the word,' he adds, 'this is the doctrine of Philo.' Because of St. Peter's friendship for Philo, 'Mark, Peter's disciple, lauded him (Philo) with his praises in Alexandria; as also afterwards the followers of Mark did.'[1]

The emperor Claudius reigned from January 24, 41 to 54 A.C. Philo went to Rome at the head of a deputation of Alexandrian citizens in the year 40, during the reign of Caligula. The emperor refused to admit the deputation, whereupon Philo composed, whether at Rome or at Alexandria is uncertain, an elaborate apology for the Jews, which was read to the Roman Senate, during the reign of Claudius, and possibly in the same or the following year. Now, in the year 41 A.C., as we tried to prove, the following portentous events occurred:—

1. Accession of Herod Agrippa I.
2. Martyrdom of St. Stephen and of St. James.
3. Imprisonment of St. Peter, his deliverance and departure for Rome.
4. Conversion of St. Paul.
5. Appointment of St. James.

Unless we are prepared to discredit the positive statement of Clement, of St. Jerome and of Eusebius, we must assert, that 'the other place' to which St. Peter fled, in that same year, was Rome. For, as he met Philo in that city; as we know that the latter was there in 40 and in 41, or later; as St. Peter had left Rome at the latest in 44, when St. Paul met him at Jerusalem; and as Philo died in 50 A.C., St. Peter must have proceeded directly from Jerusalem to Rome in the year 41. This is confirmed by the ancient Roman tradition recorded in the so-called Recognitions of Clement, according to which St. Peter went forth to teach all nations in the seventh year after the crucifixion, that is, after Easter 41 A.C. Simon Magus rose as his adversary, and St. Peter pursuing him, went from Cæsarea to Tripolis and Antioch.[2]

---

[1] Strom. ii. 29, text and note.　　[2] Recogn. i. 43; ix. 29, &c.

In addition to Philo and Simon of Samaria, St. Peter met Aquila at Rome. For when St. Paul came to Corinth, he 'found a certain Jew named Aquila, born in Pontus, lately come from Italy, with his wife Priscilla, because that Claudius had commanded all Jews to depart from Rome.' St. Paul 'abode and worked with them,' Aquila being, like St. Paul, 'a tent-maker.'[1] It is important to consider, that Aquila may have been converted by St. Peter in Rome. Had he not been a Christian, St. Paul would hardly have lived and worked in Aquila's house at Corinth, for a year and six months, and probably also at Ephesus, to which place Aquila accompanied St. Paul. Thus Aquila may have formed a link between St. Peter and St. Paul. He certainly formed a link between these Apostles and Apollos of Alexandria, ' an eloquent man and mighty in the Scriptures,' who ' was instructed in the ways of the Lord,' was ' fervent in the spirit,' and ' spake and taught diligently about Jesus,' *although* he knew 'only the baptism of John.' Apollos, probably the writer of the Epistle to the Hebrews, 'began to preach boldly (freely) in the synagogue,' lived with, and became a disciple of Aquila and Priscilla, ' who expounded unto him the way of God more perfectly.'[2] On his return to Alexandria Apollos would confer with Philo, the friend of St. Peter, if the philosopher was still alive. Apollos must have known him, but was probably a Therapeut, a disciple of John the Baptist, the Essene. Philo was not a member of this sect, but states that ' this kind of men is everywhere scattered over the world, for both Greeks and barbarians should share in so permanent a benefit.'[3]

Whilst St. Peter was at Rome, St. Paul was in Arabia, and whilst the Roman tyrant and Jewish zealot, Agrippa I., and his Sadducean high priest, ruled at Jerusalem; whilst the Christians were persecuted, wherever Agrippa had the power to do so, the Apostles at Jerusalem, ' James

---

[1] Acts xviii. 1-3.   [2] Ibid. 24-26.   [3] H. E. ii. 17.

and the brethren'[1] were not persecuted. This we must try to explain. Before his return to Jerusalem, after Agrippa's death, St. Peter probably visited other places with Mark, and there he possibly met St. Paul, in whose company we find St. Mark after Herod's death. For when, at that same time, in 44, St. Paul went to Jerusalem, he went to see St. Peter, as if he had met him before. We assume that St. Peter had just returned to Jerusalem, and those among 'the Apostles and brethren' who were 'of the circumcision, contended with him' for having eaten with Gentiles. At the head of this Judaizing party in the Apostolic body, was 'James the brother of the Lord,' whom St. Paul likewise saw at Jerusalem in that year. For we shall prove, that this overseer of the Apostles was not one of the original Twelve, that he was not even a disciple of Jesus before the resurrection, and that, for some time, he continued to live as a Jew, a Sadducee, and a Nazarite.

It is highly probable, that St. James 'the son of Alphaeus,' that is, of Cleophas or Clopas, is identical with St. James 'the brother of the Lord.' His mother was Mary Cleophas, sister of Jesus' mother. We may assert, that there are strong reasons for assuming, that this same Cleophas, the father of St. James, and whom Eusebius mentions as a native of Emmaus, is one of the two disciples to whom the Lord appeared on their way to that village. As St. Paul refers to an apparition of the Lord to James, and as he never mentions any other James than 'the brother of the Lord,' the probability of James accompanying his father to his home, favours the above hypothesis, which is likewise confirmed by a tradition recorded by St. Jerome, according to which St. James fasted after the crucifixion till the risen Lord bade him eat. But if this conclusion is accepted, it is impossible to identify this James with the son of Alphaeus the Apostle. For on their return to Jerusalem they found 'the eleven and them that were with them.' Moreover, if before the

---

[1] Acts xii. 17.

death of St. James, the son of Zebedee, there had been among the Twelve, not only St. James the son of Alphaeus, but also St. James the brother of the Lord, and if the latter became the presiding chief of the Apostles, only eleven would have been left, and we should have heard of another Apostolic election, like that of Matthias. There were only two, and not three James's among the original Twelve Apostles, and James the brother of Jesus was not one of them. Apart from the probable identity of this James with the not named second disciple of Emmaus, the following facts conclusively prove the above assertion. It is recorded in the fourth Gospel, that, whilst the Twelve declared, through Peter, their belief in Jesus as the Christ, 'his brethren did not believe in him,'[1] but considered him mad.[2] With his brethren, as, on this occasion at least, with his mother, Jesus had, according to his own words, 'nothing in common.'[3] Here, however, a distinction must be made between the unbelieving brothers of Jesus, and his mother, the 'blessed among women.' In her anxiety about the possible consequences of her Son's doings, she, for once, became a tool in the hands of her unbelieving nephews. Moreover, by allegorically explaining the record about the marriage of Cana, we may assume, that Mary is there introduced, as also in the Apocalypse, as the representative of the Jewish Church. The fact remains the same, that his brethren did not believe in Jesus. A confirmation of this fact is St. Luke's hidden reference to St. James in the account about the disciples of Emmaus. For when St. Luke's Gospel was written, it would not have been safe, to describe in such a manner the character of so influential a person as St. James, to whom, as Eusebius wishes us to believe, 'the episcopate at Jerusalem was committed by the Apostles.' St. Luke shows, that both disciples of Emmaus were like those whose heart was hardened, who had eyes and saw not, and ears and heard not; to whom consequently

---

[1] John vi. 67-70; vii. 5.   [2] Mark iii 21.   [3] John ii. 4.

the mysteries of the kingdom of heaven were not made known. If St. James, the overseer of the Apostles at Jerusalem, had been clearly identified with one of the disciples of Emmaus, the conclusion must have been drawn, that he was 'a blind leader of the blind,' that is, of the Jews and Jewish Christians in Judea.

All these traits correspond with the description of James 'the brother of the Lord,' given by Hegesippus, 'who flourished nearest to the days of the Apostles.' Like John the Baptist, who came in the way of legal righteousness, and probably like some of the Rechabites and the Nazarites, St. James was destined ' from his mother's womb' to the ascetic mode of life which many considered necessary for holiness. 'He drank neither wine nor fermented liquors, and abstained from animal food; a razor came not upon his head, he did not anoint himself with oil, and did not use the bath.' His mode of fasting was, therefore, like those ' hypocrites of a sad countenance,' who disfigured their faces, and, as the words of Jesus imply, abstained from washing and anointing their head. In the face of these hypocritical rites, Jesus commanded his disciples : 'But thou, if thou fastest, anoint thine head, and wash thy face.' He praised the woman who had given him a bath for his feet, and had anointed his head with oil.[1] He declared that no food defiles the man, and he showed by his daily life that he objected to the restrictions which many imposed on 'eating and drinking.' What could Jesus have in common with a Nazarite, as St. James must have been? 'The Son of Man came eating and drinking.' Although a Kenite by descent, he was not a Nazarite. There must have been Nazarites among all parties.

The Acts prove that St. James the Nazarite continued to uphold the practices of the Nazarites as tests of orthodoxy. It was probably about the year 60, or five years after the Apostolic Council, that St. Paul, though warned

[1] Luke vii. 44–46.

by the Spirit that spoke through the disciples at Tyre, went to Jerusalem, and appeared before St. James, in the presence of 'all the elders,' that is, of the Apostles, and possibly of other members of the Church. For in the Acts the Apostles are, on one occasion, distinguished from the elders.[1] St. James presided over the assembly of the elders, just as the high priest Ananias, or Annas, is in the Acts recorded to have done on a similar occasion, when St. Paul was publicly accused by Tertullus.[2] The judgment of St. James on the vexed question of the Gentiles, is given by him as the representative of the Apostles, and as the chief organ of the Holy Ghost.[3] St. Paul is informed that there were many thousand Jews who believed, being nevertheless 'all zealous for the law;' that they 'must needs come together,' and will want to know, whether it be true, that St. Paul taught the Jews among the Gentiles to 'fall away' from Moses, and to abstain from circumcision, and not to walk 'according to the customs.' This accusation was unfounded. For St. Paul writes: 'Unto the Jews I became as a Jew, that I might gain the Jews; to them that are under the law, as under the law, that I might gain them that are under the law.' St. Paul's keeping the Sabbath as well as the Sunday confirms his anxiety to avoid every needless offence. He had for 'a year and six months' preached in Corinth, persuading both Jews and Gentiles; yet to the Jews he only preached 'that Jesus was the Christ.' This could be believed by all Jews except by the Sadducees, who, not believing in a spiritual element, never could believe in a man anointed by the Spirit from above. The Gentiles were by St. Paul persuaded 'to worship God contrary to the law,' as his accusers maintained. But in reality St. Paul developed from the 'flinty rock' of the law the life-giving stream of the Spirit. Through the liberty whereby Christ made men free from the bondage

---

[1] Acts xv. 6, 23.    [2] Ibid. xxix. 1.    [3] Ibid. xv. 13, 19, 28.

of the law, St. Paul so interpreted the law, as to undermine its outward observance by inward sanctification, the letter by the spirit, misunderstood symbols by the revelation of their hidden meaning; the statutes that were 'not good,' though proclaimed on Divine authority, by the true and the interpreted 'oracles of God.' He wished both Jews and Gentiles to go no longer backward but forward.[1] This was 'heresy' in the eyes of those who 'were of the circumcision.' Such there were even among the Apostles and elders, and they had contended with St. Peter at Jerusalem. For this reason St. James had sent a deputation to Antioch, to which St. Peter yielded, but not St. Paul.

The Sadducees maintained that the performance of the works of the law was sufficient for salvation; St. Paul declared that justification is by faith, 'without the deeds of the law.' Did he or did he not 'live as do the Jews?' Did he regard all the injunctions of the law as binding on his conscience; did he believe that a man can be 'blameless' by living 'according to all the ordinances of the law?'[2] Or did he show, by his mode of life, that he was an apostle, a heretic, and a perverter of the people, who spoke to 'all' against the people, the law, and Jerusalem? Was the 'Pharisee and the son of a Pharisee' among the 'many thousands of Jews' whose belief in Jesus as the Christ did not prevent them from being 'all zealous for the law?' A public confession, that he had been a sinner against the law, and that he believed in justification by the deeds of the law, was demanded of St. Paul by St. James, who pointed to the expected clamour of the people as an excuse for this demand. St. James 'the Just,' or the 'Zadok,' and the Nazarite, called upon St. Paul to purify himself, according to the law respecting Nazarites, together with five men, who were about to accomplish their Nazarite obligations. In order to confirm still more

---

[1] Comp. Jer. vii.; Ezek. xx. 25; Rom. ii. 28, 29; iii. 1, 2; Acts xxv. 14.
[2] Acts xxi. 28.

forcibly the people in the conviction that he had not
ceased to regard all Jewish ceremonies as essential to
salvation, St. Paul was advised by St. James not only to
join some Nazarites in their acts of purification, but, as
an additional proof of his zeal for the outward observances
of the law, to share with them, or pay for them, the cost
of the sacrifices and of the shaving of the head. As St.
Paul (if not Aquila) had at Cenchrea shorn his head according
to 'a vow,' which had probably been enforced on
him by the Jews, and for the same reason, so St. Paul
submitted at Jerusalem to this humiliating ordeal, in order
to save his life. Not being a Nazarite, he acted as if he
were one, that is, he admitted himself to be 'an unclean
person,' or a 'captive.'[1] Thus the Nazarite overseer of
the Apostles had an opportunity of making St. Paul act
either the part of one who had, at last, been forced to
'give place by subjection' to St. James, or the part of a
'hypocrite' and of a 'Jew,' both of which epithets had
been at Antioch addressed by St. Paul to St. Peter and to
those 'Jews' whom St. James had sent, to prevent St. Peter
from joining St. Paul and thus from living as the Gentiles.

From another statement of Hegesippus we learn, that
St. James, the brother of the Lord, was not only a
Nazarite, but also a Sadducee and a priest, if not a high
priest. 'He alone might go into the holy place; for he
wore no woollen garments, but linen.' In the book of
Ezekiel the command is recorded, that 'the sons of
Zadok' were 'to be clothed with linen garments, and no
wool shall come upon them.'[2] Again, 'sons of Zadok'
were alone to enter the sanctuary, 'the most holy place,'
that is, they were exclusively to be high priests, in accordance
with the promise of eternal priesthood, made to
Phinehas the ancestor of Zadok, and confirmed in the
time of Eli, the first usurper of God's heritage. St. James
was called 'the Zadok,' or the Just, because he was a de-

---

[1] Deut. xxi. 12.      [2] Ezek. xliv. 15–17.

scendant from Zadok, and thus a Sadducee. This is confirmed by the otherwise inexplicable fact, that St. James alone was allowed to enter the holy place. We may conclude that there were, for a time, as in the days of the high priest Zadok, two high priests in the early Apostolic age. Thus we find Annas and Caiaphas mentioned in the Gospels as contemporary high priests, before both of whom Jesus had to appear. We have seen that a son of Annas, bearing the same name, was high priest at the time when St. Stephen and St. James were put to death, and when, as is probable, St. James 'the Zadok' was placed as overseer at the head of the Apostles. But whereas, in the time of David, the high priests Zadok and Abiathar respectively represented the two Aaronic lines, the senior line to which Zadok and his descendants the Zadoks, or Sadducees, belonged, was exclusively in the possession of the high priesthood at this time. Both Annas and St. James, the brother of Jesus, were Zadoks. According to Hegesippus, the latter was called the Zadok 'from the time of the Lord.' He may have been called 'the brother of the Lord' because all the Apostles, after the resurrection, were called Galileans, whilst Jesus was of Judah. The distinction between 'James and the brethren' may point to his not having been an original disciple, and to his non-Galilean and non-Kenite origin. And yet Mary Cleophas, the mother of St. James, and Mary the mother of Jesus, were sisters. St. James was cousin-german by the mother's side, with Jesus, although there was no connection between Joseph and Cleophas. Cleophas was a Hebrew, and so was his son. The two families appear to have inhabited one house at Nazareth and at Capernaum. Although St. James was not a disciple of Jesus, but an unbeliever, before the resurrection of the Lord, and though he continued his Nazarite habits of life, we have every reason to assume, that, before his death, St. James '*became* a faithful witness,' as Hegesippus declares. Such he was, without sharing all the views of

St. Paul, on the sufficiency of faith without the works of the law, which, in his Epistle, the former condemns in plain terms.[1] This Epistle, like that of Jude, 'the brother of James and of Joses' (the latter words added in the Syriac version), is acknowledgedly written at a very early period, yet even the Epistle of St. James, the first in order of all Apostolical Epistles, indirectly refers to St. Paul, though both were probably written in Palestine, and for the Hebrew Christians, between whom and the believing Jews no more distinction is here made than in the Acts. To be a believing Jew, or a Christian, was, on the authority of St. James, quite compatible with being zealous for the law. Because of his zeal for 'all the commandments of the law,' St. James, like Zacharias, was 'a devout man and a just;' his brother Joses was also called 'the Just,' and was identical with Joseph Barsabas, who, together with Matthias, was proposed for the Apostleship in the place of Judas Iscariot, as eminent among those who had gone 'in and out' with Jesus and the Apostles.[2] Again, St. James' brother Simon, his successor in the Apostleship, was called the zealot, as probably also his third brother Jude.

At the time when St. James was raised to the presidency of the Apostolic Council, the ruling Herod Agrippa I. was himself a zealot for the Jewish law, so that the party of zealots in Palestine had reached the zenith of its power. Jesus had nothing 'in common' with such zealots, and least of all with one of his four brethren according to the flesh, who considered him mad, in consequence of his having 'a devil,' or evil spirit, such as was supposed to be working among the Samaritans. Yet St. James was among those who had gone 'in and out' with the Apostles 'all the time that the Lord Jesus' had walked on earth, and his brother Joses was all but chosen to take the place of Judas Iscariot. Other circumstances favoured the choice

---

[1] James ii. 14-17.   [2] Comp. Acts xv. 22.

of St. James. He was a priest, and possibly of high priestly descent. As a son of Zadok, the Sadducean high priest allowed him to enter the holy of holies. He was constantly seen alone in the temple, praying 'upon his knees, so continually for the people's forgiveness,' that his knees grew dry and thin.' These acts were accounted to him for 'exceeding righteousness,' by the people and its spiritual rulers. The name of James was superseded by that of the Just.[1] Like 'Simon the Just' in the days of old, a son of Aaron was seen in his glory. St. James, 'when he put on the robe of honour, made the garment of holiness honourable.' And as Simon had taken care of the temple, that it should not fall, and fortified the city against besieging,[2] so St. James, according to Hegesippus, 'was called "Oblias," which means in Greek, "the bulwark of the people" and "righteousness," as the prophets declare of him.' He was regarded as the Zadok, the righteous or 'just' servant of God, who 'by his knowledge' justified many. The historian tells us, that 'all (Hebrews) who believed, believed through James.' What then was his 'knowledge,' of which others were ignorant, and which was necessary to belief?

On this point no doubt can exist. It was the doctrine of resurrection and of the Lord's second coming, in which the Sadducees did not believe, but in which St. James had been confirmed, if not initiated, by the apparition on the way to Emmaus. Some of 'the sects' connected with the party of the Sadducees, the chiefs of which were the ruling members of the senior Aaronic line, 'the sons of Zadok,' came to St. James and enquired of him 'what is the door of Jesus,' or, in what sense did he say that he was the door, that is, 'the way, the truth and the life?' How could it be taught, 'that the law was given by Moses, but grace and truth came by Jesus Christ?' This was the knowledge which St. James taught to the Sadducees, to

---

[1] Epip. haer. 78, 14.   [2] Ecclus. l. 4, 11, 13.

which he belonged, but from whom on this point he had been led to differ. Of those unbelieving but ruling Sadducees, who asked him after the way to salvation, all who believed, believed through James. That these words refer exclusively to the Sadducees, follows from the recorded fact that only unbelievers in the resurrection asked him the question, and it is confirmed by the remark of Hegesippus, that through St. James 'many of the rulers believed.' For at that time the Sadducees only seem to have been considered as rulers, since in the fourth Gospel the rulers are distinguished from the Pharisees.[1]

In consequence of many of the Sadducees having been converted by St. James, 'there was a disturbance among the Jews and Scribes and Pharisees, saying: "There is a risk that the whole people will expect Jesus to be the Christ." They came together, therefore, to St. James and said: "We pray thee, stop the people, for they have gone astray after Jesus, as though he were the Christ. We pray thee, to persuade all that come to the Passover, concerning Jesus; for we all give heed to thee, for we and all the people testify to thee, that thou art just, and acceptest not the person of man. Persuade the people, therefore, not to go astray about Jesus, for the whole people and all of us give heed to thee."' Hereupon, according to the apostolic tradition recorded by Hegesippus, St. James was by the Scribes and Pharisees placed upon 'the gable of the temple,' and he was thrown from the eminence on which they had placed him. If this passage be taken in its parabolic sense, it explains who it was that set up St. James on the high eminence, which St. James, the son of Zebedee, one of the three 'pillars,' had occupied before him. This interpretation is confirmed by the further details supplied by Hegesippus. Having heard that St. James confessed his belief in Jesus almost in the same terms in which St. Stephen had done so just before his

---

[1] John vii. 48.

martyrdom, the Scribes and Pharisees said to each other: 'We have done ill in bringing forward such a witness to Jesus.' Whether St. James was bodily thrown down from a pillar, or whether he, whom Paul mentions as seeming to be a 'pillar,' was by the Scribes and Pharisees set down, in each case we may assume that these same Jewish rulers had brought him forward, or set him up. And this hypothesis is raised to a fact by the Acts not referring to another apostolic election in the place of the son of Zebedee. Unbelieving Jewish zealots, with the consent of Heród Agrippa, the Sadducee and zealot for the Jewish law, set up James the Zadok as one of the three pillars of apostolic tradition, and they threw him down from that eminence when they had perceived that 'even the just was gone astray,' and that the writer of the Catholic Epistle was 'displeasing' unto them.

Hegesippus has recorded another incident connected with the martyrdom of St. James. Whilst he was being stoned 'one of the priests of the sons of Rechab, a son of the Rechabites to whom Jeremiah the prophet bears testimony, cried out and said: 'Stop, what are you about? the just one is praying for you!' The Kenite priest interfered for the son of a Kenite woman.

The Gospels prove that St. James, the son of Zebedee, was one of the three more intimate associates of Jesus, and that 'the brethren' of Jesus were unbelievers till after the resurrection. This obliges us to accept with caution what Eusebius has recorded on the authority of Clement of Alexandria, that Jesus imparted the gift of 'knowledge to St. James the Just, to St. John and St. Peter after the resurrection,' and that 'these delivered it to the rest of the Apostles, and they to the seventy.' St. Peter, St. James, and St. John not only 'seemed to be,' but actually were, up to the year 41 A.C., the 'pillars' of tradition, the keys of which Jesus confided to St. Peter, commanding him to feed the flock. The above statement of the historian bears the marks of inaccuracy, inasmuch as he has quoted, just before, another passage from the same work of Clement, in which St. Peter is mentioned before St. James, and St. John as the last, whilst, in the passage we are considering, 'St. James the Just' is named first, and St. Peter last. As the Greek Church always insisted upon it, that St. James, 'the brother of the Lord,' was not one of the original Twelve; as the tradition seems to have been generally believed, that Jesus, in harmony with the parable of the talents, had more fully confided his mysteries to three Apostles; and as the Acts prove St. James, the brother of Jesus, to have been set over the Apostles before the year 44 A.C., the popular tradition had gradually been formed, that the second St. James was the chief organ of tradition. To this unhistorical tradition we must also assign the statement of Eusebius, likewise given on the authority of Clement, that St. Peter, St. James and St. John, 'after the ascension of our Saviour, though they had been preferred by our Lord, did not contend for the honour, but chose St. James the Just as Bishop of Jerusalem.'[1] And a century later, Theodorete referred to St. James a passage in the Epistle to the Hebrews,[2] which it is much easier to refer to St. Peter.

Had St. James been elected by the Apostles, this fact must have been mentioned in the Acts. His probable accession to power at the commencement of the Herodian persecution of the Christians, and the statements of Hegesippus, permit us to assume that he was chosen as overseer of the Apostles at Jerusalem, because of his connection with the Sadducees, then in the zenith of their power. We may regard St. James as a special instrument of Divine Providence. Without his protection, all the Apostles would have been persecuted. St. James could not prevent the martyrdom of the brother of St. John, nor the imprisonment of St. Peter; but had the

[1] H. E. ii. 1.  [2] Heb. xiii. 7.

latter ot known how St. James would rejoice in his escape and in his departure for Rome, St. Peter would not have commanded the household of Mary, the mother of St. Mark, 'to go and show these things unto James and unto the brethren.' St. James was a secret friend of St. Peter, six years after the crucifixion of Jesus, and he who had been an unbeliever till after that event, 'became a faithful witness both to Jews and Greeks, that Jesus is the Christ.'[1]

[1] Euseb. Hist. Eccl. ii. 23.

## CHAPTER XXI.

#### THE APOCALYPSE OF THE APOCRYPHA.

'THE revelation of the mystery kept in silence since the world began,' is pointed out by St. Paul, as the characteristic feature of 'the preaching of Jesus Christ,' and of the gospel which was revealed to the Apostle of the Gentiles. 'The mysteries of the kingdom of heaven' were not at once revealed, even to those of the unlearned to whom they were first given to know. The chosen disciples could not bear to hear all that their Divine Master had to tell them. The spirit of truth would lead into all truth those who desired to come to the light. The light then dwelling with men, was to be in them. As in St. Peter, so in St. Paul was God, 'the Father of the Spirits of all flesh,' pleased to 'reveal his Son.' And Apollos could say, that what 'in the beginning was made known by the Lord,' had unto them 'come down with accuracy (certainty), from those that heard (it), God having at the same time borne witness with signs and wonders, and with divers powers, and bestowals of the Holy Ghost, according to his will.'[1] God continued to do, what he had done in all ages, that is, to speak in man, ' in manifold measures, and in manifold fashions.'

This mystery, which had been kept secret since the days of Eden, for a time ceased to be the exclusive birthright of privileged classes, and was revealed to the poor and unlearned. The 'good news' of the kingdom, that

[1] Heb. ii. 3, 4.

is, of the rule of God's Spirit in man, the seed of the 'Word' sown by the Son of Man, began to spring up and to bear fruit. The tree of knowledge, the tree of life, had been transplanted from the barren soil of Palestine into the Gentile world, the kingdom was taken from Israel and 'given to a nation bringing forth the fruits thereof.' This mystery, the things belonging to the peace of Jerusalem, were hidden from her eyes, although the eternal Christ had so 'often' desired to gather the children of Israel under the uniting standard of truth, universally revealed to rich and poor, Jews and Gentiles. Nor was the veil removed by the preaching of the Apostles, by the blood of the martyrs, or by the destruction of Jerusalem. Israel was to become a witness unto all nations. The tradition of the Kenites, notwithstanding the opposition of the Hebrews, was to be engrafted on mankind. The nation of catholicity was to bring about the catholicity of the nations.

That one 'faithful servant,' to whom the keys of knowledge, the keys of David's tradition, were confided, is to give, 'in due season,' to all servants of God, to all believers, 'what is their due,' thus putting an end to the 'mystery' of Babylon, and restoring to the people 'the key of knowledge,' which the Jewish hierarchy had 'taken away.' St. Peter was to 'seal up,' and not to write down at once, the revelation of things hidden, the Apocalypse of the Apocrypha. 'The mystery of God' was not to be 'finished' immediately; but at some future time.[1] Even St. Peter, St. James and St. John were once heavy with sleep, and did not see the 'glory' of Christ, till they awoke.[2] Being converted, and that gradually, St. Peter was to 'strengthen the brethren.' He for whom Jesus prayed, that his faith might not fail, was to let the tares grow by the side of the wheat; he who was identified with the rock, was to remember, that his Divine Master would himself build the Church on the rock; that 'he

---

[1] Rev. x. 4, 7.   [2] Luke ix. 32.

that is holy, he that is true,' is also the one who hath 'the key of David, he that openeth and no man shutteth, and shutteth and no man openeth.'[1] Christ will continue to reveal 'the mystery which was kept in silence since the world began.'

Not all those who were of Israel, were Israel. What the Kenites asserted, the Hebrews denied. The revelation of the truth was opposed by the hiding of the same, the principles of common brotherhood, by caste privileges, universality by exclusiveness and separation. The time had come, when the Kenites, the disciples of Jesus, were called Christians, whilst the Hebrews were called Jews, a name which originally pointed to Judah, the tribe of the Kenites. Five years after the crucifixion of Jesus, St. Peter had founded the Christian Church in Rome. More than twenty years later St. Paul tried, by his Epistle to the 'called of Jesus Christ' in that city, to impart to them 'some spiritual gift,' that one of 'the fruits of the Spirit,'[2] which that Church, although 'filled with all knowledge,'[3] needed above all others, the gift of peace.[4] Kenites and Hebrews, Christians and Jews, were to live together as brethren in unity.

St. Paul did not write to the Roman Church as he wrote to any other. Even in his time, 'the faith' of the Roman Christians was being 'proclaimed throughout all the world.'[5] As Abraham bowed before Melchizedec, so St. Paul bowed before St. Peter, when he apologised to the members of the Roman Church, for his venturing to write to them 'rather more boldly in some parts,' as one who brought back to their recollection, who again reminded them of what St. Peter had first taught in their congregation. For the Apostle of the uncircumcision lays down the rule which regulated his conduct. He has 'striven to preach the Gospel where Christ's name was not known,' lest he should 'build upon another man's

---

[1] Rev. iii. 7.      [2] Gal. v. 22.      [3] Rom. xv. 14.
[4] Rom. x. 15; xiv. 17, 19; xv. 13, &c.      [5] Ibid. i. 8.

foundation.' His Epistle to the Romans forms the only exception to this rule, and he apologises for thus boldly venturing to address himself to those of his 'brethren' who 'are full of goodness, filled with all knowledge, able to admonish one another.'[1] Even the 'spiritual gift,' which he wishes that Church to possess, whether it be peace, or another grace of God, the members of the Roman Church would not stand in need of, if they followed the great Apostle, who then cannot have been at Rome. Although St. Paul would have been equally considerate in writing to a Church founded by any other of the Apostles, yet as, even during the rule of St. James at Jerusalem, St. Peter and St. Paul were acknowledged as leaders of the circumcision and of the uncircumcision, we may perhaps connect St. Paul's exceptional apology with an exceptional deference, if not submission, to St. Peter. The same Apostle who declares that there is no respect of persons before God, admits that the Jew comes first.

It is a confirmation of the above interpretation of the spiritual gift which St. Paul desired to impart to the Roman Christians, that he so strongly urges the Separatist, or Hebrew party at Rome, not to oppose the catholic principles of the Kenite or Gentile party among them. The majority must have been formed by Hebrews, generally called Jewish Christians, as distinguished from Kenites, generally called Gentile Christians. At the time to which the Psalm-book of Solomon refers, after Pompey's capture of Jerusalem in 63 B.C., when the Maccabean or Sadducean, that is, the Hebrew rule was ended, when Herod the Idumean, the friend of the Kenites, commenced the persecution of the Hebrew leaders, of the Sadducees, that is, between the years 63 and 48, a numerous colony of Hebrew Israelites was founded in Rome. Augustus, the friend of Herod, liberated the greater part of those whom Pompey had made prisoners of war, and granted them

---

[1] Rom. xv. 14-20.

the Roman citizenship. So rapidly had the Jewish colony increased in numbers, that when Varus had permitted the Jews in Judea to send an embassy to Augustus, the fifty ambassadors were accompanied by 'above eight thousand of the Jews that were at Rome already.'[1] The Epistle to the Romans clearly shows that there were two antagonistic camps in that Church. And this is confirmed by the Acts.[2] We distinguish them as Hebrews and Kenites. In Rome, as elsewhere, a Hebrew, or Separatist Israelite was called a Jew, and a Kenite, or catholic Israelite was called a Christian. But as Hebrews and Kenites belonged to the same nation, they probably continued, for some time, to assemble in the same synagogues. The first Christian Church at Rome must have been a synagogue. But from thence the catholic Jews spread among Gentiles the good news of Kenite principles applied. Such became the influence of the Jews at Rome that Seneca, the philosopher under the four successors of Augustus, and the declared enemy of the Jews, wrote: 'When meanwhile the state of that most abominable nation so far recovered itself, that it was received into every country, the conquered gave laws to the conquerors.'[3]

Gentiles were added to the Roman Church before St. Paul wrote his Epistles, when the separation of the Christians from the Jews, to which the Acts refer, must already have taken place. 'For I say to you Gentiles, (that) inasmuch as I am the Apostle of the Gentiles, I (admit that I) magnify my office, (to see) if by any means I may provoke the zeal of those that are my flesh, and might save some of them. For if the casting away of them be the reconciling of the world, what shall the receiving of them be, but life from the dead? But if the firstfruit be holy, the lump is also holy; and if the root be holy, so are the branches. But if some of the branches

---

[1] Ant. xvii. 11, 1.     [2] Acts xxviii. 21, 22.
[3] Seneca, in Aug. de Civ. Dei, vi. 11.

were broken off, and thou, being a wild olive tree, wert graffed in among them, and with them partakest of the root and fatness of the olive tree, boast not against the branches. But if thou boast against them, then know, that thou bearest not the root, but the root thee. Thou wilt say then, the branches are broken off, that I might be graffed in. Well! They were broken off because of their unbelief, but thou standest because of faith. Be therefore not highminded, but fear. For if God spared not the natural branches, he will also not spare thee. Behold therefore the goodness and severity of God; on them which fell, severity, but toward thee goodness of God, if thou wilt continue in his goodness, otherwise, thou also shalt be cut off. But they also, if they abide not in unbelief, shall be graffed in, for God is able to graff them in again. For if thou art cut out of the olive tree which is wild by nature, and art graffed, contrary to nature, into a good olive tree, how much more shall these, who are by nature (his branches) be graffed into their own olive tree? For I will not keep this mystery from you, brethren, lest ye should consider your own selves as wise, that hardness in part has befallen Israel, until the full number of the Gentiles has entered in. And so all Israel shall be saved, as it is written: Out of Sion the deliverer shall come, and shall turn away ungodliness from Jacob, and this is my covenant with them, when I shall blot out their sins. According to the Gospel (it is true, they are) enemies, for your sakes, but according to election beloved ones, for the sake of the fathers. For the gifts of grace and the calling of God, are not such as can be repented of. For as ye once were disobedient towards God, yet have now obtained mercy through their unbelief, even so have those also now become disobedient, that through your mercy they might also themselves find mercy.'[1]

St. Paul magnified his office whilst especially addressing the Gentiles of the Roman Church, who formed the mi-

[1] Rom. xi. 13-31.

nority, and were new comers. This conduct is apparently contrary to his catholic principle, to that peace which is necessary to catholicity, and the imparting of which, if our suggestion is right, has caused him to compose this Epistle. The Apostle takes the part of the Gentiles, for the purpose of provoking emulation among the Jews, that is, among the Hebrew party. For between Gentile converts and Kenite Israelites there can have been no difference, if we have succeeded in establishing the foregoing conclusions. Gentiles and Kenites knew something about the mysteries of the kingdom of heaven, but these good news were hidden from the Hebrews by their spiritual rulers, the Sadducees, enemies of tradition and catholicity. Yet even the members of the enlightened part of the Roman Church, are not to consider their own selves as wise. There are mysteries which St. Paul knows, and which they do not know. One he reveals to them. There is a not-enlightened party in Israel, the Hebrew party, the members of which, afterwards exclusively called Jews, will not come in, like the elder son in the parable, till the Gentiles, represented by the younger son, and by the Kenites, have fully entered. Then there shall be no difference between Hebrews, Kenites and Gentiles, but all Israel shall be saved. The test was not a genealogical one, but a spiritual one. In Abraham's seed of faith, in Abramitic tradition, not only in the writings of Moses, all generations of the earth are to be blessed. The first and catholic covenant cannot be made of none effect by the second and separate one. The tree of life had been transplanted into Gentile soil, but it had to be plucked up by the root in Palestine, where it had first been planted. The sons of Abraham in the flesh fulfilled only in so far the Abramitic promise, as they accepted the Abramitic tradition of their Kenite brethren, descendants from Melchizedec. They and the Gentiles generally, went in before the Hebrews. Thus the Mosaic written law was reduced to its proper level. 'The end of the law is Christ, for every one that believeth.'[1] To have the spirit of Christ, is to be a Christian.[2] The catholicity of Israel, the Abramitic promise, is realised through a part of Israel, through the Kenites; the God of the Hebrews is also the God of the Kenites and of the Gentiles.[3] All this has been accomplished through the 'one man Jesus Christ,' who, as 'concerning the flesh,' came from the Israelites, inasmuch as he was 'made of the seed of David,'[4] of the Kenite king.

The party in the Roman Church which opposed the principles of St. Paul, opposed the principle of catholicity, as the Hebrew party in Israel can be proved always to have done. The antagonism was as great when the Epistle to the Romans was written, probably from Corinth in the year 62 A.C., as it was three years later, when the chief of the Jews declared St. Paul to belong to a party 'everywhere spoken against.'[5] But, for the reasons which we have considered, St. Paul does not venture to censure the Romans as he did the Galatians. It is because of the Kenite branch of Israel, to which he belonged, that the Apostle entertained the hopes which he has expressed in the eleventh chapter. It is the Kenite principle of catholicity which has enabled St. Paul to be 'unto the Jews as a Jew,' though he was not 'under the law.'[6] The majority in the Roman Church was formed by Hebrews, or Ebionites, the minority by Kenites, joined by Gentiles; and yet both parties together formed Israel. Because the majority maintained, by incessant risings, the principle recorded in Deuteronomy, that 'no stranger' who is not a 'brother,' shall be set up and recognised as ruler, therefore the Jews had so often to be banished from Rome. St. Paul warns them to be subject to the appointed rulers, and to pay tribute. Finally, the Apostle of peace instructs 'the strong' how to act towards 'the

---

[1] Rom. x. 4.     [2] Ibid. viii. 9.     [3] Ibid. iii. 29.
[4] Ibid. v. 15; ix. 5; i. 3.
[5] For the contrary opinion, see Mangold, 'der Römerbrief,' 1866.
[6] 1 Cor. ix. 20.

weak.' The latter are unquestionably the Essenes, who abstained from meat and from wine, and also rigidly abstained from work on the Sabbath. St. Paul, as a Kenite, belonged to those 'that are strong,' and therefore did not sanction the austerity of either of these rites. Yet, for the sake of peace, even the weak are to be received. The warning not to enter into 'doubtful disputations' with that party, confirms the view, that they were Essenes. In all these questions, touching outward things, in all non-essentials, charity is to rule, and not uniformity. But in essentials, individual conviction is to be the rule; not so, however, as to hinder peace. 'The faith which thou hast, keep thou unto thyself before God;' for 'whatsoever is not of (or, issues not from) faith, is sin.' In spite of Hebrew opposition, St. Paul believed, that 'obedience of faith,' not obedience of mere works, obedience through 'faith which worketh by love,' that the peace, the catholicity of the Church had become possible, by the 'revelation of the mystery kept in silence since the world began,' by the Apocalypse of the Apocrypha.

What St. Paul's Epistle failed to accomplish, even the presence of that Apostle in the Roman prison could not bring about. Those who regarded the Christians as 'a sect everywhere spoken against,' the 'chief of the Jews,'[1] added afflictions to the bonds of St. Paul, by fanning, instead of extinguishing party spirit. Whilst some preached Christ 'of good will,' and 'of love,' others preached Christ 'of envy and strife,' and 'with a party-spirit.' The great Apostle wished to die, and to be with Christ, who is the true peace of men.[2] He having died the death of a martyr, St. Peter personally presided over the Roman Church for a few years, till he also glorified God by his death. About this time, probably before the martyrdom of St. James, his brother Jude wrote an Epistle, in which one party in the Church is warned against another, against 'certain men crept in unawares,

---

[1] Acts xxviii. 17, 22.     [2] Phil. i. 15-17, 23.

who have long been written down for such judgment,
godless men,' who 'have gone in the way of Cain, and
have thrust themselves, for the sake of reward, into the
error of Balaam, and perished through the contradiction
(antagonism) of Korah.' The identity of the Kenites
and Korahites, and their connection with the Kenite
prophet, which we have proved, is here strikingly confirmed. The continued rivalry and antagonism between
Kenites and Hebrews, a few years before the destruction
of Jerusalem, is removed from all doubt. We repeat
our assertion, that what is generally called the Judaizing
party in the Christian Church of the Apostolic times, is
the Hebrew party, and the so-called Paulinic party, is
the Kenite party in Israel. Jude, like St. James, the
unbelieving Sadducee who was set over the Palestinian
Apostles, and became, in this position, a faithful witness of
Jesus, belonged to the Hebrew party of Israel's commonwealth. As in other Hebrew Scriptures, the matrimonial
metaphor is freely used in the Epistle of Jude to designate the falling away, the separation of the Kenites. Jude
refers to the destruction of 'the unbelievers' by the Lord,
after that he had saved the people out of Egypt. Thus
the writer evidently refers to the recorded destruction of
Korah in the wilderness. As if to oppose this too narrow
restriction of those Israelites with whom God was alone
displeased, St. Paul points out that the many who were
'overthrown in the wilderness,' in various ways, and at
different times, did tempt Christ, the spiritual rock which
followed them. Apollos still more pointedly corrects the
statement of Jude. God was 'grieved forty years' with
all that sinned, 'whose bodies fell in the wilderness,' to
those who, because of their unbelief, did not enter into
the promised rest.[1] Among all that came out of Egypt,
from twenty years old and upward, only two entered into
the promised rest. These two, Caleb and Joshua, who
had been 'perfectly obedient to Jehovah,' and of one of

---

[1] Jude 5; 1 Cor. x. 5; Heb. iii. 16–19.

whom it is said, that he had been led by 'another spirit' than the other grown-up Israelites; these two, who alone received possessions in the land of promise,[1] were not Hebrews, were not ancestors of Jude, but of the Kenites, of those whom Jude denounces as having gone in the way of Cain.

There existed, in the Apostolic age, certain Scriptures, called Apocrypha, referring to the good news of the kingdom, and which were yet not recognised by the Church, not having been received in the Canon, before it was closed in the fourth century. Nevertheless they had their value; for verbal tradition has always preceded its record. Now, if it was the immediate proclamation of the hidden wisdom, first revealed by Jesus, which constituted the difference between the Gospel which, for a time, St. James insisted upon at Jerusalem, and the 'other' Gospel of St. Paul, it was in the interest of the Church to omit or to explain away all such Scriptures or passages, which referred to that difference, and thus to secret tradition not published. The omission, in the Acts, of the scene at Antioch between St. Peter and St. Paul may be thus explained. For Tertullian, the leader of the anti-Pauline Montanists (a party similar to the Essenes) does not scruple to diminish the force of St. Paul's attack against St. Peter and the other 'Jews,' by stating, that St. Paul likewise, and as it were in the same breath, censured certain 'false Apostles.' He writes: 'Marcion having got Paul's Epistle to the Galatians, who blames the Apostles themselves as not walking uprightly according to the truth of the Gospel, and also charges some false prophets with perverting the Gospel of Christ, set himself to weaken the credit of those Gospels which are genuine, and published under the names of Apostles, and also of Apostolic men.'[2] In another passage he shows that the Apostle who made such a charge against the Twelve was not in a position to know more than they did. 'They are accustomed to say that

[1] Num. xiv. 24; xxxii. 11, 12.     [2] Adv. Marc. v.

the Apostles did not know all, urged on by the same madness, with which they again turn their words into: they knew all, but did not deliver the whole to all. In either case they cast a reflection on Christ, as having sent forth Apostles, either not sufficiently instructed, or not sufficiently singleminded. He himself taught, that a candle was not hidden under a bushel, but set upon a candlestick, that it might give light to all that are in the house. The Apostles either disregarded, or totally failed to understand this, if they did not fulfil it, if they hid something of the light, that is, of the word of God, and the sacrament of Christ. They were afraid of no one, so far as I know, neither (of) the violence of the Jews, nor of the Gentiles. Therefore, surely, those men preached freely in the Church, who held not their peace in synagogues and public places.'[1]

Between the time of the publication of St. John's record of those sayings of Jesus which referred to secret tradition, that is, between the middle of the second century, and the closing of the Canon in the fourth century, the word apocryphal seems to have been first used. If, up to that time, all doctrines were considered as unorthodox, which could not be supported by the public sayings of Jesus, as recorded in St. Matthew's Gospel, henceforth, at least in some Churches, unorthodoxy was whatsoever went beyond the four Gospels. Yet many turned to unrecognised or apocryphal Scriptures, as to authorities, in the time of Origen.[2] This traditional reverence for the ever reconstructing agency of the initiated, could never be quite eradicated. Eusebius probably placed the Apocrypha of the Septuagint on a par with those New Testament Scriptures which, like the Epistles of St. James, of Jude, the latter Epistles of St. John, and the second Epistle of St. Peter, were by him classified as 'controverted, and yet familiarly used by many.' St. Athanasius admits that

---

[1] Praesc. Haer. xxii. 26.   [2] Comp. in Matt. xxii. 29; iv. p. 826.

there were other ecclesiastical books not included in his collection of the Old and New Testament, which were 'framed by the Fathers to be read for the benefit of those who are just approaching (Christianity), and wish to be instructed in the word of piety.' These he wishes, therefore, to distinguish from 'apocryphal books,' which are a device of heretics. As was later done by St. Augustine, already St. Athanasius distinguishes between the larger class of 'Divine,' and the narrower class of 'canonical' Scriptures. The latter formed a selected part of the former. St. Athanasius states that none of the books included in the Canon, or of those read in the Churches like the above, 'are mentioned anywhere as apocryphal books.'

Some held that the Apocrypha ought to be read by those who were perfected, but not by all; others referred to the recorded saying of Jesus, that he had said nothing in secret, and defined the apocryphal writings neither as hidden nor as genuine, but as 'absconded Scriptures.' St. Augustine states in one place, that they were called apocryphal because their origin was unknown, and in another, because they were not inserted in the Canon. Yet he states that the book of Wisdom and Ecclesiasticus having 'been deemed worthy to be received into authority, they must be reckoned among the prophetic books.'[1] If a Scripture was used by the majority of the Churches, it was to be regarded as canonical. Minorities in the Church continued to revere uncanonical Scriptures. In the middle of the fifth century, bishop Turribius of Asturia, wrote to Pope St. Leo the Great, that some even greatly preferred the apocryphal to the canonical writings, the former being, however, exclusively within reach of a few adepts. Shakespeare recorded a still living tradition, when he wrote that 'the spells of Apocrypha' juggled men into 'strange mysteries.'

[1] De Doctr. Ch. ii. 12, 13.

As after the closing of the Old Testament Canon, under Ezra, the further record of tradition was prohibited, and rendered impossible by the Masoretic School, so after the closing of the New Testament Scriptures, virtually under Eusebius, though the end of the second Gospel dates from a later period, further records of the hidden Wisdom were not recognised. Written Apocrypha of later times were, rightly in most cases, called apocryphal, in the sense of not genuine, and consequently of not inspired. The rule of secrecy, the 'disciplina arcani,' was instituted, and the unrevealed Apocrypha, or secret tradition, formed the mystery of the chief guardians of the Church.

Not only does Jude quote a prophecy from the book of Enoch,[1] which St. Jerome admits to 'be a quotation' from that work,[2] but Jude's Epistle refers to the dispute between Michael, the archangel, and the devil, about 'the body of Moses.' Both Origen and Didymus of Alexandria declare this to have been drawn from a scripture entitled 'the Assumption of Moses.' In addition to these authorities, the Scripture is used by Clement of Alexandria, St. Clement of Rome, the writer of the Acts of the Nicene Synod, or by others; whilst it occupied the fifth place among the Apocrypha in the Synopsis of the holy Scriptures by St. Athanasius. The Assumption of Moses was written in Greek, probably at Rome, by a Jew, after the year 44 A.C., during the reign of the Emperor Claudius. The importance of this undoubtedly genuine Scripture cannot be overrated, if we have rendered certain the meeting of St. Peter and Philo at Rome in the year 41. We, therefore, first give a translation and interpretation of 'the Assumption of Moses,' as transmittted to us:[3]—

---

[1] Jude 14.      [2] In Tit. i. 708.
[3] Translated from Hilgenfeld's 'Novum Testamentum extra canonem receptum,' 1866.

## The Assumption of Moses.

1. . . . which is the two thousandth and five hundreth year from the creation of the world;[1] for 'according to those who are in the East (it is) the thousandth and thousandth and five hundreth (year) from the departure of the phœnix,[2] when the people went out, . . . . after the departure which was made by Moses unto Ammun, the prophecy which was made by Moses in the book of Deuteronomy, he called to himself Joshua (Jesus) the son of Nave, a man approved by God, that he should be his successor to the people, and to the tabernacle of witness with all his saints, that he might lead the people into the land given to their tribes; that there might be given them by a testimony and an oath, that which he said in the tabernacle that he would give through Joshua, saying to Joshua this word: Promise according to thy diligence, that thou wilt do all things that are commanded, so that thou mayest be blameless. Wherefore the Lord of the whole earth[3] saith these things: For he created the world for his own people, and the creature itself took not that beginning. And from the beginning of the world he made it known that therein the nations might be convicted, and might humbly, with disputations among themselves, convict one another.[4] Wherefore he devised and found out me, and I was prepared from the beginning of the world, that I should be the mediator of his covenant.[5] And now declare I this unto thee, because the time of

---

[1] Eupolemus reckoned, that the Israelites left Egypt anno mundi 2,569, and that Moses died 2,609. The dates given for the death of Moses in the book of the Jubilees, or the Little Genesis, and by Josephus, also nearly agree with the date in 'the Assumption of Moses.' The writer subsequently gives the reason for his date.

[2] According to Gutschmid's proposed restoration of the passage, it would mean, that 'according to the year, when the people that are in the East went forth, it was the 437th year of the departure to Phœnicia,' that is, to Palestine. This era commences with the departure of Abraham from Ur.

[3] Comp. 2 Esdr. vi. 55; vii. 11; xiv. 31.   [4] Comp. Rom. xi. 15.

[5] Gal. iii. 19, 20; Acta Syn. Nic. xi. 18.

the years of my life is fulfilled, and I pass to the sleep of my fathers. And before all the people do thou teach it. Moreover do thou take (or learn) this scripture for the preservation of the books which I shall deliver thee, which thou shalt arrange and embalm in cedar,[1] to lay them up in earthen vases, in a place he made from the beginning of the creation of the world; that his name may be invoked continually unto the day of penitence,[2] in the regard in which the Lord regards them in the consummation of the end of days.

2. But now they shall enter through thee into the land which he decreed and promised to their fathers; in which thou shalt bless them, and thou shalt give to each one, and establish to them a lot therein, and thou shalt establish to them a kingdom, and shalt appoint for them magistrates of places, according as it shall please the Lord, of them in judgment and in righteousness. But . . . (seven?) years after, they shall enter into their own land.[3] And after that, they shall be ruled by princes and tyrants for eighteen and nineteen years.[4] For two tribes shall come down and transfer the tabernacle of witness. Then the God of heaven shall make plain the (courts?) of his tabernacle and the temple of his sanctuary, and two tribes of holiness shall be established.[5] For the ten tribes shall establish for themselves kingdoms, according to his ordinances. And they shall bring victims for twenty years.[6] And seven shall fortify the walls and I will surround nine.[7]

---

[1] Pliny speaks of 'libri cedrati.'
[2] Proves that the book was written before the destruction of the temple.
[3] Josh. xiv. 10.
[4] Gutschmid explains that the book of Enoch gives the key, where the derivation of reigns is marked by hours. The eighteen years refer to Joshua, the twelve Judges, Eli, Samuel, Saul, David and Solomon; the nineteen years to the nineteen kings of Israel, from Jeroboam to Hosea.
[5] Benjamin and Judah, the tribes of the two Aaronic lines. According to the book of Enoch, 'the righteous and chosen one will let appear the temple of his church.' Enoch liii. 6, 7.
[6] The twenty kings of Judah.—Lipsius.
[7] Judah's prosperity to increase under the seven reigns, from Rehoboam to Athaliah. The following nine from Joash were to be protected by God. Under the last four Judah fell.

And they shall go to the covenant of the Lord, and pollute the end (or boundary, or definite agreement) which the Lord made with them; and shall immolate their own sons to strange gods, and shall place idols in the sanctuary, serving them. And in the house of the Lord shall they do wickedly, and shall carve many images of all animals.'[1]

3. In those days there shall come from the East a king,[2] and shall cover their land with horsemen, and shall burn their colony with fire, together with the holy temple of the Lord, and shall take away all the sacred vessels, and cast out all the people, and shall lead them into the land of·his own country, and shall lead the two tribes with him. Then shall the two tribes call upon the ten tribes, and shall roar like a lioness in the plain, covered with dust, hungry and thirsty with our children; and they shall cry: 'Just and holy is the Lord; for because ye have sinned, we also are brought into captivity with you.' Then the ten tribes, hearing the reproachful words of the two tribes, shall implore them and say: 'What shall we do for you, brethren? Hath not this affliction befallen the whole house of Israel?' And all the tribes shall implore, crying to heaven, and saying: 'God of Abraham, and God of Isaac, and God of Jacob, remember thy covenant which thou madest with them, and the oath which thou swearest unto them by thyself, that their seed should never fail from the land, which thou gavest unto them.' Then shall they remember me that day, tribe saying to tribe, and man to his neighbour: 'Is not this that which Moses testified with us in the prophecies, who suffered many things in Egypt and in the Red Sea, and in the wilderness forty years? He called to witness, and invoked unto us heaven and earth as witnesses, that we should not transgress his commandments, in which he was the mediator unto us; which came to us from him, according to his own words, and according to his own affirmation,

---

[1] Ezek. viii. 10.     [2] Nebuchadnezzar.

as he testified unto us in those times, and which are fulfilled, in that we are carried away captive into the quarter of the East.' Who also shall be in slavery seventy-seven years.[1]

4. Then shall there enter one, who is over them,[2] and he shall stretch forth his hands, and kneel and pray for them, saying: 'Lord Almighty, king in the lofty seat, who rulest for ever, who hast willed, that this people should be to thee an elected people, was it not thy will to be called their God, according to the covenant, which thou madest with their fathers? And they are gone away captive into a strange land, with their wives and their children, and they are about the door of people of another kindred, and where there is great sorrow. Look upon them and pity them, O Lord of heaven.' Then shall God remember them because of his covenant, which he made with their fathers, and shall manifest his pity in those times, and shall put it into the mind of the king to pity them, and he shall dismiss them into their own land and country. Then shall certain parts of the tribes go up and shall come into their own appointed place, and shall wall and repair it. But two tribes shall remain in their established faith, sad and lamenting, because they shall not be able to offer sacrifices to the Lord God of their fathers. And the ten tribes shall increase, and shall come down to their sons in a time of tribulation.[3]

5. And when times of convicting shall come, and vengeance shall arise against the kings who partook of wickedness and punished them, they also themselves shall be divided as to the truth, on account of what was done. They shall avoid justice, and proceed to iniquity, and defile with pollutions the house of their servitude.[4] And that because they shall commit fornication after strange

---

[1] In chapter vii. the writer adds seven years to the seventy weeks of Daniel. The same number is in Luke's genealogy, iii. 23 f.
[2] Dan. ix. 4-19; 2 Esdr. viii. 20-36.
[3] 2 Esdr. xiii. 39-47.  [4] Purim Massacre.

gods. For they shall not follow the truth of God, but some shall defile the altar with gifts which they shall offer thereupon to the Lord, not being priests, but slaves born of slaves.[1] For they who are in authority, their teachers in those times, shall be respecters of persons, of cupidity, and of the receiving of gifts, and they shall sell justice by accepting reward. And therefore their settlement (colony), and the bounds of their habitation shall be filled with crimes and pollutions.[2] . . . They who do not after the Lord, shall be impious judges, they shall be in the temple (fanum?) to judge as each man shall desire.

6. Then there shall arise kings[3] ruling over them, and these shall be called as priests of the most high God, working impiety from the holy of holies. And to them shall succeed a violent king[4] who shall not be of the line of the priests, a rash and wicked man, who shall cut off their principal men[5] with the sword, and shall bury their bodies in unknown places, that no man may know where are their bodies. He shall kill the old men and the young men, and shall not spare. Then shall the fear of him be bitter among them in their land and he shall execute judgment among them, as the Egyptians did, for thirty and four years, and shall punish them. And he shall beget sons succeeding him for shorter times,[6] until enemies shall come into their coasts, and a mighty king of the West who shall take them by storm, and lead them captive, and shall burn part of their very temple with fire, (and) some shall he crucify round about their settlement.[7]

---

[1] Joshua and the Kenite priesthood.  [2] Eliashib, Tobiah, Manasseh, &c.
[3] Maccabees.
[4] Herod the Great, who though made king B.C. 40, did not really obtain the kingdom before the taking of Jerusalem by C. Sosius B.C. 37, according to Josephus (Bell. Jud. i. 33, 8).
[5] Sadducees.   [6] Archelaus, Herod Antipas, and Philip.
[7] In the reign of Augustus, as Gutschmid has proved, in the first year after Herod's death, Varus, the governor of Syria, began to put down a Jewish rebellion. He took Jerusalem by storm, and left Sabinus there, against whom the Jews rebelled for a second time. (Bell. Jud. ii. 3, 1 f.) Part of the temple was destroyed by fire, and the treasure plundered.

7. After which the times shall be ended in a moment, the course of the years shall be ended, the four hours shall come, the seven last of the world, from the beginning of tribulation to the end. Nine about the beginning, three sevens in the second, three in the third, two in the fourth hour.[1] And afterwards pestilent and impious men shall reign, saying, that themselves are just; and these shall excite the anger of their minds, pleasing themselves, false in all their dealings, and in every hour of the day,

Varus came up with his army. His son, governor of Galilee, having taken Sepphoris, made slaves of the inhabitants and burned the city. (Ant. xvii. 10, 10; Bell. Jud. xi. 5, 1.) Varus liberated the legion, which was blockaded in Jerusalem, and hunted down the leaders of the rebellion, two thousand of whom he crucified.

[1] Hilgenfeld thus restores the text. 'Immediately after these things, the times shall be fulfilled, the courses of the year shall be fulfilled. Four hours shall come; the seven last weeks of the world, from the beginning of the tribulation to the end, shall be drawn to a close (or shortened); the beginning is about nine. The second hour is three weeks, the third hour is three years, the fourth hour is two.' Gutschmid first gave the key to the interpretation. He begins from the reduction of Judea into a Roman province. The 'nine near the beginning' refer to the nearly nine full years of the reign of Augustus after the above event, from A.C. 6 to the 14th Sept. of the year 14. This will be the 'beginning of tribulation.' The 'three sevens of the second hour' refer to the reign of Tiberius (14-37), who died (Ant. xviii. 6, 10) 'having held the empire twenty-two years all but five months and three days,' or as the same historian states, all but six months (Bell. Jud. ii. 9, 5). Thus his reign only exceeded the three weeks of years by a very little.

The 'three years in the third hour' refer to the reign of Caligula, which lasted three years, ten months, nine days (38-41), or three years and eight months, according to Josephus (Bell. Jud. ii. 11, 1). As to 'the two years of the fourth hour,' Gutschmid makes them weeks, and thus gets fourteen years instead of two, which he refers to the reign of Claudius (41-54), which lasted thirteen years, eight months, and twenty days (Bell. Jud. ii. 12, 8; Ant. xx. 4, 1). But Hilgenfeld keeps to the text, asserts that the word dual was the numeral B in the original, which might be turned as well into *duo* (anni) as into *dual* (hebdomades). Thus interpreted, the passage refers to two years of the fourth hour, that is, of the reign of Claudius, the fourth emperor. If so, the book was written at the beginning of the reign of Claudius, soon after the meeting of Peter and of Philo in Rome, and on the accession of Herod Agrippa II., whose cruel father died (44) when Claudius had scarcely reigned two years. The year 44, when St. Peter and St. Paul returned to Jerusalem, and when Judæa was again reduced to a Roman province, was regarded as the commencement of the end by the Jewish writer of this book.

loving banquets, devourers, slaves of their gullet, . . . devourers of other men's goods, saying that they do these things for the sake of pity ; who also seek out those who eject, deceitful, concealing themselves, that they may not be known to be impious ; abounding in wickedness and iniquity, from the East unto the West, saying: 'We will have banquettings and luxury, eating and drinking ; and we thought ourselves as princes, we will be (so).' And their minds and their hands handling impure things, and their mouth shall speak great things, and they shall say moreover. . . . .

8. And quickly shall there come upon them vengeance and wrath, such as was not among them, from the beginning of the world up to that time.[1] And at that time he shall rouse against them the King of the kings of the earth, and authority from the great power, who shall hang upon the cross those that confess circumcision, for (while) those who deny it he shall torture, and deliver to be led bound into prison.[2] And their wives shall be given to savage nations, and their sons shall be cut in the groin by surgeons, and they shall make them uncircumcised. For they shall be punished in those (times?) with torments and fire and sword, and shall be openly compelled to carry their abominable idols, so that they are equal to those holding them, and they shall be compelled, by those tormenting them, also to enter into their secret place, and they shall be compelled by pricks to blaspheme the word contumeliously, immediately after these things, and the laws which they had upon their altar.

9. Then at his (God's) command, a man of the tribe of Levi, whose name shall be 365,[3] who having seven sons shall speak to them, asking : 'Ye see, my sons, behold, a second vengeance is come among the people, cruel, foul,

---

[1] Matt. xxiv. 21. Comp. 2 Esdr. ix. 1 f.
[2] Persecution of the Jews by Claudius (Acts xviii. 2) ; comp. Suetonius, Dion Cassius and Tacitus. Hilgenfeld, p. 114.
[3] Comp. Rev. xiii. 18.

and a leading into captivity without pity, and they exceed all measure. For what nation, or what country, or what people of those who have been impious against the Lord, who have done many wicked things, have suffered so great evils as are come upon us? Now, therefore, my sons, hearken unto me; for ye see and know, that never did our parents, nor their fathers tempt God, that they should transgress his commands, for ye know that this is our strength. And this will we do. We will fast three days, and the fourth day we will enter into a cave which is in the field,[1] and let us die rather than transgress the commandments of the Lord of lords, the God of our fathers. For if we shall do this, and shall die, our blood will be avenged before the Lord.'

10. And then shall appear his kingdom in all his creation, and then the devil shall have an end, and, with him, sorrow shall be taken away. Then shall be filled the hands of the messenger who is set upon high,[2] who shall straightway avenge them of their adversaries. For the heavenly One shall arise from the seat of his kingdom, and shall go forth from his holy habitation with indignation and wrath, because of his sons; and the earth shall tremble, it shall be shaken unto the ends thereof, and the high mountains shall be brought low, and shall be shaken, and the vallies shall fall, the sun shall not give light, and the horns (rays) of the moon shall be turned into darkness, and be broken, and she shall be wholly turned into blood,[3] and the orbs of the stars shall be disturbed, and the sea shall shrink to the bottom thereof, and the fountains of waters shall fail, and the rivers shall be greatly afraid,[4] because the most high God shall arise, eternal, alone, and shall come manifestly, and shall punish all the nations, and destroy all their idols. Then blessed shalt thou be,

---

[1] Comp. 1 Macc. ii. 29-38; 2 Macc. vi. 11, 39.
[2] Comp. Dan. xii. 1. Moses, however, is here, and afterwards, meant.
[3] Is. xiii. 10; Ezek. ii. 7; Joel iii. 3 f.; Matt. xxiv. 29.
[4] 2 Esdr. vi. 24.

Israel, and thou shalt mount up upon eagles' necks and wings, and (these things) shall be fulfilled.¹ And God shall exalt thee, and make thee to cleave to the heaven of the stars, to the place of their habitation.² And thou shalt behold from the height, and shalt see thine enemies on earth, and shalt know them, and rejoice, and give thanks and confess to thy Creator. And now do thou, Joshua, son of Nave, keep these words, and this book. For there shall be, from my taking up unto his coming, two hundred and fifty times,³ which shall come to pass, and this is the course of them, which they observe, until they shall be accomplished. But I shall go to the sleep of my fathers. Thus, therefore, Jesus, Son of Nave, hath God solemnly chosen thee to be my successor in the same covenant.

11. And when Joshua had heard the words of Moses, thus written in his own writing, all that he prophesied, he rent his clothes, and cast himself at the feet of Moses, and prayed with Moses, and lamented with him. And Joshua made answer to him and said: Why shouldst thou hide from me, my Lord Moses, and in what manner is hidden from me the thing concerning which thou hast spoken with a bitter voice, which proceeded out of thy mouth, which is full of tears and groans? Because thou departest from this people . . . what place . . . shall receive thee? Or what shall be the monument of thy burial? Or who shall dare to carry thy body from hence, as that of a man, from place to place? For the burials of all who die in the course of their age, are in the earth; while as to thy burial, from the East to the West, and from the South to the bounds of the North, the whole world is thy sepulchre, oh my Lord, from henceforth. And who shall nourish this people of thine? or who is there,

---

¹ 2 Esdr. xi. xiv. 18.  ² Comp. Matt. xiii. 43.
³ Weeks of years = 1,750 years, from the assumption of Moses to the year 45 A.C., supposed by the writer to be the last of the world, which had been created 4,250 years ago.

who shall pity them? And who shall be to them a leader in the way? Or who shall pray for them, not keeping patience even for one day, that I may lead them into the land of the Arabians? How shall I be able (to rule) this people as a father his only son, or as his daughter, a lady, a virgin, who is prepared for such a husband,[1] who is fearful, keeping her body from the sun, and her feet lest they should run unshod upon the earth. At their will shall I be able to give them food and drink according to the will of their pleasure . . . For there were 600,000 of them, for they had increased so much through thy prayers, my Lord Moses; and what wisdom or understanding is in me in the house, . . . to show or to make answer in words? Yea, moreover the kings of the Amorites, when they shall hear of it, will drive us out, believing that there is no longer with them a holy spirit worthy of the Lord; a manifold and incomprehensive Lord, faithful in his word in all things, a Divine prophet (known) throughout the world, a teacher fulfilled for ever, is no longer among them. They shall say: Let us go unto them: if our enemies have once hitherto done impiously against their Lord God, there is no defender for them, who may offer prayers for them to the Lord, as Moses was a great messenger, who at all hours, days and nights, had his knees fixed in the earth, praying, and beholding the Almighty of the world, with pity and justice, calling to mind his covenant with their parents, and with an oath appeasing the Lord, yea, they will say: He's not with them, let us go therefore and confound them, from off the face of the earth. What therefore will become of thy people, my Lord Moses?

12. And when Joshua had finished these words, he fell a second time at the feet of Moses. And Moses took him by the hand, and raised him, and set him on a seat before himself, and said unto him, Joshua, despise not thou thy-

---

[1] Is. vii. 14; 2 Cor. xi. 2.

self, but show thyself confident, and mark my words. All the nations that are in the world, God hath created, and he hath foreseen us, them and us, from the beginning of the creation of the world to the end of time, and nothing hath been neglected by him even to the smallest thing. But he hath foreseen and foreknown all things with them. For the Lord hath provided for all things which should be in this world, and behold he is brought near. The Most High hath appointed me for these and for their sins, . . . and that not for my strength or weakness, but the longsuffering of his mercy and his patience have reached unto me. For I say unto thee, Joshua, that not because of the piety of this people shalt thou exterminate the nations. All the firmaments of the heavens were made as they were well-pleasing to God, and are under the ring of his right hand. Wherefore in doing and performing the commandments of God, they (the Israelites) increase and follow out a good way. For the good things which are promised shall be lacking to those who sin and neglect his commandments ; and they shall be punished by the nations with many torments. For it cannot be, that he should root them out utterly, and forsake them. For God hath gone forth, who hath foreseen all things for ever, and his covenant is established, and by the oath which . . . .

(*The rest is wanting.*)

It is from this Scripture that Jude extracted the passage referring to the dispute about the body of Moses. Whilst Origen distinctly asserts this, his predecessor Clement of Alexandria refers to a more complete text of the Assumption of Moses, after which he thus describes the end of Moses : 'Agreeably to this moreover, Jesus the son of Nave saw Moses twice during his assumption, once with the angels, and again upon the mountains, by the ravines, demanding burial. Jesus saw this sight below, being lifted up in spirit, and with him also Caleb. But they did not both see equally, but the one descended sooner than the other, attracting to himself much that weighed him down, while the other, descending later, related the glory which he had beheld, having been able to gaze more closely than the other, as having been more pure. This story means, in my opinion, that knowledge does not belong to all, since some look at the body of the Scriptures, the phrases and the words, like the body of Moses, while others regard the thoughts, and the things made known by the words, making more of Moses with the angels.'[1]

On the same subject Evodius, in a letter to St. Augustine,[2] writes: 'Although both in the apocrypha, and in the secret writings of Moses himself, a Scripture which lacks authority, when he ascended the mountain to die, it came to pass by the strength of his body, that part of it was committed to the earth, and part went in company with the attendant angel.' Again, Œcumenius, in his dissertation on the Epistle of Jude says:[3] 'The dispute about the body of Moses is this: It is said, that Michael the archangel had the care of the burial of Moses; but that the devil did not allow this, but brought an accusation on account of the murder of the Egyptian, saying, that Moses belonged to him, and therefore would not agree that he should have the usual burial.' Didymus of Alexandria, writing on the Epistle of Jude says:[4] 'Though the adversaries of this view object to the present epistle, and to the assumption of Moses, on account of that passage, where is signified the word of an archangel, made to an angel concerning the body of Moses.' In the Acts of the Nicene Synod it is stated:[5] 'In the book of the Assumption of Moses, Michael the archangel, disputing with the devil, says: "For from his holy spirit we were

---

[1] Strom. vi. 15, 132, p. 806.
[2] Augustine Epistles, 259.  [3] Page 348.  [4] Bibl. Patrum, iv. 326.
[5] Acta Syn. Nic. ii. 20, p. 33.

all created." And again he says: "From the face of God went forth his spirit, and the world was made." The philosopher who is introduced in an argument, replies, "I never heard before of the Assumption of Moses, so pray make clear to me the connection of what you say."'

From this evidence we come to the following conclusions :—

1. In the second and later centuries, more complete copies of the Assumption of Moses existed, than that transmitted to us, the first part of which has been lately discovered, in a corrupted Latin version.[1]

2. The original was written before the Epistle of Jude, before the destruction of Jerusalem, and therefore before the Greek version of the Gospel after St. Matthew transmitted to us by manuscripts of the fourth and later centuries.

3. The Jewish writer, residing in the West, and probably in Rome, wrote the work after the death of Herod Agrippa I., in the third year of the emperor Claudius, 44 A.D., and before the expiration of the year 45, when the writer predicted the end of the world.

4. The writer's doctrinal principles coincide with those of the Hebrews or Sadducees, as opposed to the principles of the Kenites or Pharisees, and of the Essenes, with which principles Christianity is connected.

5. The antagonism between Hebrews and Kenites, heightened by the crucifixion of Jesus, by the consequent rising of the Samaritans under Simon Magus, by the martyrdom of St. Stephen and St. James, by the general persecution of the disciples of Jesus, excepting the Apostles at Jerusalem, by the persecution of the Hebrews, in the reign of Caius-Caligula and Claudius, explains the exclusion of Kenite doctrines in the Assumption of Moses, and in the Epistle of Jude as also the strong condemnation of the Kenites in both Scriptures, although Jude calls

---

[1] 'Monumenta sacra et profana ex codicibus præsertim bibliothecæ Ambrosianæ' by Ceriani, Milan, 1861.

himself a 'servant of Jesus Christ,' and refers to the words spoken by the Apostles of 'our Lord Jesus Christ.'

6. The Assumption of Moses proves, that allegory, aided by the mysticism of cyphers, was the only form in which it was possible for a Roman Jew to refer to the leading events of the time. Thus is confirmed the view we have taken about the allegorical record referring to the Purim massacre.

7. The calculation of fifty Jubilees, also accepted by the writer of the book of Jubilees, confirms our explanation about the meaning of the seventy weeks in the book of Daniel.

8. The passage about the body of Moses is by Clement of Alexandria explained, as referring to the secret tradition, more or less divulged by the body of Mosaic writings, according to their being understood in a literal or in a figurative sense.

9. The two persons who were, above the rest, initiated in the mysteries of Moses, were the Kenites Caleb and Joshua, the only two grown-up Israelites that came out of Egypt, and who were permitted to enter into the promised land. Thus Kenite tradition is connected with Moses, who received his call whilst he was in the service of Jethro, the Kenite priest.

10. The Assumption of Moses is directly opposed to the principles enunciated in the so-called Clementines, although parts of the same may have been written in the same place, and about two years earlier, by St. Mark, the interpreter of St. Peter. According to the former scripture, Moses is the only prophet, in the latter he is one of many. These two scriptures, in their original form, were records, respectively of Hebrew and of Kenite tradition. They would suffice to prove, why the Jews, as a nation, rejected Christianity.

## II. *The Apocalypse of Moses.*

'The Apocalypse of Moses,' or 'the little Genesis,' or 'the book of the Jubilees,' written in Palestine, and in Hebrew, about the middle of the first century A.C., confirms our interpretation of the book of the law of Moses which was brought to light in the time of Josiah, and of the importance attached to jubilee periods, at a time when the Messianic expectations of the Jews were at their height. It is a targum, intended for the lower grades of the initiated, and especially of the Essenes.[1] It refers to the theoretical part of Jewish tradition, which was called 'history of creation,' as distinguished from the practical part, called 'history of the chariot.' From first to last its doctrines are anti-Sadducean, and yet it opposes likewise the Pharisees, in so far as they permit the Sanhedrim to determine the festal cycle in accordance with the new moon, instead of the jubilee. Even this commentary on Genesis is based on the festal cycle of seven times seven, or forty-nine years. The sanctity of the number seven is further demonstrated by the most rigid injunctions about observing the Sabbath, for which asceticism the Essenes were celebrated. Like the future Jerusalem, the Sabbath was created in heaven for angels. The Mosaic law is a record of Abramitic tradition. Already Abraham celebrated the feast of Tabernacles, and thus sanctioned the veneration for the number seven, for the Sabbatical week, and for the jubilee period. But although, according to the Mosaic ritual, on the feast of the Tabernacles, the doctrine, that 'it is the blood that maketh an atonement for the soul,'[2] was to be demonstrated by successive bloody sacrifices, the writer abhors blood altogether, as the Essenes and the Nazarenes are known to have done. 'Beware of blood, beware much. Dig it into the ground, and eat no blood, for it is the soul; absolutely avoid to eat blood . .

---

[1] See Jellinek, 'Bet ha-midrash,' p. x. f.   [2] Lev. xvii. 11.

that thou mayest be preserved from all evil.' This was
going beyond the written law of Moses, which required
to be interpreted by the light of Mosaic and Abramitic
tradition. The spiritual sacrifice was thus enjoined in the
words which were, probably already at that time, attributed
to Jesus. 'I am not come to take away anything from
the law of Moses, but to add to the law of Moses am I
come.'[1] 'I am come to destroy the sacrifices, and except
ye cease from sacrificing, wrath shall not cease from you.'[2]
The writer's expectations of the Messianic kingdom are
directly connected with the moral progress of Israel, and
thus with the transformation of 'this world' into 'the
world to come.' He evidently knew the book of Enoch.
As he expects the kingdom to last a thousand years, as
he waits for the fiftieth jubilee, and as he interprets the
seventy weeks of Daniel as seventy jubilee periods, we
may assert, that our interpretation of the Millennial expectations, to which we shall presently refer, is directly
confirmed by the writer of the book of Jubilees.

### III. *The Apocalypse of Ezra.*

'The Apocalypse' or 'the prophecy' of Ezra, forming
part of the second (or fourth) book of Ezra, originally
written in Greek, is altogether of Roman origin. The
author is neither an orthodox Jew, nor a Christian, but
an Essene, who does not regard Jesus as the promised
Messiah, and who lives in the time of Nerva. The last
date to which the work can refer, is the year 96 and 97
A.C. It is quoted in the 'epistle of Barnabas' as the work
of a prophet; and Clement of Alexandria refers to it
as the work of 'the prophet Ezra.'[3] St. Irenæus and
Tertullian respectfully mention it, but in the time of St.
Jerome it had fallen into disrepute. It never formed
part of the Alexandrian Canon, a fact which goes far to

[1] Ev. Naz. to Matt. v. 17.  [2] Ev. Heb. to Matt. v. 23, 24.
[3] Strom. iii. 16, 100.

confirm its Roman origin. The council of Trent did not recognise it.

This apocalypse strongly resembles the book of Daniel. Ezra is called the 'brother' of Daniel. What was 'not expounded to Daniel, was declared to Ezra by the Highest,' in answer to prayer. The knowledge thus acquired is regarded as a hidden wisdom. 'Thou only hast been meet to know this secret of the highest. Therefore write in a book all these things that thou hast seen, and hide them, and teach them to the wise of the people, whose hearts thou knowest may comprehend and keep these secrets.' Thus it is proved, that in the Apostolic age some Christians were regarded as prophets, who taught a hidden wisdom to a few, who had been prepared by learning, and bound by secrecy. Clement of Alexandria, whilst he refers to the writer of this apocalypse as a prophet, quotes from 'a certain gospel' called 'the preaching of Peter,' according to which, in the form transmitted to us in the so-called Clementines, Jesus taught that which from the beginning had been secretly communicated to those only who were 'worthy.' Again St. Peter is here recorded to have urged upon St. James the necessity of communicating only to a few, and under the oaths of secrecy his (St. Peter's) sermons, which he had preached in Rome.

If, then, there existed in the first century an organisation for the gradual proclamation of a hidden wisdom; if the same was headed by one or more prophets; if Ezra the prophet is called the brother of Daniel; and if to the former was revealed what had not been expounded to the latter, then the direct connection between the visions of Ezra and those of Daniel, proves the continuity of tradition. The following facts confirm this assertion. Whilst the two last chapters of the second book of Kings were probably written by Jeremiah, and the last chapter of the second book of Chronicles, as well as the first of the book of Ezra, were written by Daniel, other parts of the latter book seem to have been written by Haggai. The contents of this apocalypse fully establish the transmission of tradition by prophets, as chiefs of a secret organisation. The glorious future of Israel, as seen by prophets, was to be preceded, according to Daniel's vision, by four successive kingdoms of the Gentiles, the last of which was evidently the Roman empire. As such it is figuratively described in the vision of Ezra, and at the same time as 'the kingdom' which was seen in the vision of Daniel. It has been fully established that the Apocalypse of Ezra refers to Roman history.[1]

The 'twelve feathered wings' of the 'eagle'[2] which are explained as kings, are the six double-winged emperors, Julius Cæsar, Octavianus Augustus, Tiberius, Caius-Caligula, Claudius, Nero. The first ruler is described, by the Essenic Israelite, as coming from the right side, that is, for him who looked to the holy land, from the West. Thus Julius Cæsar came from Gaul, to reign 'over all the earth,' but suddenly to fall. Of the second ruler, of Augustus, it is said, that he would, like the first, rule to his 'end,' without opposition, that he 'had a great time,' that he bore 'rule over the earth so long,' and that none after him should attain to his time, 'neither unto the half thereof.' After the death of the sixth ruler, of Nero, 'great strivings,' or contentions arose, and the kingdom shall 'stand in peril of falling, nevertheless it shall not then fall; but shall be restored again to his beginning.'[3] So it was, for now the two wings of Galba are set in motion. 'Then I beheld, and lo, in process of time the feathers that followed stood up upon the right side, that they might rule also; and some of them ruled, but within a while they appeared no more. For some of them were set up, but ruled not.'[4] Again Galba rose on the right side of the seer, that is, from Spain, not as a legitimate successor, but as opposition-emperor. He

---

[1] Volkmar, 'das Vierte Buch Esdras,' p. 36 f.  [2] 2 Esdr. xi. and xii.
[3] 2 Esdr. xii. 18.  [4] Ibid. xi. 20, 21.

maintains the unity of the empire; but after six months from August 68 to January 69 A.C., Galba's reign ended. How clearly is this described! 'And I beheld, and lo, the feathers that were under the wing, thought to set up themselves, and to have the rule. And I beheld, and lo, there was one set up, but shortly it appeared no more. And the second was sooner away than the first.'[1] The second usurping ruler was Otho, whose reign lasted three months only. Another vain attempt to rule was made by the two remaining wings, they 'thought also in themselves to reign.' And when they so 'cogitated' on the government, 'one of the heads that were at rest,' the first head of a new dynasty, of the Flavii, Vespasian, arose, having rested so long.

This 'head was turned,' or 'turned himself,' with them that were with it, 'and did eat up the two (remaining) feathers under the wing,' that is, Vitellius. Indeed Vespasian 'turned himself' from Palestine against Vitellius in Italy, and, in combination with his sons Titus and Domitian, devoured the kingdom of the last usurper. Whilst Titus did his work in Palestine, Domitian opposed Vitellius in Rome, and accepted the people's acclamations of joy for Vespasian, as for their emperor. The Romans 'celebrated with a festival at once his establishment on the throne, and the overthrow of Vitellius.'[2] Vespasian is in the vision called the head 'that was in the midst,' and that which 'was greater than the two other heads.' Yet he was not the second, but the first of the Flavian emperors. As the head of the new dynasty, the place of honour among the 'three heads' of the eagle was due to him. Moreover Vespasian's rule, especially in the eyes of an Israelite, had 'put the whole earth in fear, and bare rule in it over all those that dwelt upon the earth with much oppression, and it had the governance of the world more than all the wings (rulers) that had been.' After

[1] 2 Esdr. xi. 25-27.   [2] Bell. Jud. iv. 11, 4.

the destruction of Jerusalem, Vespasian rode in the midst of his two sons, when he made his triumphant entry into Rome.[1] No Israelite of any party would ever forget this. The vision probably refers to this incident. He 'suddenly appeared no more.' And indeed, according to Suetonius and Dio Cassius, Vespasian suddenly died after a brief illness. In the interpretation of the vision it is stated that he 'died upon his bed, and yet with torments.' The emperor's fever may have been regarded by the writer as a symbol of the torments of hell that awaited the destroyer of the holy city. According to the vision 'the head upon the right side devoured that which was upon the left side,' that is, Domitian put an end to the life and rule of Titus. Although this trait is not historical, it is an echo of the well-attested tradition that connected the death of the one with a crime of the other.[2] If any doubt could exist on this point, it would be removed by the Aramean text, where it is added that the one head devoured 'and poisoned' the other. In the interpretation an error is committed, a very pardonable one for an Israelite in Rome, in that both Titus and Domitian are declared to have been 'slain with the sword,'[3] which is correct only as regards Domitian. 'In like sort,' like the other Flavii, Domitian 'ruled upon the earth, and over those that dwelt therein.'

But now the time of the writer's hopes has come. The end of Israel's bondage, like that to which the unknown prophet of the Babylonian captivity referred, is at hand. The lion of Judah will come, and to him will belong 'the obedience of the nations.' In the vision it is 'a roaring lion, chased out of the wood,' who addresses the eagle in the name of the Highest, rebuking her for her unrighteousness. 'Art not thou it that remainest of the four beasts, whom I made to reign in my world, that the end of their

---

[1] Bell. Jud. vii. 5, 5.
[2] Suet. Dom. ii.; Dio Cass. Hist. lxvi. 26; Sibyll. x. 120 f.
[3] 2 Esdr. xii. 27, 28.

times might come through them? And the fourth came, and overcame all the beasts that were past, and had power over the world with great fearfulness, and over the whole compass of the earth with much wicked oppression, and so long dwelt he upon the earth with deceit. For the earth hast thou not judged with truth.' It is declared that the 'abominations' of the beast are ended, and the eagle is commanded to 'appear no more,' that 'all the earth may be refreshed, and may return, being delivered from thy violence, and that she may hope for the judgment and mercy of him that made her.' Although another pair of wings arises, 'their kingdom was small (poor), and full of tumult.' The reign of the aged Nerva confirms this. By many he was not recognised,[1] and even among the prætorians who had raised him a ferment existed, and wars threatened in many directions. The writer expected the Messiah and the promised return of the Jews, as most Essenes, or disciples of John the Baptist, probably did. He would not have done so in the autumn of 97 A.C., when the setting up of Trajan proved the errors of the vision and of the interpretation, as far as it did not belong to the past. But the past, the present, and the future had been so mystified, that very few only can have understood the hidden meaning of this Apocrypha. At a time when 'no man spake against' Rome, 'no, not one creature upon earth,' it would have been impossible to have referred to the events of those times in a less mystic form. For this obvious reason the number of the kings, like that of the wings, is doubled in the interpretation. Three heads and twenty kings! Who should decipher this? It was too much for Roman censorship. And yet nothing flies with less than a pair of wings.

We now refer to the doctrines of the entire book. It is more than probable that the first two, and the last two chapters belong not to the original book. But the

[1] Dio Cass. lxviii. 2, 3.

addition, whenever made, does not essentially change the doctrinal character of the work. The fourteen chapters which were written in the last years of the first century, confirm the existence of St. Matthew's and St. Luke's Gospels, of St. Paul's Epistles, and of the Apocalypse of St. John. But they do not prove that the final deposit of Gospel tradition had already been made, or that the seer at Patmos saw what was entirely hidden from others. The leading ideas and symbols are the same, both apocalyptic writers had been brought up in Kenite doctrines, and as Essenes, but St. John believed in the Messiahship of Jesus, whilst Ezra did not. In the part which refers to the Apocalypse of Ezra,[1] it is stated that God has made the world to come 'for few,' that though many are created, few shall be saved. And yet, in answer to prayer, God gives seed unto man's heart, and culture unto his understanding, that there may come fruit of it.[2] Every one of those whom God has sanctified for himself 'from the beginning' shall be saved 'by his works and by faith.'[3] It is implied, that although ever since the time of Moses the kingdom of God, the kingdom of the indwelling Word, was by some known to be near, that is, in the heart of man, yet that this key of knowledge had been taken away. Even thirty years after the destruction of Jerusalem, when this scripture was composed, 'the truth which had been so long without fruit,' had not been publicly declared.[4] Having shown 'the multitude of wonders,' which God will do in the last times, 'the Highest' said to Ezra: 'These things have I not showed unto all men, but unto thee and a few like thee.'[5] The prophet addresses the Most High, reminding him, how he had declared himself to Israel in the wilderness, saying: 'I sow my law in you, and it shall bring forth fruit in you, and ye shall be honoured in it for ever.' Yet they that received the law perished, 'because they kept not the

---

[1] 2 Esdr. iii.-xiv.     [2] Ibid. viii. 1-6.     [3] Ibid. ix. 7, 8.
[4] Ibid. vi. 28.     [5] Ibid. viii. 62.

thing that was sown in them.' Still, 'the law perisheth not, but remaineth in force.'[1]

Now follows the description of a vision, in which the prophet saw 'a woman' who mourned and wept, 'and was much grieved in heart, and her clothes were rent, and she had ashes upon her head.' Ezra, trying to console her, is told: 'I thy servant have been barren, and had no child, though I had an husband (a ruler) thirty years. And those thirty years I did nothing else . . but make my prayer to the Highest. After thirty years God heard me, thine handmaid, looked upon my misery, considered my trouble, and gave me a son, and I was very glad of him; so was my husband also, and all my neighbours, and we gave great honour unto the Almighty, and I nourished him with great travail. So when he grew up and came to the time that he should have a wife, I made a feast. And it so came to pass, that when my son was entered into his wedding chamber he fell down and died. Then we all overthrew the lights, and all my neighbours rose up to comfort me; so I took up my rest unto the second day at night. Then I rose up by night and fled and came hither into this field, as thou seest. And I do now purpose not to return into the city, but here to stay, and neither to eat nor drink, but continually to mourn and to fast till I die.' The seer knows that the woman cannot be the representative of any Jewish community then existing. He, therefore, points out to her how unreasonable it is to mourn in such a manner for only 'one son,' and adds: 'if thou shalt acknowledge the determination of God to be just, thou shalt both receive thy son in time, and shalt be commended among women.' The woman replies to this advice about returning to 'the city' and to her husband: 'That will I not do; I will not go into the city, but here will I die.' The city can only be Rome, and her husband the Roman ruler, as in the narrative of

[1] 2 Esdr. ix. 31-37.

the woman of Samaria, her five husbands refer to the five kingdoms of Babylon, Cutah, Ava, Hamath and Sepharvaim. Rome was no more the husband of the woman of Judea, than Assyria was the husband of the woman of Samaria. The independence of both had ceased.

The seer urges the woman to reconsider this, and to be comforted by comparing her affliction with that which has befallen Zion. There is no remnant of the holy city, but there is a remnant of the holy people, which scattered remnant is represented by the woman. The national 'God with us,' the nation of priests, shall yet be born, and the renewed Israel shall be the blessed among the nations, though the Roman plough has passed over the hallowed ground. 'Our sanctuary is laid waste, our altar broken down, our temple destroyed, . . the light of our candlestick is put out, . . the seal of Zion hath now lost her honour, for she is delivered into the hands of them that hate us.' Suddenly the woman is transfigured before the eyes of the seer. 'Whilst I was talking with her, behold, her face upon a sudden shined exceedingly, and her countenance glistered, so that I was afraid of her, and mused, what it might be. And behold, suddenly she made a great cry, very fearful, so that the earth shook at the noise of the woman. And I looked, and behold, the woman appeared unto me no more, but there was a city builded, and a large place (the future Jerusalem) showed itself from the foundations.' Having cried for the presence of the angel Uriel, who had caused him to fall into many 'trances,' the same came unto him, found him lying 'as one that had been dead,' and whose understanding had been taken from him. The angel took him by the right hand, and comforted him, and set him upon his feet, and comforting him asked after the cause of his state. The seer declares that he went to the field to which the angel had directed him, where he has seen, and still sees, what he is not able to express. Having been promised further advice, he says to the angel: 'Speak on, my Lord, in me;

only forsake me not, lest I die frustrate of my hope. For I have seen that I knew not, and hear that I do not know. Or is my sense deceived, or my soul in a dream? Now therefore I beseech thee, that thou wilt show thy servant of this vision.' The angel invites him to hear, for that 'the Highest will reveal many things' unto him. The woman whom he saw, and after whose disappearing 'a city builded' had appeared, must be identified with that city. There will be no independence of Israel, till the future Jerusalem, seen by the prophets, has been built. The time has now come, for the thirty years, after the destruction of Jerusalem by Titus, have been foreshadowed by the thirty years which preceded the building of Solomon's temple, when 'the barren did bare a son.' So shall now the new Jerusalem and its temple arise, 'in the brightness of her glory, and the comeliness of her beauty.' One son, one people, one nation, has died with 'the destruction that came to Jerusalem.' Another son, another people, another nation, another Israel, will be born. The Jerusalem shown in the year 96 A.C., is the Jerusalem which is above. 'In the place wherein the Highest beginneth to show his city, there can no man's building be able to stand. And therefore fear not, let not thine heart be affrighted, but go thy way in, and see the beauty and greatness of the building, as much as thine eyes be able to see. And then thou shalt hear as much as thine ears may comprehend. For thou art blessed above many other, and art called to be with the Highest, and so are but few.'[1]

Like Enoch, the seer is to be translated, and the things which 'the Most High will do unto them that dwell upon the earth in the last days,' are described in general accordance with the visions recorded in the book of Enoch nearly three centuries earlier. Heaven and earth unite in the Messianic days. The Anointed, the Messiah, who has

---

[1] 2 Esdr. ix. 38-47; x. 1-57.

not yet come, but is kept unto the end by the Highest, is
no longer described as 'one like a son of man,' or, as in
the book of Enoch, as 'the son of man' and 'son of God,'
but as 'that man' who 'waxed strong with the thousands
of heaven.' Thus the seer clearly refers, as Jude had
done a few years earlier, to the description in the book
of Enoch about the coming of the Messiah 'with ten
thousand (myriads) of his saints.' All things trembled at
his look, and his voice burned them that heard it. The
seer then 'beheld, and lo, there was gathered together a
multitude of men out of number, from the four winds of
the heaven, to subdue the man that came out of the sea.'
He had 'graved himself a great mountain, and flew up
upon it,' but the prophet could not see where it was.
Instead of fighting against the multitude, 'he sent out of
his mouth as it had been a blast of fire, and out of his
lips a flaming breath, and out of his tongue he cast out
sparks and tempests.' Thus the whole multitude was
burned. Afterwards the seer saw 'the same man come
down from the mountain, and call unto him another
"peaceable multitude."' In the angel's interpretation it
is said, that in 'the latter days' the 'Most High' shall
come, 'to the astonishment of them that dwell on the
earth. And one shall undertake to fight against another,
one city against another, and one realm against another.'
After the fulfilment of the signs shown to the prophet,
'shall my son be declared, whom thou sawest as a man
ascending (the mountain). And when all the people hear
his voice, every man shall in their own land leave the
battle they have one against another. And an innumer-
able multitude shall be gathered together, as thou sawest
them, willing to come and to overcome him by fighting.
But he shall stand upon the top of the Mount Zion. And
Zion shall come, and shall be showed to all men, being
prepared and builded, like as thou sawest the hill graven
without hands.' This 'multitude of the nations' will he
destroy 'by the law which is like unto fire.' But 'the

peaceable multitude' which he gathered unto him, consists of the 'ten tribes carried away in the time of Hosea the king,' but who left the heathen and went 'into a further country where never mankind dwelt, that they might there keep their statutes, which they never kept in their own land.' As God dried up Euphrates for them to pass, so will he 'stay the springs of the stream' again, that they may 'go through' when they return in the latter time. They will be the people of God that remain, after the destruction of the Gentiles.

The coming of the Messiah, of him 'that should come' was considered 'nigh at hand' in the year 96, as is shown by the vision about the eagle. Another vision shows, what are to be the signs of his coming. 'Concerning the tokens, the days shall come, that they which dwell upon earth shall be taken in a great number, and the way of truth shall be hidden, and the land shall be barren of faith. But iniquity shall be increased above that which now thou seest, or thou hast heard long ago. And the land that thou treadest upon, shalt thou see wasted suddenly. But if the Most High grant thee to live, thou shalt see after the third trumpet, that the sun shall suddenly shine again in the night, and the moon thrice in the day. And blood shall drop out of wood, and the stone shall give his voice, and the people shall be troubled. And even he shall come whom they look not for that dwell upon the earth. Behold the time shall come, that these tokens . . shall come to pass, and the bride shall appear, and the coming forth shall be seen, that now is withdrawn from the earth. And whosoever is delivered from the foresaid evils shall see my wonders. For my son Messiah[1] shall be revealed with those that be with him, and they that remain shall rejoice within four hundred years. After these things shall my son Messiah die, and all men that have life. And the Most High shall appear upon the

---

[1] The Ethiopian text has 'Messiah,' not 'Jesus.'

throne of judgment, and misery shall pass away, and the long-suffering shall have an end.'[1]

It is impossible to assert what passages may have been altered at a later period, but on one point there can be no doubt: the Messianic future is connected with 'a city builded,' and with a man, the Son of the Highest. The prophecy of Isaiah about the woman Israel that is bearing a son, and the prophecy of Zechariah about 'the man whose name is the Branch,' were combined. The Messiah shall have a people, and that people, the Israel of all nations, catholic Israel, shall possess the new Jerusalem on earth, which, like the ark, is built after a heavenly pattern. Already in the book of Enoch the revelation of 'the temple' by the Messiah is described, and in the Assumption of Moses, which the writer likewise knew, the revelation of the tabernacle is also referred to. The Messianic Jerusalem is built in heaven, and is transferred to the earth. Nothing less could be expected, if Enoch's Apocalypse was regarded as a prophecy awaiting fulfilment. For there heaven and earth are described as united in the latter days. The righteous of all ages will arise from their graves, clothed in 'garments of life,' they will join the 'elect' upon earth, the assembly in Zion, the limited company of 'the righteous,' whose 'number' has been 'fulfilled,' who have not 'denied the Lord of Hosts and his Christ,' that is, 'the Son of God' who was 'chosen and hidden' in heaven 'before the world was created,' whom 'the wisdom of the Lord of Hosts hath revealed to the holy and to the righteous,' to those who are 'saved by his name.' The Lord of Hosts and his Son, accompanied by 'myriads of holy ones,' will for ever unite themselves with holy ones at Jerusalem. 'The chosen and holy children will descend from the high heavens, and their seed shall unite itself with the sons of men,' praising, lauding, and magnifying 'the ancient of days,' and saying:

[1] 2 Esdr. vii. 26-33.

'Holy, holy, holy is the Lord of Hosts, he filleth the earth with spirits.'[1]

The Messianic kingdom, beginning with the renewed creation of heaven and earth, is to last for ever, according to the Apocalypse of Enoch. In the Apocalypse of Ezra this period is limited to four hundred years. Had the writer been a Greek instead of a Jew, he would have limited the time to three hundred years, which number, according to a tradition recorded in the 'Epistle of Barnabas,' and by Clement of Alexandria, was explained as a mystic type of the name Jesus.[2] But according to the Hebrew symbolism of numerals, the letter *tau* like a cross, represents 400 and not 300. It was the *crux ansata* of the Egyptians, the symbol of immortality, and was of the same form as the Nile-measure, or the key, attached to the head of Amun, the God of concealment. The Essene looked for a revealing Messiah, and yet did not believe in Jesus as he that should come. As the Apocalypse of the seer at Patmos must have been known to him, his not accepting the thousand years is remarkable. The connection of the Millennium with the seventy weeks of the book of Daniel is proved beyond the possibility of serious contradiction. The writer has established, almost in the exact words attributed to Daniel, a parallel between the person of Nero and that of Antiochus, between the blasphemies, the persecutions, the compulsory worship, the duration of persecution, and the destruction of these two enemies of God.[3] He then draws a parallel between the last twenty of Jeremiah's seventy years, and the last twenty of Daniel's weeks, reckoned as jubilee periods, that, is, with the Millennium. In both cases the fall of Babylon precedes Israel's liberation.

The writer is as far from Christianity as John the Baptist was from being a disciple of Jesus. Since the

---

[1] Hidden Wisdom i. 99 f.   [2] Barn. ix. Strom. i. 91.
[3] Clearly pointed out in Journal of Sacred Literature, October, 1864.

disciples of the Essenic prophet, according to the Acts, continued in their separation, the conjecture that the writer was an Essene is highly probable. The lasting value of the Apocalypse of Ezra is, that by the light of Daniel's prophecy about the four monarchies, it interprets the history of Rome during part of the last pre-Christian, and the first Christian century, and thus forms an invaluable introduction to the Apocalypse of the seer at Patmos. The two Apocalypses centre in the Messianic expectations. Both regard the Messiah as the Son of God, but the one expects him as he that should come, the other as he who had come, and will come again. In both, the woman represents not an individual, but a people.

## CHAPTER XXII.

### SYMBOLS, MIRACLES AND CREEDS.

SYMBOLS are intended to elevate, not to lower mankind. History shows that this object was seldom realised, that symbols became idols. The most dangerous symbol was the word. By defining instead of suggesting an idea and its application, the spiritual was imprisoned by the material, the life-giving spirit by 'the letter that killeth,' heaven was chained to the earth, the soul to the body. The law, the whole law, and nothing but the law, this Sadducean symbol has acted like a leaven in the Jewish and in the Christian Church. But if the word of Moses had become a stereotyped symbol, prophets were its interpreters. What prophets foreshadowed was finally accomplished by the founder of the Christian Church. The law came by Moses, truth and grace by Jesus Christ. To the form, to the appearance of godliness, the power of godliness was added,[1] the hidden things were revealed, to the poor the Gospel was preached. Even that which was hidden from the wise and intelligent was revealed to the unlearned, but not without symbols. The practice of the prophets was not to be abolished at once. It would have been impossible to have done so. 'What the prophets said and did,' writes Justin Martyr, 'they veiled by parables and types, so that it was not easy for all to understand the most (of what they said), since they concealed the truth by these means, that those who are eager to find out and learn it might do so with much

---

[1] 2 Tim. iii. 5.

labour.'[1] In a figurative form, in parables first, more plainly afterwards, 'the mysteries of the kingdom of heaven' were proclaimed. St. Paul preached the eternal and yet hidden wisdom in 'a mystery,' even 'to them that are perfect,' and not at all to those who had to be instructed in the elementary principles of that wisdom. Those who did not even know the symbol of the written word could not be taught its interpretation. Scripture was always a popular epitome of tradition.

There existed at all times a key to the symbols of Holy Writ. 'The key of knowledge' had been taken away from the people, but it was restored to them. They possessed the Scriptures, the symbols, but not their key. This restoration was to be a gradual one. A steward of Divine mysteries was appointed, to whom 'the keys of the kingdom of heaven' were given. All apostles and evangelists shared in the responsibility of adapting the form of their Gospel proclamations to the exigencies of the time. As in the time of Ezra, by vowel points, interpretation was partially engrafted on the letter, so, in the apostolic age, the symbol of the word was still further explained. But the mystery never did cease. The surviving apostle St. John was commanded to 'seal up,' to bind, and not to loose. 'The mystery of God,' symbolised by a 'little book,' is to be finished, when the mystery of Babylon has fallen. It was St. Peter, to whom his Divine Master conveyed the power and entrusted the mission, to bind and to loose, to seal and to unseal, to shut and to open. St. Peter was to feed the flock, that is, to interpret the symbols. Few of the sayings of Jesus were published at Jerusalem, during the rule of St. James. To these, others were added, which St. Luke recorded, probably in Rome; but the most important were recorded by St. John; and it has been rendered probable, that this Apostolic record was confided to the safe keeping of St. Peter's

[1] Dial. 90.

successors, who amplified, revised, and published it, less than a century after the Apostle's martyrdom. Thus the mysteries of the Gospel were more and more revealed, the symbol of the word was more fully interpreted, yet not without error.

Historical facts had been recorded in a figurative form. Consequently there was in every symbol, especially in the word, an historical and an ideal element. This referred especially to the record of miracles. Unless people saw 'signs and wonders' they would not believe. It was 'an evil generation' which sought after a sign. The Hebrews who did so, were told, that 'no sign' should be given them, except a sign, a symbol, a mystery, the interpretation of which would be hidden from them. Jonah was a mystery to the Ninevites, and still they repented; the queen of the South came to Solomon not to see or to read, but to hear and understand 'the wisdom of Solomon.' The symbols which Jonah and Solomon interpreted were no longer understood, in the time of one greater than Solomon, and had become idols. So the unbelieving Jews, the Hebrews, saw the miracles of Jesus, and yet many believed not. They interpreted them carnally, and thus imbibed not their spiritual meaning. Their rulers kept tradition to themselves, and thus the people knew not the things belonging to their peace. But there were a few of the initiated, like Nicodemus, who became convinced, that every miracle was a symbol, an outward sign of an invisible power. Miracles and symbols conveyed the fact, that God is with man. Those who believed in Jesus because of the miracles which he did, were not by him given to know the mysteries of the kingdom of heaven; he did not commit himself unto them, they did not become his disciples, he knew them not. And yet he, as also others, worked miracles by the Spirit of God, to see whether he could not thereby suggest to them the great mystery of God's Holy Presence in man. The bodily infirmity was to point to the spiritual infirmity. In order to heal the soul, Jesus had often first to heal the body. He had to act on matter before he could act on the spirit. In so doing he identified himself with all human infirmities, even with ignorance and blind prejudice. Not only did he act on matter, but he acted also *with* matter. Even the spittle and the clay, and the pool of Siloam, which were by many venerated as efficacious means of healing, Jesus did not despise, nor reject, for he would not quench the smoking flax, but kindle a flame in the breast of the incipient believer.

This high example was followed by the Church. Not all the seed sown by Jesus, his Apostles and other disciples, sprung up at once and was ready for harvest. As the parabolic teaching of Jesus had preceded his plainer and fuller teaching, so the Church could not at once abolish the symbolical form. Holy scripture was at all times the symbol of holy tradition. The Bible never was, it never was intended to be, a substitute for tradition. There was always, there is now, and there will ever be, death in the letter 'that killeth.' And yet it was a necessary means for conveying tradition. There never was any authority for believing that the mission of tradition, and the gift of performing miracles, had ceased at any given time. Miracles continued to be performed, beyond the time of the last Apostle's death, according to the unanimous testimony of witnesses, whose moral qualities we have no right to regard as inferior to those of the men who attested and who recorded the miracles in the Apostolic age. The difference between the earlier and the later miracles can only have been one of degree. Fiction there was in the records of both, as the initiated knew well. Moreover, what was considered as miraculous in one place, or at one time, was not regarded as such in another. Knowledge was engrafted on ignorance, light on darkness, in such a manner as fallible man deemed most conducive to the gradual enlightenment of the individual and of the masses. Outward signs continued to be conveyancers of spiritual gifts. The symbol first attracted the senses, and then the soul. The more the real meaning of symbols was understood, the less were miracles required. As the uninterpreted symbol had become a miracle, so the interpreted miracle became a symbol. The night which followed upon the setting of the sun of righteousness, necessitated an increase, and not a decrease of symbolism. Soon the mysteries kept in silence for ages past, were proclaimed on the housetops, symbols were better understood, and, in course of time, miracles ceased to be regarded as absolutely direct and isolated acts of the Creator's intervention. The conviction gained ground, that miracles were visible attestations of the fact, that God works by means, through the instrumentality of his creatures, and of laws which are imperfectly known to us. Even the Apostles had to undergo the symbolical process of washing their feet, the meaning and efficacy of which, directly connected with the Paschal rite, and an accessory of the latter,[1] was to be afterwards revealed to them. They could not then bear what their Master had to tell them, though he had ceased to speak in parables, and spoke plainly. Had they understood the meaning of the symbol raised by Moses in the wilderness, had they known, that the fiery serpent symbolised the ever present healing agency of the Word or Spirit of God, as 'the Saviour of all,' as the Christ that accompanied the Israelites, then the symbol of the cross would not have been misunderstood by them. The cross of Christ was a stumblingblock to the Jews, it became a symbol to some Christians, a miracle and an idol to others. Ignorance was the cause of this.

The cross of Christ became a new symbol in the Church. The baptism with fire was understood by the initiated to mean the baptism of the Holy Ghost, the emblem of the

---

[1] The 'pedilavium;' St. Aug. Epist. ad. Jan. 118.

Holy Presence. The human body was declared to be a symbol of the Divine temple, the holy of holies, where God communes with man, where the Spirit of God, symbolised by fire, testifies to the spirit of man, that he is a child of the Highest. By the perfect obedience of one man, this mystery had been proclaimed and manifested. Jesus was not only a human teacher of the Divine Christ, but he had shown, by his entire life and by his death, that God's Spirit, if unresisted, is able to transform sons of men into sons of God. Thus Christ had become incarnate, Jesus had become the Christ. 'The temple of his body' was lifted up, like the serpent in the wilderness, as an emblem of salvation realised. It had been realised by flesh and blood. The death of the anointed Jesus must not be separated from his life, that is, from his blood. 'The blood of his cross' is the symbol of human 'obedience unto death,' and the cross is the symbol of the yoke which, by self-denial, the follower of Jesus is to 'take up daily.' The death of Christ, as a symbol, was substituted for the miracle. In course of time, all miracles centred in that miracle, all mysteries in that mystery.

The symbol of the cross became an idol. It was first represented without the image of the Crucified. The crucifix was not a symbol of the earliest Church; no trace of it can be found in the catacombs. But the Jewish Passover continued, for centuries, to be observed by the Roman Church, as by the Armenian Christians. The Pope and eleven cardinals solemnly partook of a lamb at Easter, as is proved by some early rituals, and other testimonies. Thus the doctrine of the Western Churches, that Christ did not eat, but was himself the Paschal lamb, was maintained, which the fourth Gospel confirmed in the middle of the second century, and which Epiphanius thus symbolically interprets: 'Christ must needs be sacrificed on the 14th day, that among them (the Jews) should cease the light which lighteneth them according to the law, the sun having arisen and overpowered the brightness of the moon. For from the 14th and downward the appearance of the moon waneth. So also in the law, from the time of the presence and passion of Christ, the Jewish congregation has become dim, and the Gospel has shone forth, the law not having been destroyed but fulfilled, the type not being made void, but exhibiting the truth.'[1]

The early Christian Church did not create, it found this ignorance, this superstition, this idolatry. Sadduceism was sown like tares among the wheat. The enemies of Christianity had done this. Israel was a divided camp, the broad way of destruction was much frequented, and few found 'the narrow way that leadeth unto life.' But the head of the Church was not commissioned to root out the tares, to do the work of angelic reapers. Being converted, St. Peter was to strengthen the brethren. Mankind was to be led through the symbol of the visible Church to the reality of the invisible. Because man is the sublimest terrestrial symbol of the spiritual tabernacle, the visible Church, the congregation of the faithful, is destined to be the symbol of the invisible Church. This high destiny of the Church was realised through and in every worshipper, who was assisted, by the symbol which he saw, to realise the connection of the same with the invisible and indwelling Spirit of God. Whilst the Jewish high priest, separated from the people, had to stand, once in the year, before the hidden symbol of Divine Presence, the priest at the Christian altar held up visibly before the assembled worshippers, before the congregation of priests, the mystic symbol of the Presence of him who promised to be with his Church 'all the days, even unto the end of the world.'

The cross was early connected with the tree of life, which we identify with the tree 'of the knowledge of good and evil.'[2] As already observed, Solomon knew

---

[1] Panar. i. 2. Comp. 'the Paschal Controversy' in Tayler's 'fourth Gospel,' 1867.

[2] About 'the Legend of the Oil of Mercy' see Dr. Piper's Essays, translated in Journ. of Sacr. Lit., iv. xi. &c.

that Divine Wisdom is 'a tree of life' to them that lay hold upon her and retain her.[1] The eternal Christ, 'the Wisdom of God,' was in all ages connected by prophets with the tree of life; and the tree of knowledge was, therefore, by them identified with the tree of life. Thus we explain the mysterious fact, that the tree of life, but not the tree of knowledge, is referred to in other Scriptures than in the book of Genesis. The root, the stem, the branches, the leaves, the fruit of the tree of life have all been directly connected with the Messianic kingdom. The Messiah will be of 'the root of Jesse.' Although the tree of life has been cut down to the roots, a branch, or rather a sucker, will sprout from the roots of the tree which David, the first Kenite king, had planted. That tree of tradition, of wisdom, of life, will bear fruit; this was the hope of prophets. The branch of the tree of life which will bear fruit, 'the righteous branch,' will be of God's 'planting.' Ezekiel announced that 'the tender branch,' cut off from the highest branches and planted on a high and lofty mountain, on paradise, that is, in the highland of Eden, will bear fruit, and 'in the shadow of the branches thereof,' birds of the air of every kind shall dwell.[2] The fruit-bearing branch of the tree of life, 'the man whose name is the Branch,' is called the crucified 'Prince of life.' Jesus visited the tree of life, the sycamore fig-tree which had been planted in Palestine, he had patience with it, but finally it was withered to the very roots, it was plucked up by its roots and transplanted in the sea, that is, on Gentile soil. The kingdom of God was taken away from the Jewish nation, and was given to a nation bringing forth the fruits thereof. The Messiah, the Man named the Branch, called himself the vine, and his disciples the branches. To be grafted on to the vine was and is to be nourished by the Divine root, which God the Father, the husbandman, has planted.

---

[1] Prov. iii. 18.     [2] Ezek. xvii. 22-24; comp. Matt. xiii. 31, 32.

The branches thus connected through the vine with the root, are 'trees of righteousness,' or rather, 'oaks of blessing,' and 'a plantation of the Lord to (his) glory.'[1] But 'every plant' which the heavenly Father has not planted, 'shall be rooted up.'[2]

We have pointed out that Christ Jesus, the incarnate Word or Wisdom of God, identified himself with the promised Branch, with the Messiah, and thus with the tree of life. He called himself the bread of life, the living water, and the well of water springing up to everlasting life. Thus he sanctioned the symbols which are connected with the tree of life in the book of Ezekiel, in the book of Enoch, in the Zohar, and in the Apocalypse of St. John. The connection between the tree of life and the water of life is almost literally reproduced in the Apocalypse of St. John from the book of Ezekiel; with this difference, that the river of the water of life is by the former connected with 'the throne of God and of the Lamb,' instead of with the temple. Again, instead of 'the tree of life' on 'both sides of the river,' Ezekiel describes 'fruit trees of every kind' on both sides of its banks. Both writers mention the monthly fruit-yielding, and the healing quality of the leaves.[3] Also, in the book of Enoch the tree of life is described as a palm-tree, the wood, leaves and blossoms of which 'do not fade in eternity,' and by the 'fruit' of which 'life is given to the elect.' The writer has recorded his expectation that the tree would be 'transplanted in the North, in the holy place, the temple of the Lord, the eternal king.'[4] The renewed earth will be 'a blessing,' every curse will be removed, an 'unfathomable fountain of righteousness' will continually flow, surrounded by 'many fountains of righteousness,' for all that are 'thirsty.' By drinking of the water of life men will become 'filled with wisdom,' and they will have 'their dwelling with the righteous and the holy and

---

[1] Is. lxi. 3.     [2] Matt. xv. 13.
[3] Ezek. xlvii. 12; Rev. xxii. 1, 2.     [4] Enoch xxiv. 4; xxv. 5.

the elect.' Then 'wisdom will be poured out like water,' and all 'unrighteousness will pass away like a shadow, and be no more, because the Chosen One is risen.'[1] Also in the Apocalypse of St. John the flowing of the water of life, and the healing of the tree of life, puts an end to the existing curse.[2] We shall now prove that this curse is the command, recorded in Genesis as given on Divine authority, that whoever eats of the tree of knowledge shall die.

On the allegory in Genesis referring to the trees in Eden, Origen writes: 'Where could a man be found with so limited an understanding as to believe that God, like a field labourer, had set trees in paradise, in the Eden which lay towards the East, that he had planted a tree of life, that gave life to him that ate from the same, and another tree which communicated to him that partook of the same, the knowledge of good and evil? I believe that everybody must regard these things as figures, under which a secret meaning lies hidden.'[3] The symbolical nature of the narrative in Genesis must be extended to the manner in which God is recorded to have spoken to man. Neither God's walking in the garden, nor his speaking to Adam and Eve can be taken in its literal sense. The Kenite prophet Elijah had made known that the Hebrew notions about the presence of God in the wind, or in the earthquake, or in the fire, must make way for more enlightened views. Those conceptions had in a figure impressed the people with the conviction of God's real presence. The time had come when the symbol must be interpreted, when the idol must be abolished. The Kenite, the pre-Abramitic tradition must be engrafted on the multitude, that God is present in the heart of man, through the Divine Spirit, that the Creator speaks to the creature through the still small voice of conscience. Elijah had been confirmed in this knowledge, and pre-

---

[1] Hidden Wisdom i. 110 f.  [2] Rev. xxii. 3.  [3] Huet, Origen. 167.

pared for his reformatory mission by the recorded fact that God came to him, as he came to Abraham, through the mediation of the Divine Word or Spirit, and spoke to him through that agency. Had 'the Father of the spirits of all flesh' ever spoken to man in any other way? Had the carnal ear ever heard a superhuman voice speak in accents familiar to the human intellect? Was it the carnal ear of Adam and Eve which made them afraid of the voice of the Lord in the garden? Was it their bodily nakedness they were ashamed of? Or are these and other expressions the symbols in which, as in a casket, the pearl of great price is conveyed? 'Who hath ears to hear let him hear.' These words do not refer to an exceptional organism of the human frame, but to a spiritual gift.

From the beginning God spake to man, and yet, in all ages there were mysteries, kept secret by those who understood them. Already in Eden certain things must have been mysterious to some and not to others. The men of learning, the initiated, the acknowledged organs of tradition, would be regarded as men of God, as organs through whom God spoke. Seeing that the knowledge of mysteries required training, peculiar gifts, and constant application of the same, those who were regarded as authorities in matters of God, would see the necessity of establishing a Divine authority for the secret transmission of spiritual mysteries, through a recognised secret society or corporation. The many must be admitted gradually to the privileges of the few. Secrecy implies selection.

In the holy records of the Israelites, the historical narrative is preceded by a command, for which Divine authority is claimed, establishing a barrier around the source of knowledge, similar to the barriers which guarded the avenues of Eden, and similar to the barriers erected around Sinai, and around the law there promulgated. Where the tree of life stood there stood also a tree, or symbol 'of the knowledge of good and evil.' Although in the beginning all trees whatsoever were planted for man's food, yet to eat of the fruit of the tree of knowledge of good and evil was to be punished with death. The rule of secrecy, the 'disciplina arcani' was rigidly enforced. Though there was a difference between the knowledge of the few, and that of the many, yet it was not so great, as to silence all opposition to the decreed concealment of knowledge by privileged castes. Human wisdom, not debarred from Divine enlightenment, opposed what human wisdom, if not human expediency, had devised. The opposition of Eldad and Medad, and of Korah, was foreshadowed in Eden. We have seen, that the serpent was originally the symbol of Divine Wisdom. Already in Eden the tradition, later recorded in the book of Wisdom, may have been known, that the Wisdom or Word of God is a Divine essence, a ray of light, which connects heaven and earth, God with man. Divine Wisdom is the source of knowledge, and the source of endless life. 'For so the ways of them which lived on the earth were reformed; and were saved through wisdom,' through the Word of God which is 'the Saviour of all.' That Divine power is granted 'according to the desire' of them that have 'need.' Already in Eden the knowledge of Solomon may have been no mystery to some, that Divine Wisdom is 'a tree of life' to all who desire her. The doctrine of caste-privilege, and of exclusive salvation, originated in party interest.

The serpent, the symbol of Divine Presence, and therefore of Divine Wisdom, opposed the decree which obstructed the avenues to the tree of knowledge. As Divine Wisdom, the eternal Christ, was called a 'tree of life,' so the serpent, which was regarded as the symbol of the former, was directly connected with the latter. The serpent was the symbol of Christ, and the words attributed to that 'wise' animal by the allegorist, are in literal harmony with the words of Jesus on eternal life. Not death, but God-like knowledge will be yours, if you taste the forbidden fruit. Your blindness will be removed, 'your eyes shall be opened, and ye shall be as gods, knowing good and evil.' The serpent appealed to man's conscience. The people, in the parable represented by the woman, 'saw that the tree was good for food, and that it was pleasant to the eyes, and a tree to be desired to make one wise.' Led on by the people, their rulers, represented by the woman's husband, also freely partook of the hidden treasure. The Apocalypse of the Apocrypha began in Eden. This allegory was used in later times, to explain the mystery about the first manifestation of evil. In the East similar narratives were used for similar purposes. The symbol was misunderstood and became an idol. But 'the mystery which was kept in silence since the world began,' was revealed in the fulness of times. The mark of humanity's high calling was proclaimed to be the accomplishment of the eternal purpose of God, to raise the creature to the similitude of the Creator. By precept and by example, by signs and wonders, Jesus, 'the Wisdom of God,' has confirmed the good news which the allegorist in Genesis has connected with the serpent, that the forbidden fruit must be eaten, that the barriers to knowledge must be removed, that there is no other way to the tree of life in the paradise of God, than knowledge of good and evil, and obedience to that knowledge in thought, word and deed; that there is no curse but what is of man's own making; that even to the unlearned, to babes, is to be revealed what is known, and even what is hidden from the wise and intelligent. The wisdom which Jesus recommended, he also connected with serpents. By so doing he indirectly affirmed, that the serpent in Genesis must be interpreted as the symbol of Divine Wisdom revealed to man. What was 'kept in silence since the world began,' the 'mystery' of Eden, must be revealed. Some had first to receive 'milk' before they could bear 'meat.' Yet 'the fountain of the water of life' was and is 'freely' given 'to him that is athirst.' 'He that overcometh shall

inherit all things, and I will be his God, and he shall be
my son.' With 'the former things' the decreed 'death
shall pass away.'[1]

The fountain of life, 'proceeding out of the throne of
God and of the Lamb,' the 'well of water springing up
into everlasting life,' is the Wisdom, the Word, the Spirit
of God, which 'surrounds the tree of life.' In different
countries, as already observed, different trees became the
symbols of Divine Presence.[2] In the East the tree of life
was the date palm, the leaves of which served for the
recording of tradition. Thus the tree of life and the tree
of knowledge were identified. In Palestine, as among
the Egyptians in the Mosaic time, the sacred tree was the
sycamore fig-tree, which bears its fruit at every time of
the year, and is never without leaves. This was the tree
of Israel which was visited during three years by Jesus,
which being barren was withered, and ordered to be
transplanted in the sea, that is, on Gentile soil, among a
nation bringing forth the fruits thereof, that is, the fruits of
the Spirit. Knowing this, the seer at Patmos made use of
the symbol of the tree of life when describing the kingdom
of God, after the abolition of the first heaven and the first
earth, as described in Genesis, with its 'curse' against the
free promulgation of knowledge. That curse, that 'death'
is to be removed in course of time. The seer kept secret,
and did not write down what was to be sealed up till 'the
mystery of God should be finished, as he hath declared
to his servants the prophets.' That time is marked in the
vision by the fall of the 'mystery,' which is connected
with Babylon, that is, with Rome, in so far as Rome is
'that great city which reigneth over the kings of the
earth.'

'The Son of Man,' the eternal Wisdom or Word, the
Christ of God, had already been described at the time
of the Syrian destruction of Jerusalem, as receiving with
his 'saints' the kingdom of the Catholic Church. What

---

[1] Rev. xxi. 4, 6, 7.   [2] Barlow's Essays on Symbolism, p. 9 f.

Babylon was then, Rome was at the time of Jerusalem's destruction by the Romans. The impetuous 'son of thunder' calls down fire from heaven. He appears to expect the Millennium to commence with the destruction of Jerusalem. The Jewish Church is the woman that has the rule in the Church at Rome. 'The chief of the Jews' regard St. Paul as the leader of ' a sect everywhere spoken against,' and they regard themselves as the sole and the acknowledged organs of Divine mysteries. The Jewish Church is 'drunk with the blood of saints and with the blood of the martyrs of Jesus.' The Sadducean rule, keeping back tradition, and opposing universality, was established in Rome, in spite of St. Peter and St. Paul. But the Separatists will not continue to rule, the mystery will fall, and the Church Catholic will be established; this was the hope of the aged Apostle. He knew, that the keys confided to St. Peter would not only bind but loose, not only seal but reveal, and thus chain 'the old serpent, which is the Devil, and Satan,' with his mysteries, and prevent him from deceiving any longer the nations of the earth. Once more the idol of the serpent will be destroyed, and the symbol of the serpent will be understood. Thus the complete harmony will be established, between the Biblical records about the serpent in Eden, and the serpent in the wilderness, as the type of the cross of Christ. The hopes of St. John about the removal of the curse, the flowing of the water of life, and the healing of the nations by the tree of life, centred in the Keys of St. Peter, in the traditional interpretation of Holy Writ.

The Apostolic tradition was faithfully recorded by Justin Martyr. The Gentiles could not of themselves have understood the mystery of the cross, 'all the things said of it having been put symbolically.'[1] 'This man, of whom the Scriptures declare that he will come again in glory after his crucifixion, was symbolised both by the tree of life, which was said to have been planted in paradise, and

[1] Apol. 4.

by those events which should happen to all the just.'[1] He regards as types of Christ 'the oil of gladness,' Aaron's rod, the rod coming forth from the root of Jesse, the righteous described 'like the tree that is planted by the channels of waters, which should yield its fruit in its season, and whose leaf should not fade;' the righteous who shall 'flourish like a palm-tree;' the 'rod and staff' of David, and other types. The symbolical meaning of the record in Genesis about the tree of life, is confirmed by the writer of the sublime Epistle to Diognetus, probably written by Marcion, Justin's junior contemporary, before the former separated himself from the Catholic Church. 'If ye take heed to this,' that is, to the knowledge of those things which ' the Word bringeth forth through whom he wills, when he wills,' then ' ye shall know what God proffers to those who love him in the right way, who have become a paradise of delight, an abundantly fruit-bearing tree, who are ornamented with manifold fruits, when they have brought up that tree within themselves to the full blossom. For in this place the tree of knowledge and the tree of life *was* planted, but not that which destroys knowledge (the curse recorded in Genesis), but which destroys disobedience. For not without meaning is that which is written, how God originally has planted the tree of knowledge and the tree of life in the midst of paradise, pointing to this, that through knowledge cometh life. Since the first men have not made a pure use of the same (of knowledge) they were, by the temptation of the serpent divested (of the life). For there is no life without knowledge, and no certain knowledge without true life, for which reason both were planted side by the side of each other. In consequence of the discernment of this meaning, the Apostle saith, whilst blaming that knowledge which is without a firm relation to life: Knowledge puffeth up charity edifieth. For he who thinketh that he knoweth

[1] Dial. 86.

something without true knowledge certified by the life, he hath not attained to any knowledge, and is seduced by the serpent, because he did not love the life. Who, however, with fear followeth after knowledge, and has his eyes fixed upon the life, he plants upon hope and expects fruit. Let therefore thine heart be set upon knowledge, and thy life upon gaining the true Word. If thou bearest a tree of this sort, and gatherest its fruit,[1] thou shalt continually reap that which is well-pleasing to God, which is not approached by any serpent, and which is neither touched by delusion, nor spoilt as Eve was, but is found firm as a virgin. And salvation manifesteth itself, the Apostles are being understood, the passover of the Lord steppeth onward, the courses of the world (heaven and earth) dovetail into each other, and that which refers to the world beyond is equalised (raised to its proper level), and the Word, which continually teacheth the holy ones, is of good courage, whereby the Father is glorified, he to whom eternal glory is due. Amen.'[2]

Although the mystery of the serpent was not understood by the writer of this 'Johannaic' epistle, yet the connection between the tree of life and the tree of knowledge is so interpreted as necessarily to imply their identity. Christ, the eternal Word, is the tree of knowledge and of life, and as he continually teaches mankind, every Christian is to bear a tree of this kind within himself. Origen points out, that Christ is the Wisdom of God, and that as the Wisdom of God is a tree of life, so Christ is the tree of life. St. Ambrose and St. Augustine held the same or similar views. The distinction which the latter makes between the common food (alimentum) and the mysterious food (sacramentum) confirms our interpretation of the *opsarium* as the manna or spiritual food, symbolised by the wafer in the Eucharist. The

---

[1] Amos was 'a gatherer of sycamore fruit,' that is, of sycamore figs, fruits of the symbolical tree of life.    [2] Hidden Wisdom, ii. 83 f.

manna was baked in pans before the wafers could be made. The symbolical meaning of these manna-wafers was conveyed, to the initiated at least, and possibly only among the Alexandrian Jews, by 'the golden pot that had (or 'with the') manna,' which, together with the budding rod of Aaron and the tables of the covenant, were placed inside the ark.[1] That golden pot may be connected with the manna-wafer, and thus with the Holy Presence. The tree of life was symbolised by the tree-like candlestick, for which the cross was substituted.

The records about the tree of life are the sublimest proofs of the unity and continuity of tradition, and of its Eastern origin. The earliest records of the most ancient Oriental tradition refer to a tree of life, which was guarded by spirits. The juice of the fruit of this sacred tree, like the tree itself, was called *Sôma* in Sanscrit, and *Haôma* in Zend; it was revered as the life-preserving essence. The fruit of the tree of life was called *cikhâyôni*, a word which means,[2] the matrix or womb of the flame, the Divine Power, from which the celestial fire originates. This name *cikhâyôni*, from which *kikayon* (not a gourd) is derived, was given to the fruit, because, from the fermented juice of the healing Hom-plant, the alcoholic liquor was produced, which served for lighting the sacred fire on the altars, and which, after consecration, was regarded as the mystic symbol of the Holy Presence. In the physical sense, the presence of God is the presence of the sun, which is the throne, or chariot, of God, and the principle of life, which also caused Jonah's *kikayon* (the fruit of the tree of life) to grow. This Eastern symbolism can be traced in the book of Jonah. The prophet of Lower Galilee has, like Cain, fled 'from the presence of the Lord,' which was directly connected with the tree of life. The allegory shows, how Jonah was brought back to the Holy Presence, and thus to the

[1] Heb. ix. 4.      [2] Mons. Burnouf, in a letter.

tree of life. During a storm, being in a Gentile ship, and, as we may assume, in a trance, he sees himself swallowed up by a large fish, one of the Indian and also Egyptian symbols, and the Christian symbol of the Divine Presence. As to Abraham, so to Jonah, the Word or Spirit of God, symbolised by the name Jonah, or dove, came 'in a vision,' and 'the horrors of great darkness'[1] came upon him.

Eastern symbolism throws much light on this part of the narrative. When the sôma is poured on to the fire, a great combustion is produced, preceded by thick clouds of smoke. From the midst of this dark cloud the flame issues forth. Thus suddenly the celestial fire was kindled in the breast of Jonah. The dove, the symbol of the Holy Spirit, came down and entered within him. This interpretation receives a remarkable confirmation by a painting in the catacombs, representing the deliverance of Jonah. The fish is a monster swimming on the surface of the waters, and the body, the fins, the head, and the jaws of this monster are exclusively formed by thick clouds of smoke, from which a flame darts forth, like a fiery tongue, at the point of which the little Jonah is represented, launched into the air, in the plenitude of the second birth, a new man, saved by fire.

Jonah experienced the same contrast of light within the cloud, and light not within the cloud, of God's Presence directly manifested or indirectly manifested, which is described in the 'vision' of the transfiguration. The Galilean longed to return to the Holy Presence. That desire was sufficient for its realisation. Even 'in the uttermost parts of the sea,' the 'right hand,' that is, the Spirit of God, led the prophet. The dove wished to return to the ark. Jonah cried 'out of the depths' unto God,[2] whether 'in the body or out of the body,' whether really in the belly of a fish or not, was unknown to him.

---

[1] Comp. Job xxvi. 8.  [2] Comp. the Vedic hymn of Kutsa.

As it were, from the darkness of the grave, separated from communion with his God, forsaken by him, he longed to behold again God's holy temple. His prayer was heard, light shone in darkness, his spirit was renewed, God led him forth from the watery grave. During his prophetic mission at Nineveh, God guarded him from the burning sun, by the fruit of the tree of life, by the '*kikayon*,' the symbol of God's Presence, to which Jonah had returned, like the prodigal son.

The narrative of Jonah represents the migrations of the principle of life, of which the tree of life was the symbol. Jonah is the first who planted the sycamore fig-tree in Gentile soil. And yet the symbol of the tree of life is of Eastern origin. In the physical sense the principle of life originates in the hot and shining sun, whence it descends and enters into the plant, which sprouts from the earth, grows up, and bears fruit. The principle of life is then in the fruit, it is extracted from the same, it is the sôma. The sôma is put in a vessel called *samudra*, that is, the sea, and the spirit of life swims in the waters. Poured on to the fire of the altar, it reappears, shining with light, and ascends towards heaven, where it disappears in invisible vapours. According to recorded Eastern tradition, 'the recompense of the faithful is, to come to the dwelling-place of the Creator of all,'[1] that is, to his presence, symbolised on earth by the tree of life, to 'paradise,' which the soul enters with 'a shining (or glorious) body,'[2] and after the expiration of 'the third night,'[3] like the flame which descends from heaven and returns to it, after having given life to plants and animals. The renewing of the spirit of Jonah led to his resurrection after the third night. This is 'the sign of the prophet Jonah,' and it is directly connected with the tree of life in 'the paradise of God.' Not the Eastern mystery,

---

[1] Yasna i. 15.   [2] Ibid. lix. 18; xlvi. 10.
[3] Farg. xix. 28, and Vist Yasht.

which the narrative of Jonah symbolised, but a much later conception about Divine Wisdom was, in pre-Homeric times, transmitted by Western mythology. At the outset, we refer to the Prometheus *Pyrphoros* of Æschylus, and to the tree of life, *narthex*, as described by him; again, to Bacchus, whose 'thyrsus' was a stick of *narthex* with a vine-leaf, and a pine-apple above. Moreover, Apollo and Artemis were conceived as personifications of the sun and of the moon, as living symbols of the uncreated light. These deities of light conquer darkness, symbolised by Python, the dragon-like serpent, barring the entrance to the Delphine oracles. In still later times Divine Wisdom was no longer symbolised by Apollo and Artemis, but by Asclepios, the son of the former, who became a famous healer, but had to be killed by lightning when Pluto accused him, before Zeus, of having restored the dead to life. Asclepios was represented with a staff, round which a serpent was coiled, the symbol of healing. His daughter Hygeia, the goddess of health, is generally represented by the side of Asclepios, and as feeding a serpent from a cup. These are all later symbols and conceptions of the Eastern mysteries, the records of which, attributed to Zoroaster, were called Apocrypha, in the sense of hidden wisdom, by Clement of Alexandria.[1] The serpent, as symbol of evil, of darkness, of winter, was well known in the East, but it was not connected as such with the tree of life in Eden. Nor was this done in the time of Moses, when the fiery serpent on the tree symbolised Divine Wisdom. The serpent is one of the chief mystic personifications of the Rig-Veda, under the names of Ahi, the Ophis of the Greek, Suchna, the dry, and others, which all represent the cloud, the enemy of the sun, keeping back the fructifying rain. Indra struggles victoriously against him, and spreads life on the earth with the rain and the shining warmth of the Father of life, that is, of Savitri, the sun.

[1] Strom. iv. 15.

We must, therefore, distinguish, in the narrative of Jonah, the symbol of the dove, the symbol of fire, the symbol of the tree of life, and the symbol of the sun, all of which are emblems of the Divine Presence. The serpent in the wilderness, and Jonah's kikayon at Nineveh, exclude the Divine origin of the decree of death, and point to the tree of the knowledge of good and evil in Eden, to the Wisdom of God, which 'is a tree of life,' to Christ the healer, 'the Saviour of all,' to 'Christ the Wisdom of God,' and the tree of life.

Egyptian monuments prove that the tree of life, first the palm, then the sycamore fig-tree, was represented, already about the time of the Eastern shepherds, as a tree, from the trunk of which a female hand issued forth holding a vessel from which flowed the water of life, which also is represented as flowing from the tree itself. Before the tree of life a woman (a Kenite or Samaritan?) is represented as kneeling, and her prayer, expressed by hieroglyphics, means: 'Give me of the water of life, that I thirst no more.' In the time of Alexander the trunk of the tree of life was represented by an entire figure, likewise dispensing the water of immortality. Because the tree of life was known to be the tree of knowledge, therefore Divine Wisdom, the Sophia, continued to be represented by a female figure. Again, because the tree of life was the symbol of human enlightenment, the birth of light out of darkness was directly connected with Juno, the female embodiment of the celestial deity, by whose side a peacock, the symbol of immortality, is often represented. The mother of heavenly light was called the queen of heaven. St. Paul having identified Jesus with the Wisdom of God, the 'blessed among women,' who was overshadowed by the Power of God and the Wisdom of God, was identified, as a matter of course, with the Divine Sophia, with the tree of life, with the queen of heaven. And when, in the fifth century, the contest began between the Alexandrian and the Antiochian churches, that is, between the Monophysites and the

Nestorians, St. Mary became the symbol of the co-existence of the Divine and the human natures in the person of Christ. The undefinable mystery of Divine incarnation was represented by a human symbol. Already before this time, though it cannot be asserted to have been the case before the end of the fourth century, St. Mary was called the 'Mother of God.' This is proved by a Scripture entitled the assumption, or the transit of 'the blessed Virgin.'[1] Even the new dogma or symbol about the immaculate conception may be interpreted from this historical point of view. In Jesus the Divine nature co-existed with his sinless, therefore immaculate, human nature. The new symbol requires interpretation, or it must become an idol; even as the mystery of the cross has been degraded by ignorance. The new dogma, interpreted as a symbol, receives its lustre from the annunciation, the grandest poem ever conceived.

Dogmas are symbols. The true, the comprehensive meaning of all dogmatic formulas lies hidden under their literal sense. Like all other symbols, the creeds, if taken to be more than mere forms of concord between contending parties; if they are to be regarded as authoritative expressions of a for-ever-binding tradition, as the exclusively true interpretation of Holy Writ; if they are to stand above Scripture; if they are to mark the limit between true and false doctrine; if they are to be promulgated as canons of interpretation, they must be interpreted by the progressive consciousness of the Church, that is, of the household of God, of the social community in the faith and for the faith. Scripture and living tradition applied must be regarded as the two co-ordinate sources of doctrine, so long as the proof is withheld, that Scripture is no more than an epitome, a skeleton of tradition, a lock requiring a key. The development in Scripture and in the creeds must be traced to the same source, that is, to the gradual proclamation of secret tradition, to the gradual application of the keys of St. Peter. The

[1] Translated in Wright's Syriac Apocrypha, 1865.

recognition of the primacy of the Pope of Rome is no more than the acknowledgment of an historical fact. Nowhere else than in the Roman Papacy can we recognise the historical continuity of an organisation, the high destiny of which can be historically proved to have been to harmonise what is written with authoritative canons of interpretation, and also, through general councils, with the progressive exigencies of human consciousness.

The supernatural character of man's spiritual nature, involves the supernatural character of Christianity, and of the Christian Church. Man is a miracle, Christianity is a miracle, the Church is a miracle. The Church is not only a 'society of the faith and of the Holy Spirit in the hearts,' but also a 'society of the outward signs of the Church.' Symbols must continue, but their true interpretation must be universally promulgated. The right and duty of national education, and of free enquiry may be acknowledged by the highest Church-authority, without fear that the obedience of faith will suffer by it. The Church contains now, as it always did, two parties diametrically opposed to each other, the party of stagnation and the party of progress, the party of darkness and that of light. The Church must avoid even the semblance of assuming, that there is a greater responsibility in using the keys of St. Peter in order to open, than in order to shut, in going forward than in standing still. The rightly interpreted, the enduring interests of a privileged sacerdotal corporation, cannot be incompatible with the acknowledged interests of mankind. Catholicity is not an ideal, to be realised by the blind submission of the many, who ask for progress, to the few who insist on standing still. Catholicity would then be a fiction enforced, instead of a reality which commends itself to the conscience of every man.

There is a gulf, and it must be bridged over. Canons of interpretation are the requirements of the age. They can only be supplied by the revelation of what is hidden, by the Apocalypse of the Apocrypha. How were the Gospels gradually composed in the form we received them from the Church in the fourth century? What became of St. Matthew's Hebrew Gospel-text, which St. Jerome translated? What became of the 'expositions of the sayings of the Lord, based upon the teachings of the elders,' by bishop Papias, to which work St. Irenæus and Eusebius refer as existing in their time? What share did St. Mark, St. Luke and St. John take in the transmission of Apostolic tradition? How are symbols to be interpreted? These are some of the many urgent questions of the day. What we know not, the successors of St. Peter, the possessors of the keys of St. Peter, of the key of David, do know; unless we assume that the tradition of the Church has become a mere fiction, and is in no sense 'the memory of the Church.' Let the mystery of Babylon fall. Let Rome speak.

History does not reveal a beneficial law of progressive unity, but a beneficial law of progressive truth, and of the gradual proclamation of the same all over the world. Darkness expelled by light; the rise and progress of light, this is what all history records. History is progressive application of tradition to the exigencies of mankind. Tradition is the father of history, and is not a mere invention of historians. Tradition has been sown, has grown, has borne and will bear fruit. Tradition is not destined merely to constitute a link between the nations of the earth, but it is inseparably connected with mankind, with human consciousness. Tradition will in future be connected with the promised 'one flock and one shepherd.' Infallibility must no longer be sought in the letter, or in its interpretation, that is, either exclusively in Scripture, or exclusively in tradition, nor in human consciousness, not even in its most exalted representatives. These three fallible sources combined, will form the tribunal of peace. The voice of the Church, human consciousness, more or less enlightened by Scripture, as interpreted by tradition, must continue to be expressed, through regularly appointed clerical and lay representatives of all national or local Churches of every creed under the sun. General councils thus organised, under the guiding presidency of the living pilot of the Church, will prove to the world, that now, as of old, creeds can be agreed to and promulgated, as human and temporarily binding expressions of the truth; that the represented minorities can live in peace and harmony with the equally represented majorities, both being united by their common representative, by the visible symbol of their unity, by the successor of St. Peter, by the living depositary of the keys of the kingdom of heaven. Thus the nearest possible approach to infallibility will have been made, and the voice of God, the 'still small voice' of the Divine Spirit in man, will be more and more heard in the voice of the Church. The future so ardently longed for, will be found in a just appreciation of the past.

The spirit of God is in man. The catholicity of conscience is an undoubted fact. Where the Spirit of God is, there is the Church, and there is liberty. The enemies of liberty cannot, therefore, be the friends of the Church. Yet human conscience alone can never be acknowledged as the arbiter in matters of God. It requires to be enlightened by the written and by the unwritten tradition of ages gone by. When these views shall have pervaded mankind,—and if they are true they will do so,—then catholicity will no longer be an ideal, nor merely a human organism, an institution for determining the relations between God and Man; but the Catholic Church will be the manifestation of the individually established union and communion with the Father, through the Son, in the Spirit. The Catholic Church will then be in full blossom, it will ever be a fruit-bearing tree of knowledge and of life, for the healing of the nations. It will be no longer *a* Church, but *the* Church of united, though not uniformed humanity; it will be the 'Holy Catholic Church' of the Apostolic Creed; not one fold, but one flock.

# APPENDIX.

## NEW DATES IN NEW TESTAMENT CHRONOLOGY.

|  | A.C. |
|---|---|
| Accession of Herod Agrippa I. | |
| Martyrdom of St. Stephen and St. James | |
| Imprisonment of St. Peter, and his first journey to Rome | 41 |
| Conversion of St. Paul | |
| Appointment of St. James, 'the brother of the Lord' | |
| St. Paul's first journey to Jerusalem | 41 |
| Apostolic Council | 55 |
| Arrival of St. Paul at Ephesus | 59 |
| His departure from Ephesus | 62 |
| St. Paul at Corinth, between | 62 and 63 |
| His last journey to Jerusalem | 63 |
| St. Paul's departure from Cesarea, (autumn) | 65 |
| Arrival in Rome, (spring) | 66 |
| St. Paul's Martyrdom, (between) | 68 and 69 |

LONDON
PRINTED BY SPOTTISWOODE AND CO.
NEW-STREET SQUARE

## BY THE SAME AUTHOR.

# THE HIDDEN WISDOM OF CHRIST AND THE KEY OF KNOWLEDGE;

## OR, HISTORY OF THE APOCRYPHA.

2 vols. 8vo. price £1 8s.

### OPINIONS of the PRESS.

'To establish theoretically the unity of religious dogmas in humanity, if this unity is not a fiction, would be the highest object and aim of the science of religions. To show that under their apparent variety these great institutions hide one and the same fundamental doctrine, would be to restore to each of them the part which they have played in history, and to annihilate, as much as it is possible, the antagonism which keeps them separate, and which through them has severed the families of mankind. Should, then, this universal doctrine, studied in its principles, be acknowledged as true, we should have won a beautiful game in that redoubtable play, which has been played for centuries; for as the sciences march with an unerring step in the ways which lead to truth, we should have acquired the certainty that religion and science, these two great offsprings of the spirit, tend towards a common end, where their theories must, at last, become identified. Such an assurance being granted, we should have an ever ready answer for those who would strive once more to renew the struggle on some new ground, and each of us would relish, within the domain of his conscience, that peace which the combats between reason and faith have so often disturbed. At the point which the science of religions has reached, and considering her advance year after year, are we still to regard such a hope as vain? I do not hesitate to say no. The remarkable book recently published by M. ERNEST DE BUNSEN, worthy successor of the celebrated Prussian minister, and other documents, of a nature to complete the work of the learned theologian, will assist me, no doubt, to engraft this hope on the soul of my readers.'

MONS. BURNOUF IN THE REVUE DES DEUX MONDES.

'The subject of Mr. DE BUNSEN's volumes is one of the highest moment. Their literary excellence is great. By the stages of an elaborate argument, Mr. DE BUNSEN goes on to show that the true Christianity, the private and secret teaching of Christ, was first proclaimed by St. Paul, openly, and alike to Jew and Greek. We do not suppose that Mr. DE BUNSEN will satisfy all his critics, but whether these critics accept or dispute his conclusions, they will see that he has found a new way to treat a problem in sacred literature; and that, whether his reasoning be considered as sound or unsound, he has brought to bear on the discussion a good temper, a fluent pen, and a cultivated mind.'

ATHENÆUM.

'To trace an idea or a doctrine through its various forms is a task requiring great sagacity and caution, as well as knowledge, even where the doctrine is one publicly professed and discussed, like the acknowledged truths of Christianity. The difficulty is, of course much greater when the doctrine is supposed to have been transmitted with secrecy, and with precautions against its becoming public. Mr. DE BUNSEN undertakes to trace such a secret doctrine or "gnosis," a "hidden wisdom," relating to the deepest and most mysterious subjects of human thought, and belief, and hope.'

SATURDAY REVIEW.

'If Mr. DE BUNSEN can induce Protestants to re-open the study of heresiarchs without the prejudices they have inherited from Rome, to re-examine books like "the Wisdom of Sirach," without the prepossessions derived from Luther, to re-discuss the question of the existence of a permanent but unwritten revelation in the heart of man, his volumes will have done a great service.'

SPECTATOR.

## Opinions of the Press.

'These opinions are curious and startling, but they are, nevertheless, put forward by Mr. De Bunsen with feelings of the friendliest interest in the mission of the Christian religion, and a sincere conviction of its truth, and of its miraculous character. The Author has brought an extensive amount of erudition to his task; his facts are well chosen, and cleverly marshalled to bear on his arguments, which are at least plausible, if not convincing to accurately logical minds.' — LONDON REVIEW.

'Modern expounders of the Scriptures persist strangely in not seeing, or seeing in not acknowledging the inconsistency of their idea, that a Divine revelation of truth for the guidance of erring mortals was vouchsafed to them in terms as equivocal and mysterious as any utterance of an ancient heathen oracle.' — MORNING POST.

'This is a remarkable book: remarkable for its earnestness and vigour of style, for the wide range of topics which it discusses, and the amount of learning and research displayed in handling them.' — MORNING HERALD.

'The Author lays before us candidly and fairly the results of his investigations, step by step, with an elaborateness which some might think not needed; but while every page is interesting, we have the advantage of being placed in a position to form our own conclusions on the bases from which the writer argues.' — MORNING STAR.

'We almost hesitate to pronounce the actual characteristics of a work displaying so much real power as well as earnestness, or devoted to so sacred a subject.' — DAILY TELEGRAPH.

'The Author is too much in earnest, much too learned a man, and much too original in his ideas, to be put down by a general anathema, or to be ridiculed as a mere enthusiast.' — BELL'S WEEKLY MESSENGER.

'The work is one which deserves the serious and careful consideration of Christians of all denominations.' — OBSERVER.

'Whatever be thought of the soundness of Mr. De Bunsen's conclusions, there can be no doubt that he has given us here a very important contribution to the study both of religious history and of theology.' — JOHN BULL.

'There is much in these two volumes which most readers will find entirely new and interesting, and throughout, the tone and spirit exhibited by the writer are sure to arrest attention.' — PUBLIC OPINION.

'The presumed platform on which the writer proceeds to present his theory is, that Cain and Abel are merely figurative representations of two "Aryan brothers," members of a small clan of Aryans, who had left their aboriginal home, and probably settled on the highest elevation of Central Asia.' — CLERICAL JOURNAL.

'Regarded as a contribution to Biblical and Patristic literature, we may view Mr. De Bunsen's volumes in another light. To the student their value is real, calling a careful attention to the LXX, to the Apocryphal books, the writings of Philo; and investing the works of the Apostolic Fathers with a new interest.' — CHURCH REVIEW.

'No words could well be more stimulating to the curiosity of the reader than those in which Mr. Ernest De Bunsen states the questions which he attempts to solve in the present work.' — WESTMINSTER REVIEW.

'It is a curious book, containing an unusual amount of heresy; but at the same time opening out, at least in English literature, an untrodden path of inquiry.' — ECCLESIASTIC.

'True Christian gnosis is not to be imported from foreign quarters.' — CHRISTIAN ADVOCATE AND REVIEW.

'One of the most important religious works that the season has yet produced.' — LITERARY GAZETTE.

'This very remarkable book, taken as a whole, has a considerable air of novelty.' — EVANGELICAL MAGAZINE.

London: LONGMANS, GREEN, and CO.

39 Paternoster Row, E.C.
London: *January* 1867.

# GENERAL LIST OF WORKS

PUBLISHED BY

## Messrs. LONGMANS, GREEN, READER, and DYER.

---

Arts, Manufactures, &c. ............ 12
Astronomy, Meteorology, Popular Geography, &c. ............ 7
Biography and Memoirs ............ 3
Chemistry, Medicine, Surgery, and the Allied Sciences ............ 9
Commerce, Navigation, and Mercantile Affairs ............ 19
Criticism, Philology, &c. ............ 4
Fine Arts and Illustrated Editions ............ 11
Historical Works ............ 1
Index ............ 21—24
Knowledge for the Young ............ 20

Miscellaneous and Popular Metaphysical Works ............ 6
Musical Publications ............ 11
Natural History and Popular Science ............ 7
Poetry and The Drama ............ 17
Religious and Moral Works ............ 13
Rural Sports, &c. ............ 18
Travels, Voyages, &c. ............ 15
Works of Fiction ............ 16
Works of Utility and General Information ............ 19

---

## *Historical Works.*

**Lord Macaulay's Works.** Complete and uniform Library Edition. Edited by his Sister, Lady Trevelyan. 8 vols. 8vo. with Portrait, price £5 5s. cloth, or £8 8s. bound in tree-calf by Rivière.

**The History of England from** the Fall of Wolsey to the Death of Elizabeth. By James Anthony Froude, M.A. late Fellow of Exeter College, Oxford.
Vols. I. to X. in 8vo. price £7 2s. cloth.
  Vols. I. to IV. the Reign of Henry VIII. Third Edition, 54s.
  Vols. V. and VI. the Reigns of Edward VI. and Mary. Second Edition, 28s.
  Vols. VII. & VIII. the Reign of Elizabeth, Vols. I. & II. Fourth Edition, 28s.
  Vols. IX. and X. the Reign of Elizabeth, Vols. III. and IV. 32s.

**The History of England from** the Accession of James II. By Lord Macaulay.
  Library Edition, 5 vols. 8vo. £4.
  Cabinet Edition, 8 vols. post 8vo. 48s.
  People's Edition, 4 vols. crown 8vo. 16s.

**Revolutions in English History.** By Robert Vaughan, D.D. 3 vols. 8vo. 45s.
  Vol. I. Revolutions of Race, 15s.
  Vol. II. Revolutions in Religion, 15s.
  Vol. III. Revolutions in Government, 15s.

**An Essay on the History of the** English Government and Constitution, from the Reign of Henry VII. to the Present Time. By John Earl Russell. Fourth Edition, revised. Crown 8vo. 6s.

**The History of England during** the Reign of George the Third. By the Right Hon. W. N. Massey. Cabinet Edition, 4 vols. post 8vo. 24s.

**The Constitutional History of** England, since the Accession of George III. 1760—1860. By Sir Thomas Erskine May, K.C.B. Second Edit. 2 vols. 8vo. 33s.

**Brodie's Constitutional History** of the British Empire from the Accession of Charles I. to the Restoration. Second Edition. 3 vols. 8vo. 36s.

**Historical Studies.** I. On Precursors of the French Revolution; II. Studies from the History of the Seventeenth Century; III. Leisure Hours of a Tourist. By Herman Merivale, M.A. 8vo. 12s. 6d.

**Lectures on the History of England.** By William Longman. Vol. I. from the Earliest Times to the Death of King Edward II. with 6 Maps, a coloured Plate, and 53 Woodcuts. 8vo. 15s.

A

**History of Civilization in England** and France, Spain and Scotland. By HENRY THOMAS BUCKLE. Fifth Edition of the entire work, complete in 3 vols. crown 8vo. price 24s. cloth; or 42s. bound in tree-calf by Rivière.

**The History of India**, from the Earliest Period to the close of Lord Dalhousie's Administration. By JOHN CLARK MARSHMAN. 3 vols. crown 8vo.
[*Nearly ready.*

**Democracy in America.** By ALEXIS DE TOCQUEVILLE. Translated by HENRY REEVE, with an Introductory Notice by the Translator. 2 vols. 8vo. 21s.

**The Spanish Conquest in America**, and its Relation to the History of Slavery and to the Government of Colonies. By ARTHUR HELPS. 4 vols. 8vo. £3. VOLS. I. & II. 28s. VOLS. III. & IV. 16s. each.

**History of the Reformation in** Europe in the Time of Calvin. By J. H. MERLE D'AUBIGNÉ, D.D. VOLS. I. and II. 8vo. 28s. VOL. III. 12s. and VOL. IV. price 16s. VOL. V. in the press.

**Library History of France**, in 5 vols. 8vo. By EYRE EVANS CROWE. VOL. I. 14s. VOL. II. 15s. VOL. III. 18s. VOL. IV. 18s.

**Lectures on the History of** France. By the late Sir JAMES STEPHEN, LL.D. 2 vols. 8vo. 24s.

**The History of Greece.** By C. THIRLWALL, D.D. Lord Bishop of St. David's. 8 vols. fcp. with Vignette-titles, 28s.

**The Tale of the Great Persian** War, from the Histories of Herodotus. By GEORGE W. COX, M.A. late Scholar of Trin. Coll. Oxon. Fcp. 7s. 6d.

**Greek History from Themistocles** to Alexander, in a Series of Lives from Plutarch. Revised and arranged by A. H. CLOUGH. Fcp. with 44 Woodcuts. 6s.

**Critical History of the Language** and Literature of Ancient Greece. By WILLIAM MURE, of Caldwell. 5 vols. 8vo. £3 9s.

**History of the Literature of** Ancient Greece. By Professor K. O. MÜLLER. Translated by the Right Hon. Sir GEORGE CORNEWALL LEWIS, Bart. and by J. W. DONALDSON, D.D. 3 vols. 8vo. 36s.

**History of the City of Rome** from its Foundation to the Sixteenth Century of the Christian Era. By THOMAS H. DYER, LL.D. 8vo. with 2 Maps, 15s.

**History of the Romans under** the Empire. By CHARLES MERIVALE, B.D. Chaplain to the Speaker. Cabinet Edition, with Maps, complete in 8 vols. post 8vo. 48s.

**The Fall of the Roman Republic**: a Short History of the Last Century of the Commonwealth. By the same Author. 12mo. 7s. 6d.

**The Conversion of the Roman** Empire; the Boyle Lectures for the year 1864, delivered at the Chapel Royal, Whitehall. By the same. 2nd Edition. 8vo. 8s. 6d.

**The Conversion of the Northern** Nations; the Boyle Lectures for 1865. By the same Author. 8vo. 8s. 6d.

**Critical and Historical Essays** contributed to the *Edinburgh Review*. By the Right Hon. Lord MACAULAY.
LIBRARY EDITION, 3 vols. 8vo. 36s.
CABINET EDITION, 4 vols. post 8vo. 24s.
TRAVELLER'S EDITION, in 1 vol. 21s.
POCKET EDITION, 3 vols. fcp. 21s.
PEOPLE'S EDITION, 2 vols. crown 8vo. 8s.

**History of the Rise and Influence** of the Spirit of Rationalism in Europe. By W. E. H. LECKY, M.A. Third Edition. 2 vols. 8vo. 25s.

**The History of Philosophy**, from Thales to the Present Day. By GEORGE HENRY LEWES. Third Edition, partly rewritten and greatly enlarged: In 2 vols. VOL. I. *Ancient Philosophy;* VOL. II. *Modern Philosophy.* [*Nearly ready.*

**History of the Inductive Sciences.** By WILLIAM WHEWELL, D.D. F.R.S. late Master of Trin. Coll. Cantab. Third Edition. 3 vols. crown 8vo. 24s.

**Egypt's Place in Universal History**; an Historical Investigation. By C. C. J. BUNSEN, D.D. Translated by C. H. COTTRELL, M.A. With many Illustrations. 4 vols. 8vo. £5 8s. VOL. V. is nearly ready, completing the work.

**Maunder's Historical Treasury;** comprising a General Introductory Outline of Universal History, and a Series of Separate Histories. Fcp. 10s.

**Historical and Chronological Encyclopædia**, presenting in a brief and convenient form Chronological Notices of all the Great Events of Universal History. By B. B. WOODWARD, F.S.A. Librarian to the Queen. [*In the press.*

**History of the Christian Church,** from the Ascension of Christ to the Conversion of Constantine. By E. BURTON, D.D. late Regius Prof. of Divinity in the University of Oxford. Eighth Edition. Fcp. 3s. 6d.

**Sketch of the History of the** Church of England to the Revolution of 1688. By the Right Rev. T. V. SHORT, D.D. Lord Bishop of St. Asaph. Seventh Edition. Crown 8vo. 10s. 6d.

**History of the Early Church,** from the First Preaching of the Gospel to the Council of Nicæa, A.D. 325. By the Author of 'Amy Herbert.' Fcp. 4s. 6d.

**History of Wesleyan Methodism.** By GEORGE SMITH, F.A.S Fourth Edition, with numerous Portraits. 3 vols. crown 8vo. 7s. each.

**The English Reformation.** By F. C. MASSINGBERD, M.A. Chancellor of Lincoln. Fourth Edit. revised. Fcp. 7s. 6d.

## *Biography* and *Memoirs.*

**Life and Correspondence of** Richard Whately, D.D. late Archbishop of Dublin. By E. JANE WHATELY, Author of 'English Synonymes.' With 2 Portraits. 2 vols. 8vo. 28s.

**Extracts of the Journals and** Correspondence of Miss Berry, from the Year 1783 to 1852. Edited by Lady THERESA LEWIS. Second Edition, with 3 Portraits. 3 vols. 8vo. 42s.

**The Diary of the Right Hon.** William Windham, M.P. From 1783 to 1809. Edited by Mrs. H. BARING. 8vo. 18s.

**Life of the Duke of Wellington.** By the Rev. G. R. GLEIG, M.A. Popular Edition, carefully revised; with copious Additions. Crown 8vo. with Portrait, 5s.

**Life of the Duke of Wellington,** partly from M. BRIALMONT, partly from Original Documents (Intermediate Edition). By Rev. G. R. GLEIG, M.A. 8vo. with Portrait, 15s.

**Brialmont and Gleig's Life of the Duke** of Wellington (the Parent Work). 4 vols. 8vo. with Illustrations, £2 14s.

**Life of Robert Stephenson, F.R.S.** By J. C. JEAFFRESON, Barrister-at-Law; and WILLIAM POLE, F.R.S. Member of the Institution of Civil Engineers. With 2 Portraits and 17 Illustrations on Steel and Wood. 2 vols. 8vo. 32s.

**History of my Religious Opinions.** By J. H. NEWMAN, D.D. Being the Substance of Apologia pro Vitâ Suâ. Post 8vo. 6s.

**Father Mathew: a Biography.** By JOHN FRANCIS MAGUIRE, M.P. Popular Edition, with Portrait. Crown 8vo. 3s. 6d.

**Rome; its Rulers and its Institutions.** By the same Author. New Edition in preparation.

**Letters and Life of Francis** Bacon, including all his Occasional Works. Collected and edited, with a Commentary, by J. SPEDDING, Trin. Coll. Cantab. VOLS. I. and II. 8vo. 24s.

**Some Account of the Life and** Opinions of a Fifth-Monarchy Man, chiefly extracted from the Writings of JOHN ROGERS, preacher. Edited by the Rev. EDWARD ROGERS, M.A. Student of Christ Church, Oxford. Crown 4to.
[*Nearly ready.*

**Life of Amelia Wilhelmina Sieve-** king, from the German. Edited, with the Author's sanction, by CATHERINE WINKWORTH. Post 8vo. with Portrait, 12s.

**Mozart's Letters (1769-1791),** translated from the Collection of Dr. LUDWIG NOHL by Lady WALLACE. 2 vols. post 8vo. with Portrait and Facsimile, 18s.

**Beethoven's Letters (1790-1826),** from the Two Collections of Drs. NOHL and VON KÖCHEL. Translated by Lady WALLACE. 2 vols. post 8vo. Portrait, 18s.

**Felix Mendelssohn's Letters from** *Italy and Switzerland*, and *Letters from 1833 to 1847*, translated by Lady WALLACE. With Portrait. 2 vols. crown 8vo. 5s. each.

**Recollections of the late William** Wilberforce, M.P. for the County of York during nearly 30 Years. By J. S. HARFORD, F.R.S. Second Edition. Post 8vo. 7s.

**Memoirs of Sir Henry Havelock,** K.C.B. By JOHN CLARK MARSHMAN. Second Edition. 8vo. with Portrait, 12s. 6d.

**Essays in Ecclesiastical Biography.** By the Right Hon. Sir J. Stephen, LL.D. Fourth Edition. 8vo. 14s.

**Biographies of Distinguished Scientific Men.** By François Arago. Translated by Admiral W. H. Smyth, F.R.S. the Rev. B. Powell, M.A. and R. Grant, M.A. 8vo. 18s.

**Vicissitudes of Families.** By Sir Bernard Burke, Ulster King of Arms. First, Second, and Third Series. 3 vols. crown 8vo. 12s. 6d. each.

**Maunder's Biographical Treasury.** Thirteenth Edition, reconstructed and partly rewritten, with above 1,000 additional Memoirs, by W. L. R. Cates. Fcp. 10s. 6d.

---

## Criticism, Philosophy, Polity, &c.

**The Institutes of Justinian;** with English Introduction, Translation, and Notes. By T. C. Sandars, M.A. Barrister-at-Law. Third Edition. 8vo. 15s.

**The Ethics of Aristotle** with Essays and Notes. By Sir A. Grant, Bart. M.A. LL.D. Director of Public Instruction in the Bombay Presidency. Second Edition, revised and completed. 2 vols. 8vo. price 28s.

**On Representative Government.** By John Stuart Mill, M.P. Third Edition. 8vo. 9s. crown 8vo. 2s.

**On Liberty.** By the same Author. Third Edition. Post 8vo. 7s. 6d. crown 8vo. 1s. 4d.

**Principles of Political Economy.** By the same. Sixth Edition. 2 vols. 8vo. 30s. or in 1 vol. crown 8vo. 5s.

**System of Logic, Ratiocinative and Inductive.** By the same. Sixth Edition. 2 vols. 8vo. 25s.

**Utilitarianism.** By the same. 2d Edit. 8vo. 5s.

**Dissertations and Discussions.** By the same Author. 2 vols. 8vo. 24s.

**Examination of Sir W. Hamilton's Philosophy,** and of the Principal Philosophical Questions discussed in his Writings. By the same. Second Edition. 8vo. 14s.

**The Elements of Political Economy.** By Henry Dunning Macleod, M.A. Barrister-at-Law. 8vo. 16s.

**A Dictionary of Political Economy;** Biographical, Bibliographical, Historical, and Practical. By the same Author. Vol. I. royal 8vo. 30s.

**Lord Bacon's Works,** collected and edited by R. L. Ellis, M.A. J. Spedding, M.A. and D. D. Heath. Vols. I. to V. *Philosophical Works,* 5 vols. 8vo. £4 6s. Vols. VI. and VII. *Literary and Professional Works,* 2 vols. £1 16s.

**Bacon's Essays, with Annotations.** By R. Whately, D.D. late Archbishop of Dublin. Sixth Edition. 8vo. 10s. 6d.

**Elements of Logic.** By R. Whately, D.D. late Archbishop of Dublin. Ninth Edition. 8vo. 10s. 6d. crown 8vo. 4s. 6d.

**Elements of Rhetoric.** By the same Author. Seventh Edition. 8vo. 10s. 6d. crown 8vo. 4s. 6d.

**English Synonymes.** Edited by Archbishop Whately. 5th Edition. Fcp. 3s.

**Miscellaneous Remains from the** Common-place Book of Richard Whately, D.D. late Archbishop of Dublin. Edited by E. Jane Whately. Post 8vo. 7s. 6d.

**Essays on the Administrations of** Great Britain from 1783 to 1830. By the Right Hon. Sir G. C. Lewis, Bart. Edited by the Right Hon. Sir E. Head, Bart. 8vo. with Portrait, 15s.

*By the same Author.*

**Inquiry into the Credibility of the** Early Roman History, 2 vols. 30s.

**On the Methods of Observation and** Reasoning in Politics, 2 vols. 28s.

**Irish Disturbances and Irish Church** Question, 12s.

**Remarks on the Use and Abuse of** some Political Terms, 9s.

**The Fables of Babrius,** Greek Text with Latin Notes, Part I. 5s. 6d. Part II. 3s. 6d.

**An Outline of the Necessary** Laws of Thought: a Treatise on Pure and Applied Logic. By the Most Rev. W. Thomson, D.D. Archbishop of York. Crown 8vo. 5s. 6d.

**The Elements of Logic.** By Thomas Shedden, M.A. of St. Peter's Coll. Cantab. 12mo. 4s. 6d.

**Analysis of Mr. Mill's System of Logic.** By W. STEBBING, M.A. Second Edition. 12mo. 3s. 6d.

**The Election of Representatives,** Parliamentary and Municipal; a Treatise. By THOMAS HARE, Barrister-at-Law. Third Edition, with Additions. Crown 8vo. 6s.

**Speeches on Parliamentary Reform.** By the Right Hon. B. DISRAELI, M.P. Chancellor of the Exchequer. 1 vol. 8vo. [*Nearly ready.*

**Speeches of the Right Hon. Lord** MACAULAY, corrected by Himself. Library Edition, 8vo. 12s. People's Edition, crown 8vo. 3s. 6d.

**Lord Macaulay's Speeches on** Parliamentary Reform in 1831 and 1832. 16mo. 1s.

**A Dictionary of the English** Language. By R. G. LATHAM, M.A. M.D. F.R.S. Founded on the Dictionary of Dr. S. JOHNSON, as edited by the Rev. H. J. TODD, with numerous Emendations and Additions. Publishing in 36 Parts, price 3s. 6d. each, to form 2 vols. 4to. VOL. I. in Two Parts, now ready.

**Thesaurus of English Words and** Phrases, classified and arranged so as to facilitate the Expression of Ideas, and assist in Literary Composition. By P. M. ROGET, M.D. 18th Edition, crown 8vo. 10s. 6d.

**Lectures on the Science of Language,** delivered at the Royal Institution. By MAX MÜLLER, M.A. Taylorian Professor in the University of Oxford. FIRST SERIES, Fifth Edition, 12s. SECOND SERIES, 18s.

**Chapters on Language.** By F. W. FARRAR, M.A. F.R.S. late Fellow of Trin. Coll. Cambridge. Crown 8vo. 8s. 6d.

**The Debater;** a Series of Complete Debates, Outlines of Debates, and Questions for Discussion. By F. ROWTON. Fcp. 6s.

**A Course of English Reading,** adapted to every taste and capacity; or, How and What to Read. By the Rev. J. PYCROFT, B.A. Fourth Edition, fcp. 5s.

**Manual of English Literature,** Historical and Critical: with a Chapter on English Metres. By THOMAS ARNOLD, M.A. Second Edition. Crown 8vo. 7s. 6d.

**Southey's Doctor, complete in One** Volume. Edited by the Rev. J.W. WARTER, B.D. Square crown 8vo. 12s. 6d.

**Historical and Critical Commentary** on the Old Testament; with a New Translation. By M. M. KALISCH, Ph. D. VOL. I. *Genesis,* 8vo. 18s. or adapted for the General Reader, 12s. VOL. II. *Exodus,* 15s. or adapted for the General Reader, 12s.

**A Hebrew Grammar, with Exercises.** By the same. PART I. *Outlines with Exercises,* 8vo. 12s. 6d. KEY, 5s. PART II. *Exceptional Forms and Constructions,* 12s. 6d.

**A Latin-English Dictionary.** By J. T. WHITE, D.D. of Corpus Christi College, and J. E. RIDDLE, M.A. of St. Edmund Hall, Oxford. Imp. 8vo. pp. 2,128, price 42s.

**A New Latin-English Dictionary,** abridged from the larger work of *White* and *Riddle* (as above), by J. T. WHITE, D.D. Joint-Author. 8vo. pp. 1,048, price 18s.

**The Junior Scholar's Latin-English** Dictionary, abridged from the larger works of *White* and *Riddle* (as above), by J. T. WHITE, D.D. surviving Joint-Author. Square 12mo. pp. 662, price 7s. 6d.

**An English-Greek Lexicon,** containing all the Greek Words used by Writers of good authority. By C. D. YONGE, B.A. Fifth Edition. 4to. 21s.

**Mr. Yonge's New Lexicon, English** and Greek, abridged from his larger work (as above). Square 12mo. 8s. 6d.

**A Greek-English Lexicon.** Compiled by H. G. LIDDELL, D.D. Dean of Christ Church, and R. SCOTT, D.D. Master of Balliol. Fifth Edition, crown 4to. 31s. 6d.

**A Lexicon, Greek and English,** abridged from LIDDELL and SCOTT's *Greek-English Lexicon.* Eleventh Edition, square 12mo. 7s. 6d.

**A Sanskrit-English Dictionary,** The Sanskrit words printed both in the original Devanagari and in Roman letters; with References to the Best Editions of Sanskrit Authors, and with Etymologies and Comparisons of Cognate Words chiefly in Greek, Latin, Gothic, and Anglo-Saxon. Compiled by T. BENFEY. 8vo. 52s. 6d.

**A Practical Dictionary of the** French and English Languages. By L. CONTANSEAU. 11th Edition, post 8vo. 10s. 6d.

**Contanseau's Pocket Dictionary,** French and English, abridged from the above by the Author. New Edition. 18mo. price 3s. 6d.

**New Practical Dictionary of the** German Language; German-English, and English-German. By the Rev. W. L. BLACKLEY, M.A. and Dr. CARL MARTIN FRIEDLÄNDER. Post 8vo. 14s.

## Miscellaneous Works and Popular Metaphysics.

**Recreations of a Country Parson.** By A. K. H. B. FIRST SERIES, with 41 Woodcut Illustrations from Designs by R. T. Pritchett. Crown 8vo. 12s. 6d.

**Recreations of a Country Parson.** SECOND SERIES. Crown 8vo. 3s. 6d.

**The Commonplace Philosopher in Town and Country.** By the same Author. Crown 8vo. 3s. 6d.

**Leisure Hours in Town;** Essays Consolatory, Æsthetical, Moral, Social, and Domestic. By the same. Crown 8vo. 3s. 6d.

**The Autumn Holidays of a Country Parson;** Essays contributed to *Fraser's Magazine* and to *Good Words*. By the same. Crown 8vo. 3s. 6d.

**The Graver Thoughts of a Country Parson,** SECOND SERIES. By the same. Crown 8vo. 3s. 6d.

**Critical Essays of a Country Parson,** selected from Essays contributed to *Fraser's Magazine*. By the same. Post 8vo. 9s.

**Sunday Afternoons at the Parish Church of a University City.** By the same. Crown 8vo. 3s. 6d.

**A Campaigner at Home.** By SHIRLEY, Author of 'Thalatta' and 'Nugæ Criticæ.' Post 8vo. with Vignette, 7s. 6d.

**Studies in Parliament:** a Series of Sketches of Leading Politicians. By R. H. HUTTON. (Reprinted from the *Pall Mall Gazette*.) Crown 8vo. 4s. 6d.

**Lord Macaulay's Miscellaneous Writings.**
LIBRARY EDITION, 2 vols. 8vo. Portrait, 21s.
PEOPLE'S EDITION, 1 vol. crown 8vo. 4s. 6d.

**The Rev. Sydney Smith's Miscellaneous Works;** including his Contributions to the *Edinburgh Review*. People's Edition, 2 vols. crown 8vo. 8s.

**Elementary Sketches of Moral Philosophy,** delivered at the Royal Institution. By the same Author. Fcp. 6s.

**The Wit and Wisdom of the Rev. SYDNEY SMITH:** a Selection of the most memorable Passages in his Writings and Conversation. 16mo. 5s.

**Epigrams, Ancient and Modern:** Humorous, Witty, Satirical, Moral, and Panegyrical. Edited by Rev. JOHN BOOTH, B.A. Cambridge. Second Edition, revised and enlarged. Fcp. 7s. 6d.

**The Folk-Lore of the Northern Counties of England and the Borders.** By WILLIAM HENDERSON. With an Appendix on Household Stories by the Rev. S. BARING-GOULD. Crown 8vo. with Coloured Frontispiece, 9s. 6d.

**From Matter to Spirit:** the Result of Ten Years' Experience in Spirit Manifestations. By SOPHIA E. DE MORGAN. With a Preface by Professor DE MORGAN. Post 8vo. 8s. 6d.

**Essays selected from Contributions to the *Edinburgh Review*.** By HENRY ROGERS. Second Edition. 3 vols. fcp. 21s.

**Reason and Faith, their Claims and Conflicts.** By the same Author. New Edition, revised and extended, and accompanied by several other Essays, on related subjects. Crown 8vo. 6s. 6d.

**The Eclipse of Faith;** or, a Visit to a Religious Sceptic. By the same Author. Eleventh Edition. Fcp. 5s.

**Defence of the Eclipse of Faith,** by its Author. Third Edition. Fcp. 3s. 6d.

**Selections from the Correspondence of R. E. H. Greyson.** By the same Author. Third Edition. Crown 8vo. 7s. 6d.

**Fulleriana, or the Wisdom and Wit of THOMAS FULLER,** with Essay on his Life and Genius. By the same Author. 16mo. 2s. 6d.

**Occasional Essays.** By CHANDOS WREN HOSKYNS, Author of 'Talpa, or the Chronicles of a Clay Farm,' &c. 16mo. 5s. 6d.

**An Essay on Human Nature;** showing the Necessity of a Divine Revelation for the Perfect Development of Man's Capacities. By HENRY S. BOASE, M.D. F.R.S. and G.S. 8vo. 12s.

**The Philosophy of Nature;** a Systematic Treatise on the Causes and Laws of Natural Phenomena. By the same Author. 8vo. 12s.

**The Secret of Hegel:** being the Hegelian System in Origin, Principle, Form, and Matter. By JAMES HUTCHISON STIRLING. 2 vols. 8vo. 28s.

**An Introduction to Mental Philosophy,** on the Inductive Method. By J. D. MORELL, M.A. LL.D. 8vo. 12s.

**Elements of Psychology,** containing the Analysis of the Intellectual Powers. By the same Author. Post 8vo. 7s. 6d.

**Sight and Touch:** an Attempt to Disprove the Received (or Berkeleian) Theory of Vision. By THOMAS K. ABBOTT, M.A. Fellow and Tutor of Trin. Coll. Dublin. 8vo. with 21 Woodcuts, 5s. 6d.

**The Senses and the Intellect.** By ALEXANDER BAIN, M.A. Prof. of Logic in the Univ. of Aberdeen. Second Edition. 8vo. 15s.

**The Emotions and the Will,** by the same Author. 8vo. 15s.

**On the Study of Character,** including an Estimate of Phrenology. By the same Author. 8vo. 9s.

**Time and Space:** a Metaphysical Essay. By SHADWORTH H. HODGSON. 8vo. pp. 588, price 16s.

**The Way to Rest:** Results from a Life-search after Religious Truth. By R. VAUGHAN, D.D. Crown 8vo. 7s. 6d.

**Hours with the Mystics:** a Contribution to the History of Religious Opinion. By ROBERT ALFRED VAUGHAN, B.A. Second Edition. 2 vols. crown 8vo. 12s.

**The Philosophy of Necessity;** or, Natural Law as applicable to Mental, Moral, and Social Science. By CHARLES BRAY. Second Edition. 8vo. 9s.

**The Education of the Feelings and Affections.** By the same Author. Third Edition. 8vo. 3s. 6d.

**On Force,** its Mental and Moral Correlates. By the same Author. 8vo. 5s.

**Christianity and Common Sense.** By Sir WILLOUGHBY JONES, Bart. M.A. Trin. Coll. Cantab. 8vo. 6s.

## *Astronomy, Meteorology, Popular Geography, &c.*

**Outlines of Astronomy.** By Sir J. F. W. HERSCHEL, Bart, M.A. Eighth Edition, revised; with Plates and Woodcuts. 8vo. 18s.

**Arago's Popular Astronomy.** Translated by Admiral W. H. SMYTH, F.R.S. and R. GRANT, M.A. With 25 Plates and 358 Woodcuts. 2 vols. 8vo. £2 5s.

**Saturn and its System.** By RICHARD A. PROCTOR, B.A. late Scholar of St. John's Coll. Camb. and King's Coll. London. 8vo. with 14 Plates, 14s.

**The Handbook of the Stars.** By the same Author. Square fcp. 8vo. with 3 Maps. price 5s.

**Celestial Objects for Common Telescopes.** By T. W. WEBB, M.A. F.R.A.S. With Map of the Moon, and Woodcuts. 16mo. 7s.

**A General Dictionary of Geography,** Descriptive, Physical, Statistical, and Historical; forming a complete Gazetteer of the World. By A. KEITH JOHNSTON, F.R.S.E. 8vo. 31s. 6d.

**M'Culloch's Dictionary, Geographical, Statistical, and Historical,** of the various Countries, Places, and principal Natural Objects in the World. Revised Edition, with the Statistical Information throughout brought up to the latest returns. By FREDERICK MARTIN. 4 vols. 8vo. with coloured Maps, £4 4s.

**A Manual of Geography,** Physical, Industrial, and Political. By W. HUGHES, F.R.G.S. Prof. of Geog. in King's Coll. and in Queen's Coll. Lond. With 6 Maps. Fcp. 7s. 6d.

**Hawaii:** the Past, Present, and Future of its Island-Kingdom: an Historical Account of the Sandwich Islands. By MANLEY HOPKINS, Hawaiian Consul-General, &c. Second Edition, revised and continued; with Portrait, Map, and 8 other Illustrations. Post 8vo. 12s. 6d.

**Maunder's Treasury of Geography,** Physical, Historical, Descriptive, and Political. Edited by W. HUGHES, F.R.G.S. With 7 Maps and 16 Plates. Fcp. 10s. 6d.

**Physical Geography for Schools** and General Readers. By M. F. MAURY, LL.D. Fcp. with 2 Charts, 2s. 6d.

## *Natural History and Popular Science.*

**The Elements of Physics or** Natural Philosophy. By NEIL ARNOTT, M.D. F.R.S. Physician Extraordinary to the Queen. Sixth Edition, rewritten and completed. 2 Parts, 8vo. 21s.

**Volcanos,** the Character of their Phenomena, their Share in the Structure and Composition of the Surface of the Globe, &c. By G. POULETT SCROPE, M.P. F.R.S. Second Edition. 8vo. with Illustrations, 15s.

**Rocks Classified and Described.** By BERNHARD VON COTTA. An English Edition, by P. H. LAWRENCE (with English, German, and French Synonymes), revised by the Author. Post 8vo. 14s.

\*\*\* Lithology, or a Classified Synopsis of the Names of Rocks and Minerals, also by Mr. LAWRENCE, adapted to the above work, may be had, price 5s. or printed on one side only (interpaged blank), for use in Cabinets, price 7s.

**Sound:** a Course of Six Lectures delivered at the Royal Institution of Great Britain. By Professor JOHN TYNDALL, LL.D. F.R.S. 1 vol. crown 8vo.
[*Nearly ready.*

**Heat Considered as a Mode of Motion.** By Professor JOHN TYNDALL, LL.D. F.R.S. Second Edition. Crown 8vo. with Woodcuts, 12s. 6d.

**A Treatise on Electricity,** in Theory and Practice. By A. DE LA RIVE, Prof. in the Academy of Geneva. Translated by C. V. WALKER, F.R.S. 3 vols. 8vo. with Woodcuts, £3 13s.

**The Correlation of Physical Forces.** By W. R. GROVE, Q.C. V.P.R.S. Fifth Edition, revised by the Author, and augmented by a Discourse on Continuity. 8vo.

**Manual of Geology.** By S. HAUGHTON, M.D. F.R.S. Fellow of Trin. Coll. and Prof. of Geol. in the Univ. of Dublin. Second Edition, with 66 Woodcuts. Fcp. 7s. 6d.

**A Guide to Geology.** By J. PHILLIPS, M.A. Prof. of Geol. in the Univ. of Oxford. Fifth Edition. Fcp. 4s.

**A Glossary of Mineralogy.** By H. W. BRISTOW, F.G.S. of the Geological Survey of Great Britain. With 486 Figures. Crown 8vo. 12s.

**The Elements:** an Investigation of the Forces which determine the Position and Movements of the Ocean and Atmosphere. By WILLIAM LEIGHTON JORDAN. VOL. I. royal 8vo. with 13 maps, price 8s.

**Phillips's Elementary Introduction** to Mineralogy, re-edited by H. J. BROOKE, F.R.S. and W. H. MILLER, F.G.S. Post 8vo. with Woodcuts, 18s.

**Van Der Hoeven's Handbook of Zoology.** Translated from the Second Dutch Edition by the Rev. W. CLARK, M.D. F.R.S. 2 vols. 8vo. with 24 Plates of Figures, 60s.

**The Comparative Anatomy and Physiology of the Vertebrate Animals.** By RICHARD OWEN, F.R.S. D.C.L. 3 vols. 8vo. with upwards of 1,200 Woodcuts. VOLS. I. and II. price 21s. each, now ready. VOL. III. in the Spring.

**The First Man and His Place in Creation,** considered on the Principles of Common Sense from a Christian Point of View; with an Appendix on the Negro. By GEORGE MOORE, M.D. M.R.C.P.L. &c. Post 8vo. 8s. 6d.

**The Lake Dwellings of Switzerland and other Parts of Europe.** By Dr. F. KELLER, President of the Antiquarian Association of Zürich. Translated and arranged by J. E. LEE, F.S.A. F.G.S. Author of 'Isca Silurum.' With several Woodcuts and nearly 100 Plates of Figures. Royal 8vo. 31s. 6d.

**Homes without Hands:** a Description of the Habitations of Animals, classed according to their Principle of Construction. By Rev. J. G. WOOD, M.A. F.L.S. With about 140 Vignettes on Wood (20 full size of page). Second Edition. 8vo. 21s.

**The Harmonies of Nature and Unity of Creation.** By Dr. G. HARTWIG, 8vo. with numerous Illustrations, 18s.

**The Sea and its Living Wonders.** By the same Author. Third Edition, enlarged. 8vo. with many Illustrations, 21s.

**The Tropical World.** By the same Author. With 8 Chromoxylographs and 172 Woodcuts. 8vo. 21s.

**Manual of Corals and Sea Jellies.** By J. R. GREENE, B.A. Edited by J. A. GALBRAITH, M.A. and S. HAUGHTON, M.D. Fcp. with 39 Woodcuts, 5s.

**Manual of Sponges and Animalculæ;** with a General Introduction on the Principles of Zoology. By the same Author and Editors. Fcp. with 16 Woodcuts, 2s.

**Manual of the Metalloids.** By J. APJOHN, M.D. F.R.S. and the same Editors. 2nd Edition. Fcp. with 38 Woodcuts, 7s. 6d.

**Sketches of the Natural History of Ceylon.** By Sir J. EMERSON TENNENT, K.C.S. LL.D. With 82 Wood Engravings. Post 8vo. 12s. 6d.

**Ceylon.** By the same Author. 5th Edition; with Maps, &c. and 90 Wood Engravings. 2 vols. 8vo. £2 10s.

**The Wild Elephant, its Structure and Habits,** with the Method of Taking and Training it in Ceylon. By the same Author. Fcp. 8vo. with Illustrations.

**A Familiar History of Birds.**
By E. STANLEY, D.D. late Lord Bishop of Norwich. Fcp. with Woodcuts, 3s. 6d.

**Kirby and Spence's Introduction** to Entomology, or Elements of the Natural History of Insects. Crown 8vo. 5s.

**Maunder's Treasury of Natural** History, or Popular Dictionary of Zoology. Revised and corrected by T. S. COBBOLD, M.D. Fcp. with 900 Woodcuts, 10s.

**The Elements of Botany for** Families and Schools. Tenth Edition, revised by THOMAS MOORE, F.L.S. Fcp with 154 Woodcuts, 2s. 6d.

**The Treasury of Botany, or** Popular Dictionary of the Vegetable Kingdom; with which is incorporated a Glossary of Botanical Terms. Edited by J. LINDLEY, F.R.S. and T. MOORE, F.L.S. assisted by eminent Contributors. Pp. 1,274, with 274 Woodcuts and 20 Steel Plates. 2 Parts, fcp. 20s.

**The British Flora;** comprising the Phænogamous or Flowering Plants and the Ferns. By Sir W. J. HOOKER, K.H. and G. A. WALKER-ARNOTT, LL.D. 12mo. with 12 Plates, 14s. or coloured, 21s.

**The Rose Amateur's Guide.** By THOMAS RIVERS. New Edition. Fcp. 4s.

**The Indoor Gardener.** By Miss MALING. Fcp. with Frontispiece, 5s.

**Loudon's Encyclopædia of Plants;** comprising the Specific Character, Description, Culture, History, &c. of all the Plants found in Great Britain. With upwards of 12,000 Woodcuts. 8vo. 42s.

**Loudon's Encyclopædia of Trees and** Shrubs; containing the Hardy Trees and Shrubs of Great Britain scientifically and popularly described. With 2,000 Woodcuts. 8vo. 50s.

**Bryologia Britannica;** containing the Mosses of Great Britain and Ireland, arranged and described. By W. WILSON. 8vo. with 61 Plates, 42s. or coloured, £4 4s.

**Maunder's Scientific and Literary Treasury;** a Popular Encyclopædia of Science, Literature, and Art. New Edition, thoroughly revised and in great part rewritten, with above 1,000 new articles, by J. Y. JOHNSON, Corr. M.Z.S. Fcp. 10s. 6d.

**A Dictionary of Science, Literature, and Art.** Fourth Edition, re-edited by the late W. T. BRANDE (the Author) and GEORGE W. COX, M.A. 3 vols. medium 8vo. price 63s. cloth.

**Essays on Scientific and other** subjects, contributed to Reviews. By Sir H. HOLLAND, Bart. M.D. Second Edition. 8vo. 14s.

**Essays from the Edinburgh and** *Quarterly Reviews;* with Addresses and other Pieces. By Sir J. F. W. HERSCHEL. Bart. M.A. 8vo. 18s.

---

*Chemistry, Medicine, Surgery,* and *the Allied Sciences.*

**A Dictionary of Chemistry and** the Allied Branches of other Sciences. By HENRY WATTS, F.C.S. assisted by eminent Contributors. 5 vols. medium 8vo. in course of publication in Parts. VOL. I. 31s. 6d. VOL. II. 26s. VOL. III. 31s. 6d. and VOL. IV. 24s. are now ready.

**A Handbook of Volumetrical** Analysis. By ROBERT H. SCOTT, M.A. T.C.D. Post 8vo. 4s. 6d.

**Elements of Chemistry, Theoretical and Practical.** By WILLIAM A. MILLER, M.D. LL.D. F.R.S. F.G.S. Professor of Chemistry, King's College, London. 3 vols. 8vo. £2 13s. PART I. CHEMICAL PHYSICS, Third Edition, 12s. PART II. INORGANIC CHEMISTRY, 21s. PART III. ORGANIC CHEMISTRY, Third Edition, 24s.

**A Manual of Chemistry, Descriptive and Theoretical.** By WILLIAM ODLING, M.B. F.R.S. PART I. 8vo. 9s.

**A Course of Practical Chemistry,** for the use of Medical Students. By the same Author. Second Edition, with 70 new Woodcuts. Crown 8vo. 7s. 6d.

**Lectures on Animal Chemistry** Delivered at the Royal College of Physicians in 1865. By the same Author. Crown 8vo. 4s. 6d.

**The Toxicologist's Guide:** a New Manual on Poisons, giving the Best Methods to be pursued for the Detection of Poisons. By J. HORSLEY, F.C.S. Analytical Chemist. Post 8vo. 3s. 6d.

**The Diagnosis and Treatment of** the Diseases of Women; including the Diagnosis of Pregnancy. By GRAILY HEWITT, M.D. &c. New Edition, with Woodcut Illustrations, in the press.

**Lectures on the Diseases of Infancy** and Childhood. By CHARLES WEST, M.D. &c. 5th Edition, revised and enlarged. 8vo. 16s.

**Exposition of the Signs and Symptoms** of Pregnancy: with other Papers on subjects connected with Midwifery. By W. F. MONTGOMERY, M.A. M.D. M.R.I.A. 8vo. with Illustrations, 25s.

**A System of Surgery, Theoretical** and Practical, in Treatises by Various Authors. Edited by T. HOLMES, M.A. Cantab. Assistant-Surgeon to St. George's Hospital. 4 vols. 8vo. £1 13s.

Vol. I. General Pathology, 21s.

Vol. II. Local Injuries: Gun-shot Wounds, Injuries of the Head, Back, Face, Neck, Chest, Abdomen, Pelvis, of the Upper and Lower Extremities, and Diseases of the Eye. 21s.

Vol. III. Operative Surgery. Diseases of the Organs of Circulation, Locomotion, &c. 21s.

Vol. IV. Diseases of the Organs of Digestion, of the Genito-Urinary System, and of the Breast, Thyroid Gland, and Skin; with APPENDIX and GENERAL INDEX. 30s.

**Lectures on the Principles and** Practice of Physic. By THOMAS WATSON, M.D. Physician-Extraordinary to the Queen. Fourth Edition. 2 vols. 8vo. 34s.

**Lectures on Surgical Pathology.** By J. PAGET, F.R.S. Surgeon-Extraordinary to the Queen. Edited by W. TURNER, M.B. 8vo. with 117 Woodcuts, 21s.

**A Treatise on the Continued** Fevers of Great Britain. By C. MURCHISON, M.D. Senior Physician to the London Fever Hospital. 8vo. with coloured Plates, 18s.

**Anatomy, Descriptive and Surgical.** By HENRY GRAY, F.R.S. With 410 Wood Engravings from Dissections. Fourth Edition, by T. HOLMES, M.A. Cantab. Royal 8vo. 28s.

**The Cyclopædia of Anatomy and** Physiology. Edited by the late R. B. TODD, M.D. F.R.S. Assisted by nearly all the most eminent cultivators of Physiological Science of the present age. 5 vols. 8vo. with 2,853 Woodcuts, £6 6s.

**Physiological Anatomy and Physiology** of Man. By the late R. B. TODD, M.D. F.R.S. and W. BOWMAN, F.R.S. of King's College. With numerous Illustrations. VOL. II. 8vo. 25s.

VOL. I. New Edition by Dr. LIONEL S. BEALE, F.R.S. in course of publication; PART I. with 8 Plates, 7s. 6d.

**Histological Demonstrations;** a Guide to the Microscopical Examination of the Animal Tissues in Health and Disease, for the use of the Medical and Veterinary Professions. By G. HARLEY, M.D. F.R.S. Prof. in Univ. Coll. London; and G. T. BROWN, M.R.C.V.S. Professor of Veterinary Medicine, and one of the Inspecting Officers in the Cattle Plague Department of the Privy Council. Post 8vo. with 223 Woodcuts, 12s.

**A Dictionary of Practical Medicine.** By J. COPLAND, M.D. F.R.S. Abridged from the larger work by the Author, assisted by J. C. COPLAND, M.R.C.S. and throughout brought down to the present state of Medical Science. Pp. 1,560, in 8vo. price 36s.

**The Works of Sir B. C. Brodie,** Bart. collected and arranged by CHARLES HAWKINS, F.R.C.S.E. 3 vols. 8vo. with Medallion and Facsimile, 48s.

**Autobiography of Sir B. C. Brodie,** Bart. printed from the Author's materials left in MS. Second Edition. Fcp. 4s. 6d.

**A Manual of Materia Medica** and Therapeutics, abridged from Dr. PEREIRA's *Elements* by F. J. FARRE, M.D. assisted by R. BENTLEY, M.R.C.S. and by R. WARINGTON, F.R.S. 1 vol. 8vo. with 90 Woodcuts, 21s.

**Dr. Pereira's Elements of Materia** Medica and Therapeutics, Third Edition, by A. S. TAYLOR, M.D. and G. O. REES, M.D. 3 vols. 8vo. with Woodcuts, £3 15s.

**Thomson's Conspectus of the** British Pharmacopœia. Twenty-fourth Edition, corrected and made conformable throughout to the New Pharmacopœia of the General Council of Medical Education. By E. LLOYD BIRKETT, M.D. 18mo. 5s. 6d.

**Manual of the Domestic Practice** of Medicine. By W. B. KESTEVEN, F.R.C.S.E. Second Edition, thoroughly revised, with Additions. Fcp. 5s.

**Sea-Air and Sea-Bathing for** Children and Invalids. By WILLIAM STRANGE, M.D. Fcp. 3s.

**The Restoration of Health;** or, the Application of the Laws of Hygiene to the Recovery of Health: a Manual for the Invalid, and a Guide in the Sick Room. By W. STRANGE, M.D. Fcp. 6s.

**Manual for the Classification,** Training, and Education of the Feeble-Minded, Imbecile, and Idiotic. By P. MARTIN DUNCAN, M.B. and WILLIAM MILLARD. Crown 8vo. 5s.

## *The Fine Arts,* and *Illustrated Editions.*

**The Life of Man Symbolised by** the Months of the Year in their Seasons and Phases; with Passages selected from Ancient and Modern Authors. By RICHARD PIGOT. Accompanied by a Series of 25 full-page Illustrations and numerous Marginal Devices, Decorative Initial Letters, and Tailpieces, engraved on Wood from Original Designs by JOHN LEIGHTON, F.S.A. 4to. 42s.

**The New Testament,** illustrated with Wood Engravings after the Early Masters, chiefly of the Italian School. Crown 4to. 63s. cloth, gilt top; or £5 5s. morocco.

**Lyra Germanica;** Hymns for the Sundays and Chief Festivals of the Christian Year. Translated by CATHERINE WINKWORTH; 125 Illustrations on Wood drawn by J. LEIGHTON, F.S.A. Fcp. 4to 21s.

**Cats' and Farlie's Moral Emblems;** with Aphorisms, Adages, and Proverbs of all Nations: comprising 121 Illustrations on Wood by J. LEIGHTON, F.S.A. with an appropriate Text by R. PIGOT. Imperial 8vo. 31s. 6d.

**Shakspeare's Sentiments and** Similes printed in Black and Gold, and illuminated in the Missal style by HENRY NOEL HUMPHREYS. In massive covers, containing the Medallion and Cypher of Shakspeare. Square post 8vo. 21s.

**Half-Hour Lectures on the History** and Practice of the Fine and Ornamental Arts. By W. B. SCOTT. Second Edition. Crown 8vo. with 50 Woodcut Illustrations, 8s. 6d.

**The History of Our Lord,** as exemplified in Works of Art. By Mrs. JAMESON and Lady EASTLAKE. Being the concluding Series of 'Sacred and Legendary Art.' Second Edition, with 13 Etchings and 281 Woodcuts. 2 vols. square crown 8vo. 42s.

**Mrs. Jameson's Legends of the Saints** and Martyrs. Fourth Edition, with 19 Etchings and 187 Woodcuts. 2 vols. 31s. 6d.

**Mrs. Jameson's Legends of the Monastic Orders.** Third Edition, with 11 Etchings and 88 Woodcuts. 1 vol. 21s.

**Mrs. Jameson's Legends of the Madonna.** Third Edition, with 27 Etchings and 165 Woodcuts. 1 vol. 21s.

## *Musical Publications.*

**An Introduction to the Study of** National Music; Comprising Researches into Popular Songs, Traditions, and Customs. By CARL ENGEL, Author of 'The Music of the most Ancient Nations.' With Frontispiece and numerous Musical Illustrations. 8vo. 16s.

**Six Lectures on Harmony.** Delivered at the Royal Institution of Great Britain before Easter 1867. By G. A. MACFARREN. 8vo. [*In the press.*

**Lectures on the History of Modern** Music, delivered at the Royal Institution. By JOHN HULLAH. FIRST COURSE, with Chronological Tables, post 8vo. 6s. 6d. SECOND COURSE, the Transition Period, with 26 Specimens, 8vo. 16s.

**Sacred Music for Family Use;** A Selection of Pieces for One, Two, or more Voices, from the best Composers. Foreign and English. Edited by JOHN HULLAH. 1 vol. music folio, 21s. half bound.

**Hullah's Part Music, Sacred and** Secular, for Soprano, Alto, Tenor, and Bass. New Edition, with Pianoforte Accompaniments, in course of publication in Monthly Numbers, each number in Score, with Pianoforte Accompaniment, price 1s. and in separate Parts (Soprano, Alto, Tenor, and Bass). uniform with the Score in size, but in larger type, price 3d. each Part. Each Series (Sacred and Secular) to be completed in 12 Numbers, forming a Volume, in imperial 8vo.

## Arts, Manufactures, &c.

**Drawing from Nature;** a Series of Progressive Instructions in Sketching, from Elementary Studies to Finished Views, with Examples from Switzerland and the Pyrenees. By GEORGE BARNARD, Professor of Drawing at Rugby School. With 18 Lithographic Plates and 108 Wood Engravings. Imp. 8vo. 25s.

**Gwilt's Encyclopædia of Architecture.** New Edition, revised, with alterations and considerable Additions, by WYATT PAPWORTH. With above 350 New Engravings and Diagrams on Wood by O. JEWITT, and upwards of 100 other Woodcuts. 8vo. [*Nearly ready.*

**Tuscan Sculptors, their Lives,** Works, and Times. With 45 Etchings and 28 Woodcuts from Original Drawings and Photographs. By CHARLES C. PERKINS. 2 vols. imp. 8vo. 63s.

**The Grammar of Heraldry:** containing a Description of all the Principal Charges used in Armory, the Signification of Heraldic Terms, and the Rules to be observed in Blazoning and Marshalling. By JOHN E. CUSSANS. Fcp. with 196 Woodcuts, 4s. 6d.

**The Engineer's Handbook;** explaining the Principles which should guide the young Engineer in the Construction of Machinery. By C. S. LOWNDES. Post 8vo. 5s.

**The Elements of Mechanism.** By T. M. GOODEVE, M.A. Prof. of Mechanics at the R. M. Acad. Woolwich. Second Edition, with 217 Woodcuts. Post 8vo. 6s. 6d.

**Ure's Dictionary of Arts, Manufactures, and Mines.** Re-written and enlarged by ROBERT HUNT, F.R.S., assisted by numerous Contributors eminent in Science and the Arts. With 2,000 Woodcuts. 3 vols. 8vo. [*Nearly ready.*

**Treatise on Mills and Millwork.** By W. FAIRBAIRN, C.E. F.R.S. With 18 Plates and 322 Woodcuts. 2 vols. 8vo. 32s.

**Useful Information for Engineers.** By the same Author. FIRST, SECOND, and THIRD SERIES, with many Plates and Woodcuts. 3 vols. crown 8vo. 10s. 6d. each.

**The Application of Cast and Wrought Iron to Building Purposes.** By the same Author. Third Edition, with 6 Plates and 118 Woodcuts. 8vo. 16s.

**Iron Ship Building, its History** and Progress, as comprised in a Series of Experimental Researches on the Laws of Strain; the Strengths, Forms, and other conditions of the Material; and an Inquiry into the Present and Prospective State of the Navy, including the Experimental Results on the Resisting Powers of Armour Plates and Shot at High Velocities. By W. FAIRBAIRN, C.E. F.R.S. With 4 Plates and 130 Woodcuts, 8vo. 18s.

**Encyclopædia of Civil Engineering,** Historical, Theoretical, and Practical. By E. CRESY, C.E. With above 3,000 Woodcuts. 8vo. 42s.

**The Practical Mechanic's Journal:** An Illustrated Record of Mechanical and Engineering Science, and Epitome of Patent Inventions. 4to. price 1s. monthly.

**The Practical Draughtsman's** Book of Industrial Design. By W. JOHNSON, Assoc. Inst. C.E. With many hundred Illustrations. 4to. 28s. 6d.

**The Patentee's Manual:** a Treatise on the Law and Practice of Letters Patent for the use of Patentees and Inventors. By J. and J. H. JOHNSON. Post 8vo. 7s. 6d.

**The Artisan Club's Treatise on** the Steam Engine, in its various Applications to Mines, Mills, Steam Navigation, Railways, and Agriculture. By J. BOURNE. C.E. Seventh Edition; with 37 Plates and 546 Woodcuts. 4to. 42s.

**A Treatise on the Screw Propeller,** Screw Vessels, and Screw Engines, as adapted for purposes of Peace and War; illustrated by many Plates and Woodcuts. By the same Author. New and enlarged Edition in course of publication in 24 Parts, royal 4to. 2s. 6d. each.

**Catechism of the Steam Engine,** in its various Applications to Mines, Mills, Steam Navigation, Railways, and Agriculture. By J. BOURNE. C.E. With 199 Woodcuts. Fcp. 9s. The INTRODUCTION of 'Recent Improvements' may be had separately, with 110 Woodcuts, price 3s. 6d.

**Handbook of the Steam Engine,** by the same Author, forming a KEY to the Catechism of the Steam Engine, with 67 Woodcuts. Fcp. 9s.

**The Art of Perfumery;** the History and Theory of Odours, and the Methods of Extracting the Aromas of Plants. By Dr. PIESSE, F.C.S. Third Edition, with 53 Woodcuts. Crown 8vo. 10s. 6d.

**Chemical, Natural, and Physical Magic,** for Juveniles during the Holidays. By the same Author. Third Edition, enlarged with 38 Woodcuts. Fcp. 6s.

**Talpa;** or, the Chronicles of a Clay Farm. By C. W. HOSKYNS, Esq. With 24 Woodcuts from Designs by G. CRUIKSHANK. Sixth Edition. 16mo. 5s. 6d.

**History of Windsor Great Park** and Windsor Forest. By WILLIAM MENZIES, Resident Deputy Surveyor. With 2 Maps and 20 Photographs. Imp. folio, £8 8s.

**Loudon's Encyclopædia of Agriculture:** Comprising the Laying-out, Improvement, and Management of Landed Property, and the Cultivation and Economy of the Productions of Agriculture. With 1,100 Woodcuts. 8vo. 31s. 6d.

**Loudon's Encyclopædia of Gardening:** Comprising the Theory and Practice of Horticulture, Floriculture, Arboriculture, and Landscape Gardening. With 1,000 Woodcuts. 8vo. 31s. 6d.

**Loudon's Encyclopædia of Cottage, Farm, and Villa Architecture and Furniture.** With more than 2,000 Woodcuts. 8vo. 42s.

**Bayldon's Art of Valuing Rents** and Tillages, and Claims of Tenants upon Quitting Farms, both at Michaelmas and Lady-Day. Eighth Edition, revised by J. C. MORTON. 8vo. 10s. 6d.

---

## *Religious* and *Moral Works.*

**An Exposition of the 39 Articles,** Historical and Doctrinal. By E. HAROLD BROWNE, D.D. Lord Bishop of Ely. Seventh Edition. 8vo. 16s.

**The Pentateuch and the Elohistic Psalms,** in Reply to Bishop Colenso. By the same. Second Edition. 8vo. 2s.

**Examination-Questions** on Bishop Browne's Exposition of the Articles. By the Rev. J. GORLE, M.A. Fcp. 3s. 6d.

**The Acts of the Apostles;** with a Commentary, and Practical and Devotional Suggestions for Readers and Students of the English Bible. By the Rev. F. C. COOK, M.A., Canon of Exeter, &c. New Edition, 8vo. 12s. 6d.

**The Life and Epistles of St. Paul.** By W. J. CONYBEARE, M.A. late Fellow of Trin. Coll. Cantab. and J. S. HOWSON, D.D. Principal of Liverpool Coll.

LIBRARY EDITION, with all the Original Illustrations, Maps, Landscapes on Steel, Woodcuts, &c. 2 vols. 4to. 48s.

INTERMEDIATE EDITION, with a Selection of Maps, Plates, and Woodcuts. 2 vols. square crown 8vo. 31s. 6d.

PEOPLE'S EDITION, revised and condensed, with 46 Illustrations and Maps. 2 vols. crown 8vo. 12s.

**The Voyage and Shipwreck of St. Paul;** with Dissertations on the Ships and Navigation of the Ancients. By JAMES SMITH, F.R.S. Crown 8vo. Charts, 10s. 6d.

**Fasti Sacri, or a Key to the** Chronology of the New Testament; comprising an Historical Harmony of the Four Gospels, and Chronological Tables generally from B.C. 70 to A.D. 70: with a Preliminary Dissertation and other Aids. By THOMAS LEWIN, M.A. F.S.A. Imp. 8vo. 42s.

**A Critical and Grammatical Commentary** on St. Paul's Epistles. By C. J. ELLICOTT, D.D. Lord Bishop of Gloucester and Bristol. 8vo.

Galatians, Third Edition, 8s. 6d.
Ephesians, Third Edition, 8s. 6d.
Pastoral Epistles, Third Edition, 10s. 6d.
Philippians, Colossians, and Philemon, Third Edition, 10s. 6d.
Thessalonians, Second Edition, 7s. 6d.

**Historical Lectures on the Life of** Our Lord Jesus Christ: being the Hulsean Lectures for 1859. By the same Author. Fourth Edition. 8vo. 10s. 6d.

**The Destiny of the Creature;** and other Sermons preached before the University of Cambridge. By the same. Post 8vo. 5s.

**The Broad and the Narrow Way;** Two Sermons preached before the University of Cambridge. By the same. Crown 8vo. 2s.

**The Greek Testament; with Notes,** Grammatical and Exegetical. By the Rev. W. WEBSTER, M.A. and the Rev. W. F. WILKINSON, M.A. 2 vols. 8vo. £2 4s.

VOL. I. the Gospels and Acts, 20s.
VOL. II. the Epistles and Apocalypse, 24s.

**Rev. T. H. Horne's Introduction** to the Critical Study and Knowledge of the Holy Scriptures. Eleventh Edition, corrected, and extended under careful Editorial revision. With 4 Maps and 22 Woodcuts and Facsimiles. 4 vols. 8vo. £3 13s. 6d.

**Rev. T. H. Horne's Compendious Introduction** to the Study of the Bible, being an Analysis of the larger work by the same Author. Re-edited by the Rev. JOHN AYRE, M.A. With Maps, &c. Post 8vo. 9s.

**The Treasury of Bible Knowledge**; being a Dictionary of the Books, Persons, Places, Events, and other Matters of which mention is made in Holy Scripture; intended to establish its Authority and illustrate its Contents. By Rev. J. AYRE, M.A. With Maps, 15 Plates, and numerous Woodcuts. Fcp. 10s. 6d.

**Every-day Scripture Difficulties** explained and illustrated. By J. E. PRESCOTT, M.A. VOL. I. *Matthew* and *Mark*; VOL. II. *Luke* and *John*. 2 vols. 8vo. 9s. each.

**The Pentateuch and Book of Joshua Critically Examined.** By the Right Rev. J. W. COLENSO, D.D. Lord Bishop of Natal. People's Edition, in 1 vol. crown 8vo. 6s. or in 5 Parts, 1s. each.

**The Pentateuch and Book of Joshua Critically Examined.** By Prof. A. KUENEN, of Leyden. Translated from the Dutch, and edited with Notes, by the Right Rev. J. W. COLENSO, D.D. Bishop of Natal. 8vo. 8s. 6d.

**The Church and the World:** Essays on Questions of the Day. By various Writers. Edited by Rev. ORBY SHIPLEY, M.A. Second Edition, revised. 8vo. 15s.

**The Formation of Christendom.** PART I. By T. W. ALLIES. 8vo. 12s.

**Christendom's Divisions;** a Philosophical Sketch of the Divisions of the Christian Family in East and West. By EDMUND S. FFOULKES, formerly Fellow and Tutor of Jesus Coll. Oxford. Post 8vo. 7s. 6d.

**Christendom's Divisions,** Part II. *Greeks and Latins*, being a History of their Dissentions and Overtures for Peace down to the Reformation. By the same Author. [*Nearly ready.*

**The Life of Christ,** an Eclectic Gospel, from the Old and New Testaments, arranged on a New Principle, with Analytical Tables, &c. By CHARLES DE LA PRYME, M.A. Revised Edition. 8vo. 5s.

**The Hidden Wisdom of Christ** and the Key of Knowledge; or, History of the Apocrypha. By ERNEST DE BUNSEN. 2 vols. 8vo. 28s.

**The Temporal Mission of the Holy Ghost**; or, Reason and Revelation. By the Most Rev. Archbishop MANNING. Second Edition. Crown 8vo. 8s. 6d.

**Essays on Religion and Literature.** Edited by the Most Rev. Archbishop MANNING. 8vo. 10s. 6d.

**Essays and Reviews.** By the Rev. W. TEMPLE, D.D. the Rev. R. WILLIAMS, B.D. the Rev. B. POWELL, M.A. the Rev. H. B. WILSON, B.D. C. W. GOODWIN, M.A. the Rev. M. PATTISON, B.D. and the Rev. B. JOWETT, M.A. 12th Edition. Fcp. 5s.

**Mosheim's Ecclesiastical History.** MURDOCK and SOAMES's Translation and Notes, re-edited by the Rev. W. STUBBS, M.A. 3 vols. 8vo. 45s.

**Bishop Jeremy Taylor's Entire Works:** With Life by BISHOP HEBER. Revised and corrected by the Rev. C. P. EDEN, 10 vols. £5 5s.

**Passing Thoughts on Religion.** By the Author of 'Amy Herbert.' New Edition. Fcp. 5s.

**Thoughts for the Holy Week,** for Young Persons. By the same Author. Third Edition. Fcp. 8vo. 2s.

**Self-examination before Confirmation.** By the same Author. 32mo. 1s. 6d.

**Readings for a Month Preparatory to Confirmation** from Writers of the Early and English Church. By the same. Fcp. 4s.

**Readings for Every Day in Lent,** compiled from the Writings of Bishop JEREMY TAYLOR. By the same. Fcp. 5s.

**Preparation for the Holy Communion**; the Devotions chiefly from the works of JEREMY TAYLOR. By the same. 32mo. 3s.

**Principles of Education drawn** from Nature and Revelation, and Applied to Female Education in the Upper Classes. By the same. 2 vols. fcp. 12s. 6d.

**The Wife's Manual;** or, Prayers, Thoughts, and Songs on Several Occasions of a Matron's Life. By the Rev. W. CALVERT, M.A. Crown 8vo. 10s. 6d.

**Lyra Domestica;** Christian Songs for Domestic Edification. Translated from the *Psaltery and Harp* of C. J. P. SPITTA, and from other sources, by RICHARD MASSIE. FIRST and SECOND SERIES, fcp. 4s. 6d. each.

**Spiritual Songs for the Sundays** and Holidays throughout the Year. By J. S. B. MONSELL, LL.D. Vicar of Egham. Fourth Edition. Fcp. 4s. 6d.

**The Beatitudes**: Abasement before God; Sorrow for Sin; Meekness of Spirit; Desire for Holiness; Gentleness; Purity of Heart; the Peace-makers; Sufferings for Christ. By the same. Third Edition. Fcp. 3s. 6d.

**Lyra Sacra**; Hymns, Ancient and Modern, Odes, and Fragments of Sacred Poetry. Edited by the Rev. B. W. SAVILE, M.A. Third Edition, enlarged. Fcp. 5s.

**Lyra Germanica,** translated from the German by Miss C. WINKWORTH. FIRST SERIES, Hymns for the Sundays and Chief Festivals; SECOND SERIES, the Christian Life. Fcp. 3s. 6d. each SERIES.

Hymns from Lyra Germanica, 18mo. 1s.

**The Chorale Book for England;** a complete Hymn-Book in accordance with the Services and Festivals of the Church of England: the Hymns translated by Miss C. WINKWORTH; the Tunes arranged by Prof. W. S. BENNETT and OTTO GOLDSCHMIDT. Fcp. 4to. 12s. 6d.

Congregational Edition. Fcp. 2s.

**Lyra Eucharistica;** Hymns and Verses on the Holy Communion, Ancient and Modern; with other Poems. Edited by the Rev. ORBY SHIPLEY, M.A. Second Edition. Fcp. 7s. 6d.

**Lyra Messianica;** Hymns and Verses on the Life of Christ, Ancient and Modern; with other Poems. By the same Editor. Second Edition, enlarged. Fcp. 7s. 6d.

**Lyra Mystica;** Hymns and Verses on Sacred Subjects, Ancient and Modern. By the same Editor. Fcp. 7s. 6d.

**The Catholic Doctrine of the Atonement;** an Historical Inquiry into its Development in the Church: with an Introduction on the Principle of Theological Developments. By H. N. OXENHAM, M.A. formerly Scholar of Balliol College, Oxford. 8vo. 8s. 6d.

**From Sunday to Sunday;** an Attempt to consider familiarly the Weekday Life and Labours of a Country Clergyman. By R. GEE, M.A. Fcp. 5s.

**Our Sermons:** an Attempt to consider familiarly, but reverently, the Preacher's Work in the present day. By the same Author. Fcp. 6s.

**Paley's Moral Philosophy,** with Annotations. By RICHARD WHATELY, D.D. late Archbishop of Dublin. 8vo. 7s.

---

## Travels, Voyages, &c.

**Ice Caves of France and Switzerland;** a narrative of Subterranean Exploration. By the Rev. G. F. BROWNE, M.A. Fellow and Assistant-Tutor of St. Catherine's Coll. Cambridge, M.A.C. With 11 Woodcuts. Square crown 8vo. 12s. 6d.

**Village Life in Switzerland.** By SOPHIA D. DELMARD. Post 8vo. 9s. 6d.

**How we Spent the Summer;** or, a Voyage en Zigzag in Switzerland and Tyrol with some Members of the ALPINE CLUB. From the Sketch-Book of one of the Party. Third Edition, re-drawn. In oblong 4to. with about 300 Illustrations, 15s.

**Beaten Tracks;** or, Pen and Pencil Sketches in Italy. By the Authoress of 'A Voyage en Zigzag.' With 42 Plates, containing about 200 Sketches from Drawings made on the Spot. 8vo. 10s.

**Map of the Chain of Mont Blanc,** from an actual Survey in 1863—1864. By A. ADAMS-REILLY, F.R.G.S. M.A.C. Published under the Authority of the Alpine Club. In Chromolithography on extra stout drawing-paper 28in. × 17in. price 10s. or mounted on canvas in a folding case, 12s. 6d.

**Transylvania, its Products and its People.** By CHARLES BONER. With 5 Maps and 43 Illustrations on Wood and in Chromolithography. 8vo. 21s.

**Explorations in South-west Africa,** from Walvisch Bay to Lake Ngami and the Victoria Falls. By THOMAS BAINES, F.R.G.S. 8vo. with Maps and Illustrations, 21s.

**Vancouver Island and British Columbia;** their History, Resources, and Prospects. By MATTHEW MACFIE, F.R.G.S. With Maps and Illustrations. 8vo. 18s.

**History of Discovery in our** Australasian Colonies, Australia, Tasmania, and New Zealand, from the Earliest Date to the Present Day. By WILLIAM HOWITT. With 3 Maps of the Recent Explorations from Official Sources. 2 vols. 8vo. 20s.

**The Capital of the Tycoon;** a Narrative of a 3 Years' Residence in Japan. By Sir RUTHERFORD ALCOCK, K.C.B. 2 vols. 8vo. with numerous Illustrations, 42s.

**Florence, the New Capital of** Italy. By C. R. WELD. With several Engravings on Wood, from Drawings by the Author. Post 8vo.

**The Dolomite Mountains.** Excursions through Tyrol, Carinthia, Carniola, and Friuli in 1861, 1862, and 1863. By J. GILBERT and G. C. CHURCHILL, F.R.G.S. With numerous Illustrations. Square crown 8vo. 21s.

**A Lady's Tour Round Monte Rosa;** including Visits to the Italian Valleys. With Map and Illustrations. Post 8vo, 14s.

**Guide to the Pyrenees,** for the use of Mountaineers. By CHARLES PACKE. With Maps, &c. and Appendix. Fcp. 6s.

**A Guide to Spain.** By H. O'SHEA. Post 8vo. with Travelling Map, 15s.

**Christopher Columbus;** his Life, Voyages, and Discoveries. Revised Edition, with 4 Woodcuts. 18mo. 2s. 6d.

**Captain James Cook;** his Life, Voyages, and Discoveries. Revised Edition, with numerous Woodcuts. 18mo. 2s. 6d.

**The Alpine Guide.** By JOHN BALL. M.R.I.A. late President of the Alpine Club. Post 8vo. with Maps and other Illustrations.

Guide to the Eastern Alps. [*Just ready*.

Guide to the Western Alps, including Mont Blanc, Monte Rosa, Zermatt, &c. price 7s. 6d.

Guide to the Oberland and all Switzerland, excepting the Neighbourhood of Monte Rosa and the Great St. Bernard; with Lombardy and the adjoining portion of Tyrol. 7s. 6d.

**Humboldt's Travels and Discoveries** in South America. Third Edition, with numerous Woodcuts. 18mo. 2s. 6d.

**Narratives of Shipwrecks of the** Royal Navy between 1793 and 1857, compiled from Official Documents in the Admiralty by W. O. S. GILLY; with a Preface by W. S. GILLY, D.D. 3d Edition, fcp. 5s.

**A Week at the Land's End.** By J. T. BLIGHT; assisted by E. H. RODD, R. Q. COUCH, and J. RALFS. With Map and 96 Woodcuts. Fcp. 6s. 6d.

**Visits to Remarkable Places:** Old Halls, Battle-Fields, and Scenes illustrative of Striking Passages in English History and Poetry. By WILLIAM HOWITT. 2 vols. square crown 8vo. with Wood Engravings, 25s.

**The Rural Life of England.** By the same Author. With Woodcuts by Bewick and Williams. Medium 8vo. 12s. 6d.

---

## Works of Fiction.

**Atherstone Priory.** By L. N. COMYN. 2 vols. post 8vo. 21s.

**Ellice:** a Tale. By the same. Post 8vo. 9s. 6d.

**Stories and Tales by the Author** of 'Amy Herbert,' uniform Edition, each Tale or Story complete in a single volume.

AMY HERBERT, 2s. 6d.
GERTRUDE, 2s. 6d.
EARL'S DAUGHTER, 2s. 6d.
EXPERIENCE OF LIFE, 2s. 6d.
CLEVE HALL, 3s. 6d.
IVORS, 3s. 6d.
KATHARINE ASHTON, 3s. 6d.
MARGARET PERCIVAL, 5s.
LANETON PARSONAGE, 4s. 6d.
URSULA, 4s. 6d.

**A Glimpse of the World.** By the Author of 'Amy Herbert.' Fcp. 7s. 6d.

**The Six Sisters of the Valleys:** an Historical Romance. By W. BRAMLEY-MOORE, M.A. Incumbent of Gerrard's Cross, Bucks. Fourth Edition, with 14 Illustrations. Crown 8vo. 5s.

**Gallus;** or, Roman Scenes of the Time of Augustus: with Notes and Excursuses illustrative of the Manners and Customs of the Ancient Romans. From the German of Prof. BECKER. New Edit. Post 8vo. 7s. 6d.

**Charicles;** a Tale illustrative of Private Life among the Ancient Greeks: with Notes and Excursuses. From the German of Prof. BECKER. New Edition, Post 8vo. 7s. 6d.

NEW WORKS PUBLISHED BY LONGMANS AND CO.    17

**Icelandic Legends.** Collected by JON. ARNASON. Selected and Translated from the Icelandic by GEORGE E. J. POWELL and E. MAGNUSSON. SECOND SERIES, with Notes and an Introductory Essay on the Origin and Genius of the Icelandic Folk-Lore, and 3 Illustrations on Wood. Crown 8vo. 21s.

**The Warden:** a Novel. By ANTHONY TROLLOPE, Crown 8vo. 2s. 6d.

**Barchester Towers:** a Sequel to 'The Warden.' By the same Author. Crown 8vo. 3s. 6d.

**Tales from Greek Mythology.** By GEORGE W. COX, M.A. late Scholar of Trin. Coll. Oxon. Second Edition. Square 16mo. 3s. 6d.

**Tales of the Gods and Heroes.** By the same Author. Second Edition. Fcp. 5s.

**Tales of Thebes and Argos.** By the same Author. Fcp. 4s. 6d.

**The Gladiators:** a Tale of Rome and Judæa. By G. J. WHYTE MELVILLE. Crown 8vo. 5s.

**Digby Grand,** an Autobiography. By the same Author. 1 vol. 5s.

**Kate Coventry,** an Autobiography. By the same. 1 vol. 5s.

**General Bounce,** or the Lady and the Locusts. By the same. 1 vol. 5s.

**Holmby House,** a Tale of Old Northamptonshire. 1 vol. 5s.

**Good for Nothing,** or All Down Hill. By the same. 1 vol. 6s.

**The Queen's Maries,** a Romance of Holyrood. By the same. 1 vol. 6s.

**The Interpreter,** a Tale of the War. By the same Author. 1 vol. 5s.

---

## *Poetry* and *The Drama*.

**Goethe's Second Faust.** Translated by JOHN ANSTER, LL.D. M.R.I.A. Regius Professor of Civil Law in the University of Dublin. Post 8vo. 15s.

**Tasso's Jerusalem Delivered,** translated into English Verse by Sir J. KINGSTON JAMES, Kt. M.A. 2 vols. fcp. with Facsimile, 14s.

**Poetical Works of John Edmund Reade;** with final Revision and Additions. 3 vols. fcp. 18s. or each vol. separately, 6s.

**Moore's Poetical Works,** Cheapest Editions complete in 1 vol. including the Autobiographical Prefaces and Author's last Notes, which are still copyright. Crown 8vo. ruby type, with Portrait, 6s. or People's Edition, in larger type, 12s. 6d.

**Moore's Poetical Works,** as above, Library Edition, medium 8vo. with Portrait and Vignette, 14s. or in 10 vols. fcp. 3s. 6d. each.

**Moore's Lalla Rookh,** Tenniel's Edition, with 68 Wood Engravings from Original Drawings and other Illustrations. Fcp. 4to. 21s.

**Moore's Irish Melodies,** Maclise's Edition, with 161 Steel Plates from Original Drawings. Super-royal 8vo. 31s. 6d.

**Miniature Edition of Moore's Irish Melodies,** with Maclise's Illustrations, (as above) reduced in Lithography. Imp. 16mo. 10s. 6d.

**Southey's Poetical Works,** with the Author's last Corrections and copyright Additions. Library Edition, in 1 vol. medium 8vo. with Portrait and Vignette, 14s. or in 10 vols. fcp. 3s. 6d. each.

**Lays of Ancient Rome;** with *Ivry* and the *Armada*. By the Right Hon. LORD MACAULAY. 16mo. 4s. 6d.

**Lord Macaulay's Lays of Ancient Rome.** With 90 Illustrations on Wood, Original and from the Antique, from Drawings by G. SCHARF. Fcp. 4to. 21s.

**Miniature Edition of Lord Macaulay's Lays of Ancient Rome,** with Scharf's Illustrations (as above) reduced in Lithography. Imp. 16mo. 10s. 6d.

**Poems.** By JEAN INGELOW. Twelfth Edition. Fcp. 8vo. 5s.

**Poems by Jean Ingelow.** A New Edition, with nearly 100 Illustrations by Eminent Artists, engraved on Wood by the Brothers DALZIEL. Fcp. 4to. 21s.

**Poetical Works of Letitia Elizabeth Landon (L.E.L.)** 2 vols. 16mo. 10s.

**Playtime with the Poets:** a Selection of the best English Poetry for the use of Children. By a LADY. Crown 8vo. 5s.

c

**Bowdler's Family Shakspeare,** cheaper Genuine Edition, complete in 1 vol. large type, with 36 Woodcut Illustrations, price 14s. or, with the same ILLUSTRATIONS, in 6 pocket vols. 3s. 6d. each.

**Arundines Cami,** sive Musarum Cantabrigiensium Lusus Canori. Collegit atque edidit H. DRURY. M.A. Editio Sexta, curavit H. J. HODGSON, M.A. Crown 8vo. price 7s. 6d.

**The Æneid of Virgil** Translated into English Verse. By JOHN CONINGTON, M.A. Corpus Professor of Latin in the University of Oxford. Crown 8vo. 9s.

**The Iliad of Homer Translated** into Blank Verse. By ICHABOD CHARLES WRIGHT, M.A. late Fellow of Magdalen Coll. Oxon. 2 vols. crown 8vo. 21s.

**The Iliad of Homer in English** Hexameter Verse. By J. HENRY DART, M.A. of Exeter College, Oxford; Author of 'The Exile of St. Helena, Newdigate, 1838.' Square crown 8vo. price 21s. cloth.

**Dante's Divine Comedy,** translated in English Terza Rima by JOHN DAYMAN, M.A. [With the Italian Text, after *Brunetti*, interpaged.] 8vo. 21s.

## *Rural Sports, &c.*

**Encyclopædia of Rural Sports;** a Complete Account, Historical, Practical, and Descriptive, of Hunting, Shooting, Fishing, Racing, &c. By D. P. BLAINE. With above 600 Woodcuts (20 from Designs by JOHN LEECH). 8vo. 42s.

**Notes on Rifle Shooting.** By Captain HEATON, Adjutant of the Third Manchester Rifle Volunteer Corps. Fcp. 2s. 6d.

**Col. Hawker's Instructions to** Young Sportsmen in all that relates to Guns and Shooting. Revised by the Author's Son. Square crown 8vo. with Illustrations, 18s.

**The Rifle, its Theory and Practice.** By ARTHUR WALKER (79th Highlanders), Staff, Hythe and Fleetwood Schools of Musketry. Second Edition. Crown 8vo. with 125 Woodcuts, 5s.

**The Dead Shot,** or Sportsman's Complete Guide; a Treatise on the Use of the Gun, Dog-breaking, Pigeon-shooting, &c. By MARKSMAN. Fcp. with Plates, 5s.

**Hints on Shooting, Fishing, &c.** both on Sea and Land and in the Fresh and Saltwater Lochs of Scotland. By C. IDLE, Esq. Second Edition. Fcp. 6s.

**A Book on Angling:** being a Complete Work on every branch of Angling practised in Great Britain. By FRANCIS FRANCIS. With numerous Explanatory Plates, coloured and plain, and the largest and most reliable List of Salmon Flies ever published. Post 8vo.

**The Art of Fishing on the Principle** of Avoiding Cruelty; being a brief Treatise on the Most Merciful Methods of Capturing Fish; describing certain approved Rules in Fishing, used during 60 Years' Practice. By the Rev. O. RAYMOND, LL.B. Fcp. 8vo.

**Handbook of Angling:** Teaching Fly-fishing, Trolling, Bottom-fishing, Salmon-fishing; with the Natural History of River Fish, and the best modes of Catching them. By EPHEMERA. Fcp. Woodcuts, 5s.

**The Fly-Fisher's Entomology.** By ALFRED RONALDS. With coloured Representations of the Natural and Artificial Insect. Sixth Edition; with 20 coloured Plates. 8vo. 14s.

**The Cricket Field;** or, the History and the Science of the Game of Cricket. By JAMES PYCROFT, B.A. 4th Edition. Fcp. 5s.

**The Cricket Tutor;** a Treatise exclusively Practical. By the same. 18mo. 1s.

**Cricketana.** By the same Author. With 7 Portraits of Cricketers. Fcp. 5s.

**Youatt on the Horse.** Revised and enlarged by W. WATSON, M.R.C.V.S. 8vo. with numerous Woodcuts, 12s. 6d.

**Youatt on the Dog.** (By the same Author.) 8vo. with numerous Woodcuts, 6s.

**The Horse-Trainer's and Sportsman's Guide:** with Considerations on the Duties of Grooms, on Purchasing Blood Stock, and on Veterinary Examination. By DIGBY COLLINS. Post 8vo. 6s.

**Blaine's Veterinary Art:** a Treatise on the Anatomy, Physiology, and Curative Treatment of the Diseases of the Horse, Neat Cattle, and Sheep. Seventh Edition, revised and enlarged by C. STEEL, M.R.C.V.S.L. 8vo. with Plates and Woodcuts, 18s.

**On Drill and Manœuvres of** Cavalry, combined with Horse Artillery. By Major-Gen. MICHAEL W. SMITH, C.B. commanding the Poonah Division of the Bombay Army. 8vo. 12s. 6d.

**The Horse's Foot, and how to keep it Sound.** By W. MILES, Esq. 9th Edition, with Illustrations. Imp. 8vo. 12s. 6d.

**A Plain Treatise on Horse-shoeing.** By the same Author. Post 8vo. with Illustrations, 2s. 6d.

**Stables and Stable Fittings.** By the same. Imp. 8vo. with 13 Plates, 15s.

**Remarks on Horses' Teeth,** addressed to Purchasers. By the same. Post 8vo. 1s. 6d.

**The Dog in Health and Disease.** By STONEHENGE. With 70 Wood Engravings. New Edition. Square crown 8vo. 10s. 6d.

**The Greyhound.** By the same Author. Revised Edition, with 24 Portraits of Greyhounds. Square crown 8vo. 21s.

**The Ox,** his Diseases and their Treatment; with an Essay on Parturition in the Cow. By J. R. DOBSON, M.R.C.V.S. Crown 8vo. with Illustrations, 7s. 6d.

---

## Commerce, Navigation, and Mercantile Affairs.

**The Commercial Handbook of France**; Furnishing a detailed and comprehensive account of the Trade, Manufactures, Industry, and Commerce of France at the Present Time. By FREDERICK MARTIN. With Maps and Plans, including a Coloured Map showing the Seats of the Principal Industries. Crown 8vo.

**Banking, Currency, and the Exchanges:** a Practical Treatise. By ARTHUR CRUMP, Bank Manager, formerly of the Bank of England. Post 8vo. 6s.

**The Theory and Practice of Banking.** By HENRY DUNNING MACLEOD, M.A. Barrister-at-Law. Second Edition, entirely remodelled. 2 vols. 8vo. 30s.

**A Dictionary, Practical, Theoretical, and Historical, of Commerce and Commercial Navigation.** By J. R. M<sup>c</sup>CULLOCH. New Edition in preparation.

**Practical Guide for British Shipmasters** to United States Ports. By PIERREPONT EDWARDS, Her Britannic Majesty's Vice-Consul at New York. Post 8vo. 8s. 6d.

**A Manual for Naval Cadets.** By J. M<sup>c</sup>NEIL BOYD, late Captain R.N. Third Edition; with 240 Woodcuts, and 11 coloured Plates. Post 8vo. 12s. 6d.

**The Law of Nations Considered** as Independent Political Communities. By TRAVERS TWISS, D.C.L. Regius Professor of Civil Law in the University of Oxford. 2 vols. 8vo. 30s. or separately, PART I. *Peace,* 12s. PART II. *War,* 18s.

**A Nautical Dictionary, defining** the Technical Language relative to the Building and Equipment of Sailing Vessels and Steamers, &c. By ARTHUR YOUNG. Second Edition; with Plates and 150 Woodcuts. 8vo. 18s.

---

## Works of Utility and General Information.

**Modern Cookery for Private Families,** reduced to a System of Easy Practice in a Series of carefully-tested Receipts. By ELIZA ACTON. Newly revised and enlarged; with 8 Plates, Figures, and 150 Woodcuts. Fcp. 7s. 6d.

**On Food and its Digestion;** an Introduction to Dietetics. By W. BRINTON, M.D. Physician to St. Thomas's Hospital, &c. With 48 Woodcuts. Post 8vo. 12s.

**Wine, the Vine, and the Cellar.** By THOMAS G. SHAW. Second Edition, revised and enlarged, with Fronti-piece and 31 Illustrations on Wood. 8vo. 16s.

**A Practical Treatise on Brewing;** with Formulæ for Public Brewers, and Instructions for Private Families. By W. BLACK. Fifth Edition. 8vo. 10s. 6d.

**How to Brew Good Beer:** a complete Guide to the Art of Brewing Ale, Bitter Ale, Table Ale, Brown Stout, Porter, and Table Beer. By JOHN PITT. Revised Edition. Fcp. 4s. 6d.

**The Billiard Book.** By Captain CRAWLEY, Author of 'Billiards, its Theory and Practice,' &c. With nearly 100 Diagrams on Steel and Wood. 8vo. 21s.

**Whist, What to Lead.** By CAM. Third Edition. 32mo. 1s.

**Short Whist.** By MAJOR A. The Sixteenth Edition, revised, with an Essay on the Theory of the Modern Scientific Game by PROF. P. Fcp. 3s. 6d.

**Two Hundred Chess Problems,** composed by F. HEALEY, including the Problems to which the Prizes were awarded by the Committees of the Era, the Manchester, the Birmingham, and the Bristol Chess Problem Tournaments; accompanied by the SOLUTIONS. Crown 8vo. with 200 Diagrams, 5s.

**The Cabinet Lawyer;** a Popular Digest of the Laws of England, Civil, Criminal, and Constitutional. 22nd Edition, entirely recomposed, and brought down by the AUTHOR to the close of the Parliamentary Session of 1866. Fcp. 10s. 6d.

**The Philosophy of Health;** or, an Exposition of the Physiological and Sanitary Conditions conducive to Human Longevity and Happiness. By SOUTHWOOD SMITH, M.D. Eleventh Edition, revised and enlarged; with 113 Woodcuts. 8vo. 15s.

**Hints to Mothers on the Management** of their Health during the Period of Pregnancy and in the Lying-in Room. By T. BULL, M.D. Fcp. 5s.

**The Maternal Management of Children in Health and Disease.** By the same Author. Fcp. 5s.

**Notes on Hospitals.** By FLORENCE NIGHTINGALE. Third Edition, enlarged; with 13 Plans. Post 4to. 18s.

**The Executor's Guide.** By J. C. HUDSON. Enlarged Edition, revised by the Author, with reference to the latest reported Cases and Acts of Parliament. Fcp. 6s.

**Hudson's Plain Directions for Making Wills.** Fcp. 2s. 6d.

**The Law relating to Benefit Building Societies;** with Practical Observations on the Act and all the Cases decided thereon, also a Form of Rules and Forms of Mortgages. By W. TIDD PRATT, Barrister. 2nd Edition. Fcp. 3s. 6d.

**C. M. Willich's Popular Tables** for Ascertaining the Value of Lifehold, Leasehold, and Church Property, Renewal Fines, &c.; the Public Funds; Annual Average Price and Interest on Consols from 1731 to 1861; Chemical, Geographical, Astronomical, Trigonometrical Tables, &c. Post 8vo. 10s.

**Thomson's Tables of Interest,** at Three, Four, Four and a Half, and Five per Cent, from One Pound to Ten Thousand and from 1 to 365 Days. 12mo. 3s. 6d.

**Maunder's Treasury of Knowledge** and Library of Reference: comprising an English Dictionary and Grammar, Universal Gazetteer, Classical Dictionary, Chronology, Law Dictionary, Synopsis of the Peerage, useful Tables, &c. Fcp. 10s. 6d.

---

## *Knowledge for the Young.*

**The Stepping Stone to Knowledge:** Containing upwards of 700 Questions and Answers on Miscellaneous Subjects, adapted to the capacity of Infant Minds. By a MOTHER. 18mo. price 1s.

**The Stepping Stone to Geography:** Containing several Hundred Questions and Answers on Geographical Subjects. 18mo. 1s.

**The Stepping Stone to English History:** Containing several Hundred Questions and Answers on the History of England. 1s.

**The Stepping Stone to Bible Knowledge.** Containing several Hundred Questions and Answers on the Old and New Testaments. 18mo. 1s.

**The Stepping Stone to Biography:** Containing several Hundred Questions and Answers on the Lives of Eminent Men and Women. 18mo. 1s.

**Second Series of the Stepping Stone to Knowledge:** containing upwards of Eight Hundred Questions and Answers on Miscellaneous Subjects not contained in the FIRST SERIES. 18mo. 1s.

**The Stepping Stone to French Pronunciation and Conversation:** Containing several Hundred Questions and Answers. By Mr. P. SADLER. 18mo. 1s.

**The Stepping Stone to English Grammar:** containing several Hundred Questions and Answers on English Grammar. By Mr. P. SADLER. 18mo. 1s.

**The Stepping Stone to Natural History:** VERTEBRATE or BACKBONED ANIMALS. PART I. *Mammalia*; PART II. *Birds, Reptiles, Fishes.* 18mo. 1s. each Part.

# INDEX.

| | |
|---|---|
| ABBOTT on Sight and Touch | 7 |
| ACTON's Modern Cookery | 19 |
| ALCOCK's Residence in Japan | 16 |
| ALLIES on Formation of Christianity | 14 |
| Alpine Guide (The) | 16 |
| APJOHN's Manual of the Metalloids | 8 |
| ARAGO's Biographies of Scientific Men | 4 |
| —— Popular Astronomy | 7 |
| ARNOLD's Manual of English Literature | 5 |
| ARNOTT's Elements of Physics | 7 |
| Arundines Cami | 18 |
| Atherstone Priory | 16 |
| Autumn Holidays of a Country Parson | 6 |
| AYRE's Treasury of Bible Knowledge | 14 |
| | |
| BACON's Essays, by WHATELY | 4 |
| —— Life and Letters, by SPEDDING | 3 |
| —— Works | 4 |
| BAIN on the Emotions and Will | 7 |
| —— on the Senses and Intellect | 7 |
| —— on the Study of Character | 7 |
| BAINES's Explorations in S.W. Africa | 15 |
| BALL's Guide to the Central Alps | 12 |
| —— Guide to the Western Alps | 12 |
| —— Guide to the Eastern Alps | 16 |
| BARNARD's Drawing from Nature | 12 |
| BAYLDON's Rents and Tillages | 13 |
| Beaten Tracks | 15 |
| BECKER's *Charicles* and *Gallus* | 16 |
| BEETHOVEN's Letters | 3 |
| BENFEY's Sanskrit-English Dictionary | 5 |
| BERRY's Journals | 3 |
| BLACK's Treatise on Brewing | 19 |
| BLACKLEY and FRIEDLANDER's German and English Dictionary | 5 |
| BLAINE's Rural Sports | 18 |
| —— Veterinary Art | 18 |
| BLIGHT's Week at the Land's End | 16 |
| BOASE's Essay on Human Nature | 6 |
| —— Philosophy of Nature | 6 |
| BONER's Transylvania | 15 |
| BOOTH's Epigrams | 6 |
| BOURNE on Screw Propeller | 12 |
| BOURNE's Catechism of the Steam Engine | 12 |
| —— Handbook of Steam Engine | 12 |
| —— Treatise on the Steam Engine | 12 |
| BOWDLER's Family SHAKSPEARE | 18 |
| BOYD's Manual for Naval Cadets | 19 |
| BRAMLEY-MOORE's Six Sisters of the Valleys | 16 |
| BRANDE's Dictionary of Science, Literature, and Art | 9 |
| BRAY's (C.) Education of the Feelings | 7 |
| —— Philosophy of Necessity | 7 |
| —— On Force | 7 |
| BRINTON on Food and Digestion | 19 |
| BRISTOW's Glossary of Mineralogy | 8 |
| BRODIE's Constitutional History | 1 |
| BRODIE's (Sir C. B.) Works | 10 |
| —— Autobiography | 10 |
| BROWNE's Ice Caves of France and Switzerland | 15 |
| —— Exposition 39 Articles | 13 |
| —— Pentateuch | 13 |
| BUCKLE's History of Civilization | 2 |
| BULL's Hints to Mothers | 20 |
| —— Maternal Management of Children | 20 |
| BUNSEN's Ancient Egypt | 2 |
| BUNSEN on Apocrypha | 14 |
| BURKE's Vicissitudes of Families | 4 |
| BURTON's Christian Church | 3 |
| | |
| Cabinet Lawyer | 20 |
| CALVERT's Wife's Manual | 14 |
| Campaigner at Home | 6 |
| CATS and FARLIE's Moral Emblems | 11 |
| Chorale Book for England | 15 |
| CLOUGH's Lives from Plutarch | 2 |
| COLENSO (Bishop) on Pentateuch and Book of Joshua | 14 |
| COLLINS's Horse Trainer's Guide | 18 |
| COLUMBUS's Voyages | 16 |
| Commonplace Philosopher in Town and Country | 6 |
| CONINGTON's Translation of Virgil's Æneid | 18 |
| CONTANSEAU's Two French and English Dictionaries | 5 |
| CONYBEARE and HOWSON's Life and Epistles of St. Paul | 13 |
| COOK's Acts of the Apostles | 13 |
| —— Voyages | 16 |
| COPLAND's Dictionary of Practical Medicine | 10 |
| COX's Tales of the Great Persian War | 2 |
| —— Tales from Greek Mythology | 17 |
| —— Tales of the Gods and Heroes | 17 |
| —— Tales of Thebes and Argos | 17 |
| CRAWLEY's Billiard Book | 19 |
| CRESY's Encyclopædia of Civil Engineering | 11 |
| Critical Essays of a Country Parson | 6 |
| CROWE's History of France | 2 |
| CRUMP on Banking, &c. | 19 |
| CUSSANS's Grammar of Heraldry | 12 |
| | |
| DART's Iliad of Homer | 13 |
| D'AUBIGNÉ's History of the Reformation in the time of CALVIN | 2 |
| DAYMAN's Dante's Divina Commedia | 18 |
| Dead Shot (The), by MARKSMAN | 18 |
| DE LA RIVE's Treatise on Electricity | 8 |
| DELMARD's Village Life in Switzerland | 15 |
| DE LA PRYME's Life of Christ | 14 |
| DE MORGAN on Matter and Spirit | 6 |
| DE TOCQUEVILLE's Democracy in America | 2 |
| DISRAELI's Speeches on Reform | 5 |
| DOBSON on the Ox | 19 |

| | |
|---|---|
| ROGERS's Correspondence of Greyson | 6 |
| ———— Eclipse of Faith | 6 |
| ———— Defence of ditto | 6 |
| ———— Essays from the *Edinburgh Review* | 6 |
| ———— Fulleriana | 6 |
| ———— Reason and Faith | 6 |
| ———— (E.) Fifth-Monarchy Man | 3 |
| ROGET's Thesaurus of English Words and Phrases | 5 |
| RONALDS's Fly-Fisher's Entomology | 13 |
| ROWTON's Debater | 5 |
| RUSSELL on Government and Constitution | 1 |
| | |
| SANDARS's Justinian's Institutes | 4 |
| SCOTT's Handbook of Volumetrical Analysis | 9 |
| ———— Lectures on the Fine Arts | 11 |
| SCROPE on Volcanos | 7 |
| SEWELL's Amy Herbert | 16 |
| ———— Cleve Hall | 16 |
| ———— Earl's Daughter | 16 |
| ———— Experience of Life | 16 |
| ———— Gertrude | 16 |
| ———— Glimpse of the World | 16 |
| ———— History of the Early Church | 3 |
| ———— Ivors | 16 |
| ———— Katharine Ashton | 16 |
| ———— Laneton Parsonage | 16 |
| ———— Margaret Percival | 16 |
| ———— Passing Thoughts on Religion | 16 |
| ———— Preparation for Communion | 14 |
| ———— Principles of Education | 14 |
| ———— Readings for Confirmation | 14 |
| ———— Readings for Lent | 14 |
| ———— Examination for Confirmation | 14 |
| ———— Stories and Tales | 16 |
| ———— Thoughts for the Holy Week | 14 |
| ———— Ursula | 16 |
| SHAW's Work on Wine | 19 |
| SHEDDEN's Elements of Logic | 4 |
| SHIPLEY's Church and the World | 14 |
| Short Whist | 20 |
| SHORT's Church History | 3 |
| SIEVEKING's (AMELIA) Life, by WINKWORTH | 3 |
| SMITH's (SOUTHWOOD) Philosophy of Health | 20 |
| ———— (J.) Paul's Voyage and Shipwreck | 13 |
| ———— (G.) Wesleyan Methodism | 3 |
| ———— (SYDNEY) Miscellaneous Works | 6 |
| ———— ———— Moral Philosophy | 6 |
| ———— ———— Wit and Wisdom | 6 |
| SMITH on Cavalry Drill and Manœuvres | 18 |
| SOUTHEY's (Doctor) | 5 |
| ———— Poetical Works | 17 |
| STANLEY's History of British Birds | 9 |
| STEBBING's Analysis of MILL's Logic | 5 |
| STEPHEN's Essays in Ecclesiastical Biography | 4 |
| ———— Lectures on History of France | 2 |
| STEPHENSON's Life, by JEAFFRESON and POLE | 3 |
| Stepping-Stone (The) to Knowledge, &c. | 20 |
| STIRLING's Secret of Hegel | 6 |
| STONEHENGE on the Dog | 19 |
| ———— on the Greyhound | 19 |
| STRANGE on Sea Air | 10 |
| ———— Restoration of Health | 11 |
| Sunday Afternoons at the Parish Church | 6 |

| | |
|---|---|
| TASSO's Jerusalem, by JAMES | 17 |
| TAYLOR's (Jeremy) Works, edited by EDEN | 14 |
| TENNENT's Ceylon | 8 |
| ———— Natural History of Ceylon | 8 |
| ———— Wild Elephant | 8 |
| THIRLWALL's History of Greece | 2 |
| THOMSON's (Archbishop) Laws of Thought | 4 |
| ———— (J.) Tables of Interest | 20 |
| ———— Conspectus, by BIRKETT | 10 |
| TODD's Cyclopædia of Anatomy and Physiology | 10 |
| ———— and BOWMAN's Anatomy and Physiology of Man | 10 |
| TROLLOPE's Barchester Towers | 17 |
| ———— Warden | 17 |
| TWISS's Law of Nations | 19 |
| TYNDALL's Lectures on Heat | 8 |
| ———— Lectures on Sound | 8 |
| | |
| URE's Dictionary of Arts, Manufactures, and Mines | 12 |
| | |
| VAN DER HOEVEN's Handbook of Zoology | 8 |
| VAUGHAN's (R.) Revolutions in English History | 1 |
| ———— (R. A.) Hours with the Mystics | 7 |
| ———— Way to Rest | 7 |
| | |
| WALKER on the Rifle | 18 |
| WATSON's Principles and Practice of Physic | 10 |
| WATTS's Dictionary of Chemistry | 9 |
| WEBB's Objects for Common Telescopes | 7 |
| WEBSTER & WILKINSON's Greek Testament | 13 |
| WELD's Florence | 16 |
| WELLINGTON's Life, by BRIALMONT and GLEIG | 3 |
| ———— by GLEIG | 3 |
| WEST on Children's Diseases | 9 |
| WHATELY's English Synonymes | 4 |
| ———— Life and Correspondence | 3 |
| ———— Logic | 4 |
| ———— Remains | 4 |
| ———— Rhetoric | 4 |
| ———— Paley's Moral Philosophy | 15 |
| WHEWELL's History of the Inductive Sciences | 2 |
| Whist, what to lead, by CAM | 20 |
| WHITE and RIDDLE's Latin-English Dictionaries | 5 |
| WILBERFORCE (W.) Recollections of, by HARFORD | 3 |
| WILLICH's Popular Tables | 20 |
| WILSON's Bryologia Britannica | 9 |
| WINDHAM's Diary | 3 |
| Wood's Homes without Hands | 8 |
| WOODWARD's Historical and Chronological Encyclopædia | 2 |
| WRIGHT's Homer's Iliad | 18 |
| | |
| YONGE's English-Greek Lexicon | 5 |
| ———— Abridged ditto | 5 |
| YOUNG's Nautical Dictionary | 19 |
| YOUATT on the Dog | 18 |
| ———— on the Horse | 18 |

www.ingramcontent.com/pod-product-compliance
Lightning Source LLC
Chambersburg PA
CBHW022107300426
44117CB00007B/627